CONGREGATION

ALSO BY GARY DORSEY

The Fullness of Wings

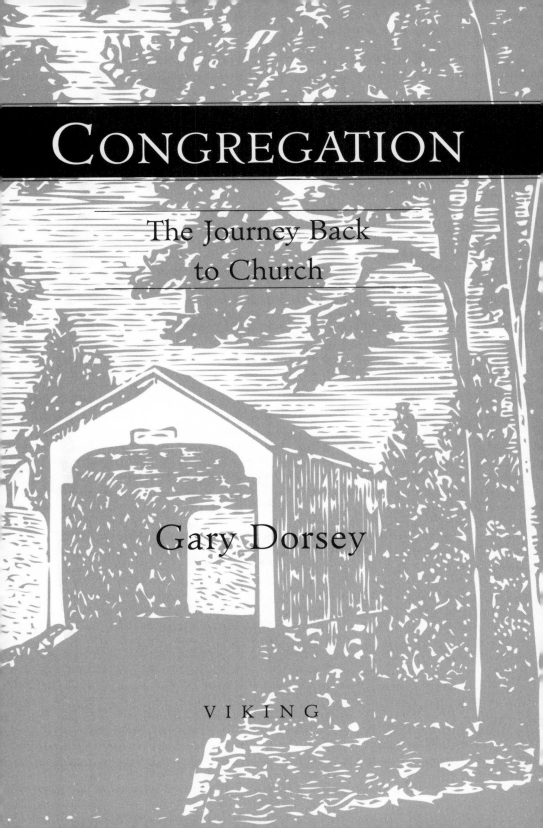

CONGREGATION

The Journey Back to Church

Gary Dorsey

VIKING

VIKING
Published by the Penguin Group
Penguin Books USA Inc., 375 Hudson Street, New York, New York 10014, U.S.A.
Penguin Books Ltd, 27 Wrights Lane, London W8 5TZ, England
Penguin Books Australia Ltd, Ringwood, Victoria, Australia
Penguin Books Canada Ltd, 10 Alcorn Avenue, Toronto, Ontario, Canada M4V 3B2
Penguin Books (N.Z.) Ltd, 182–190 Wairau Road, Auckland 10, New Zealand

Penguin Books Ltd, Registered Offices:
Harmondsworth, Middlesex, England

First published in 1995 by Viking Penguin,
a division of Penguin Books USA Inc.

1   3   5   7   9   10   8   6   4   2

Grateful acknowledgment is made for permission to reprint an excerpt from "Love, like the
yellow daffodil," Sydney Carter, *In the Present Tense, Book 5*, © 1981 Stainer & Bell Ltd.

ISBN 0-670-83776-8

CIP data available

This book is printed on acid-free paper.
∞

Printed in the United States of America
Set in Minion
Designed by James Sinclair

For

Ella Smith, Kate Smith Dorsey

&

Ella Winburn Dorsey

(Generation to Generation)

Author's Note

As part of an initial agreement with First Church in Windsor, the author has obscured certain details of members' lives as they appear in this book. An effort has been made to assure them privacy within their community while at the same time adhering to the truth of their stories. For the same reason, the senior minister and his associate were asked to read a draft prior to publication and given an opportunity to recommend modifications to the author. Except for the three ministers, the spiritual director, and the church organist, every church member's name has been changed.

Contents

Pilgrim

That is all the help I need; to speak to you. For I am at a moment in my life past which I can no longer see my way. Yet this is not exhaustion. The point is I can no longer understand. I need to speak, I tell you. The capacity to get free is nothing; the capacity to be free, that is the task.

—Andre Gide,
The Immoralist

Prologue

In the spring of 1988, after traveling to Greece for a book about mythology and aeronautics, I came home to Connecticut and settled down. I married a second time, bought a home in the country, and hired out to a good magazine. I might have found more comfort or happiness at midlife, but then nothing satisfies like the next risk. For instance, I could have stayed home on Sundays. Instead, I went back to church.

I am a journalist, which is not to say I am a man of insight or original thoughts. So there is no need to wonder whether I will turn this story into a conversion narrative or preach to you or reveal too many of my life's secrets. I am not a serious or complicated person at all. I have no interest in "ancestor worship," no regard for religion's frozen bolts of paradox or biblical injunctions chiseled in stone. Probably like you, I am mostly curious, oblique, undisciplined, largely unoriginal.

Perhaps also like you, I have attended churches at different times in my life. Born and baptized Protestant, I became an agnostic, turned mystic, self-actualized, individuated, joined the Quakers, opted out— the usual course for my generation in the American psycho-religious carnival. Of course, it never takes long in our culture to grow weary of religion's failures and conceits. You leave the carnival for a while, and then, when you grow grim about the mouth, like an itinerant Ishmael, there you go, off again, onto another ride.

Oddly enough, the ride that becomes a journey often begins in a church. And so, that is where my story begins.

Before our marriage, my wife, Jan, joined a little Presbyterian church in rural eastern Connecticut. A place of hard pews and stale air. The church attracted a troop of elderly devotees and their children, who were the first friendly people she had met in New England. Their sanctuary smelled like an earthen vessel, a homely pot of ancient scents left over from one hundred years of ham-and-bean suppers. Molting palm fronds, spicy bathroom disinfectants, and old ladies' perfumes tinged the air. On Thursday nights they sold dinners of homemade cabbage soup and garden salads prepared by a small group of women who never seemed to leave the kitchen. On Sundays, they met in a cold sanctuary to sing hymns and hear meditations from an Irish interim minister or his anemic female associate. It was surprisingly quaint and pleasurable. On a sensual level alone, their experience together was irresistible. Delightfully sweet. Curiously erotic.

At first, Jan had to whisper in my ear on Sundays to refresh my memory with names of deacons, trustees, or choir members with whom we shared table on Thursdays. But even after faces became familiar, their services remained a puzzle to me. One morning, I remember grabbing fresh palm fronds during the first hymn and following the red-robed adult choir out the back door, singing, into the parking lot. We marched in the cold, damp morning air, circling twice in our suits and spring dresses, waving green palms, warbling, "Ride On, Ride On, in Majesty!" and then we marched right back into the church. I felt completely foolish.

"We have a real treat today," a deacon was saying as we sat down. "Three young women in the church have a special offering for us." While we paraded through the parking lot someone had jury-rigged a small, portable sound system around the pulpit, and then a young woman whom I recognized from the weekday dinners solemnly strode barefoot down the aisle.

"Patty Pandolfo," Jan whispered.

"Patty Pandolfo?" I sputtered.

She was dressed in a thin, shimmering white robe and wore a thick, green wreath of pachysandra on her head. She stopped at the chancel, whirled and lifted her cold, pink hands up to the cross on the wall. Somewhere in the vestibule a record needle tapped into a scratchy track of "inspirational" music and two more women in white robes came fluttering into church. They did not dance so much as sway. They did not sing or speak or look at one another. Rather, they gazed soulfully at the cross and ceiling, and moved their hands like slow fish in water. I thought of nineteenth-century New England virgins doing a hula, but the bulletin described them as a "Rhythmic Choir."

When the music stopped, the women made one final lurch toward the cross, and froze in a beseeching pose. I looked around to see if anyone else was as embarrassed for them as I. Nope, not one.

Women sniffled quietly. Men, heads lowered, glasses removed, handkerchiefs in hand, wiped their wet cheeks. Patty's father sobbed. The associate minister smiled radiantly. "Praise the Lord!" she said.

"Let's get out of here," I said.

"Hush!" Jan said.

Erotic might not be a word you would ordinarily associate with a church. But the old interim minister suddenly introduced the idea after the women's little dance and, oddly enough, I caught myself listening.

"*Eros*," he said, "is a Greek term signifying longing and desire, a 'daemon,' as they say in seminary, prodding people toward fulfillment or union or completion. Could be sex; could be religion. In fact, some churches are in such a slow heat for God's love that their hallways, offices, and worship spaces produce the most eccentric sounds and smells—a faint droning from the crevices, a musky whiff from the carpets."

I looked around when he said this. The little Presbyterian church was such a place. Balanced against the erotic mysteries of the Rhythmic Choir and the Thursday-night suppers, the congregation had created a place of uncommon intimacy. And here they were again celebrating in a Sunday-morning roadhouse: white-and-green felt banners hung from the rafters; hand-stitched quilts presented a pictorial history of the congregation; hand-hewn pews groaned as people shifted in place; the young associate minister wore a brilliantly colored African prayer shawl; the senior man was dressed like a shepherd; the silver service, forged from coins during the Civil War, shimmered under the flicker of flesh-colored candles. The scents were mysterious. Windows framed scenes drenched in light.

Critically and methodically, peering over a set of black-framed glasses that hung at the tip of his nose, the interim continued to speak dryly, fashioning ideas that seemed meant for a stranger like me.

"When worshipers participate in past events, whether it's Palm Sunday, Easter, Pentecost, or Christmas, they do more than remember history," he said. "A rhythmic choir or congregational march through the parking lot waving palms acknowledges the living reality of biblical stories in our lives, with implications that far exceed literal interpretations. Our physical participation with cryptic symbols, in dance and song and meditation, allows a release of psychic energy to explore emotionally what is grave and constant in all human experience."

Something in his eyes caught my attention, a glint, a glimmer, a hint of amusement that matched my own. I actually thought I understood what he was saying.

"The complex discourse of our gatherings, the symbols and rituals, the holy scripture we read, the gossip we share, the stories we reenact . . ."

It took some time for me to see what was happening. Over the weeks, even though the place remained mysterious, its pleasures had grown in intensity, like the slow unlayering of a lover's charms. After savoring delicious homemade pie at Thursday-night suppers and going back on Sunday mornings to sing out loud and glad-hand with the congregation, I had found myself looking forward to our meetings. Jan was pleased to have me beside her in the pew. I, however, was becoming more confused, slowly coming undone like a silly, lovesick Benedick.

Later that day, I thought much more about the congregation and its story—about the significant deaths, divorces, the loss of beloved ministers, failed building campaigns, and dwindling membership rolls. As we had become intimate, I had learned there was no better place to hear the story of the disciples' walk on the road to Emmaus than in a small, rural church of Bible believers. Even though the interim minister kept sentiment at bay, still, when I joined the tinny choir singing "Amazing Grace" and then followed his interpretation of congregational life, I thought we had just struck upon the most accurate juxtaposition of intellect and innocent parochialism. Under the roof of Sunday worship, we enjoyed an undisturbed kind of truth. For the first time in my life, I felt clued into the secrets of the living, breathing practice of religious community.

Later the next week, on Sunday morning, after another fascinating sermon, about the "narrative vision of church life," and the final hymn—"I Love to Tell the Story"—I walked out of the sanctuary with tears in my eyes.

Jan and I attended through Easter and early Pentecost. We would be there still, perhaps, except that the interim minister left in midsummer. The reverend, whose academic style seemed to suit my thinking so well, returned to Cambridge to teach theology at a distinguished seminary, and the congregation hired the female associate full-time. After a few Sundays, I remembered why I hadn't been back to church in twenty years. It turned out she was a fundamentalist, a Bible literalist. In just a few weeks, my romance with the church ended. The spell broke.

I am not sure when I started to think about writing a book. I am not a person with much insight into matters of the Spirit. But I do think that sometime during our stay at that little church my midlife pilgrimage began. All the stories we heard—biblical myths, the congregation's story, individual tales of family struggles—continued to play in my mind long after we left. Eventually, in interviews with other ministers and religious scholars, I managed to put together a bibliography that explained more about this narrative vision of church life, and as I studied, an extravagant vision appeared.

The Church became an object of intense curiosity for me. In my imagination the composition of ordinary stories took on larger meanings. I continued reading—mythology, religion, theology, sociology, biographies of saints, stories of congregational life. Eventually I came across a quote from Martin Luther that created, to my surprise, a great stirring of heart:

> *Let every one of us stay each in his own parish, where he will discover more useful work than in all the making of pilgrimages, even if they were all combined into one. Here, at home, you will find baptism, sacrament, preaching, and your neighbor; these are more important to you than all the saints in heaven.*

Now, this is strange, I thought. I began to wonder whether what I found at the little Presbyterian church could be found almost anywhere. Could there really be so many such places in America? Our original shrines of folk art? As common as convenience stores?

As I set out from Sunday to Sunday, I often thought of those words of Martin Luther. Stepping through arched doorways, passing through the Gate of Dreams, I looked for one special minister in his Customhouse to be my subject. I wanted to find a man rumpled, laughing, caught between attending a funeral service and counseling a couple for marriage. I searched for someone who did not show a bit of interest in theology or myths or theoretical notions, a minister with a dog at home, a hiccupping mimeograph machine in the office, and a line of small children toddling by the doorway.

Scholars and theologians had done the hardest work, that was certain. An early movement of intellectuals convinced me you could enter a congregation the way you would a novel, meeting characters and engaging in stories as a way of understanding the foundation of community life. At night, I spent hours underlining passages and making notes in their books, attending local lectures on Biblical literature and thumbing through my Bible. During the day, I left the studies at home and simply went traipsing through churchyards.

For the first time in my life I decided I could go to church not as a seeker but as a journalist. With the Bible as only a subtext, with religion as only a subplot in my plan, I hoped to find a place that suited my latest preoccupation, a congregation whose religious calendar would present an ongoing literary event, a simple community reeling in the full erotic mystery of an innocently ordinary, intentionally purposeful life. I went out into the world, for once, driven by more than a sense of mere curiosity or financial need. The desire to understand the mysteries of church life had become my mission.

Holy Week

Despite our aspirations, congregations are not time-less havens of congenial views or values. By congregating, human beings are implicated in plot, in a corporate historicity that links us to a specific past, that thickens and unfolds a particular present, and that holds out a future open to transformation.

—James F. Hopewell,
Congregation

CHAPTER ONE

A long line of cars parked at the edge of the cemetery on Palm Sunday morning. Van Parker watched from his bedroom window as people hustled in for eight-o'clock Communion. His hair, still wet from a douse of water, looked unkempt and matted on one side from his pillow. He thumbed a Bible and reached for his notes. In a moment, he would step out the back door and jog across the lawn like an old relief pitcher called up for the final inning. Sarah Wilton was dead. Ed Newberry lay in intensive care. The capital funds drive lagged way below its goal.

As usual, he would break the drowsy stillness by absently dropping his notes at a lectern. The crowd would awaken to a brisk rehearsal of the ten-o'clock sermon. He would call them into a standing circle for a couple of humans. They would share Communion by dipping bits of home-baked honey wheat bread into a mysterious well of Welch's grape juice, sing "Kumbaya," and say the Lord's Prayer. Finally alert, Van would run home for a cup of hot tea and a quick turn through the gray columns of Sunday's *Times* before the main service began.

At five till eight, Van went to the downstairs bathroom to brush his hair, hiked up his britches, and then left by the back door. His wife, Lucille, watched him limping across a dewy stretch of the ancient burial ground and realized that he had again let a week pass without repairing the hole in his shoe.

"The old bird," she said.

Two other buildings came to life. Next to the parsonage, the minister's middle-aged associate, Bill Warner-Prouty, grilled bacon and flipped pancakes in the industrial-size kitchen at the parish house. The sticky-sweet smell of warm maple syrup and the sizzle of hot bacon greeted latecomers sauntering in. As Bill served up steaming plates of hotcakes, people helped themselves to a fresh ballast of coffee and sat down for a final lesson on Old Testament geography.

At the same time, two members of the Prudential Board circled around the fourth building on the grounds, the Pierson House, a decrepit, three-story colonial on the northeast-corner lot. They had arrived early to discuss chopping down one old sycamore in the yard and to decide on the need for pruning others. But as they marched round and round, their attention was drawn to the gray house itself. Rotted steps, flaking paint, and warped shingles demanded attention. Despite the pleasant landscape of white pines, evergreens, a canopy of maples, and great expanses of lawn covering nearly three acres, the entire campus was sullied by a distracting shabbiness. What had certainly once been an elegant, historic New England layout now looked frowzy and neglected. It reflected poorly on them all, the men agreed, and, shaking their heads, they wondered aloud why something had not been done long before.

The morning unfolded as scripted. At nine-fifteen Van went home to his newspaper. Lucille joined the choir doing vocal exercises in a practice room at the rear of the meetinghouse. Traffic began to bunch and crawl along Palisado Avenue. An off-duty police officer made his way into the street to signal directions. Andy McCarthy smoked a pipe on the steps of the parish house and greeted Wilson Keefe, who had lost his job and hoped to drum up freelance carpentry work at coffee hour. Back at the church, a group of new deacons clustered around a breaker box in the vestibule, rehearsing a sequence of maneuvers to light the sanctuary through the week. A moment later, Andy ambled over to the church, where he grabbed a thick line of coarse, yellow rope dangling thirty feet through the ceiling into the belfry and tugged with all his weight. A dull chime rang out over the grounds. The tower's unearthly inhabitants—bees, mice, and an old owl—flapped and buzzed and scurried into motion. It was exactly nine-forty-five. Andy walked over to the door to pick up a pack of bulletins and waited for the crowd.

Five minutes to ten: the organist and choirmaster, Fran Angelo, took his position in the loft, setting stops on a panel to control tones and harmonics on a brilliant set of towering pipes. Cast into a raised deck decorated with artificial columns and a sculptured set of three-foot-tall bronze angels, Fran's Casavant Frère, Limitée, encompassed the entire back wall of the balcony. When Fran began to play, the organ roiled to life, rasping a clean breath of chords across the handsome, blue-barreled ceiling.

Suddenly they came striding across the yard, dodging traffic in the street, strolling through the cemetery, dressed in dark suits and wooly red-and-blue tartans: the old guard, a batch of newcomers wearing boutonnieres, widowers and newlyweds, alcoholics and mothers of alcoholics, winners in the stock market, women battling breast cancer, men fighting mental illness, successful doctors, lawyers, accountants, engineers, husbands without jobs, a few former ministers, a solitary stranger whose wife had died just the day before. One hundred, two hundred, three hundred shuffled noisily through the arched red doors into a cushion of warmth. From the balcony, I watched them circulate, chattering in a bright prism of morning light angling in from twenty-four tall windows, antique twelve-on-twelves, and rare Tiffany stained glass. They stormed in searching for friends or a regular pew in the hollow, luminous hall. Fran's fingers did a spidery dance on the organ keys and the meetinghouse shivered under a complex web of notes. My, were they loud!

"Prepare for the invasion!" shouted Van's black-robed associate, Bill Warner-Prouty. "The children are coming!"

Van jumped up from a gold divan next to Bill behind the pulpit. Fran struck the opening chords of no. 155, "All Glory, Laud, and Honor," and heads turned as dozens of children came dancing, running, and marching down the aisles banging drums, shaking rattles, and waving palms.

They sang it twice—*All glory, laud and honor / To thee, Redeemer King / To whom the lips of children / Made sweet hosannas ring!*—as Sunday-school teachers led celebrants into the front four rows where they could all be seen and prized and cooed over while the ministers struggled to get through the morning announcements. When Van looked down at the wiggling crowd of kids, he grasped the pulpit so hard that his hands paled.

Van led them through the opening prayer, another hymn, and the reception of twenty new members. Over the years, he felt he had become an observer of this process even as he led it. He preferred to be free from the nuisance of a recording system and microphones and every semblance of ceremony (although the rejection of any one of those would not have been an option anymore). He already had decided that in a few years, when he retired, he would skip these ten-o'clock performances altogether. "Bunch of hoo-ha," he would say, privately. But he did like to preach, and when he finally bellied up to the pulpit, he looked, like the rest of them, excited and almost unnaturally happy to be there.

Tall and slender, with a slight slackness about his waist, Van might have made a compelling figure at the front of a church except that he had a habit of nervously straightening a wild wisp of brown forelock and constantly shuffling his notes. His face, smooth and hairless, had earned the folds of age. A wet, toothy smile, large ears, a round robust nose, and active, surprisingly trenchant eyes gave him the friendly appearance of a man who could be grasped at a glance. His hands looked like soft mitts slapping at the air when he preached, as if he were swatting bees. His dark robe hung limply and his face turned pink and warm as he started to speak.

Van always preached with a jerky, unsynchronous glance at his wristwatch, giving himself precisely ten minutes to preach, no more, no less. Nothing worse than a slow service or a dull minister, he would say. Three hymns, a responsive reading, two scripture lessons, an anthem, a response, a four-page sermon, forty-five seconds of silence, an offering, a greeting of peace, the benediction, and a closing verse. No one fidgeted more than he.

During the sermon, he quoted the love song of Don Quixote, the wisdom of Bishop Desmond Tutu, and a line from *To Kill a Mockingbird*. Straightening his collar, squeezing his hands, drawing his fingers into a claw, ducking, feinting, accidentally smacking the microphones, he raised and lowered his voice with a dramatic flair. It was said that he counted them secretly while he preached, that he saw them when they dozed or when their eyes wandered, that he knew who was there and he knew who was not. But watching him work, you would have thought he had nothing on his mind but the message.

"The best thing said about the early church," he cried, "was not 'See how successful they are!' or 'See what good ideas they have!' No, it was 'See how they love each other.' Words like *faithfulness, loyalty, experience,* and *wisdom* sometimes seem irrelevant in our world. And the connecting impulses of peace, reconciliation, and mutual appreciation seem very fragile. Yet hasn't the gospel always seemed foolish? Hasn't the call for simple trust and mutual love always appeared naïve? And isn't this naïve gospel the one that has the power to heal and break down the walls that divide us?"

Van hit his stride and then his voice dropped to a conversational tone. Time to pack in an anecdote and a cliché. Head down the homestretch. Recalling Isaiah, he lowered his voice to a whisper: *"Morning by morning, he wakens—wakens my ear to listen as those who are taught. The Lord God has opened my ear."*

He saw a cloud of grief lift briefly over Nick Wilton, who had buried his wife just the day before. Van had noticed the grave this morning, still fresh and brown at the southwest corner of the cemetery. He thought of his last few visits with Nick, when the man's touching confessional had begun. Joan Rockwell was crying quietly in the balcony. Probably seeing visions again. Allison Denslow, who had come back to church after a long absence, was staring out the window. Maybe she was recalling her own childhood, when she had sat in a Congregational church whispering into her mother's pack of dental floss, "Beam me up, Scotty." Van watched her gazing out on the veil of woods as everyone stood for the final hymn. He wished that a new path might open for her. Maybe he should send Lucille for a visit.

"Go to Dark Gethsemane," they sang. When Fran began a polyrhythmic "Le Chemin de la Croix" ("Jesus Is Condemned"), with a dark descension of chords, the congregation turned and Andy McCarthy rang the bell. People shuffled out as loudly as they had entered, and long lines formed to shake hands with the two ministers on the sunny portico.

Not bad, I thought. Relatively painless. I glanced at my watch. Five past eleven. Time for coffee and cake. Time to pick up the latest gossip. Time to count the money.

There are eighty-nine First Churches in Connecticut, fifteen in Hartford alone. I had set out to find mine a full sixteen months after leaving the little Presbyterian church, going as aggressively as a sightseer, stopping to scan the primly trimmed grounds of Congregational churches and seeking tours from ministers or their associates. They were easy enough to find. At once quaint and stately, the First Congregational church of any town often resides at the geographic center of a historic district. Within a short drive from my home, going east or west of Interstate 91, I often saw from almost any ridge two or three old white spires peeking out of a green, leaf-ruffled landscape. Like ancient broadcast towers, they often stood at the highest point of a myriad small towns from Northampton to New Haven. After three months, I could predict the setting at every turn. Drive into town, pass the pharmacy, the bank, the town hall, a doddering old movie theater, and there it would be: white clapboard, stone wall, crippled gravestones. Pass them on any weekday, in city, town, or countryside, and I would find them hollow but for a skeletal staff who, in one way or another, appeared busy serving traditions with an outmoded personal computer and a distressed office copier beaten down by overwork.

I chose the United Church of Christ denomination because in New England it offered traits that suited my own leanings: theologically liberal, pervasively Anglo-Saxon, democratic, autonomous, and generally middle-class. The membership was formed partly from what remained of the old Congregationalist churches. In the religious tradition, one would say Congregationalists evolved from the Puritans. They did not become the elite. They *were* the elite. In the American literary tradition, they mark a strain that begins with Nathaniel Hawthorne's Dimsdale and ends, or perhaps reaches its most notorious decline, in John Updike's fictional biographies of the spiritually undernourished Harry Angstrom. At various times, Congregationalists have taken credit for everything good and virtuous in our society. From the origins of American democracy to the moral underpinnings of American civic life, Congregationalists, like Presbyterians and Episcopalians, claim to have been at the center of things since the very beginning.

There I was one Sunday, for instance, sharing a hymnal with a young black woman in the back row of Center Church in Hartford. Before the morning was out, I learned that in the 1630s, the Reverend Thomas Hooker had developed the earliest themes for American democracy right on that spot. On a short drive north, I discovered another congregation in Northampton where, during the 1730s, Jonathan Edwards sparked the first Great Awakening by spreading his powerful ideas on experiential religion. On successive Sundays I came across other churches in the valley where, in the early 1800s, the sermons of Yale-educated ministers stirred congregations to life in what is commonly known as the Second Great Awakening, a potent evangelical revival that gave birth to the uniquely American good habits of voluntarism, benevolent associations, missionary societies, and reform movements. How could I not have known?

But then I did not know that the *Reverend* Thomas Gallaudet created the American School for the Deaf in Hartford; that Harriet Beecher Stowe, who wrote *Uncle Tom's Cabin*, was the wife of a Congregationalist professor in Hartford; that Horace Bushnell, who preached for decades at Old North Church in Hartford, set loose the first impulse of religious liberalism ever to stir the nation; that Congregationalists founded Harvard College and Yale College and seminaries long renowned as touchstones for neo-orthodoxy, political activism, and the nurture of human community.

But here in this same valley, still resonating with the legacy of an important intellectual and cultural history, what I wanted to find was not the revivalist sounding an alarm or a modern prophet on the march. The scut work of day-to-day religious life was what interested me, and

that had always been the domain of a relatively undistinguished and forgotten class of parish ministers. The modern-day lighthouse keepers, pe-
destrian harbor masters, and small-time politicians were my targets. I
looked for those who still survived on the inheritance of parochial tradition, a group of general practitioners whose greatest claim to fame was
that they were the last of any professional clan still making house calls.

It was a sunny February morning when I finally met Van Parker.
Nearly five months after my search began, I drove into the Connecticut
River town of Windsor, ten miles north of Hartford, and found him sitting by a drafty window where he had worked every Thursday morning
for the past twenty-two years comparing scripture to anecdotes and
punching out inspiration on a manual Olympia spattered with Wite-
Out. Van was hammering out Sunday's sermon when I arrived. Old
tunes played through a dry, windy whistle from his lips. He riffled a red
Pilgrim Hymnal and listened for an uplifting chord. While I waited in
the church office for the formal tour, I heard him laughing out loud as
he typed and then watched, amazed, as the church secretary peeked
around the corner to scream at him. "Fletcher Van Gorder Parker!" she
shouted. "You are not supposed to be having fun in there! Get back to
work!" I could tell immediately, here was a man who enjoyed his
vocation.

And I already liked the appearance of his church. From the street, the
three-acre pastoral layout looked elegantly shabby. Perfectly appropriate,
I thought, for a Congregationalist. Perched atop the steep northern
slope of the Farmington River, the long white portico of the meetinghouse caught the morning sun, which exposed fractures and cracks in
the facade. The square tower and surmounting belfry lifted the church
over the ragged edge of old maples. Simple architectural details, en-
riched by modillions, beveled quoins, and large moulded architraves,
made a starchy expression of Protestant simplicity. High Greek Doric
columns, heavy, arched Gothic doors at the entrance, and an underpin-
ning of red sandstone appealed to my tastes. Dates cut into the corner-
stones read 1794 and 1757, the latter date, I imagined, taken from an
even earlier First Church structure. Yes, I liked that, too: a salute to
continuities.

Behind the meetinghouse, sloping gently north across several acres, stretched the town's ancient burial ground, heavily seeded with granite and sandstone markers. Geer, Loomis, Mather, Sill, Pinney, Wareham, Huit . . . Gravestones claimed the largest spread of sacred space, designating births and deaths of church members and townspeople since the 1600s. The cemetery looked like an enchanted stone forest. A few broken headstones and discarded beer cans did not disturb the profound sense of a long-settled, civilized community.

I scouted out other buildings on my way in. The handsome Russell House, marked by a brittle plaque at the front door, built in 1755 by the Reverend William Russell, was a roomy, staunch-shouldered three-story colonial where I assumed the minister and his wife lived. Next to it, a simple brick parish house, with its cozy church offices, industrial kitchen, nursery school facilities, library, auditorium, and Sunday-school rooms, built, by my reckoning, during the Protestant heydays of 1950s. Then, on a northeast corner, I noticed a second rundown, three-story colonial, the Pierson House, a building whose purpose was not immediately clear. I was not surprised to learn later that parishioners used the term "campus" to describe their handsome, somewhat decrepit surroundings.

But despite these general attractions, something else drew me in. An endearing informality? An off-centeredness? During a heavy binge of church shopping along the Connecticut River valley, I had encountered finer structures and more impressive men, some of whom boasted reputations that echoed louder and longer than Van Parker's. There was one place known as "the fastest-growing church in New England," and another boasting that its minister was "the most impressive preacher in Connecticut." Some men tagged the title "the Reverend Doctor" to their names, and others operated out of swank offices filled with large, professional staffs. But Van Parker and his church in Windsor had more of what I wanted—personality, a mysterious charisma, a wholesomely attractive and ordinary setting.

At the Hartford Seminary and around the conference office of the United Church of Christ, Van had a reputation for being a radical among mainline ministers. People described his congregation as healthy, hearty, robust—an activist church with special interests in Central America, liberation theology, and the urban poor. At the same time, an outreach minister and a spiritual director had just joined the staff, making First Church not only one of the few Protestant congregations in the country to recognize spiritual direction as an ongoing part of its service, but also the only one with a salaried minister running a homeless shelter.

Honestly, I had expected to meet a moderately hip, left-wing intellectual hard at work in the minister's study. But Van surprised me. He was older than I had guessed. Sixty, to be sure. He did use the occasional Zen phrase—*a beginner's mind* was one—to characterize his ministry in its third decade, and he said his own spiritual director had once described the Parker style as "purposeful drift," a phrase I thought sounded as if it might have been borrowed from one of the Beat poets. But when I pressed him, Van disagreed about how "purposeful" he had ever been.

"More like just 'drift,' " he said, with a goofy chuckle.

As he gave me the tour, I did my best to gauge him, but he could not be pinned down.

Yes, he said, he had experienced a spiritual rebirth in Nicaragua in 1985, but it was a very private conversion, and although it had affected him deeply, he did not believe in one-shot, lightning-bolt transformations. Born-again Christians who'd undergone jackpot conversions had about as much credibility with him as Protestant ministers who complained about being lonely or misunderstood.

"Why, that's all a lot of BS," he said. "Heck, when ministers get so hung up with being solitary and individual, they're in the wrong business! In fact, I think they're probably sick! Why don't they just go do something else!"

Skipping past the topic of conversion, I asked about credentials. I supposed the Reverend Fletcher Van Gorder Parker had taken some advantage from the full weight of his name and training at Ivy League schools, as did many other ministers around the state. His father had been a well-known minister in Hartford before the Second World War. His brother, now deceased, was once an admired Congregational minister in Vermont. But, no, Van downplayed family history and he had little to say about his own association as an alumnus of Middlebury College and Yale University. In fact, he said he found himself becoming, much to his relief, more and more ordinary as he aged.

Then what about spiritual mentors? I asked. He answered with names of parishioners, his wife, Lucille, and his children Susan, Beth, and Doug.

What about theologians? Educators? Mystics? He could not think of a single one.

From the way he padded around happily from building to building, he gave no appearance of being less than satisfied with his present job, title, or station in life. In fact, after spending a week with the man, I found that nothing about him fit his reputation of radicalism. Instead, he spent his days lunging for the phone, arranging hours for weddings, ordering flowers, and offering his help for funeral services. His calendar was congested with mundane committee meetings. He had letters to write, hospitals to visit, funds to raise.

"Churches have to be practical and pragmatic and real and caring in local ways," he told me one day, "but at the same time, a local parish can't afford to be parochial. You're only truly local when there's a universal quality about your life."

Oh yes, he also showed a propensity for one-liners, which often emerged as he attempted to answer one of my questions several days after I asked it. Without prompting, he would look at me thoughtfully and deliver: "Religion's like politics—it's all local." Here they came fully gestated, popping out wholly formed like a hen's egg: "Religion's not some dogged personal affair!" he would shout. "Come on! Relax! There's no party line in this church! ... Theology comes from below, not from above! ... I don't care what you write about us, you can't kill this place! ... What's the big deal about spirituality? It's as mundane as ham and eggs. It's not some—oh wow, man!—ghost that goes bump in the night ..."

Before long, I was at his side every day, wondering like the rest of them why, three weeks before Easter, Van Parker kept telling people life felt new again. Not an unexpected sentiment from a minister, you might say, especially at the end of the Lenten season. And to the rest of the staff it might have sounded like just another pronouncement from the boss man on one of those typical March mornings when the whorl of activity turns Holy Week to Hell Week. Still, I noticed, even when everyone else rolled their eyes and sighed, Van forged ahead, insisting that the days to come promised something good.

At first, I thought maybe a rash of small events suggested possibilities to him. It wasn't just the presence of a professional fund-raiser who had set up office in the Sunday-school room, or the spiritual director, whose fledgling ministry sent a silent stream of conferees questing by his door. For instance, he announced one day that, after twenty-two years, he had finally landed a spot on local radio—one of the worst times imaginable, twelve oh-five a.m. on Sundays—to preach the Good News to nightowls in Hartford County.

"We'll finally reach the insomniacs!" he howled.

When one of his newest members stopped by one morning to ask about starting a prayer chain, he reacted in kind.

"I don't know what the heck you're talking about, a 'prayer chain,' " Van admitted. "But let's put it in the bulletin, anyway, and see what happens. This could be great!"

He even found a sign of hope in a wildly undisciplined dog that Lucille brought home one day. All around the church now you could hear Daisy, a black Labrador puppy, barking in the yard. She danced on a long chain and dug pits in the gardens. As Holy Week continued, Van and Daisy went for long, rambling jaunts around the cemetery, pushing and pulling each other, seemingly blessed by the same spirit, though no one—not even his wife or secretary—knew what kind of spirit it was or whether one or both of them had fallen under its spell.

Within a few weeks, I came to a decision. Preferring plain daily practice to transcendental performance, the minister and members of First Church might have been judged "low church" in the trade—a definite slur in many places around the Connecticut River Valley. But in Windsor? No, Van Parker said he considered that a compliment if he ever heard one.

There was something funny going on here, I thought. Didn't know what exactly. First Church seemed like a good place, where the mark of liturgical seasons could still be used to chart a congregation's journey.

Van vowed to give me access to every aspect of church life, and the groundskeeper snuck me a set of keys so I would have complete run of the place for the next year.

"I'm sorry, I guess I don't know why you're interested in us," Van told me on the day we made an agreement. "We don't have anything profound to say. What we do here is just the steady, undramatic task of ordinary days."

But I just wrote that one down, too, adding it to a list that had grown longer and more curious by the day.

CHAPTER TWO

One Thursday in early March I watched Van as he typed, looking up often to study the action on snow-crusted Palisado Avenue. Big Henry Holcombe, a physical giant of a man and the congregation's single most impressive contributor, had phoned to say he would drop by to make a pledge call before lunch. Van wanted Henry to kick off the campaign with a ten-thousand-dollar pledge. But the idea of asking for that much money made Van nervous. He fidgeted and wriggled anxiously by the window.

Janet Filer had insisted the campaign start with this one meeting—a symbolic conjunction of pastor and steward—so Van couldn't duck out. But Henry's potential reaction bothered him less than the thought of his own contribution. Sometime around noon, he guessed, Henry would hand him a blue three-by-five pledge card with the names "Van and Lucille Parker" inscribed on it, and ask for about three thousand dollars. He had heard that the committee wanted at least that much from him. Sounded like plenty to Van. Combined with their annual pledge, it would put him and Lucille well beyond a ten-percent tithe. Except for Henry, practically nobody else at First Church tithed.

Unfortunately, Lucille kept insisting that they give even more.

"Van," she'd said again that morning at breakfast, "you're the minister. You have to set the pace."

"Lucille, we are naturally frugal people," he said.

"No, Van Gorder, you know three thousand dollars is not enough! Being tight is no excuse."

When he came to work that morning, he reviewed a few rough pages from next week's sermon. He kept returning to the scripture lesson from Genesis: *God saw everything that he had made, and indeed, it was very good. And there was evening and there was morning, the sixth day.*

Maybe Lucille was right, he thought. None of it is ultimately ours. He typed the line into his draft.

"Nne of xxit is ultmitely prs."

As he slipped another blank page into the carriage, a rapid tap of high heels echoed down the hall.

"Janet!" he shouted.

Janet Filer spun quickly and walked back to the minister's doorway. He leaned in and smiled. "Today's the day, Van," she said.

"What time did you say Henry was dropping by?" Van asked.

"Before lunch," she said.

"He's a saint!" Van said.

"So you think you're ready for him. Have you pre-prayed?"

" 'Pre-prayed'?" Van repeated. "Oh! Yes, of course!" Henry suggested that everyone "pre-prayer" before pledge calls.

Just then a large, burr-headed figure lumbered up the parish house steps and slung open the front door.

"Too late," Janet said.

"Well, Reverend, ready for the dunnin'?" Henry Holcombe loomed behind Janet, wiggling Van's pledge card in the air.

"Come on in," Van said. "I've been pre-praying all morning."

The men excused themselves, then shut the door quietly to begin.

The pyramid scheme would unfold from the top down, just as Janet had planned. She had assured everyone this would be the best way to start, a very rational way to raise $750,000.

Janet walked back to her temporary office at the end of the hall. She thumbed stacks of green, white, and blue pledge cards prepared for more than four hundred First Church families ("giving units," as they were known in the trade), and proofread the final galleys for a glossy, black-and-white brochure called "Building the Household of God."

She looked like a professional golfer: short, straight brown hair, tawny skin, a pug nose, a rugged frame. When she walked, it took some effort for me just to keep up. Her "office" in the Sunday-school room looked a little strange, I thought, consisting, as it did, of a set of tables and chairs sized for kindergarteners. A bulky, black rotary-dial telephone and several simple cardboard files filled with financial statements rested along the window sill. Life-size, handpainted murals depicting stories from the Old Testament surrounded her, making the busy production appear charmingly naïve.

But despite the surroundings, the techniques used for "Building the Household of God" sounded remarkably prescriptive. The process looked vaguely scientific; her spreadsheet, astonishingly businesslike. Sitting down in one of those little chairs next to printouts of four hundred families' private pledge accounts. I imagined the campaign as my own personal gold mine, a clear, quick opening into the true obstructed core of church life. Janet saw my eyes wandering down the lists and quickly shuffled them into a folder. Then she explained her plans like this:

"This system's been used for fifty years in hundreds of churches, colleges, and hospitals. But before you build the pyramid, first, you have to call in a kind of focus group—a small meeting of church leaders. I start by giving them a list of names of all the people in the congregation. Then I tell them they will be responsible for setting a goal for every single member. It's a once-in-a-lifetime gift for some people, so there's no other reference. Unfortunately, there's no other way to make the assessment. All I can do is give them an idea of the scale we're looking at. To raise $800,000, for example, we need one pledge for eighty thousand, two for forty thousand, four at twenty thousand, eight at ten thousand, and many, many smaller pledges.

"Then I ask them to begin with themselves—'What can I give?'—and I tell them to write that figure down on a sheet of paper. Then, I say, 'Now, think beyond yourself. What can the minister do in relation to your gift? Write that down. What can our chairperson, Henry Holcombe, do? Write that down, too. What can the other people in this room do? Now put those numbers down.' And so it goes until we've got a list of pledge requests for every family in the church.

"Sure, it can be a difficult meeting. The first reaction is, 'You're asking me to judge my neighbor's lifestyle!' and then, 'How should I know what somebody else can afford?' I had one woman here come up to me afterward and say, 'Well! If this is the way we set pledges, then I'd better not drive my Mercedes to church anymore.' And I said, 'Well, honey, if you don't need it, why don't you just donate it to the campaign?' "

Janet laughed nervously. If her voice had an edge, it wasn't just because she risked her reputation at First Church. In New England, she said, unlike the Bible Belt, people generally do not talk openly about money in church. At best, the subject is never discussed; at worst, it serves as material for gossip or operates under a minister's singular control. Even at First Church, only a few years had passed since the days when the treasurer routinely stashed each Sunday's offerings in a bag after church and carried them home to hide behind a brick in her fireplace until she could deposit them in a bank on Monday morning. Such eccentric arrangements usually masked an old Yankee attachment to money, a relationship characterized by privacy, stinginess, and a noticeable lack of spiritual depth. In all her years of raising money for churches—seventeen in the past five years alone—Janet had never run a campaign in her own church, though, and more than anything else, she felt responsible for easing the congregation through the transition.

She had been a member of First Church for only a year when the idea came up. Naturally, her name was mentioned to lead the effort. She had spoken up often at early meetings, encouraging the congregation to raise the goal five times higher than the original target of $150,000. She had also urged that the church set aside five percent of the total for Habitat for Humanity, a home-building project for poor families in Hartford. She had even boasted that they could raise the money in just six weeks. When the offer came, she greeted it enthusiastically.

Now, as Van and Henry met, Janet finished plotting her schedule for the next six weeks. A dozen "captains" from the original focus group would ask for pledges from one hundred people they knew, and then those people, in turn, would become "canvassers" and spend three weeks running around Windsor to call on the remaining church families at home. A complete harvest, collected by Easter, could bring in as much as a million dollars.

At twelve thirty, Henry and Van came clamoring down the hall and Janet turned away from her accounts. They appeared in the doorway grinning like boys just baptized on the banks of the Farmington River.

"So. I could hear you two giggling all the way from the office," Janet said.

Henry rubbed his head shyly. Van laughed, shoving his hands deep into his pockets, and nervously jangled a lump of change.

"What's the matter, Henry?" she asked again. "Didn't Van give enough?"

He handed Janet their cards. Van's card showed $7,200 and Henry's exceeded the $10,000 request Van made. Henry squatted down into a tiny plastic chair; Van leaned up against a mural of Moses in the bullrushes.

Janet looked at Henry's card again, and then drew a fresh batch out of a blue stack on the table. Henry cleared his throat and leaned over the table grinning.

"So," he said slyly. "Who's next?"

"Honestly, Mr. Holcombe," Janet said, turning the stack over in her hands and fanning them like a deck of playing cards, "I would say you can take your pick."

In truth, dry rot and demographic trends convinced people of the need to raise money. The enthusiasms of Van, Henry, and Janet Filer only served to promote the plan. Van actually had a little interest in the project initially. He never wanted to be remembered as curator of a living museum along Palisado Avenue, and he had no desire to raise money for the sake of historic preservation. In fact, he would say as much out loud. Once during a meeting with the property committee, when the discussion about church architecture started to sound like a high-toned missive, he fired off his own blunt opinion: "We're a church, dammit, not a historical society!"

But not everyone agreed. In fact, some people thought Van deserved the blame for letting their fine old buildings decay. Just two years before, an analysis by engineers and architects had detected so much neglect at the congregation's two-hundred-year-old meetinghouse and parsonage that the congregation felt forced to call a special committee to assess the needs.

For years, surface inspections on Sunday mornings must have been sufficient to satisfy the property committee, known formally as the Prudential Board. Their reports regularly gave the buildings and grounds passing marks. Until the professional engineers' tour, the Prudential Board had somehow failed to see lead paint peelings in the children's playground, dim lighting in hallways, distressed stairways, strangely pocked ground around gravesites, and rickety foundations. Occasionally, someone commented on bits of brittle shingle from Van's roof found scattered around the sidewalks on Sunday mornings, but no one recognized that Van's own dining room had become uninhabitable—termed "hazardous" in the professional report. Rotting joists and decayed beams lay beneath the floor. It should not have taken a trained engineer to discover a foundation wall caved in underneath the sanctuary. Evidence that the leaching field for raw sewage had backed up into the church's 360-year-old cemetery was unthinkable, but there it was, as clear as daylight on Easter morning—an explosive matter, for sure, should certain families' ancestors come washing up.

With fresh demographic figures in hand, a new property committee sounded a note of prophecy. Their reports would begin, "In light of the coming millennium . . . ," and go on to remark about the need to "hold market share" of Windsor's churchgoers, and predict a "potential downsizing of pledges." They needed money to repair the property, more members to raise money, more money to meet the needs of new members. Suddenly, everyone was feverish about growth. A case of millennial fever struck in Windsor, and the congregation startled awake, seeing its future suddenly in doubt.

And so it was that the pressure of prudent capitalization, not God, finally caused Van to accept the one job he had avoided throughout his career. The time had come, at last, for a major fund drive, and though Van was not pleased by the thought, he offered to work alongside Henry Holcombe and Janet Filer, as a good sport, to wheedle and cajole for the cause.

As usual, Van started to wonder whether God had perhaps given him a new opportunity, and after making his pledge to Henry, he told Janet he felt an excitement that he had never imagined possible.

"It was a little painful," Van said. "But that's a sure sign of growth."

Janet saw the eager look in his eyes.

"Okay," she said, "but before we start going through these decks, you need to know one thing."

"I know what you're going to say," Henry said.

"In the next few days we're going to be dealing with all those people who weren't invited to the original goal-setting meeting."

Van cocked his ear.

"That's right," Janet said. "Word gets out, and people will say we've judged their lifestyles and assessed them a fee."

"Well, where else were we going to get the information?" Henry asked.

"I know," Janet said. "But when people start talking, they're going to come in here privately to talk, and they'll make excuses: 'I have this situation or that . . . We're retiring . . . We're putting our children through school . . . We can't possibly afford this much, and, besides, our finances are none of your business!' Once the campaign begins on Sunday, we'll be putting out fires for a week. I guarantee it. I just want you both to be prepared."

"Pre-prayered," Van corrected, glancing at Henry.

"Okay," she said. "Cut it out."

"Go ahead," Henry said.

"All right. First, I'm concerned about Miles Carrington." She handed Henry one of the blue cards, which designated the largest requests.

"It's true," Van said, angling over her shoulder to see the figure. "He hasn't been to church for a while."

"Do you think he's upset because of the cross?" Janet asked.

"I don't know, but we sure don't want to mention it if it's not true," Van said. "Maybe we should just make a note for whoever takes the call."

During the year, Van had convinced the congregation to let him hang a plain wooden cross on the wall behind the pulpit, the first time in anyone's memory that the symbol had ever appeared at First Church. Old-line Congregationalists regarded a cross as Catholic, a reminder of why their pilgrim ancestors had left England 360 years before. The mighty King James Bible, not the cross, was the most exalted icon for Congregationalists. For men like Miles, groomed under old-line doctrine, a cross, if not exactly pagan, definitely breached the canons of good taste.

"Yes, well," Henry said, "Miles was upset about the cross. You know, there hasn't been a cross in the church for some time . . . a hundred years, at least!"

"At least!" Van repeated.

"So it was a bit of a shock to him, and I can tell you there were a few others upset about it. But I don't think it'll make him turn his back on the fund drive."

"Okay, then what about Kate and Ken Tabor?" Janet asked, handing Henry another card. "Kate stopped me in the hallway last week and said she didn't think the drive was being conducted at the right time. So I set up an appointment so we could talk about it, and she didn't show up. I just wonder if they're worried about being asked for more than they can afford."

Henry looked at the Tabors' card. "It's a big request," he said. "Actually, you know Ken's been sick. Maybe they're worried that as they get older, they won't be able to make these big pledges like they have in the past."

"No," Van said. "They've been big supporters for years."

"Well, what about this outreach business?" Henry said. "You know, I've heard that Ken's not too happy about giving money to Habitat for Humanity. And neither is Miles. And neither is Paul Price."

Paul Price. The treasurer. The name seemed to vibrate with hidden meaning.

Janet continued riffling through the cards, and pulled out another.

"All right then," she said. "Seems like you two are on top of it. Why don't we start with someone less controversial. Look. Here's one. Forrest Clarke."

Henry took the Clarkes' card, printed with a five-figure sum. He showed it to Van.

"Fifty's okay," Van said. "You don't want to insult him."

"Who knows, he might be flattered," Henry said.

"Great!" Janet said. "Then he's the next block in the pyramid, and we'll ask for fifty thousand. But maybe you should check it out first, Van. You know, loosen him up, tell him we're thinking about asking for this amount from certain people and see how he reacts."

"What harm can it do?" Van said.

"He can always say no," Henry said, picking up another stack off the table. "So who's going to take this one?"

"How about this one?" Van asked, snapping a card from the blue deck.

"Whoa! Here's one you should be careful with," Henry said.

Then Henry came across two that caught him short. He showed them to Janet and then to Van.

"I might tackle these myself," he said, smiling.

"Henry, you know we can't send someone who pledges ten thousand to get thirty thousand," Janet teased. "They'll look at you and say, 'Are you crazy? Who in his right mind gives that much money to the church?' "

Henry palmed the two cards and thought for a second. "You know, my wife got a call from an old college roommate of hers this weekend, and she's married to a four-star general. And she said they're having problems with the capital campaign at their church up in Maine. The trouble is, her old general's ordered, 'No visitations! I don't want any solicitation at my house!' Now that's real trouble. Who in the church has the nerve to solicit a hostile four-star general?"

"And . . . ?" Janet said.

Henry puffed out his chest and stood up. "And? Well, the general's a pretty big fellow!"

Janet laughed.

"Of course, I was just a little old private in the army," Henry said, "but then I told my wife, 'Now wouldn't that be fun! Tell them, I'll hit up the old general! It'll be good practice. Let me do that job! I'll be up there tomorrow!' "

Henry reached out and grabbed a thick bundle of cards off the table. "So, Janet, if you've got any tough ones in there just give 'em to me! Because I don't care who it is or how much we're asking for. For the church, I'll knock on anybody's door!"

Van suddenly burst out laughing and flapped his arms, sputtering in such pleasure that he couldn't get a word out. The laugh rose in fits and starts. Janet and Henry began to smile, and then they looked stunned as Van's body shook and rocked. His mouth broke wide open, exposing tooth and gum, then he froze and the laughs cascaded.

By one-fifteen, the first block of the pyramid fell neatly into place. The sound of laughter and shouts echoed down the hallways. Henry tucked two more cards in his coat pocket, and Van joked about his own niggardliness at the breakfast table with Lucille.

By the end of the day, they had a clearer sense of their targets, and when Mrs. Tabor and Mr. Carrington called to complain about the campaign, Janet knew precisely how to respond.

"We've been very eager to hear your concerns," she said. "In fact, I think Van and Henry Holcombe will be calling you soon. One of them will probably be dropping by your house sometime tonight."

The congregation met routinely at the parish house after Sunday services, in a broad, putty-colored auditorium known as Nelson Hall, a room as large as a skating rink, a place named for the beloved sixteenth pastor, the Reverend Roscoe Nelson (1892–1932).

An enormous handmade quilt, stitched with colorful scenes commemorating special moments in First Church history, hung in a Plexiglas case at one end of the hall, and a grand piano, placed at the foot of a raised stage, anchored the other end. Significant social occasions left the linoleum permanently scuffed: Women's Club luncheons regularly lured one hundred or more; church suppers, Weight Watchers, Confirmation classes, nursery-school fitness programs, magic acts, First

Church fairs, and fashion shows came and went. For weeks, I watched them parade in and out. This is their erotic place? I wondered. It did appear to be, as one of my books said, "the place where a congregation intensifies its quest for communion."

In any case, I often saw famished crowds drain the punch bowls and coffeepots, wipe out platefuls of cookies, and vanish by noon. I thought it was a sort of "slam, bam, thank-you, ma'am" kind of eroticism, but probably a meaningful encounter to a Congregationalist's way of thinking.

On Palm Sunday morning, however, the customary feast was interrupted by an announcement.

"May I have your attention, please!"

Janet, wearing white pearl earrings and a shimmering cobalt-blue dress, stood on the stage and waved her hand at the crowd. "We will soon begin our first accounting for the capital funds drive. And while I get set up here, I'd like to ask Henry Holcombe to say a few words about the campaign."

Henry ambled up to the serving table looking like a sumo wrestler in a Brooks Brothers suit. He stroked his chin shyly and then filled the room with his husky, formal, sonorous voice. Quoting a verse of scripture, he silenced the crowd and then he tried, awkwardly, to tell a couple of jokes. Janet disappeared and soon returned wheeling a blackboard filled with a matrix and long lists of members' names. The crowd thinned out in a hurry.

"Looks like we're starting to lose a few," Van whispered, handing Janet an electronic calculator.

The machine started to whir in her hand as she poked a few buttons to test the paper readout.

"Don't worry, Van," she said, and then she called out with a strong, flat voice that cut through the auditorium.

"Okay, thank you, Henry," she said. "Let's start with our captains. Now where's Ralph Stoot? Ralph! What's your total?"

"My canvassers called in twenty-one hundred dollars this week!"

"Andy McCarthy!" she shouted.

"Eighteen hundred dollars."

"Tony Gillette!"

"I got one card back. Eighteen hundred."

She read down the list with commanding efficiency, smacking the blackboard with clean strokes, filling in lines with a blur of figures. A crowd of the church's most prominent and influential supporters stood back, watching like precinct workers comparing tallies on election night.

"Forrest Clarke?"

"I've got nine cards, for a total of fourteen thousand . . ."

Van took over at the blackboard to fill in digits as Janet kept calling names. For the next several minutes she clamped down on the calculator, summing toward a total.

"This isn't so bad," she said. "With only one hundred and two cards in, we have $473,855. That's really on target, in terms of percentages. Of course, there are still three hundred cards outstanding."

"Three hundred?" someone said. "That means seventy-five percent of our people haven't pledged!"

"Now there's no need to worry. We just need to pin them down!" Janet said.

"I know we'll get it," Van said, looking out at his parishioners. Streaks of chalk smudged his coat.

"There's no question we'll get it," Janet repeated. "But we're going to lose steam if we pass our target date next Sunday. Call me for the tough ones. Or call Van. It's important for us to hear about your visits."

Elizabeth McCarthy, the head deacon's wife, fidgeted by the coffee table, apparently eager for an invitation to speak. Her hand went up, waving furiously.

"Then I have to tell you one thing," she said, her voice aquiver. "I have just been very disappointed! Even considering all my years on stewardship, this has not gone well. People are coming in at one-third to one-sixth the amounts we've set. Besides that . . ."

"Elizabeth! Elizabeth! We don't want to know everybody's circumstances," Van said. "Besides, I think we should just hold up the good experiences and move on."

"That's right," Janet continued. "Does anyone have a positive story they'd like to tell?"

Positive? Elizabeth shuffled in place. Her eyes cast around the crowd. Anne Carrington, Miles's wife and a prominent attorney in the area, caught Elizabeth's arm.

"I'd just like to say this has been a good opportunity to visit people in their homes, and it gives them a chance to say some things they haven't said before," Anne said. "But one thing I'd like to know is, how will their comments be addressed? I don't know if there should be one person or if we need a whole new vehicle—"

Van jumped again.

"Anne," he said, "I'd suggest that anything that has to do with the building fund should just be referred to Bill or me."

Anne had not said a thing about the building fund.

"But Van, it seems to me," she countered, her voice rising, "that maybe something else needs to go on. Beyond the two of you. There have been certain issues raised by certain people and they need to be addressed!"

Certain issues. Certain people. Janet's brow furrowed. The story I had heard during the past week involved a certain private, prestigious benefactor who was apparently holding back on a pledge because he had some beef with the outreach committee. I never heard a name, and the details from my sources—Van, essentially—were always sketchy. All I knew was that he and Janet had been on the trail for days.

"I . . . I think you're . . . you're certainly right!" Janet said, searching for an upbeat note. "Especially when I get back pledge cards and they're full of zeros. I want you to tell me about it. Not that we all need to know the gory details. But we do need to know how to follow up. Sure . . . we need to know . . . and maybe . . . Well, maybe even Van needs to know. But is it just one person with an issue or is it thirty? And I think we need to give some thought to that before we get too worked up."

Anne looked around the hall. You had to read Janet like a hieroglyph.

"Go ahead," Elizabeth whispered.

"Well," Anne said, taking a step forward, "I don't know if it's just one person, but one thing I do know is I've heard throughout this campaign that people are concerned about how we're handling our money. And when certain people give money for a certain thing, they would like to see that money used in the way it was originally intended."

Van flinched. Anne took another step toward the blackboard. She suddenly raised her arm emphatically and said, "Frankly, Van, I think this calls for an evaluation! We need a group to sit down and say, 'Okay! Just what's going on here?' Yes, I know, we have our Cabinet and we have our Prudential Board. But maybe we need a group without any connections to things like that. Do you hear what I'm saying?"

She paused and looked around the room. What was she saying?

"Just so we can look at an issue like this and analyze it and throw it out here and say that the Moly—"

"Anne!" Van shouted.

"Anne," Janet repeated. Then, calmly emphasizing her words: "The first thing you can do is let me know what you're hearing and then I can give a report back to Van and then we can talk about it."

There was a pause. A voice came from another part of the room. "I have to agree with Anne."

Then another. "I've heard the same complaints."

Janet started. "Okay," she said, "that's three."

"But it's not just three," Anne said. "There is a family in this church who is not happy with the way the Molyneaux estate is being administered, and I think . . ."

Here it came. Briefly, precisely, Anne Carrington broached the name traveling the grapevine for weeks. It had eluded Van and escaped Janet. But now Anne would tell everybody: Word was out that portions of a fund from the Molyneaux estate, supposedly set aside for property expenses, had been siphoned into outreach programs. "If it's true," she said, "an explanation is in order."

I knew that ministers sometimes reveal secrets to embarrass the larger congregation. For instance, if a church regularly falls below budget and there's no other way to balance the budget, a minister might report actual pledge figures to shame people into increasing their donations. But this was the first time I'd heard of a parishioner unleashing a secret to shame the minister. Van looked pale.

"All I know is," Anne continued, "these people were good friends with the Molyneauxes and they do not think the church should be using money set aside for the buildings in any way we choose regardless of—"

"No, no, no!" Van shouted.

Anne leaned over to look him in the eye. "You should hear what this family says! As soon as they heard about the campaign they flipped on their answering machine. They're monitoring every call that comes to the house."

Van looked shocked. Anne smacked her hands together and shook her finger. "Look, I'm just saying this is a big family who has the potential to be a major contributor in terms of pledges or endowments—"

"Can I say something?" Van said, raising his hand toward Janet. "Okay, can I speak now?"

He stopped for a breath and turned to the crowd. His voice changed timbre.

"You know, money wields a lot of unseen power in our society because we don't talk about it. We make it private. And I feel that the more we talk about it—not in an overbearing way, but in a confessional way— the easier it's going to be. That's true in my own life. And I know it can be true in this church. That's a positive step.

"And the next thing I want to say is this: Last week I got a call from Louisa Mircalos, who must be our poorest member. But she still gives two or three dollars a week to the church, which is about all she can afford, and beyond that she is a very faithful member. Well, Louisa called me up last week and said, 'Van, I got a letter from the church and I think I can add another ten dollars a month to my pledge.' And I said, 'Louisa, that's wonderful. That really means something.' And she said, 'Van, everyone thinks I'm crazy to give away as much as I do but I've always found that when I give stuff away I get back more than I give.' And I thought that was one of the best stewardship sermons I'd heard in a long time. From one of our poorest members. But rich in other ways. And I think whether we're giving ten dollars more or ten thousand dollars more, that's the spirit behind whatever we do and . . . and . . . Well, I'm sorry. I just had to say that . . . And the last thing I want to say . . ."

He was preaching again. Packing in an anecdote and a cliché. Heading down the homestretch. Van's best strategy in a conflict: the well-timed filibuster.

Nonetheless, as he talked, it was also clear that at least one layer of gossip had eluded them. They thought they had taken care of the Tabors and Carringtons and Prices—headed them off before the calls went out. But with only one week left in the campaign, the "Household of God" was short $300,000, and certain rumors were running faster than either Janet or Van could keep up with. If they didn't act quickly, the ethos of Christian charity and homecoming, developed slowly from Sunday to Sunday and day to day over an entire career, could be damaged in a single season of discontent.

For a minute, Van started to say something about the foundation of church life, that it is not the intimacy of friends that matters so much as the capacity of strangers to share a common territory, common resources, and common problems. That was what he'd said, in one way or another, for the past five Sundays, ever since I started coming to his church. But then he was suddenly quiet.

Anne walked back to the stage and sat down next to Elizabeth. Van, still flushed with excitement, looked at Janet. Janet looked at Henry.

I snapped off my tape recorder and placed it securely in my leather briefcase. I knew I was onto a good one. The narrative that had begun during Holy Week had started to thicken, and the conflicts that I had anticipated would now begin in earnest.

CHAPTER THREE

By Thursday, the office sounded like a train depot. Van cranked out a prayer, a Good Friday meditation, notes for a funeral service, and an Easter sermon. The ink-spitting mimeograph machine burped out bulletins for six services. Peggy Couples, the church secretary, fielded a final round of calls for lily and tulip memorials, her hands spattered with black ink. The rest of the staff marched through the cramped office like baggage handlers and ticket punchers calling out schedule changes for the final string of Holy Week events.

Late in the morning, Van walked down the hallway toward the sunlit Sunday-school room. The walls of the corridor were pasted with green cardboard. Golden crepe-paper angels dangled airily among postings of winter's gray financial reports.

Van tapped on the door. Janet had been on the phone tracking down rumors about the alleged mishandling of funds. The subject had cropped up again at Monday night's deacons' meeting.

"Cómo está?" he said, cheerily.

"Oh, Van," she said. "I'm starting to see church people drive by my house at night." She sounded weary.

"They're what?"

"Honestly, I can sit by my living room window and practically count members as they go around the block."

"They're just naturally going to be curious," he said.

"I know, but thank God I live in a modest home in a middle-class neighborhood."

"I wouldn't worry about it," Van said. "After Sunday, it's going to be almost over anyway."

"Maybe. But how much money do they think I'm making here?"

Janet sat at the kindergartener's table, her knees tilted sideways to compensate for the height. The mass of paperwork seemed to have tripled over the last few days as more pledge cards came in. She was swamped.

"Anyway, I wouldn't count on it ending soon," she said. "The good news is we have enough money pledged to request bids for work. The bad news is we're still about one hundred fifty thousand dollars short. The campaign's definitely going to drag on way beyond Easter."

She handed Van the latest batch of cards.

Van pulled up a chair and shuffled through the decks. From time to time, he stopped to pluck a few and set them aside.

"I guess it's a pretty good thing I hid my Jaguar in the garage," she said.

When he finished thumbing the blue deck Janet pursed her lips, as if she wanted him to take a second pass before commenting. She brushed her brown hair out of her face and sat back in the chair.

"Well, it is surprising to see who stretched and who didn't," he said, seriously.

"Yes, a little surprising," she said. According to the usual formula, eighty percent of the money should have come from the top twenty percent of members—those designated by the stack of blue cards. Ten percent of the congregation would probably not give any money at all, and the rest would pledge the remainder in one or more shares of the twelve-hundred-dollar average.

"Unfortunately," Janet said, "we're not doing so well on those blue cards. They're way low."

He finished going through the final deck and silently nudged the cards across the table.

"What's the matter?" she asked.

Van thrummed his pale fingers against the cards he had plucked, then sifted through a few, a mix of lowballers and unsigned pledges. They included a few prominent members.

"I don't know," he said. "Maybe I've just totally misread the congregation."

"What about me?" she replied. "I'm afraid these people will never speak to me again."

He shrugged his shoulders. He sighed, then clapped his hands together.

"How about a glass of iced tea?" Van said. "Come on, you need a break."

"Sure," she said. "But we still have to talk about a few things. This Habitat issue opened a scab."

"Where did you hear that?"

"I don't know where it's coming from. It's like these stories about the Molyneaux funds."

"Oh, Paul Price again," Van said. He reached over to get the door for her. "So it keeps coming back to outreach?"

"Yes, but I think you and I have the same idea about where it started. We've got some real characters out there, Van."

"Real characters!" Van repeated, as they started down the hall toward the kitchen. "I think Abraham Lincoln once said, 'God loves all the real characters; otherwise, he wouldn't have made so many of them.' "

They slipped into the kitchen. Van mixed two large plastic cups of instant tea and filled them with ice. Then they went into his office and shut the door. If rumors and gossip and a smattering of scurrilous talk had obstructed the flow of funds, something would have to be done soon. Especially if the church treasurer was involved, they would have to act fast.

———

Ten miles to the south, on a cold gray plaza in front of Hartford's city hall, a young minister slung a sandwich board over his shoulders and joined a revolving circle of picketers.

"Homeless, not helpless!" they shouted. "Homeless, not helpless!"

Television crews and newspaper reporters drifted through a grumbling crowd of street people huddled together like survivors of an earthquake. The homeless picketers left grocery carts and paper bags filled with clothes strewn around the sidewalks. They stomped their feet to keep warm, blew air into their hands, and passed bottles of wine disguised in paper bags to fight a sharp wind. When police cars pulled up to the curbside, dozens of the protesters ascended the front steps of the municipal building. The minister turned when he reached the heavy front doors and waved overhead to three men standing behind a glass door inside the second-floor city council meeting room.

Suddenly, the glass flung open. Three men stepped out onto a narrow balcony and unfurled a bedsheet painted with the words SAVE OUR HOMELESS PEOPLE. Cheers erupted from around the plaza. A set of loudspeakers mounted on aluminum posts were lifted up out of the crowd. A microphone crackled to life.

At thirty-two, with pouting, fleshy lips, large blue eyes, and a thick, well-sculpted head of wavy blond hair, John Gregory-Davis looked at least ten years younger than anyone present. His polite demeanor might have allowed him to pass as a gentleman farmer from Vermont, if not a young seminarian, and ordinarily the tone of his voice had a bridled quality, as soft and as precise as a prayer. But as the hollow sound of homeless men's chants droned on, his voice became charged. He grabbed the microphone and shouted angrily.

"For the eighth straight year," the minister said, "when the Immaculate Conception shelter is forced to close on Good Friday, many of Hartford's homeless men will have no place to go. For most people in this city and in Hartford's prosperous suburbs, Holy Week will end with a beautiful Easter sunrise service, but for many of the people who stand with me here today, there will be no resurrection. Holy Week will end and they will go back into the tomb! Back into the tomb! . . . Back into the tomb!"

The chant rang out and John passed the microphone to a young black man who, a moment earlier, had been standing on the balcony with his fist raised.

As the crowd grew more agitated, two Hispanic men wearing sunglasses and black nylon jogging suits disappeared around the side of the building, entered through a back door, and came around to the lobby. Inside, the gilded entryway looked bright and cheery. Large clusters of white Easter lilies lined the corridors. John stood there waiting.

"Yo! John!" The men waved at the minister and motioned to the elevator that would take them to the second floor.

"Looks like you went all out today," one of the men said, pointing at John's plastic collar.

"I hate these things," John said as they stepped into the elevator. He tugged at the clerical collar digging into his neck. "I'd never wear this at First Church. But for TV, it's a prerequisite."

Although no one from Windsor had shown up to support the action, John's position as First Church outreach minister and director of the Immaculate Conception homeless shelter in Hartford gave the dramatic takeover at city hall the one element it needed most at Easter—a religious symbol. Although it was his own shelter's closing that would turn seventy or eighty homeless men back to the streets on Good Friday, he had managed to take the moral high ground. With his blessing, the men of his shelter had planned the first organized political campaign ever led by homeless people in the city. In the past week, they had elected officers, published press releases, demanded appointments with city council members and the mayor, and worked with a veteran union organizer to train in civil disobedience techniques.

For a month, John repeatedly used a single image to characterize the living paradox of Holy Week: "Back into the Tomb." At First Church in Windsor, he could not stir a response. Lately, he only snickered cynically when members of the congregation grimaced at the phrase. He warned them that on Good Friday, when guests at his shelter in the Immaculate Conception church were turned out (as they were every March for six months when the Catholic congregation needed more space) there would be no beds at the city's other shelters. His men would disappear into parks and abandoned buildings around downtown Hartford. Inevitably, many of those men would take sick, and by summer, some would die.

"Think about it," he would say. "Would you send Christ, who was also a homeless man, back into the tomb to die?"

Still, the Windsor congregation had refused to join the effort, and now, as the rally continued outside, he was alone with a cadre of homeless men and a couple of Hartford's usual leftist rabble-rousers heading into a meeting in the city council chambers.

I stepped onto the elevator with them. A few men were already in the mayor's office. When we arrived, John and his entourage hustled over to the second-floor window to watch the action down below.

I searched the faces in the crowd. For the past week, I had observed as this bedraggled, besotted assembly formed a team. Most nights in John's basement shelter many of them seemed as if they could hardly draw a breath with ease. Most were drug-addicted, a few suffered from AIDS. In the last few nights, while they trained in nonviolence and prepared to speak to the press, I had seen them stone drunk, psychotic, trembling, hyperactive from cocaine, sometimes so out of their minds that their conversation was incomprehensible and John had to interpret and steer the meetings for hours. I could not imagine how any one of them would lead a protest. But here was Bobby Ware, who had bounced from abandoned trailers to city shelters in Hartford for years, a man who did not normally express two words about anything, looking clean and attentive, speaking directly to the police chief about what would happen next. An unlikely crowd of the city's homeless, alerted by word of mouth, passed a microphone and distributed press releases to reporters. Compared to what I'd seen during the week, these men had nearly returned from the dead.

"We won't start by talking about civil disobedience," John said. "But I hope the city's prepared."

At five o'clock, when city hall closed for the holiday weekend, a dozen homeless men with bedrolls snuck inside and joined John in the council chambers. They met the mayor and demanded accommodations. If their needs went unmet, on Good Friday morning they would gather again at John's shelter to continue the assault.

As the mend opened negotiations, John drifted to the back of the council chamber, out of the view of television cameras, and, crossing his arms, waited for events to unfold.

Early that evening, a dozen choir members slipped into First Church to practice the darkest, saddest service of the year. Tenebrae, a symbolic re-enactment of the Last Supper, would go on, as it did every year, with mournful anthems, melancholy solos, and the passing of Communion bread under slowly diminishing lights. Despite quickly dropping temperatures outside, the meetinghouse was warm and the last angles of sunlight swept over the interior. Everyone inside looked comfortable and calm.

The choir practiced vocal drills—*Homo-nomo-homo-nomo-noooo! Mumma-mumma-mumma-mumma-maaaaa!*—tackling scales faster and louder while a crew of deacons rushed through the choir room with silver trays of bread and grape juice. Two women stood at a window talking, gazing out on the cemetery where tombstones and granite obelisks cast longer and larger shadows across the yard.

"You're holding back!" Fran Angelo crowed. "Enunciate! 'When Jesus weh-eh-ept!' Listen! Listen! Again . . ." Joan Rockwell snuck away from the soprano section to stand over the floor vent. Straddling the grate, she let warm air billow her robe and rise beneath her skirt while the choir sang. Just outside the view of her friends, she spun slowly and spread her arms in a graceful dance.

The meetinghouse filled with generous gusts from the furnace, creating the largest, most welcoming public space in town that night. By seven o'clock, it would appear from the street like a hollow lantern, all cordiality and luster. The muffled sounds of choir practice would still be echoing in the sanctuary at seven fifteen when the first worshipers arrived.

At the parish house, Bill Warner-Prouty wrapped a gift for a boy he had guided through Confirmation class that year. He marked a scripture passage in his Bible to read during the evening. *Rise up on wings of eagles . . .* A dozen fourteen-year-olds had completed the Warner-Prouty seven-month program of Protestant indoctrination, and tonight each would pair off with a sponsor guide and be confirmed as a First Church member.

The kid Bill had paired himself with was at home dressing in a light-blue oxford shirt, sockless loafers, dark slacks, and a navy blue jacket. By the time he arrived at the church with his parents, he would look neat and preppy. At the last moment he would drop a necklace over his head to let a small silver cross dangle discreetly against his chest. Many generations removed from his famous ancestor Jonathan Edwards, young Jon Powell had decided, with Bill's help, that he could believe in something, even if he still couldn't reconcile history with myth. Standing alone, the few facts of Jesus' life presented a scattered puzzle; read as fact, the imaginative stories of Jesus insulted the boy's intelligence. After months of debate, he had finally settled on a cosmic prop—the symbol of a cross—as a way of acknowledging and accepting the mysteries of the Christian story. Some parents simply forced their kids to sign the requisite faith statements, but Bill and Jon had gone at each other with heavy theological arguments until Jon made a leap of faith. "He's a smart kid," Bill thought, as he wrapped the gift, a recording of Bach organ pieces.

At seven thirty, a small crowd settled into the pews. The choir was seated. Six deacons drew chairs up to the Communion table at the foot of the high white pulpit, while two others manipulated lights from the breaker box in the vestibule.

"On the night that he was betrayed . . ."

While Bill read the story of the Last Supper from the Gospel of Matthew, two deacons whispered directions in the vestibule, trying to hit the appropriate switches to douse lights.

"Left and right choir," one said, and the balcony fell into darkness. "Okay, wait now, right and left cove . . . No, that's the chandelier! Here, try this one." The new deacon reached over to the breaker box and flipped a black switch. Pews along the far walls were drowned in shadows.

Six young confirmands climbed the stairs to the pulpit and took Bill's place reading scripture. Jon Powell leaned into the microphone. More lights burned down. His shadow grew large and significant on the wall behind.

"When it was evening, he came with the twelve. And when they had taken their place and were eating, Jesus said, 'Truly I tell you, one of you will betray me, one who is eating with me.'"

The cove lights clicked off, ancillary lights in the choir blinked and shut down. Individually, deacons, sitting like apostles in symbolic positions, blew out one candle after another until only one flame flickered on the table. A single bright beam from the pulpit allowed the kids to continue reading the story of communion and betrayal, and soon the images of deacons carrying silver plates of grape juice and bread to the congregation rose on the walls in the darkening hull.

When the last lights went out with a pronounced click, Joan Rockwell sang "Pie Jesu," as she did every year, and then all that could be heard was the steady breathing of the furnace and Fran's Casavant pipes. The congregation sat for a full, uncomfortable minute in silence.

"'But see, the one who betrays me is with me, and his hand is on the table.' Then they began to ask one another, which one of them it could be who would do this."

Van stood to say a prayer. They sang one hymn. Andy McCarthy tugged at the long rope. A few lights switched back on. Under the direction of a dull chime from the belfry, everyone rose to go home, somber and quieted.

At that moment, thirteen homeless men and protesters went face-to-face against the Hartford city council.

"Like, all you got homes and stuff," said one of the ragpickers, pointing at police officers. "You, you, you, you, you! It could happen to anybody in this room. That guy over there. All you rich politicians! All you high-class people who look at us like we scum. But let the stock market fall tomorrow and every one of you be out here with us."

"That's right," said another, wearing a floppy broad-brimmed black hat. "Like hey, we homeless. You white, I'm black. You die of cancer, I die on the street."

"Tell it, Cowboy!" the other men shouted.

"Next week, we be sleeping on park benches. The next week, we be in your doorway. Next thing you know the city gonna tell us, 'We don't have no place for you.' Look, man, we need a bed! We need food!"

A chant started: "One, two, three, four, we want more than just a floor!"

A homeless man wearing green and gold marching-band trousers flashed a scroll of dirty papers.

"I got my hospital records!" he cried, and slammed them down on the council table. "Last year we lost five guys who didn't live through the summer!"

"Tell him, Eddie!" someone yelled.

"Twenty-five guys got knocked in the head. M'fuckers got rolled on the streets . . ."

"Tell him, Eddie!"

I marched with them that day lifting picket signs that said, WE'RE HOMELESS, WE'RE HUMANS and SIXTY HOMELESS MEN WILL BE WITHOUT SHELTER ON EASTER. Now, just as the First Church choir was hanging up its robes, a group of homeless men with nicknames like Tiny, Cowboy Joe, Frenchy, and John the Baptist stood in the city council room and explained to Hartford police that they would spend the night sleeping right there on the floor. "We have nowhere else to go," they said.

By the time the confirmands unwrapped their gifts and headed home with their parents, John and his protesters had presented city politicians with a set of options. By the time the lights of the church shut down for the night, John and the homeless men were making impassioned arguments for housing.

A dozen men, all residents from John's shelter, joined his circle. They smelled bitter like woodsmoke and sour wine. In the quiet light of the council chambers, their rough faces looked bloated from alcoholism and their bodies drifted whenever anyone spoke, as if they were suspended in liquid tanks. John, by contrast, tall, pale, and as thin as a post, looked clean and well-pressed in his crisp blue shirt and dark corduroys. He finished negotiating with astonishing expertise.

"Last year," he said, pointing forcefully at the deputy mayor, "the city had no emergency plan when our shelter closed, and our men went out on the streets again with no place to live. In the meantime, the city of New Haven has been to court and faced a test case that should change the way you do business this year.

"The issue is this: Does a town have a legal responsibility to provide shelter to homeless people? And the answer is yes! The Superior Court has ruled that cities and towns in Connecticut do have an obligation. We see a precedent, and when we close the Immaculate shelter tomorrow morning—on Good Friday—we believe the city of Hartford will be under a legal—not to mention moral—obligation to find shelter for these men. And, as you can see, if you put us out tonight, they'll be on the streets immediately with no place to go."

One of the men took off his sunglasses and John turned to him.

"We can speak for ourselves!" the man said. "My name is Bobby Ware and after tomorrow, I'm going to be homeless again. But I'm not helpless."

"Tell it, Bobby!" shouted men around the room.

"Preach on!"

While the pietistic Tenebrae service in Windsor ended in silence, the homeless men were told repeatedly that they would have to go. Bobby Ware made his speech, turned to his small, select gathering of men in the council chambers.

"Okay, guys, this is it," he said. "What we getting ready to do is what they call civil disobedience. The police might take physical control over us, but they can't control what we think. And the power we have is the power of truth. We got the juice!"

Speaking truth to power. John's eyes sparkled.

Thirteen men unfolded blankets and lay down on the floor of the chamber.

As police officers lifted bodies off the floor and carried them out into the hallway, John Gregory-Davis sneered at the city's director of social services, calling him a "jellyfish" for not finding the men shelter, and then ended the evening in a shouting match. The deputy mayor called John a "creep" and told a reporter than if John Gregory-Davis and his homeless men did not like Hartford then they should move on. John told a reporter he felt like throwing a punch. By nine o'clock, thirteen homeless men were handcuffed, fingerprinted, and taken to jail.

That night at home before bedtime, Van watched a report of the events on the eleven-o'clock news. The mayor of Hartford had little to say, not much more than a weary comment. "We absorb so many problems in this city," she said. "We're about to explode."

What was it about that John Gregory-Davis? Van wondered. Why was he always picking a fight?

Early the next morning, John went back to work. No one from First Church had called. Even though he had told Van and the rest of the First Church staff about his plans during Monday morning's staff meeting, no response came from Windsor. The news stories on TV and in the morning's front-page coverage by the *Hartford Courant* had not mentioned John's association with First Church. But John said he expected at least to get a call from Van.

At one o'clock Bobby Ware showed up at the shelter with a bundle of copies of the morning's *Hartford Courant*. While John answered calls from reporters, Bobby clipped color photos from the front page showing Cowboy Joe holding a picket sign.

"Did you guys see the governor's called for 'a day of fasting and prayer'?" John said.

"Great, so why don't we get a six-pack of root beer and celebrate," Bobby joked. "On the other hand, why don't we just get a six-pack of beer!"

"What we really need is to regroup before we lose momentum," John said.

"Yeah? Well, what I really need is a six-pack!" Bobby said.

"I wonder where we can get a bus," John said. "We've got to keep pushing—we're gonna rally on the deputy mayor's porch tonight."

"You got no sense of humor," Bobby said.

Of course, Van would not call, John thought. The poor Puerto Rican neighborhood where he ran the shelter was still too unfamiliar to First Church members. Their lives revolved around stately historic neighborhoods and glistening, frost-covered tobacco lands. Here, the streets were thick with black and Hispanic poor, teenage mothers pushing strollers, drug dealers making sales, prostitutes and young gang toughs hustling a living.

Just a few blocks from the new sixty-million-dollar state legislative office building, the Connecticut Supreme Court, and the vast brick and granite home offices of the nation's largest insurance companies, the young minister worked out of an old Catholic church where few Windsorites ever visited. The bridge John had been called on to create between First Church and the homeless shelter, a job he'd been hired specifically by Van to perform as a staff member of the Windsor church, spanned only a few miles. But after six months, it was clear they remained an ocean apart. John understood precisely why it was so hard to attract suburbanites to the city, but he still could not fathom Van's own reluctance to get involved.

The truth was that only a few members of First Church took the homeless mission seriously. Even Van seemed intolerant of the liberation Gospel John preached. Over the last six months, John and Van had had more than a few confrontations about John's approach to Hartford's housing problems. John's solutions always involved strategies of civil disobedience and public demonstrations. Van insisted on reconciliaton and working through systematic channels.

Sometimes you could hear them arguing in Van's office after Monday-morning staff meetings—a hostile father and son locked in a showdown. Why Van ever hired John remained a puzzle to me.

"I've got to keep that guy on a shorter leash," Van would sometimes say after one of their fights.

"Van's a lot of talk," John would tell me, privately. "A typical liberal. He means well, but you can't expect any action."

By midafternoon John had spent most of the day either out on the street looking for homeless men or back in his office flipping through the yellow pages for a place to rent a vehicle. He needed transportation to get to the next protest site. He phoned the Red Cross, but was refused. Greyhound was on strike. He had contacts at the Loomis-Chaffee School in Windsor, but they weren't likely to give him permission. His own friends had left to spend the day at the annual blood-dumping on nuclear submarines in Groton.

"What about your church?" Bobby said.

"I guess I could call Van," John said, finally. "We've got to have some way to get you guys up to the North End tonight. We might as well use the church bus as anything else."

"What's the choice?" Bobby said, sarcastically. "Connecticut Limo? No, I got an idea! We'll rent a dump truck."

At five thirty, John called First Church. He flipped the conference-call button on his phone so Bobby could hear, too.

"It's a long shot," he said.

In a moment, Van answered.

"Yes, Reverend Gregory-Davis," Van said, sounding enthusiastic. "I see you've been busy in Hartford."

"We have," John said. "And we're trying to keep it going for one more night. But we need transportation and . . . I was wondering if we could borrow the church bus tonight. Things are really hot down here."

The front page of that morning's *Courant* flashed in Van's mind.

"We really need it about six thirty to start moving our people," John said.

"I wish we could work something out, John, but it would be a lot of red tape, and at this point, it's probably too late. I wish you had let us know earlier."

"We didn't know earlier," John said.

"Not tonight, John," Van said. "I'm afraid it's just so much . . . bureaucracy. We'd have to go through the Prudential Board and then there

are all kinds of liability issues that have to be worked out and ...
and ..."

There was a pause. John said nothing.

"What time do you need it?" Van asked.

"About six thirty."

"So, I guess that means you're not going to be able to make the Good
Friday service tonight?"

John shrugged. "Guess not. You might say we're holding our own services down here."

When he hung up, John looked at Bobby. "See what I'm saying? It's
that capital funds campaign. I'm sure of it. Van's getting spooked by you
guys."

I thought John was probably right. By the afternoon of Good Friday,
two days before Easter, financial problems at First Church had consumed Van's thoughts. The campaign's five-percent apportionment to
help build low-income housing in Hartford had caused a stir in some
quarters. Just that morning, I had overheard the treasurer expressing his
disapproval to Van and Janet. Even I could see the dynamics of that: no
bus for the homeless.

"Well, we've got to keep our momentum," John said.

He strapped on the plastic collar and, a few minutes later, Bobby followed him out into the street again to look for foot soldiers.

"Cowboy! Cowboy!" John said, as they passed behind a dumpster off
Park Street. "C'mon, Cowboy, we don't have time for this shit!"

A body shifted underneath the Dumpster and a head tilted up, tooth-
less, boozy, eyes sunken.

"Yo, Cowboy!"

"We got the juice!" the body mumbled.

"Muster the troops," John said. Bobby clapped John on the back, then
they grabbed the drunken homeless man, hoisted him to his feet, and
went off to look for more.

By mid-evening, temperatures had dropped below freezing and snow
was forecast. John and twelve homeless men hitched rides to the home

of Hartford's deputy mayor. Crowding onto the man's front porch, they presented a set of written demands at the door, and then staged a press conference on the sidewalk. Under the glare of camera lights, the continuing question from news reporters went like this: "How do we know you people are really homeless?"

Once again at eleven o'clock the protesters appeared on the late news, reading prepared statements, and making a final Easter appeal. And once again for those to whom the ancient story must have been most familiar—for Van and his absent congregation—the scene of betrayal and communion passed unnoticed.

It was nearly midnight when John returned to the shelter and unlocked the doors to let the twelve men sleep on the floor for one last evening. Clasping Bobby and Cowboy Joe around the shoulders as they descended down the vaporous entrance to the basement, I heard John whisper, kindly, "Brothers, I guess this means we'll have one more meal together."

Maybe those were the words that finally did it for me. Sometime during the weekend, before Saturday night, almost every one of the homeless men disappeared. On Easter Sunday at First Church no one asked John Gregory-Davis about the protests, the jailings, or the outcome of their struggle. Van read scripture lessons on Easter morning and a brass and string ensemble performed a rousing serenade. This final piece of a weeklong drama presented itself—if only to John and me—as a paradox, suddenly unknowable and unexpectedly profound. The men would vanish, the apostles would wander.

Another cunning twist, one more clever turn, and, I thought, I would soon become more than an observer on assignment.

The Word

In Exodus 3:14, though God also gives himself a name, he defines himself (according to the AV) as "I am that I am," which scholars say is more accurately rendered "I will be what I will be." That is, we might come to understand it as a verb and not a verb of simple asserted existence but a verb implying a process accomplishing itself. This would involve trying to think our way back to a conception of language in which words were words of power, conveying primarily the sense of forces and energies rather than analogues of physical bodies.

—Northrop Frye,
The Great Code

CHAPTER FOUR

Easter left me with vague anxieties. After browsing old First Church records, I began to see images from the seventeenth-century diary of young Roger Clapp intruding on worship services. On Sundays I would see us, like passengers in the belly of a boat, merchants, mariners, medics, millers—"and so we came, by the Hand of the Lord, through the Deeps comfortably; having Preaching or Expounding of the Word of God"— traveling in a spell of Eurocentric wonder.

Here we go: the same hollow, wooden sounds; the identical round, pink faces. Stair-step melodies and cramped English verses.

Young Clapp had assembled with 139 others from the west country of England for the first services at Plymouth Harbor the day before Palm Sunday in 1630. The little boat simply called *Mary and John* formed a sanctuary that crossed the ocean. Within five years they had settled Windsor, a kind of harbor town, where they built their own *para oikos* (the Greek root for *parochial*, literally, the "house next door") on the banks of the Farmington River. Worship had continued, uninterrupted, from Sunday to Sunday—from Plymouth to Massachusetts Bay to Windsor—for three hundred sixty years.

Did the old pilgrims still contribute to the spiritual life? I wondered.

I could sense the spirit of their ocean journey in the creaking of the drafty meetinghouse. I imagined their traditions generating a physical power over us, like a magnetic field that could be sensed only by ghostly intuition. Were those adventurers still the true cosmic center of First Church, the real source of its influence and order? Were these Congregationalists still shaped more by the celebrated story of English pilgrims who civilized a wilderness than by the stories of Abraham, Moses, Jesus, and the disciples? After what I witnessed at Easter, I had to wonder.

The congregation had certainly evolved a pleasant but impenetrable style. Gray matrons shaped like milk bottles came and went with a mysterious air, serving coffee and making a smiling appearance as sponsors of every significant event. Who were they? I wondered—so friendly yet so remote. In the activity of standing up and sitting down, singing and making vows, even an astute observer would never have a clue about what attracted them there. Anonymity was prized. Even during the one moment of Sunday's service called "Joys and Concerns," when people were allowed—implored—to reveal themselves, the congregation remained as hushed as a snowdrift.

"Does anyone have something to share?" one of the ministers would ask aloud every week. "An announcement? . . . A concern?"

I listened many weeks for one personal tale—a husband's grief, a mother's celebration, a mystic's dream. What of illnesses, childhood discoveries, epiphanies? Never a word from the crowd. Even at coffee hour and during weeknight suppers, I failed to crack the facade. They were like strangers on a voyage, as young Clapp had noted three centuries before, "amassed in intimate proximity."

I turned to history. Bookish detail, I thought, might make churchgoing not only a more quaint and indelible experience, but connect me to unspoken depths. Especially if the past continued to reveal itself in the architecture and the worship service, there must be something in blind tradition that led everyone to church so regularly. Surely, a window would open into the secret, elusive life of their community.

At evening meetings of the church Cabinet, Prudential Board, and Board of Deacons, I learned the extent to which people still prized the past. Apparently, Van's effort to hang a plain wooden cross had stirred more discontent than the minister was willing to acknowledge. The truth was that Van had first attempted to bring a cross into the church twenty years ago. As a young minister, when he and Lucille moved into the parsonage, Van's effort to install a simple cross behind the pulpit had met a storm of protest. Van beat a retreat. So ferocious had the opposition been, that he waited twenty years—until most of the old-timers literally died off or left for nursing homes—before he attempted to raise the subject again.

The fact that the buildings—authentic American monuments, in a sense—had been allowed to fall into disrepair also created a storm of discontent that I had just begun to fathom. At both the Cabinet and Prudential Board meetings, I heard the issue blamed for continued resistance to the capital funds campaign. The deacons actually believed the faltering fund drive, stalled nearly $100,000 short of its goal, pointed directly to where the allegiance of the church lay. Several families had designated their pledges for upkeep of property only, barring the church from giving any portion of the funds to Habitat for Humanity. Conservators of tradition formed a powerful bloc.

Touring the property, I looked for further evidence. Most symbols of the church were not religious in nature at all, but historical. Stone plaques or vintage prints depicting the church or Windsor village commanded the most prominent spaces on walls. Heavy slabs of engraved marble hanging next to the pulpits listed names of every First Church minister since the seventeenth century. Nineteenth-century diagrams of the sanctuary, with names of members penciled in at specific pews, greeted visitors in the vestibule. A few original Currier and Ives prints of a meetinghouse that looked very much like First Church hung in committee rooms. Portraits of bearded First Church ministers, Old Yalies with expressions of tight-lipped concern, peered around corners. Nothing more. Nothing remotely religious appeared, not even a dime-store print of the Last Supper or a blue-eyed Jesus looking skyward.

In conversations, I noted that the cemetery was considered by the ministers and congregation to be the most sacred space of all. Revered as a historical treasure, a plot marking the remains of their original English minister, John Warham (1630–1670), rested in the south end of the

First Church cemetery beneath a shattered sandstone marker. Large monuments loomed over the bones of a few famous statesmen, a former United States Supreme Court justice, and an important early American poet. Interestingly, the same surnames continued to appear on membership rolls today. Right here, every Sunday, Susannah (Warham) Beardsly sat in the fifteenth pew in quiet contemplation. The Ellsworths, a family whose ancestor, the honorable Oliver Ellsworth, had been named chief justice of the United States Supreme Court in 1796, had their regular pew. His tombstone had a prominent place in the cemetery. Then there were the Loomises, the Barbers, the Drakes, the Phelpses, the Gillettes, the Sills . . . , original settlers represented now by family cemetery plots, and, of course, by present-day members of the First Church finance committee, Prudential Board, or other bodies of influence.

As opportunities for getting to know people were so limited, and members so guarded, it was my hope that the most telling details of history might soon add up and explain more clearly who these people were and why they kept returning. I searched their most valuable documents. Handsome bicentennial and tercentenary publications produced in paperback contained a trove of detailed information. A dusty file of Women's Club records was unearthed. I even signed up for a ten-day summertime expedition to England with two dozen members of the congregation. I rooted around for nuggets.

Still, nothing of value. From the vantage of Monday mornings, Sundays began to look to me like little more than amateur snapshots, a collection of moments that became memorable only when something—or someone—went awry. With nothing else to connect me to the congregants' lives, I watched quietly from Sunday to Sunday, waiting for any awkwardness that might reveal the place. Snug in my balcony perch I took notes, like a satellite doing reconnaissance.

The sight of the choirmaster's children and the associate minister's boy mocking services provided moments of amusement. Mimicking soloists and yawning over the sermons, they turned any act of piety on its head. I once observed a couple of kids on either side of the balcony tossing an orange ball across the pulpit during a somber announcement for a healing service, and more than once I saw a paper airplane drift from a child's hand into a pew below. Ministers' children and their heathen friends could always be counted on to hurry along the spiritual quickening of any moment.

I also learned that I could chart significant events in people's lives. For instance: the day Trudy Crandall walked in wearing a wig signaled the effects of chemotherapy; Nick Wilton's sudden and continued presence in pew number six seemed to inaugurate a determined search toward something important following his wife's death; two mentally retarded women started bringing boyfriends to the deacons' bench in front and turned their pews into the liveliest corner of the church; Joan Rockwell, who still sometimes cried quietly during the services, started a practice of coming to church early on Sundays to meditate and pray in the choir loft. What was her problem?

Van always gave an enjoyable performance. Especially after the fund drive stalled, you could measure his dismay by counting the number of dull objects that suddenly became animated on his person. Driven by the shock of financial distress, Van sent ballpoint pens and notepads leaping from his hands. Sometimes, over one hour, his comb, handkerchief, grocery list, names of shut-ins, sermon topics, phone numbers, and addresses would all hit the floor. His hearing aid sounded off like a pitch pipe at times, and one Sunday, looking down from the balcony, I noticed him speaking from a set of notes all typed in red. I realized that his jackhammer typing style finally had frayed the black ribbon on his Olympia, and rather than spending a dollar to replace it, he had jumped the cartridge to pound on the red side alone, making every word look like the scarlet verse of Jesus.

Then there was Rufus Wedemeyer, the eighty-five-year-old deacon emeritus who appeared sporadically at ten-o'clock services. There was something at once funereal and yet strangely reassuring about taking a bulletin from Rufus's silky white hand, and funny how the musky, warm fragrance of his old deacon's breath lingered long into the day. But this title: deacon emeritus. What the hell was that?

In time, I vowed that no change would go unnoticed. Even a person's absence tickled my imagination. I took pages of notes. Charted seating arrangements. Quietly attended the journalistic enterprise. Unlike my own childhood experience of churchgoing, the more often I attended and took notice of every little action, the more engaging the whole affair became.

Eventually, turning heads and outstretched hands began to greet me. Tenors in the choir motioned for me to join their section. Allison Denslow would sit down and snatch my notepad away—"Can't you quit doing that!" she'd whisper, teeth gritted. The ministers would look up and nod kindly.

Still, nothing of any consequence happened on Sundays. Not really. Congregationalists were as steady and unchanging as an association of—I don't know—birders or philatelists.

"Now you know why they call them 'God's Frozen People,' " Jan said to me one Sunday when I came home, once again, perplexed and annoyed.

"That's '*Chosen* People,' " I answered. "And besides, they're very nice, despite everything else."

"Yes," she said, this time mocking me. "Nice. As nice as nice can be."

I ignored her. Maybe, I thought, I needed more development, just like any other new churchgoer. First, you take notes and memorize names. You attend a roast beef dinner. You teach Sunday school. You visit a family in their home. You volunteer for a committee and slowly work your way onto the deacons or the Cabinet. I kept telling myself that it takes time merely to discover one's self in the midst of so many irrepressible, symbolic affairs. Modest acts of discovery, I thought, may be the reason churchgoing favors—even requires—a habit. Patience must eventually pay off with a special kind of knowledge—of respectability, belonging, community, civility. What was it I wanted but could not yet name?

After Easter, I asked to join the healing committee. I volunteered to take notes at meetings and offered to publish their monthly newsletter. A few members resisted, initially. But, as everyone knows, a church committee never refuses a volunteer. True, I was not altogether sincere or clear about my motives. To become a participant offended my professional ethics. But there was no other way. I vowed to be a good listener and promised myself never to be so cynical as to call any one of them *hypocrite* or *clown*.

"We must make this sound very ordinary. Bread-and-buttery, not weird and wonderful."

Sifting through a pile of books and articles strewn at her feet, balancing a lapful of papers, Priscilla Drake gave orders with impressive alacrity.

"And as for music, I do not want scratchy-tacky," she said, her light accent appropriately tart. "I do not want New Age fuzzy."

Born and reared in the West Country of England, where the First Church congregation originated, Priscilla brought a special authenticity to the job of chairperson of the healing committee. It was not just her melodious accent or exacting attitude that gave her authority. Her extravagant nest of prematurely gray hair, which she swept back into a bun, and her dressy executive woman's business attire put her a notch or two in class above the rest of us. From the square of her shoulder pads to the smart, brown glint of her loafers, Priscilla looked well appointed to her role.

For weeks, as we struggled to plan the best form for a service that would be liturgically correct, she demanded punctilious discipline. And yet even after so much planning, at the eleventh hour, just days before our first service, the idea of spiritual healing still posed many weighty dilemmas. The thought of printing a program, for instance, created a panic.

"Priscilla, let's just skip the tunes. Anything's gonna sound like elevator music in this setting," said Ted Alford, the high school baseball coach. She had watched him scroll her agenda into a tight wand and use it to bat the bottom of his shoe.

"So what do you suggest, Ted?" Priscilla asked.

"Why don't we just have a little silence."

"But how much silence?"

"Five or ten minutes."

"Well, Ted, you're awfully mature in your ability to handle silence," Priscilla replied.

"Actually, I prefer silence, too," said Allison.

"I've got no problem with silence," Nancy said.

They sat in their usual circle, in their usual parlor, the Morrell Room, named after the nineteenth pastor, Herbert B. Morrell (1948–1958). Priscilla Drake, Allison Denslow, Joan Rockwell, Ted Alford, Nancy Fitch, David Weston, and Van. A small group, middle-aged, grown comfortable enough to snipe. Allison, the black-haired one, about my age, was taking notes. Joan, the blonde, a little older, listened with her eyes closed. Nancy, who left a trailing scent of bathpowder or perfume when she came to sit down, kept a book open while they talked.

"Okay, silence 'tis," Priscilla said. "Now, where shall we hold the service? In the choir room or church? And if it's in the church, shall we hang some panels or flags so we won't feel like an ant in a barn?"

"No, no," Ted said. "In the church."

"And bring a candle," Allison added.

"One single, chunky, white candle," Priscilla said, penciling out a list.

"And, please, no flags," Ted said.

"Fine, no flags." She added an asterisk to the list. "Now, Joan has volunteered to pour the grape juice," Priscilla said. "But should it be in cups or in a single silver chalice?"

"I wish we weren't so self-conscious," Ted mumbled.

"I beg your pardon, Ted?" Priscilla said.

"I said, the less analytical, the better," he barked. Ted hadn't shaved today, I could tell that much. Probably just midterm exams and his twentieth baseball season catching up with him. David, the group's single sullen psychiatrist, was substantially buried in his chair, legs crossed, immovable, also apparently distancing himself from the growing list of particulars.

"Can we go back to the silence?" asked Allison. "I know we just decided on quiet without music. But maybe we should just read some scripture to give focus."

"A welcoming!" Priscilla said, delightedly. "Van, you could do that."

"It's not my service," Van said.

"Oh, yes," Nancy said, shutting her book. "We're supposed to be 'empowered,' aren't we? We could read something from Bernie Siegel or . . ."

"Scripture's better," Allison said, scratching down an outline on her notepad.

"Yes," Ted said. "Christ is the healer. Then we can have Communion, and it will bring everything together."

"All right," Priscilla said, "I'll call this part silent reflection. Followed by a greeting . . . Communion . . . But if we sing hymns, must we use those clunky hymnals?"

"We've got to get healing in here somewhere!" Van insisted.

"Yes, yes," Priscilla said. "But if we're going to sing 'Let Us Break Bread Together' we must settle the logistics. Do we sit or kneel? Do we stand up? We want to avoid the impression of false bishops."

False bishops?

"I don't really like this term *laying on of hands*," Allison said. "I prefer *compassionate touch*."

Ted shifted uncomfortably in his chair.

"Gosh! That reminds me," Van said. "Gordon Bates wants to bring a group from his church in Glastonbury to observe. I thought since he helped some of us get this group going . . ."

"I have strong feelings about that, Van," Allison said. "This is our church and I don't want to turn people off by having visitors here to watch. It's like . . ."

"How do you feel about it, Joan?" Priscilla asked.

Joan Rockwell sat on the green divan, back straight as a yardstick, bare feet tucked beneath her hips, cross-legged, as silent and contemplative as the Buddha. She looked completely different from the straitlaced, buttoned-down woman who sang solos in the choir on Sundays. She was wearing dirty blue sweatpants. Her light hair was falling down over her shoulders.

"I'm trying to see how I feel," she whispered, closing her eyes again.

"Well, I'm afraid they're coming unless we disinvite them," Van said, moving on.

"Oh, I see," Priscilla said.

"Is Gordon's congregation farther along than we are?" Allison asked.

"They haven't even started, actually," Van replied.

"Well, neither have we," Priscilla said.

"That's just my point!" Allison said.

"This 'stranger' business doesn't bother me, Allison," Priscilla said. "Having gotten into groups as a stranger myself, it's hard for me to say this is only for those free, white, and over twenty-one. I mean, just as long as they don't sit there and tap their toes and say—"

"Ahem!" Joan said, suddenly awakening, demonstratively pointing a finger around the room. "I see that one didn't work! That one didn't work! Oh my! That one was a miserable failure!"

Everyone laughed, as Joan continued her performance, pointing at imaginary lepers, cripples, arthritic crones stumbling about. Yes, that was the problem. Dramatically observed.

"I'm sorry, Priscilla," Allison said again. "But I do feel strongly about this."

"I hear you, Allison," Priscilla said sympathetically.

"And I hear you, Priscilla," Allison echoed, in all seriousness. For a moment, I thought they looked like an Anglican mother and daughter, engaged in polite debate.

"I'm glad we're hearing each other," Van said, "but I just want to say one more thing, and then I'll be quiet."

"Van!" Allison said.

"I think a minute or two of silence is enough."

"Are you back on that?" Nancy said.

"Come on, Van, you won't even give us a minute of silence in church," Joan complained, rocking her hips to root herself more firmly into her yoga position. "You call that centering down? A minute or two of silence!"

"Okay," Van said, "it's not my service. But I've also decided I don't want to do the scripture readings. I mean, I'll do whatever you want, but you never know, I'll probably be the one who ends up sitting in that chair for you to heal."

"We're not *doing* the healing," Ted said, wearily. "We're *declaring* the healing."

"Yes, yes," Priscilla said.

"I don't even think this is my gift particularly," Van said.

"Well, I don't know why we can't be more spontaneous," Ted said again. "We need to be comfortable with spontaneity."

They were hardly what I had expected. If I had joined the healing group with the intent of infiltrating the mysterious culture of the church, I very quickly found its members to be a natural source of middlebrow entertainment—chaotic and Chaplinesque—despite themselves.

Though they hardly showed it at the moment, these men and women had serious reputations in the church. Their spiritual curriculum vitae suggested a great depth of experience: shamanic journeys, training in massage and dance therapy, civil rights activity, prosaic Bible study, formal seminary education, professional psychiatric training, and small-group contemplation of the Word. They had enjoyed many years of spiritual activity together, and as I learned, some of them had even traveled abroad on foreign missions. Over time, they had each passed a kind of initiation through psychotherapy, and though they all used words like *journey* and *quest* and *sojourn* to chart lives that had sometimes taken startling turns on the spiritual path, everyone was rooted in the parochial life of Windsor, where they held jobs, tended gardens, raised families, and made it a practice to wait now, at times beyond belief, for what they insisted were three simple gifts of fulfillment: stillness, patience, and mystery.

These monthly discussions had been underway for more than a year. Begun out of a sense that the God of their fathers had grown obsolete, the group sought, in a most general way, an authentic encounter. They complained that the language for addressing an objective God had become meaningless, and once a month they gathered to plan for an experience they assumed could be more assertive and significant: to stand in the mysterious ocean of the unknown God and call on the healing Spirit.

Many books had passed among them during that year, popular works on spiritual healing by authors such as Bernie Siegel, Morton Kelsey, Norman Cousins, and Agnes Sanford. They clipped articles, subscribed to journals, attended weekend retreats. Still they groped along in an almost inarticulate fashion, confusing the metaphors of the New Age with biblical parables and spiritual formation with Jungian psychoanalysis. They kept hoping they would find something in the Protestant tradition to account for larger dimensions of spirit in the healing process, and yet they fumbled through the existing literature, finding it surprisingly void and useless. The healing committee was left only with these bumbling acts of self-discovery.

I knew the awkwardness was not their fault. Mainline churches had long ago disestablished healing as a ministry. The most familiar language and ceremonies had been forged by Christian fundamentalists—irrational Appalachian snake-handlers, nomadic tent revivalists, and fraudulent TV evangelists—while many New Testament stories of Christ's healing powers were ignored or treated as metaphor by the more sophisticated, liberal congregations. The only hope was that gradually, as the general ideal of good health took on a more holistic connotation, the spiritual dimensions of healing would become more accepted. In some communities, as reported in national Protestant journals and newsletters, members of prayer groups had already come face-to-face with the need for healing services. Most of the time, it started in prayer groups, where people were sometimes asked to pray for someone else's healing. Consequently, members of the prayer groups encountered their own important questions about faith, and, not surprisingly, healing ministries formed where people first discovered holiness linked with wholeness, and wholeness with health.

I understood. Really, I was sympathetic. But who could blame me if I also thought they were extremely amusing in the meantime?

"Okay, I'll do the scripture reading," Ted said. "I'm driving back from spring training in Florida with the team that day, so I'll be pretty tired. But I really need to be here for the service."

Priscilla stopped shuffling her papers. Ted looked either angry or depressed. You couldn't tell.

"Are you sure?" she said.

"Yes, I want to do it," he snapped.

"Is there something bothering you about this?" Priscilla leaned over to find his eyes. He looked away.

"I have a friend," he mumbled.

"What are you saying, Ted?" she asked, quietly.

"I'm saying I have a colleague."

"And?"

"And I want to sit in the chair for him. He's sick. That's all. I don't think he'd show up for himself."

"But you must know what's the matter . . ."

Ted shot her a cold look.

Priscilla stopped herself.

"It's just . . . a friend," he said. "He has a kind of cancer."

I was astonished by the awkward silence. All night they never once broached the name of anyone who was sick.

"Look, we don't want any Oral Roberts type of service where people come in and throw down their crutches," Van said. "That's not who we are here."

Over the next hour, Priscilla applied the force of logic and propriety at every step of the way, and then when it seemed as if there could not be a moment unaccounted for, Allison let out a gasp.

"We've forgotten something! What are we going to do if you-know-who shows up?" she said.

"Oh my gosh!" Nancy said, hiding a giggle behind her book.

"I'm serious," Allison said.

At the committee's first experimental service, held weeks before by an experienced lay minister from Vermont, an enthusiastic participant— this mysterious "you-know-who"—had joined the circle when the call for healing came. When the laying on of hands was called, he nearly mauled the poor woman who had taken a seat in the healing chair. Horrified members of the committee had never suspected that *Gregory Lankester* masked a latent urge of Pentecostal fervor. But there he was, demonstrating a technique as subtle as a policeman's frisk—grasping, pawing, rubbing, thumping. The healing committee had been mortified. They had feared a congregational uproar would force them to disband overnight.

Of course, there had been no uproar except on the committee. The scene apparently was not as extreme as they imagined. But just in case the mysterious "you-know-who," or someone like him, should appear again, Priscilla wanted to be prepared. As soon as Allison mentioned the name, Priscilla reached into a folder and extracted photocopies of a note she prepared just that afternoon: *"In the event of 'untoward physical contact' with the person seated in the chair for healing, a team member should elect to go forward, followed by other team members, and they should gently but firmly position themselves to shield the recipient from any further unsuitable touch. Members of the team should remember to touch only the head or shoulders, or simply stand nearby."*

"Great!" Nancy said, as she read the memo. "We won't have to block and tackle."

"Let's just hope he doesn't show up," Allison said.

"Hey," Joan said with a laugh, "you know, this reminds me of the time Jim Coughlin came to talk to us about his sweat lodge."

"Oh!" Nancy giggled. "That was too much!"

"Remember," Joan said, "he told the story of a woman who had come to see him before her wedding. He invited her into his tepee—"

" 'Bright with burning coals, choking with thick steam,' " Allison mocked.

"And tried to induce a rise of sweat out of her. What was it— premarital jitters or something?"

The Reverend Coughlin, who ran a small parish in western Massachusetts, had created an uproar at one of the committee's earliest meetings when he came to discuss his own experiences in spiritual healing. The pastor, apparently fancying himself something of a storyteller, had used the scene of a young woman's healing both as an introduction to his work and as a springboard to commence the tale of his own spiritual journey. In the middle of his presentation, however, the story took a strange twist and awkwardly turned into a tale of the minister's own two-and-a-half-day sojourn in the Appalachians, where he sat alone, naked on a cold mountaintop, and came to receive the name High Eagle.

"It was so confusing!" Joan said, finally uncurling her legs.

"At one point," Allison said, "it sounded to me like the minister and the bride were actually sitting naked in the sweat lodge."

"No way," I said.

"Well, they were!" Nancy said.

"I know! I couldn't believe it!" Allison said.

"Then he got to that part where he and the bride were circling around the fire and the woman was shouting, 'I can't let go! I can't let go! I can't even sweat!' " Nancy said. "And then he pressed his bare back against hers . . ."

"That's where I lost it!" Priscilla said.

"Then when he shouted, 'I want to enter you!' " Nancy said.

The women were talking all at once now, red-faced, laughing hysterically, slapping their hands together.

"I looked at you and . . ." Allison was laughing so hard she couldn't finish.

"You thought they were still hopping around in the sweat tent!" Nancy said, whacking her book on her thigh.

"Well, I was mortified," Priscilla said.

"Appalled," Allison said.

"I saw you flinch, and I thought, My gosh! what was going on in there?" Nancy said.

" 'I want to enter you! I want to enter you!' " Allison cried.

Only Van seemed to have followed most of the young man's ramblings accurately to the end, when he told how he had bravely "entered" the healing spirit of an Eagle, brought its life force back to the woman in the tent, pecked out the slime he found on her soul—metaphorically, of course—and when it was all done, fell by the coals and literally vomited on the floor.

I looked over and saw Van's face turning a brilliant shade of scarlet. Nancy collected herself while the others howled, and she turned to fill me in on the joke.

"Van," she said, "thought all along this guy was describing the woman's wedding, not his sweat-tent healing bit. So while we're all sitting here dumbstruck about what we imagined was going on, Van pipes up and says, very matter-of-factly, 'Hey, that must have been quite an interesting wedding!' "

Now I was howling. Van, trying desperately to control himself, sputtered and quaked. "Good gosh!" he said. "Must've been this darned hearing aid. I didn't hear him say 'sweat tent.' "

They teased Van for the next five minutes, and I realized that the meeting was over. The endless haggling over an appropriate order for the service, debates about selecting the proper symbols, and discussing how best to light the sanctuary were forgotten.

So they could laugh, I thought. Thank God!

When we finished, it was almost ten thirty. Priscilla invited everyone to stand and join hands in a circle. We bowed our heads. The breathing calmed. All fell silent. For the first time, I noticed the murmur of an old aluminum coffee pot plugged in on a dessert tray for refreshments. It made a ghostly sound. A train whistle blew. A dog barked outside.

For the longest time, no one said a word. Then came a name, followed by silence. Then another name. Then a prayer spoken aloud, lightly, reverently. For a friend, they would say. For a family member. From my collection of "awkward particulars," Sunday's faces came into view.

"For Tom Dibble," Oh, yes, I remembered—whose wife had died recently.

"For Nick Wilton." Whose wife had died.

"For Bea Rossiter." I had met her, the lady who thinks her children have abandoned her.

"For Charlie Squires." Who has been fighting thoughts of suicide.

"For Ed Newberry." Who collapsed before Easter and was now in Mountainview nursing home, unconscious.

"For Cloris." Who is Ed's wife, alone suddenly, and frightened.

"For Stella Wright." Who fell and broke her hip last week.

"For my husband." Who is suffering with depression.

"For my brother, William." Who faces sentencing for drunken driving tomorrow.

"For the people of Bangladesh." A country again ravaged by storms.

"For the black people of South Africa. Bring an end to the conflict."

"A prayer of Thanksgiving for the ministers of First Church."

"A prayer of Thanksgiving for the Spirit that works among us."

"Accept our prayers, Creator God, and be with us as we pray together using the traditional words that Jesus taught his disciples to say: Our Father, who art in Heaven . . ."

An hour later I surprised myself, standing outside under the icy black limbs of an elm tree, shivering with Priscilla and Allison as they talked endlessly by their cars. They were no longer timid or indefinite. Together, they issued a stream of stories about people who had touched their lives at church lately, stories of child abuse and incest, alcoholism and marital troubles that at one point began to pile up and sound so unnatural that I had to speak.

"You wouldn't think there could be all these problems right here," I said.

"We're no different from anywhere else," Priscilla insisted.

"Oh well." Allison glanced at her watch.

"Forget it! Who cares what time it is?" Priscilla said.

They looked around at the empty lot, faint and blue under the illumination of a full moon. They were quiet for a moment, long enough for me to notice the cold vapor from their lips, and their cheeks, still gaining color. In the stillness, the evening's work settled. The litany of names, the final order of a service, the frozen sky—all peacefully clear.

"Well," I said. It was past time for me to be home. "It's a weeknight, you know." I wanted to tell them about something that was on my mind, about the news I'd received that day from Jan about her visit with the doctor. We had never expected to be an infertile couple. But I quickly chased away those thoughts and said good night, leaving them there to talk.

I had been moved. I had seen in their faces a flash of wonder and excitement. I don't think I had ever before seen expressions that tender, so certain, light, and confident. It was almost midnight when I left, as they immersed themselves again in stories of the church and moved to the verge of a new universe of prayer and participation with something they believed to be infinitely powerful. I had felt peculiar standing in a suburban church parking lot with those two, experiencing a flash of feeling like that. I am ashamed to admit it. Embarrassed. I feel foolish even now. It was so charming and childlike. But the feeling held promise. I was lightened by their words: peace and wonder, health and wholeness.

I grew solemn on the ride home. Would I risk common sense and test their healing powers? I don't know how long it had been since I had tried to pray, but that night when I crawled into bed with Jan, I knew I had to do something for her. It wasn't her fault. I drew close to her and she grabbed my hand.

I fully expected to return to my heart, to reexperience the feelings of peace and holiness that came during the committee's prayers. I wanted to speak silently with God about our own needs—Jan's and my loss. About childlessness. But as I tried I drew, instead, on one lame metaphor after another. Lamps and Radiant Clouds, Father God Lord, Rock of Ages, Spirit, and Endless Mystery. Every utterance a childish cliché. Journeyman journalist, writer, man of words—I lay there next to my wife, mute, frozen and indefensible, deaf even to the silence. I tried, but when I finally made the return, it was not to heart but to the accustomed place. Another solitary evening. The usual ditch of dreams.

CHAPTER FIVE

Shortly before seven one morning, Van rose from bed and hurried into his clothes. (Discount trousers. Polyester tie. A shoe with a hole in the bottom.) He poured a cup of hot tea, penned Lucille's dog, Daisy, in the yard, and trod the short path from kitchen door to parish house, a distance he covered in about twenty-two steps.

All around town, people were out in shirtsleeves enjoying the early sunlight. Fishermen picked their way into treeless dry spots along the stubbled banks of the Farmington River and cast lines for shad. Pink-and-purple-haired teenagers, dressed in black leather, loitered outside the Donut Shoppe. Ninety-nine-year-old Mary Bartlett reached up to her clothesline to hang damp white draperies.

Springtime, at last: *The flowers appear on the earth; the time of singing has come, and the voice of the turtle is heard in our land.*

"Train's leaving the station," Van said, passing the church secretary on the way to his desk.

Peggy Couples shrugged. "Mornin', Poopsie!"

Van snatched a dog-eared directory and dialed one number after another, making appointments with half a dozen new members before they left for work.

For fifteen years, Peggy had held the title of Assistant in Christian Education, but she also ran the office and single-handedly maintained
calm against the chaos in Van's office, to her right, and Bill's office, to
her left. As the first person at work every morning, she straightened the
mess from the night before, reviewed ministers' schedules, and met
whoever appeared at the parish house door.

"Well, *Claudia Rabbit!*" she would say, if, for instance, a certain Mrs.
Rabbit dropped by to visit. Loud enough to alert the ministers, Peggy
would dig for a nugget of news. You could often hear a rustling in one
of the near offices. "And how are your little ones—*Flopsy, Mopsy, and
Cottontail?*" More rustling. And then she would go for one telling detail:
"And *Peter*—I hope he's *feeling better.*"

By that time, Van or Bill would be up from his desk, seemingly organized, and come to the doorway appearing properly ministerial. Without being formally briefed, they would pick up the conversation with all
the facility of a close friend.

It also helped that Peggy's husband fixed cars in town for a living, her
daughter sold ads for the newspaper, and her son worked with both the
ambulance service and fire department. Among them, news of all kinds,
from deaths and births to affairs, stray cats, and broken solenoids, made
its way into her household—and into the church office. Add random reports from the police scanner Peggy kept next to her reading table at
home, and this dear, sweet woman, with her sunflower scarfs, New Age
crystals, and Native American jewelry, accessed a higher power unavail-
able to either minister. Peggy was also amazingly discreet and, in a way
unknown to most of the congregation, a force to be reckoned with.

Today, however, she kindly left Van alone and greeted people as they
arrived for the Monday staff meeting. Fran Angelo, John Gregory-Davis,
Joan Rockwell, and finally Bill wandered in, poured themselves cups of
coffee, and talked quietly around Peggy's desk. A new six-week series on
inclusive language created a buzz. While they waited for Van to finish his
calls, Peggy whispered.

"If I know Van, we'll get through the seminar, then he'll appoint a
committee, and we won't hear another word about it."

"I think he'll wait at least until the fund drive is over," John said.

"He can't do that!" Joan said. "I won't let him sweep this one under the rug."

"Don't count on it," Peggy said. "Look at the hymns he picked out this Sunday." There they were on her desk: "Dear Lord and Father of Mankind" and "O God, Beneath Thy Guiding Hand."

" 'our exiled fathers crossed the sea . . . ,' " Bill sang.

"Sexist!" John said. "As long as we keep using that old *Pilgrim Hymnal,* he'll have every excuse."

"Just my point," Joan said.

Bill only wanted the boss to meet his guest that afternoon. Dr. Shannon Clarkson, a member of a team that had just published a new Bible edited for sexist and racist language, had agreed to lead a seminar at First Church. Bill thought if Van would at least make a symbolic gesture of support, then Dr. Clarkson might feel more comfortable about leading a study group. Van's blessing would help Bill avoid an immediate backlash from certain members of the church.

Soon Van called them in.

"The last capital funds letter goes out this week," Van said. "Top priority. We've got another hundred thousand bucks to shake out of this congregation, and I'm anxious to get the darn thing over with. Why don't we have a prayer?"

He scratched his forehead and began the meditation with a tired sigh. "Lord, it's been a busy year . . ."

"Van, Dr. Shannon Clarkson's coming in today to help us plan a series on inclusive language," Bill said as soon as the prayer ended. "I've scheduled six weeks—"

"Good Gosh!" Van said. "That must mean we have six or eight meetings here tonight." He thumbed his pocket calendar. "Deacons, Weight Watchers, Boy Scouts. . . . Today's Armenian Martyr's Day. We've got some kind of group scheduled for that tonight. And what about the anonymous groups, Peggy? And I see there's a school group wanting to meet in the Dinosaur Room."

"But, Van—" Bill said.

"I also understand the annual bus trip to Tanglewood is filled up. And the women's retreat is booked for the end of the month."

"Van—" Bill said.

"Peggy, isn't the healing service tonight?" Van asked. "I might need you to sit in for me, Bill."

Van held a stack of new members' cards in his hands. Without looking up, he shuffled through them anxiously. "What else is going on around here?" he asked. "Bill, you got any weddings coming up?"

Bill flipped a page in his calendar. "Four weddings scheduled the second weekend in June," Bill said dryly. "How's that?"

"What about you, Joan?"

"I'm still helping our Ukrainian friends get settled. When they asked us if they could plant a garden on our property, I had forgotten what *garden* means in the Soviet Union. Looks like we'll have a half acre of potatoes and onions this summer."

"You'll feed the multitudes! What about you, John?"

"The Homeless Association is going strong," John said. "The guys have done a teach-in at Trinity College and a sleep-in in Farmington, and I'm starting to drum up some support from First Church for helping us find a new shelter space."

"Sounds like an exciting time to me," Van said, whacking his thigh with the cards. "I don't have anything else to add. Why don't we get to work?"

Peggy shot Bill a stern look.

"Van," Bill said again, "you know, this inclusive-language series—"

"Oh my gosh!" Van thumped his chair. "That reminds me. Did anyone hear about the Little League schedule? The town's set it for Sunday-morning games again!"

"Van, Bill was talking about the inclusive—" Peggy said.

"The recreation department in this town is like a many-headed monster! If it's not Little League, it's soccer. If it's not motocross it's something else! Don't they understand what this means? I'm just about fed up. What can we do to get them to listen!"

"Maybe you could—" Bill said.

"No!" Van said.

"We could just try to—"

"No!" Van said again.

"Listen, Van," Bill said, sounding almost desperate. "There's not much we can do about the Little League schedule. But we could think about trying to reach out to these kids. We could have a service constructed around children. You know, make it *inclusive* and try something with sports and parents—"

"Sunday morning's our time!" Van said.

"It's our time but it's their time, too," Bill said. "Why not reach out to people who wouldn't ordinarily be in church? A very *inclusive* service—a special prayer, invite the kids to come in uniform . . ."

"What are we going to do, send them out and say, 'Consider yourself blessed'? Blessed for what? 'Bless you, child, as you go forth today to steal second base.' " Van laughed out loud.

"Oh!" Fran said, turning to Joan. "I disapprove of the town's scheduling. And I've already told my two boys they have no choice. 'No baseball for the Angelos.' We have church on Sundays."

"You did?" Joan said.

"I don't want heathens living under my roof."

Van and Bill continued to argue.

"I'm going to write a letter to the town and get this off my chest once and for all!" Van said.

"Van Gorder!" Peggy admonished.

"In a peaceful, irenic way," Van said.

"Oh, of course, *irenic*," she muttered.

"But all we have to do is hold one special service," Bill said.

"I'm sorry, I've been fighting this town's athletic department for twenty years. Before some of you people were even born."

"We just need a little more communication with the town," Bill said.

"They're dumb!" Van said.

"They're just not church people, Van."

"It's a secular society! I was listening to the radio yesterday and they said, tomorrow's going to be a nice rainy Sunday, why don't you just stay inside and relax and read *The New York Times*? I thought, Dammit! Why don't you go to church?"

"It has been a very busy year so far, hasn't it?" Joan said, trying to change the subject. "By the way—I don't mean to interrupt—but since

I was out of town, I never heard how the Lenten series went. What was it called? 'Questions of Faith.' "

"All questions of faith were settled!" Van said.

"Van passed a resolution and sent it to a higher committee," Bill said.

"On to the next controversy!" Peggy said. "Which, by the way—"

"Now that's going to be very interesting," John said. He looked at Bill. "I can't wait for that inclusive-language series to start."

Inclusive language? The words finally penetrated Van's thoughts.

"Oh, yes," Van said. "You know, I can't say where that will lead us, John." He set his pledge cards down on a side table. "Lucille keeps talking to me about this inclusive-language thing, and she says, 'Why can't you drop it for now and just enjoy life a bit?' And I tell her, 'Lucille, you can't stop the process. We've got to keep moving. We have to keep working to consolidate our programs, make people aware of the values of stewardship, be conscious of the world outside our own, keep our outreach healthy, help new members feel welcome . . .' "

"Will someone tell him to quit preaching!" Peggy said. "Van, you sound just like your father."

"Sometimes I don't even know what kind of animal we are," Van continued, "but we're constantly evolving, like an organism . . ."

"He can't help it," Joan said.

"What!" Van said. "Was I preaching again?"

He laughed at himself and then kept loudly repeating, in a pompous, overly mannered voice, one of his favorite phrases. "Let no dog bark before I speak!"

Bill closed his calendar and stood up. The morning fairly boasted springtime by now. From behind the bright, sun-streaked windows where the staff met for the first Monday morning in May, Van's voice was booming.

Afterward, when they were back in the main office, Bill asked Peggy, "Do you think he heard anything?"

"What did I tell you?" she said. "I'll bet he's already decided who's going to be on the committee and, believe me, he won't be here this afternoon when Dr. Clarkson arrives. No way, José. He's at least three steps ahead of the rest of us right now, and in his mind, it's a done deal. He's staging his own plan. The whole nine yards."

Van knew that the eminence of language in the Protestant tradition could not be denied. Particularly among Congregationalists, who regarded the Word as perhaps the ultimate authority, the ministers' responsibility to safeguard the language of the Bible meant that legitimate objections deserved a fair hearing. Particularly when the work of archaeologists supplied new evidence of bias in the scriptures, and scholarly examinations of texts revealed prejudices that distorted original meanings, the minister was obliged to educate. The people of First Church were, at least in theory, people of intelligence, after all. *En arche en ho logos,* the declaration that began the Gospel of John ("In the beginning was the Word"), was an unwritten creed. The mystery of the Word and the ongoing quest for precision, clarity, and coherence in the Word had made Protestant culture a society based on scholarly enterprise. The arrival of the New Revised Standard Version Bible, which Bill's seminar would illuminate, reasserted that honored discipline. The church would be well within the scope of its tradition to review linguistic changes.

The only problem was, Van would say, that even in the breakdown of a patriarchal culture, some people would not accept a change from the masculine deity. If the seminar introduced radical notions about Gaia and Earth Mothers and the Goddess Within—as it was sure to do, given his staff's prejudices—he could see trouble ahead. He had not meant to be coy at the staff meeting, but he felt there was no choice about masking his own intentions. Integration, not alienation; consolidation, not confrontation. Those were the hallmarks of pastoral leadership.

"Why, for God's sake, can't we at least wait until Cloris Thrall dies?" Van would ask Peggy. "She's a hundred and three years old and she doesn't need any one of us telling her she has to change her old Father God into a hummingbird or a Goddess or anything else mysterious and arcane! Why, she's been happy with 'Father' all her life! Frankly, some of these ideas sound as foreign to me as quantum physics!"

Van had already studied the arguments for remaking hymns and church services. He knew Bill was right when he would say the congregation would never make a change unless someone took them back to the text and exposed evidence of blatant sexism. Scholarly authority was important. Van also knew people would trust Bill probably more than anyone. Bill had intelligence and a pedigree (he was an alumnus of both Yale College and Yale Divinity School). Bill could be trusted to insist on credentials and the legitimate stamp of expert authority before issuing a proposal.

But even if every idea stood up as intellectually sound and historically valid, there was still the matter of timing. Congregations often react poorly to changes in worship. People had barely warmed up to the "Passing of the Peace" on Sundays—the awkward, informal, ten-second ritual that required members to shake hands with strangers in neighboring pews. With the capital-funds drive and John Gregory-Davis's antics and everything else, an effort to stamp out sexist language might appear like yet another radical move by Van Parker. And then what? Add it to the list of complaints? Give people another excuse for withholding pledges from the fund drive?

No one but a minister could really understand the dangerous crosscurrents at work in mainline congregations nowadays. It would be so much easier for Van just not to rock the boat. What happened in church hardly seemed to matter so much to society, anyway. The big events in town no longer occurred around a churchyard. Just as long as he kept up the property and celebrated the big seasons from Rally Day to Christmas to Easter, most members would think Van had fulfilled his obligations. After Easter, especially, it was the town's job not the church's to keep people amused and busy.

It was true this year already, I noticed. In May, the Windsor Shad Festival drew people together for the glory and honor of a greasy, boney, particularly inedible fish. The Shad Festival took over during Pentecost as the biggest, most thrilling quasireligious event of the season: a shad spawns, the people celebrate. A Shad Queen would be crowned. Fishing rodeos overtook the banks of the Farmington River. Street carnivals and outdoor concerts attracted hordes of otherwise housebound New Englanders. You'd see deacons and choir members on the streets guzzling a cold beer with the best of them. In coming weeks, as corner-lot ballfields grew green and dusty under the sunlight of longer days, softball season would return. Little League would take over. Gentleman farmers would till tobacco lands to let the brown soil breathe and bake for seasonal plantings. Church people from all over would leave for the beach, fly to Aruba, backpack in Maine. Congregational life would soon recede, not to return until September.

Ordinarily, Van thought, the seasonal lull might have presented the right time for controversial subjects. Most people would be otherwise engaged. But this year at the big white church on Palisado Avenue, where azaleas bloomed and scents of honeysuckle and mowed grass mingled, when celebrations ended, the congregation still buzzed with gossip. The property looked as tumbledown as it had all winter—paint chipping, tree limbs dangling, storm drains pooling over. Van's promise of new life after Easter, his annual refrain in April, had been forgotten in protracted shove-and-duck rounds of church politics. Prospective donors to the fund drive clammed up tighter than Martin Luther's sphincter. Bill's inclusive-language seminar was starting rumors that the words to the Lord's Prayer would change. Paul Price, the church treasurer, had worked up a head of steam and was organizing a private campaign to stifle spending for outreach missions.

Now, on gorgeous black nights when stars linked in clear, regular alignment over the parish house, Van sat inside growing crusty and quarrelsome. Church meetings lasted longer than twilight doubleheaders. They kept him stranded in the Morrell Room, captive to sprawling, meandering, endless analysis.

The deacons were the worst. Tony Gillette, the assistant head deacon, conducted a series of meetings billed as "A Post Mortem of Holy Week." A deadly affair. The deacons exploded into action anatomizing services. Long, fervent reports on ice rings, boutonnieres, and plastic Communion cups followed. Following Robert's Rules of Order, Tony "honchoed" new deacons to help at the startup healing service and "ID'ed" the "key drivers" for a successful Communion Sunday. Whenever they finished a line of new business, he would scratch it off his list with a sharp stroke. "Done deal!" he'd say. "What else we got on the plate?" Off they went, casting for trifles.

I watched poor Van catalogue their concerns during the most butt-numbing meetings of the year.

Van, the new deacons asked, can we buy frozen bread for Communion? Van, how do you shut off the lights under the eaves? Did anyone think the coffee tasted a little dry on Sunday? Why can't we recycle the bulletins? What's the poundage on a ream? Who has a calculator? What happened to the dead mouse we found in the balcony after Easter? Should we hang the Koshenevskys' handmade scarf from the pulpit or leave it on the Communion table? Do we use the red cups for John Warham Sunday? And if we pass out name tags, should we do it after church or before coffee hour? Don't forget the big items: Lemons—slices or wedges? And tablecloths—paper or linen?

How, I wondered, could Van lead an authentic spiritual journey in a place where the rehearsal and preparation for any event could no longer be separated, even by death or miracles, from the steady downpour of timebound courtesy and customs? How could he continue to promise new growth if the congregation kept getting mired in the sucking mud of church politics and bad theology? Worship-making wore on and on like a particularly vile brand of Protestant water torture.

"Who's going to pour punch on John Warham Sunday?" one deacon asked.

"The ministers' wives always pour the punch!" an old-timer said.

"I think the librarian should pour the punch."

"Do we mix the usual ginger ale punch or the special pineapple–grape juice punch? . . . How much food should we make?"

Finally, when they asked Van questions, he just picked at his shoe and nodded.

"Fine, fine," he would say. "That would be fine." When they kept on, he simply repeated their questions as an exclamation—"What kind of punch!"—and let someone else answer. Sometimes, even after three and a half hours, the new deacons still would not have come out of their stupor.

Even outside church, Van could not escape complaints. When he dropped into a nursing home, he suffered an upbraiding from old women.

"I'm a little upset about what effect that new work will have on the church," eighty-eight-year-old Eloise Lilly told Van one afternoon, meeting him at the door of Kimberly Hall nursing home in her wheelchair. "I don't want to see the road graded so the church doesn't appear to be set on a hill."

She shot him a cold look, her cataracts gray and glinting. Van wondered how she knew.

She rustled a fresh copy of *The New York Times*, which rested in her lap, and curled the corners with her shriveled hands. She paused a moment.

"But I've decided I don't mind the cross so much, Van."

"Eloise, I'm glad I finally have your seal of approval," Van replied.

"I didn't say I approve!"

Van noticed an increase in gossip after Easter, when a new group took charge. Seasonal turnover on the Prudential Board brought in a new team of good old boys—oh, yes, there were also two women versed in real estate and architecture—to run the property committee. Complaints and rumors sprang up like weeds. On Monday nights the men parked their trucks and four-by-fours out on the street and ambled down to the Morrell Room to play "hardball" with the ministers.

At first I thought it was just a coincidence when almost every one of them came in wearing khaki shorts and Hawaiian shirts. But soon it looked very much to me like the start of an ongoing Monday-night poker match. Put your cards on the table, boys, they seemed to say, we're going down 'n' dirty.

The Prudential Board showed more skill than other committees in the art of church politics. The first few times I attended, I wondered why they spent so much time arguing over the use of certain words. They spent hours on *re-siding*, for example. It seemed niggling and tedious. But soon I realized the real discussions were taking place "out of church," so to speak, and when the members met on Monday nights, they came prepared to stitch a veil of rhetoric over a grander design.

They knew, for instance, that one could not use the word *re-siding* in public at First Church without raising hackles. In time, after much debate, the phrase *replacing clapboards* was chosen, allowing the property committee to move a resolution through the rule-making process and eventually past the town historical society. The question of whether they intended to wrap the buildings with bands of prosaic "siding" rather than with the more charming but expensive alternative—wooden shingles—never came up. With the right choice of words, the committee avoided dissent and had its way.

The discussion of *alternative plantings* took the same course, as the committee deemed it best not to give any hint that they would take down the old cedar trees that loomed over the spot where they wanted to build a parking lot. The Women's Club's Pennies for Perennials committee would certainly be up in arms, and Carla Pike, who maintained an American flag on that spot for war veterans, was capable of marshaling a strong defense if riled. Scrubby evergreens took on a sacred mystique in some minds. No matter how scraggly, once planted in a churchyard, a tree was a verdant symbol of the Everlasting. Thus, *alternative plantings* replaced *evergreens* in reports to the larger congregation, and plans for a parking lot continued apace.

Over a period of weeks, haggling over certain words and rituals left Van looking like he'd been struck with a blunt-edged instrument. Circles rimmed his eyes. His hopes for New Life dwindled. I wondered how many years he had come away from Easter with the same hopes, and within weeks gone reeling back into his corner, blindsided by the proclivities of well-meaning church people who sanctified every bland object and plant in sight. When the time came for Bill's inclusive-language series, I thought Van's reluctance was understandable. His members were keenly attuned to nuances in language. But they were not interested in change so much as in making sure everything stayed generally in its place.

In the first weeks of spring, Van also acted more and more like a solitary servant, a shopworn keeper of the institution. He beat a path running back and forth from his kitchen to the office carrying books, Cup O' Soup boxes, hefty, ice-clattering plastic cups of freshly minted instant tea, and bunches of mail. More rumpled and bedraggled than ever, he bounced up the porch steps to the parish house, grasping at his pocket calendar, chewing on the caps of cheap ballpoint pens. As he passed through the yard, Daisy would leap up on him, leaving muddy prints on his pants. Van's face turned pale and swollen, wrinkled from worry and lack of sleep. His doctor warned him that his blood pressure had climbed too high. He needed to lose weight. But he could not slow down. Pastoral calls took up his afternoons, meetings consumed every night.

After the Monday-morning staff meeting, Van told me, privately, about his own plans for inclusive language. One day soon, he said, he would appoint a committee. Let Andy McCarthy run it. Send a report to the deacons. Ask them to study the issues. File another report. They could modify the doxology during the summer when attendance was light. Print up a few new hymns and insert them in Sunday's bulletins. Go ahead with Bill's seminar, but not make any promises about what could come next. Besides, he wasn't sure he trusted his own staff to lead an experiment in language without becoming doctrinaire. If there was one thing he could not tolerate, most of all, it was people who seemed to have all the answers.

"The language of fundamentalism comes in many disguises," Van said. It didn't matter to him whether the words came wrapped in the glossy rhetoric of a Harvard theologian pushing feminist images of God or of a Carolina evangelist vilifying the liberal agnostics. "I don't care what their reasons are, and I don't care what kind of credentials they have. We don't separate the sheep from the goats at First Church. And I'm not going to excommunicate anybody around here because they happen to think of God as a man."

Sounded to me like Peggy had been right all along.

Dr. Shannon Clarkson arrived at First Church that afternoon. Bill met her on the front steps, beaming with pride. They shared the same dusty and restrained look. Dr. Clarkson wore rimless glasses and a muted tweed suit. She presented herself with a kind of finicky reticence that theologians often bring into churches. Bill, who was plump, bearded, and also bespectacled, guided her around looking like an Irish rabbi. His red beard and radiant corona of blond hair added to his look of a man bred for learning and teaching. Together they made a curious pair wandering the halls—curious but informed, like archaeologists in a wilderness cave.

At three o'clock, the group met in the Morrell Room. Ordinarily, you would encounter people of breeding and intelligence at First Church. Old cheerleaders and punchbowl hosts, educated coffee brewers, vitamin takers and wholesome do-gooders. Greeting guests in warm, clockless rooms, smiling and nodding across a varnished table, they made gatherings delightfully easy. Whether sitting on hard folding chairs eating molded jello salads or circulating with cups of decaf and sugar cookies at coffee hour, they did quite well with the old "How d'you do?" or the standard "grip 'n' grin."

But today, with summer around the corner, there was no regular parade of sweet-faced strangers around demonstrating the old niceties. Instead, Dr. Clarkson met with the staff, those who called for a more primitive religious experience. Joan and Peggy, John and Bill joined her alone.

"I'm not usually invited into churches until things get thorny," Dr. Clarkson said. "So I want to applaud your early efforts. But I also want you to understand that I do not see myself coming here to recommend changes for your church or to review your liturgy for standing examples of sexist language. That would be not only presumptuous, but ill-advised."

"Yes, well, I won't sing a lot of the hymns anymore," Peggy said. "I just sit there and count all the men in those songs. He's, Hims, Fathers, Lords, fellows . . ."

"I don't even feel like we were created in God's image on Sundays," Joan said. "There are an amazing number of names for deities that we never hear from the pulpit."

"I just want to see some action around here," John said.

Dr. Clarkson maintained her calm. Preceded by the King James Version in 1611, she said, the American Standard Version in 1911, and the Revised Standard Version in 1952, the New Revised Standard Bible had only discarded sexist language in those cases where bias had originated in English translations. Still, the courageous sixteen-year effort by a consortium of Protestant, Jewish, Roman Catholic, and Orthodox scholars, of which Dr. Clarkson had been a longtime member, was generating a groundswell of debate internationally. Perhaps the best result of their work had been the theological objections raised about cultural bias in religious language. Handled skillfully, the handsome new Bible could be presented to introduce the issue of sexism without making ministers appear militant.

Not appearing militant was an important point. Inclusive language hit some congregations like kerosene on fire, she said. She did not want to be near First Church when—if—that happened. By giving simple lessons from her committee's academic enterprise, she could leave First Church with a juggernaut to crack the issue open. But beyond that, if they wanted to play with fire, they were on their own.

Everyone seemed to appreciate Dr. Clarkson's advice—a thoroughly responsible, suitably conservative approach would suit First Church. Dr. Clarkson would stay fundamentally within the tradition, and—this much was apparent without her having to promise it—her delivery would be so dry that anything she said on the subject would probably pass without much notice among churchgoers.

After a long discussion, a date was set for the series. Bill would publicize the event using the bland title, "Language and the Bible." With or without Van's blessing, the little group would soon challenge the gray Father God figure who had dominated First Church for centuries.

CHAPTER SIX

I drove to Windsor one morning thinking of my father, my brother, my nephews. Imagining the sounds of wolfpacks and the high timbre of melodic drums, I waited on the sixth sense. An emotional shakedown with New Age clichés rattled the door open as I sped faster up the highway.

I knew enough about sitting still to recognize a meditative state. Each breath deepened. Light itself changed tones. Muscles relaxed. Images moved out of mind, and words that might have clustered escaped attention. God did not require this—I did, flowing dangerously through rush hour on the interstate north.

I don't need this shit. For twenty years, it's been the same discipline. "If you were driving a cart and it didn't move, would you whip the cart or the ox?" Attention! Cite thirteen ways of looking at a blackbird! Enjoying the eros of an open road? Ha, ha, ha, ha. Rub the Buddha's belly and win a prize!

My usual religious practice had become this kind of solitary confinement. If religion had been cruel and unusual when I was a child, the adult practice of meditative disengagement had become a chilly ride through the preserve of dead poets and dharma bums.

Psychoreligious America . . . freaky, free-ride carnival . . . like an itiner-

*ant Ishmael grown grim about the mouth . . . tired of one ride? Hitch an-
other . . .*

In the fundamentalist world of North Carolina, where I was raised,
religious spectacles rivaled Ringling Brothers. Nothing like New Englanders, Southerners invited geeks and zealots into the midway. Within
a five-hundred-mile radius of my childhood home, I could visit the
birthplace, pulpit, or broadcast studio of the Lord's evangelical advance
team for Armageddon—Jim and Tammy Bakker, Billy Graham, Jerry
Falwell, Pat Robertson. Charlotte marked the nation's epicenter of religious malpractice. By the time I was a young teenager, I thought of it as
Redneck Vatican City. Led by silver-tongued Daddy Graces and sticky-
fingered Jimmy Swaggarts, church people carried on in style, blindly following a corrupt tradition administered by vulgarians and bigots. As a
child, you were either dragged along to prayer meetings and tent revivals
and indoctrinated with Biblical "truths," or you attended lovely middle-
class churches that trivialized religion to smithereens.

That was how I thought of it as a teenager, anyway. At home, my
mother favored the saber rattlers, my father, the Republican Party at
prayer. Lucky me, sampling both.

Is it any wonder that so many children leave the church? It took me
years to expunge the doctrine of fear taught by my mother's fundamentalist friends—Satan was the lurid monster of my childhood. To satisfy
the hunger left unmet by our otherwise tepid mainline connections, I left
the church altogether. By the time I was old enough to think for myself,
I started the solitary practice—a "deconditioning of attitude"—taught by
dharma poets. A familiar discipline today, it was once exotic and strange.
One grows spiritually by giving up control, it is said. Develop a taste for
paradox, acquire a tolerance for contradictions, desire moments of emp-
tiness. Beat poets as emancipators, as authentic as the Christ.

The poetic exercise stems from Flaubert, who taught that the "ordi-
nary is extraordinary." It was inherited by Ezra Pound and William
Carlos Williams, and was popularized for my generation by Allen
Ginsberg and Gary Snyder. The Children's Crusades fed the fad during
the sixties, spreading simple truths as far as a VHF broadcast traveled.
Every middle-class adolescent got a free kernel of the discipline. A child

of mass culture, you listened to the Beatles, you watched TV, you sang folk songs with the neighborhood Young Life group. Eventually, you knew something important that your parents did not. Beyond that, all you had to do was read. The tantric wisdom of the hip fathers, the Ferlinghettis and Creeleys and Blys, taught you to see the minute particulars of a moment. Sooner or later, I and everybody I knew was doing TM, talking anthropology, wearing a downy beard and ceramic beads, running in packs—the Love Children of Independence Boulevard, the Sons and Daughters of Freedom Drive.

At least meditating on the highway was better than being at home listening to Jan sob. I was fleeing back to church now. My own home was either lonely, sad, or otherwise miserable these days.

Actually, I had left the house that morning angry. Jan could not quit talking about the doctor's awful bedside delivery, the way he had dished out his diagnosis. In one day, a few weeks after Easter, a brief visit to his office had ended any thoughts we had for producing children. "He was so cold!" Jan shouted. (It was as if he had poked her like a pig and hung her up to bleed. "Premature menopause," he said, with a thin smile. "Unusual, but not serious.")

"He sat there listing all the changes in my system like I was a lab rat!" Jan cried. "I felt like throwing up. The smug bastard kept reciting case studies and talking about loss of bone mass!"

Every day was like that now. Crying in the morning. Hysterical at night. Irritable. Complaining. Obsessed with the wicked doctor. I couldn't handle it.

"I've got to go," I told her. "There's a church meeting at ten."

Church meeting?

I parked my car under the pine trees next to Van and Lucille's house, and took a minute to compose myself. Maybe, I thought, this group will be different.

Down the hall in the parish house a dozen questers sat in the Morrell Room, hands folded, heads bowed. The flame of a white candle fluttered on a coffee table and the sound of a strong wind sang from a cassette deck in the corner. JoAnne motioned me into the circle. Only two men. Me and Jesus. The rest, women.

God!

I found a seat and shut my eyes.

Another hen party? Or an encounter group? What am I doing back in a place like this?

I should have known women would predominate. As symbolic space, the Morrell Room had retained its prim qualities as a "ladies' parlor" for more than thirty-five years. A flourish of green cotton, silk, and rayon fabrics was fashioned into heavy Victorian floral drapes for the windows. Lush, forest-green, velvet-covered, spindly-legged settees. A series of water colors of the meetinghouse hung on the light green and peach-colored walls. Leafy green plush pile for the wall-to-wall made the room quiet and warm. The women sat in Queen Anne chairs, or settled into sumptuous pink-upholstered high-backed armchairs. Table lamps with ivory pleated-fabric shades and a gilt-edged mirror balanced one end of the room; a sturdy lady's writing table decorated with fresh flowers centered the other. The late Reverend Morrell's memorial was the most elegant room on campus.

Not many years ago, only certain members of the Women's Club had been allowed entry here. In recent times, officers of the club stored the antique silver service on a corner shelf, and cared for the room with compulsive concern. They worried now over beatings the furniture took from overuse almost as much as they fretted privately about "crumbunions" (technically, pieces of bread left floating in the Communion chalice) and the need to organize committees of "carpet beadles" (i.e., volunteers to pick up crumbs after Communion). These were not, however, the same women who now focused attention on the wind and steadily meditated on a small flame. In recent months, there had been a turn in tradition.

Market research hinted that the incremental changes I witnessed at First Church reflected a larger trend. Nationwide, pollsters recorded a rising tide of baby boomers returning to church, women and men less interested in religion than in "spirituality." National data analyzed by sociologists at Hartford Seminary showed that, while one-third of baby-boomers had settled into traditional church memberships and another third spurned religion entirely, the rest of us—apparently fussier than our parents—shopped like heathens in a cafeteria of broadening options. A full twenty percent of us attended spiritual growth seminars or sought personal fulfillment through new forms of meditation, Eastern traditions, New Age techniques, and amalgams of science and mysticism. Sociologists of religion suggested that the more individualistic trends might make the future of denominations and ecumenical movements more tenuous, though, paradoxically, they also might make individual congregations healthier.

Yes, paradoxically. Religious cultures, it has been said, persist because they have the capacity to generate moral and symbolic power across long stretches of time. But during the mainline's present transition, fin de siècle, liberal denominations were losing members, experiencing an erosion of prominence as Establishment institutions. Struggling with the issue of identity, some members raised questions about whether new forms of worship and a less rigid moral code might not awaken sleepy congregations.

For more than a decade, zesty currents of new knowledge worked their way through the mainline. Jungians had a field day. But not only Jungians. In Windsor, nuns practiced yoga in Nelson Hall. Buddhists on an antinuclear walk stopped by to teach. Meditation groups came and went. Van, in particular, traveled to visit more vital communities outside New England—at Koinonia Farms in Georgia, at Christian base communities in Nicaragua, among the Protestants in Northern Ireland, with the Taizé in France and the Iona community in Scotland. Throughout the 1980s, he brought back foreign symbols that would have been unimaginable in the old meetinghouse ten years before. "Vaya con Diós!" he would say at the benediction, while little gray heads turned quizzically. He met routinely with a "spiritual guide" and, when no one was looking, he replaced Warner Sallman's old *Head of Christ*, the blue-eyed Jesus in his office, with a colorful portrait of an unmistakably Hispanic Francis of Assisi.

At the same time, ministers at First Church noticed a rise in reports of mystical occurrences. Parishioners claimed to be seeing visions. They yammered at ghosts, experienced private conversions, and discovered illumination through dreams. Increasingly, as Van and Bill went on their rounds, they heard astonishing tales and drew a blank. What do you say when a woman insists she has seen her deceased husband lumbering silently around the living room at night? ("Don't worry," Van told her, "Rudolph never did have much to say!") Or someone claims he died and came back to life? Sometimes Van wanted to laugh out loud. But these were not the visions of lunatics. These were earnest, sophisticated, college-educated adults with graduate degrees and grown children; older, traditional, long-rooted grandparents with pensions and ever-present travel plans; single and divorced professional men and women with impossible schedules. He heard from people of all kinds. Sometimes, he thought, it seemed as if they were all emerging from three hundred years of solitude, but he still did not know what it meant or exactly how to respond.

By coincidence, in 1988, just as these issues were bubbling up, a small, wistful-looking woman named JoAnne Taylor came to First Church. In her late fifties, JoAnne had just that year completed a two-year program in spiritual direction at the Shalem Institute in Washington, D.C., and was beginning work on a book about the spiritual life of children. Van knew her and her husband, who was also a minister, through the state conference. In the spring of that year, he persuaded the Board of Deacons to invite her onto the staff. Every week, JoAnne parked her red sports car at the curb in front of the parish house and hung a sign outside the library saying, THE SPIRITUAL DIRECTOR IS IN. She distributed her home phone number to church members and set aside days to conduct group and individual sessions. Before long, several dozen people signed up to see her, including, it was said, Van's wife, Lucille.

Word had it that JoAnne could produce a well in dry souls. Behind the closed library door, she listened to indecipherable accounts of mystical dream sagas, laughed or cried with people, and held hands. She taught adults how to pray. Because her service sounded vaguely psychological, parishioners who met with her tended to keep quiet about their visits. Only thirty or so people now used the service, but occasionally you'd hear recommendations from respectable sources. Allison Denslow used the word *phenomenal.* Bill Warner-Prouty told me he'd found their meetings to be very useful. Tony Gillette, an engineer with a major defense company, let it slip at a deacon's retreat that JoAnne had taught him how to love.

Her conferees demonstrated incomparable devotion. But they also held a strict silence about JoAnne's work. Too personal, I assumed. Too close to the bone.

The spiritual director nourished mystery. She kept the shadowy profile of a gypsy. Indeed, she looked like the proprietor of a church boutique rather than the spiritual director of a large colonial meetinghouse. JoAnne was the type of woman who carried woolly handbags half her size and wore bright Indian silk scarves and black, hand-sewn sandals. She practiced a gentle detachment that served her well leading the dramatis personae of Spirit. I noticed, for instance, that she rarely attended worship services. She distanced herself from operational jobs. She made it a rule never to discuss money or church politics or anyone's private or professional life. At the same time, the fact that she had just published a book on the spiritual life of children using verbatim interviews and crayon drawings of children's images of God—a full year before Harvard sociologist Robert Coles published his book using similar techniques— heightened her profile within the larger community. The book also nailed her reputation within the Connecticut conference and enhanced her credibility for doubters such as I. She was, in a word, exceptional—a quiet, enigmatic presence in the congregation. The first time I interviewed her, she described her mission as "undoing an epidemic of bad theology." Churches, she believed, could—and often did—damage and confuse people rather than guide them. "Especially when you associate religion with ethics or morality, it's a real killer," she said. "It's a killer in the true sense of death."

Over twenty years, after working as a minister of children's education at a local church, occasionally traveling and sometimes living in other parts of the world, JoAnne, like Van, began to compare her work in Connecticut churches with that in developing countries. One year, for instance, she and her husband lived in South America. During the past decade, they had traveled in Central America, Jamaica, Haiti, and other impoverished Caribbean islands. On every tour outside North America, JoAnne had found Christianity to be a much livelier and more meaning-ful faith. The return home always left her more alienated than before and, in time, she lost interest in her work. She became critical and de-manding. The desire grew to pick away at the flimsy layers of the thin mask of Protestant mainline religion; before long, she entered a time of personal crisis.

"I finally realized what I cared about did not carry weight profession-ally," she told me. "What I felt was really missing from church person-ally, and what I observed other people getting outside the institution, was a deeper appreciation for life. I saw how 'religion' crushed the spir-itual lives of adults when they were children. I became more aware of what the world was like outside our town, and working in a mainline church, I knew that most people just were not aware. People were com-ing to church to be entertained! And I'd think, 'This is not a village fair, folks! This is not some kind of sideshow!' Maybe that sounds harsh, but it was true.

"I was also tired of churches. It became more and more painful to me to be in these 'great, historic places.' You know, we can have a past and know who we are historically and celebrate who we are but, frankly, it gets really old after a while. Church becomes a kind of town meeting rather than an acknowledgment that we're here to be in the presence of God."

If the association of religion with history, the misplaced emphasis on ethics and morality damaged people, then an alternative was required. JoAnne wanted to shift the focus from morality, piety, judgment, and psychoanalysis, to peace, justice, and daily practice. As a spiritual guide, she thought she could gently aid the transition in a particular place. At an age when most people began to think of retirement, she went on a mission.

By the time she came to First Church, JoAnne had developed her own simple tasks for kindling the spirit. To meet with members and tend the most remedial aspects of spiritual life would be enough, she thought.

She scheduled weekly appointments with people and asked a few basic questions over and over. Like a valued friend, she would listen keenly to the stories her questions evoked.

"What were your earliest experiences of church? . . . What are your most pressing questions about God? . . . Where do you feel God is working? . . . Where do you feel an absence of God? . . . Where is God? . . . How do you pray? . . . Where are you finding joy in your life?"

Besides meeting one-on-one, she also quickly formed two groups. The idea was to allow people an experience of how God acts within community. With few rules or guidelines, the groups joined her monthly to pray or talk about spiritual matters.

"Find a picture that reflects or appeals to your spirit," JoAnne said, pointing to a spread of photographs on the coffee table. "Then we will take time to center and emphasize our being called together in God's presence."

And so, as I joined them for the first time, I anticipated an adventure. Even though the room still looked like a formal parlor with its Nottingham lace, varnished lamp stands, and silver serving bowls, the meditative stillness spoke of naturopathy, self-actualization, wholeness, and, if I wasn't mistaken, the first faint murmurings of confession.

In the silence, I heard the sounds of anxious women—feet waggling, stomachs burbling.

I had seen nearly everyone in the room at Dr. Shannon Clarkson's lectures. Over several weeks, we had traced the ascent of sexism in the English language, starting in the sixteenth century, when the prejudices of British grammarians inflicted masculine authority across entire English-speaking cultures. In 1850, we learned, an act of British Parliament officially made *he* the legislated standard of reference in cases of mixed gender (as in, "If my mother or father calls, please tell him I've gone out").

Was it significant?

An increasing fundamentalism had crept into biblical translations. After the act of Parliament, in fact, Bibles were even more sexist than before. The Revised Standard Version, produced in our modern era, eventually led an even more doctrinaire use of sexist language than had the mighty King James.

A few men and women in our crowd acted appalled. Some asked what difference did a few male pronouns make?

Dr. Clarkson started on page one of Genesis—the story of Adam and Eve. For instance, she said, consider the word *rib*—as in "Adam's rib," the one used by God to create Eve. The word, as it originally appeared prior to translation, was *tslea*. Interestingly, she said, the committee that created the New Revised Standard version had discovered that the word *tslea* never appeared anywhere else in the Bible. Other than that one creation story, there was no other place where context could offer translators a comparison. *Tslea* was Adam's rib? Perhaps not. Without another context, its true definition was anybody's guess. Thus, in the act of translation, biblical scholars had reported God's creation of Eve by performing their own, so to speak, stab in the dark.

But what did that have to do with sexism? we asked.

Dr. Clarkson went on: When one again looked carefully at the language, it appeared that Adam himself may have been a hoax. As the name underwent scrutiny by the NRSV committee, a new interpretation of the creation story emerged. Since the Hebrew word for "humankind" or "earth creature" was the word *adam,* and the words for man and woman—*ish* and *ishah*—were entirely different, it was possible that the original creation story did not mean that God created woman from man. If one thought of Adam as the genderless *adam,* then the rib from which Eve was created came not from man at all. This would make Eve man's predecessor, not the other way around. If this were true, she teased, then this good fellow, Adam, was not a man at all, and Eve was not representative of the "second sex," as "his-story" told it, but of the first.

Outbursts of applause and grunts of disapproval occasionally interrupted her lectures, as Dr. Clarkson went on and on with examples from the committee's archive. Soon the evidence grew so vast that it was wearying, and the lecture turned into a tart discussion. Over time, First Church members revealed their own personal images of God. I catalogued them—a magician, an Episcopal bishop, Humpty Dumpty, Santa Claus, Zeus, Captain Kirk, the church organist, the Wizard of Oz, a fingerprint, a woman giving birth. A fascinating variety of images, but also a clue that perhaps some people's God had stopped growing with them in adolescence, something I never would have imagined while watching them at worship on Sundays, and a thought I did not dare express at the time.

On the night of the last seminar, Van announced he would appoint a "task force" to study the issue. Headed by Andy McCarthy, it would report to the Board of Deacons. A report would be issued. Then, later perhaps, they would decide what to do.

"You've never been a minority, have you, Van!" Peggy snapped.

"I don't like the words *task force*," Joan said. "Sounds like we're going to war!"

"Sounds evangelical," Dr. Clarkson said.

"The E word!" Priscilla exclaimed.

"Now, now," Van said, "*evangelical* is a word that's often narrowly construed . . ."

John Gregory-Davis and his wife both mentioned something about their own frustrations with First Church worship services, and then Bill and Van exploded.

"That's unfair!" Bill said. "You can't say we've done nothing to change around here."

"I didn't say that," John said.

"We didn't say that," his wife repeated.

"Well, I heard it!" Bill said.

"And I felt it!" Van snapped.

Then, as quickly as it began, the conflict abruptly ended. The spectacle of ministers fighting in public silenced the crowd. Van changed the subject. Turning the attention back to Dr. Clarkson, Bill reached for a gift, tucked beneath his chair, and thanked her for "spiritual guidance on a difficult subject." Then Andy, seizing the moment, politely acknowledged the ministers for planning the series, and John Gregory-Davis scooted out into the hallway with his wife.

Dr. Clarkson did not stay to chat after the meeting broke up. She packed her new Bibles and disappeared in a rush. Bill and John met privately in the hall to discuss a special service with feminist liturgy. Andy and his wife, Elizabeth, went home wondering if the seminars might result in a "sneak attack" on the congregation. Elizabeth, in particular, was furious.

"Who does that John Gregory-Davis think he is?" she fumed. "All that nonsense about his 'Mother God' and 'giving birth to the universe.' What the heck does he know about giving birth?"

Kerosene on fire. Within days of the last lecture, the effect of Dr. Clarkson's presence had already been tantamount to allowing Mother language into the life of First Church. It was as if someone were about to loosen a wild dog in the sanctuary on Sundays. On the list of rumor items, this was soon number two, just after the capital funds campaign.

As I sat in the Morrell Room now, lost in thought, I looked at JoAnne and wondered. Almost every person in this room had attended Dr. Clarkson's lectures. Almost all of them were on the healing committee, too. Were these the rabble-rousers? Mother God lovers? Somebody had to be responsible for what was beginning to happen in this congregation. What, I wondered, did these women really talk about in their little group with JoAnne after all?

JoAnne had a thin, weathered face. She was tanned and quite pretty, and as she spoke, she moved with a stealthy efficiency, like a cat in tall grass. As usual, she was dressed in a blowsy, Indian-print skirt and peasant blouse. She sat slightly apart from us, comfortably stationed by the picture window. After a while, she prayed aloud: "God, we come from many places this morning, with many needs. We hear the wind like a common language. Whether it calls us to submit or relinquish or just to be still, help us be aware that, like the wind, you are always present in most powerful and unexpected ways when we take time to wait on one another and listen."

I peeked. Each person's face held a vastly different expression. A profound sadness. A frozen smile. A wistful gaze. An ironic twist. Then there was Nancy Fitch, a puff of white powder and florid cheeks. A woman desperately aglow.

"Oh! Joanne! Where did you get that tape!" Nancy exclaimed when the winds subsided. "It's wonderful! You know that reminds me of something I heard at a retreat in Boston last February when I went to that conference with Bernie Siegel."

"Didn't he produce a wonderful, healing visualization?" Priscilla said.

Visualization! I silently ran the word across my tongue. Was I being bad again? In the healing committee, I had already pegged Nancy as the elusive prattler. I started to imagine what other styles might emerge over the hour. The ambivalent waffler? The profuse intellectual? Flighty eccentrics, detached anglers?

"Why don't we start with the pictures you've selected," JoAnne said. "I'd like you to use these to express where you are at this moment in your journey. And I'd like to ask you to consider how you have been praying. How is your prayer life? What has been effective or not effective lately?"

Traditional courtesies might evoke a story or two. Or the women might hide in theological abstractions. I laid low.

"I'll go first," said Allison, holding up a dark photograph. "I've been standing at the edge of this cliff for quite a while."

For more than ten minutes, we listened to her unload. JoAnne glanced around. Through the windows I watched the light silhouette of pine trees shiver. Dust flew as a breeze sifted through the yard.

To sit silently was not enough for this crowd. The wind tape was supposed to lead to stories of compulsions, sad tales of desperate acts, private revelations. I understood: JoAnne fished to recover an experiential tradition. Reclamation of the awful subjective. The realignment of religion with ordinary life. We would disgorge our feelings, share them with the group, sort through the clammy remains.

Allison's voice shook. "I've been on the verge of something . . . destructive," she said. "I've wanted to fly the coop."

She seemed entirely different from the young woman who baked bread for Communion and served coffee on Sundays. She looked even younger here. Early thirties, I guessed. Her dark hair, parted straight down the middle, glistened and curled fashionably just above her small shoulders. She was quite still even as she spoke, like a deer alert, looking for something that was not apparent to the rest of us.

As one of the youngest adults active in the church, Allison always appeared to me to have the most integrated life. The enthusiastic mother of three boys. A physician's wife. English teacher at a private school in West Hartford. Deacon. In church, she carried herself with distinction, an easy kind of grace that suggested good parentage and an exceptional education.

"I know myself well enough to ask for help, and I've had some problems with depression in the past," she said. "So I'm taking time now with prayer, thanks to JoAnne. I've become more involved in church, as you all know, and in the community. It's helpful to be busy. But after fifteen years of marriage and raising kids, it's just become very hard to find something . . ."

What? What was this whiny, self-pitying blather? How could she find something better than the cushy life of a physician's wife?

". . . to become clearer? I really don't know. I suppose that's why I'm here."

Silence followed her.

Okay, I understood. You could stagger-step to revelation with this crowd. Perfectly acceptable to duck and hide. I rested more easily on the settee.

JoAnne said nothing. No one spoke until Nancy blurted out: "Well, I'm feeling more renewed this week!" Her false-cheery smile was repulsive. "Having just returned from that marvelous Monet exhibit in Boston with my daughter."

"And I've been journaling for the first time," said another, adding, "Thanks to JoAnne, I'm getting my anger out."

"Oh, Jane, isn't it liberating to allow yourself to be angry rather than being the usual fixer-upper of the household?" Nancy said. "The always cheery and helpful one."

"Well, I seem to be stuck in my prayer life," Priscilla said. "I realized lately that I've only prayed one prayer over the last six years. Only one!

But it has been regular and consistent, and that was, 'Dear God, don't let my mother end up in a nursing home.' "

"And, of course, you just had to take your mother to Kimberly Hall," JoAnne said.

"Yes! And now we have to sell the house, and sell all her belongings and begin the visits every day, which she expects. And she always wants me to be cheerful and to pick up her spirits, just like I've done all my life."

"How old is she?" Allison asked.

"Eighty-five. We have never really gotten along. Every day I have to muster the strength to be jolly and try to please her and make her happy when all she really wants to do is die and all I want is for her to die. Isn't that awful? But do I feel ashamed? No, I just try to be cheerful. Just like Jane, always cheerful, always good."

"That's it exactly," Jane said. "The other day I was driving back from the nursing home and while I was passing through town, I saw a bumper sticker that said, ANTICIPATE MIRACLES. And I thought, 'That's what I need right now.' I'm right there with you, Priscilla."

"I hear you," Priscilla said.

I hear you, my ass!

The chatter went on. I watched Joan Rockwell on the sofa, pulling her legs up under her into a half-Lotus, distant and pensive.

For at least two months, I had wondered about her. Somehow, like Allison and Priscilla, she appeared to be at the center of things in the church, making crafts with children in the day school, singing in the choir, preparing healing services. And yet, I could not forget seeing her cry in the balcony on Sundays or finding her alone in the choir loft praying before anyone else arrived. In the short time I'd been here, I could have sworn I had watched her undergo a metamorphosis. The pleasant middle-aged lady who wore a blond pageboy haircut and Ann Taylor dresses, who kept her nails glossy with a red sheen, looked more and more like a poor stray. She had not slept well, you could see that, and her wardrobe ran more toward blue jeans and flannel shirts. I had heard that she planned to go back to school or leave her family to travel in Central America, but no one really knew.

"Joan?" JoAnne said. "You've been very quiet."

Joan looked at me, I thought, judging if I could be trusted. She began tentatively. For months, she said, she had experienced the same disturbing dreams, the kind that foretell a change—swampy, murky, important dreams. Just like that. Without a warning.

Last night, she said, she had dreamed of herself riding in a careening school bus. The driverless vehicle, full of spectators of some kind, lost control on a mountain road, went barreling down a winding highway, suddenly swerved off the shoulder, and tumbled off an embankment. When it came to rest, the bus was lodged between large rocks on a river.

Who was there with her? the women asked. Family? Friends?

"Joan?" Allison said.

"They are like visions," she said.

At times, as she spoke, I had the impression that she was still vividly inside the dream. She gesticulated as she talked and narrowed her eyes dramatically.

"Everyone climbed out of the bus," she said. "Water was rising up, arms and legs were churning. But as I jumped out the back door, I looked around, and I saw a baby squirming against one of the windows. People kept yelling, 'We won't wait!' like a threat. An ultimatum. But I turned and went back anyway. I grabbed the little girl up in my arms and then I had to swim across this raging river with the baby and once we got to land, the ground was soupy and I had to struggle over to the mountainside and then climb a rocky path to reach the road. It was incredibly difficult.

"Apparently, the group had taken a more circular route or something, but they all looked clean and happy when I first spotted them. They were laughing and having a good old time when I came straggling up the path. And when I finally caught up they said, 'Oh, hi! What's up' as if I hadn't just been through the most awful experience of my life, as if nothing had happened. And I said, 'Well, I'm sure glad to see you folks again!' Like nobody cared about the infant or my struggle to save her. Then I realized there was no baby in my arms. There hadn't even been a bus crash. The 'baby' was me, and while everybody else was just walking down this road, I had somehow gone off a cliff, fallen into a river, and saved myself. It was as if I had gone off this ledge and was working very hard to save a baby, but no one else cared. Nobody even realized!"

"That's the way it is on our journey sometimes, isn't it?" Priscilla said.

Give me a break! Which Flannery O'Connor short story did you step out of?

"That's the way it is in my life!" Joan said. "Not that I want to go into any details. Obviously. Those of you who know me will know. Some days it feels like I'm actually giving birth to myself."

Jesus!

She kept looking at me as if I were an interloper. I couldn't care less. Not about her or Allison or Jane or Nancy. Enough! I felt anxious and irritable. It was like being trapped with a group of shamans, neurotics, and palm readers. They sounded off like an echo: I, I, I, I, I . . . And I felt silly for having come. I folded my arms to enjoy a fine sulk.

My father, my nephew, the sound of drums, a circling pack of wolves . . .

"Lottie, you haven't said anything," Joanne said. "Not that you have to."

Lottie looked genuinely surprised to hear JoAnne call her, as if she never expected to be included. She was the one with the frozen smile, the oldest person in our group. Yes, I thought, Lottie has the face of an old church volunteer, a dutiful silver polisher. She had the familiar, solid expression of grandmotherly kindness forcefully pressed into her face. She wore thin wire-framed glasses. During the entire hour, she had sat quite properly with her ankles crossed and hands delicately folded, like a cloth napkin, in her lap.

"Oh!" she said. "Well, nothing. I've just been wanting very much to tell our writer friend over there"—she motioned at me—"about our wonderful church. And how lucky we are to have such a caring fellowship."

She looked back at me with that dreadful smile. I arched an eyebrow and smiled back. Force of habit.

"Gary," she said, "you know, when my husband died, I received flowers from this church for four or five months! And the meals! I think people kept bringing meals for weeks. And Van . . . but not just Van! The women of this church are wonderful! And after David died, I really learned . . . I learned about . . . I learned . . ."

She looked at JoAnne and her smile broke.

"How long ago was that?" JoAnne asked gently.

"Two years."

"And you're really doing better?"

"Oh yes. . . . Fine. Really. I'm much better. This church . . ."

"Keeping busy?"

"Better. I'm busier than before," she stammered.

"Oh," Priscilla sighed. "Poor thing."

"No, really," Lottie said. "I knit afghans."

"That's nice," Joan said.

"It's better than watching TV," Allison added.

"I don't like TV, either," Lottie said. "So really, it's fine. I've knitted eight or nine afghans since January."

Before I noticed, a box of Kleenex started around the circle. Several women started to cry.

"It's okay to feel that here," JoAnne said, and then Lottie choked back a sob.

I looked to my left. Nancy wrapped both arms around her stomach and slouched down in the pink armchair like a nauseated sailor. If anyone could have broken the spell with a chirpy anecdote and an off-the-wall remark, I thought, it would have been her. Instead, she began to cry and then spoke of her needs at home—the perfect family struck by alcoholism, her son suffering from skin disease, her daughter in trouble with the law. Then Priscilla, our unflappable healing committee leader, commenced to sob—troubles at home, illness in the family, more of the same.

I thought of my empty prayers again, and came up against the indifferent God who abandoned lonely widows to their afghans and mutely regarded people's griefs from afar.

"I don't know how to pray!" I blurted. My hands shook and my voice sounded angry, but it was too late to muffle myself.

They looked at me with phony interest.

"What?" JoAnne said. "Where did that come from?"

"In the past few months, my wife and I have been trying to get pregnant and we just discovered that she's infertile. What am I supposed to do? I try to pray. I try to imagine myself holding her in a bath of light. I ask God for healing. I spend a lot of time listening to her because this has hit us very hard and she's going through a terrible time. She's grieving and angry. But that's all she can do. I can't even pray for myself. I don't know how. It's always false. Every time I close my eyes to begin, I can't find an honest word. I don't have a way to say . . ."

"You're angry at God," JoAnne said.

"What?"

"I said, you're angry at God."

"Okay."

"And you don't think God's big enough to hear that?"

What? What did she know? Did they want a confession? Poor Lottie. Poor Nancy. Poor Joan. Poor Allison. Poor Jane. But not me. No, I wouldn't give them the pleasure.

"What?" I said.

"Maybe your God's too fragile," JoAnne said. "Is that it? The God who is all powerful and all loving will do what with your anger? Why not let God have it! Go right up to God and shake the cage. Have you ever thought of that? Shaking God's cage?"

I glanced at her. Sounded vaguely sacrilegious.

"You're stuck," she said. "Maybe your God is too small."

I looked away. Stuck with this pathetic crowd. I tried to change the subject, quickly switched to talking about my father and nephews, something about Sam Keene and "men's spirituality." But I felt humiliated in front of all those women.

Soon the group became chattier and I grew more solemn. In my mind, I imagined headlines that would tell the story:

SOJOURNER JOURNALIST
GAGGED BY GHOULS.

Neither Lottie nor I said another word, and when the group broke up after a prayer over the small flame on the coffee table, she hit the door first and I quickly followed, not once thinking the attention of the group would remain with us. To say the least, I was not grateful for having come. I left feeling alarmed and disoriented.

A few days later, I found a letter addressed to me in the church office. It was from Priscilla, who worked with Joan in the downstairs nursery school. The note said, in part:

> *I burn with outrage at the injustice of where you are; at the irony of com-*
> *ing closer to your father and your wandering nephews, and of the hope*
> *and possibility of growing into parenthood yourself, but having it so sud-*
> *denly and rudely and unjustifiably slipping away from you. . . . I cannot*
> *"know how you feel." We all carry our own unique "baggage" of reac-*
> *tions; and neither I nor the others in the spirituality group can "make it*
> *better." But I want you to know that I hear your distress, I witness and*
> *validate your anger, I rage with you over the unfairness, I grieve with*
> *you at the irrevocable nature of it all. I listen, and I care very much.*
> *What truth can lie in such bitter matters? I don't know. But I know you*
> *matter. You are of value to me.*

The pieties of church women displeased me. I didn't want to remember mentioning either my father or my nephew that morning. Her "validation," "witness," and cliché-filled concern only made me feel more inept and off-balance.

I refused to answer Priscilla's letter or acknowledge her act of kindness. The formal, polite monologues that I once prayed from my heart became more impertinent and challenging and indecorous. I did not need church women to care for me.

Save it for your old mother, I thought. Leave me alone. Go away.

Then, at night, my prayers suddenly started to change.

"Fuck you!" I would pray. Over and over, the same message. Could the all-powerful, all-loving God absorb that kind of anger? Was there a language He could understand?

"Bastard!" I'd pray. "Stupid shit! Come here, you lousy son of a bitch! Answer me now or leave me alone!"

CHAPTER SEVEN

Piney Woods, Georgia, 1961.

"Hellfire! Satan wants your soul! He don' care 'bout your mommies and daddies! Satan don' care 'bout you or me! And when the Judgment comes the Lord gonna take those wise enough, the Lord gonna take those who one night said, 'Yes, Lord.' The Lord gonna come back to those who say tonight in this hot Georgia church . . . who come to the altar and say . . . who get up out of their seats right now and cry . . . who step to the front with me and give their life to Jeee-suss! Forgive me, Lord. Bless me, Lord! Save me, Jesus! And the rest will burn in hell. Too late then! Too late, old man! Too late, adulteress! Too late, vain chil'ren! For you'll burn in hell forever! So say the scriptures! Let the little chi'ren come to me now. Blessed be the meek. Blessed be the poor in spirit. . . . Come now and repent. . . . Come to the altar and be forgiven. Your time is here. Jesus calls you to the altar. He waits with a word for your redemption."

"As hot as blue blazes," my mother said on the way home, calmly flapping a fan she had picked up from the pew.

"We'll be there in a minute," Daddy said. "Get out of these wet clothes."

Dear God, I prayed in the back seat, thank you, Jesus, thank you, Jesus.

Thank you, Jesus. Jesus loves me this I know . . . Thank you, Jesus. Thank you, Reverend. Thank you, God, I am saved!

"How old were you when that happened?" JoAnne asked. Our first session together started off on a tear.

Seven or eight, I could not remember. Every summer we'd drive down to see my grandparents in Georgia, and if we hit it during revival week we'd go to the church and listen to guest preachers. Every night, fire and wickedness, the story of the Last Days. Lust and lies! The battle of demons and saints. Sermons always led to a dramatic call to come to the altar and be saved.

Jesus saved me three or four times, at least. I could think of it now as a primitive ritual, perhaps, but in those days, all across the South, it had been as common as cantaloupes at breakfast. In the Southern culture where I was brought up—and more so for older people like my parents and grandparents—being born again marked the high point of religious life. Revive! Repent! Be saved! Just like when you killed your first deer, and they'd smear blood on your face and chest, being born again scored the beginning of a new life.

"These were the kind of places where people spoke in tongues?" JoAnne asked.

"No," I said quickly.

Actually, they might have been speaking in tongues, for all I knew. I only remembered the first time with much clarity. The old preacher would not let up with news of the Apocalypse and I thought the only way we could stop him from raging would be if everyone went up to the railing in front of the church and surrendered. I was surprised so few stepped forward. It was hard for me, just a boy, trying to overcome the ambivalence and embarrassment of going it alone. The wild-eyed stranger wanted to damn the whole world. But when my parents didn't get up, nor my uncle nor aunt, nor my grandparents, I must have figured it was up to me. At that moment, I must have felt so frightened that I didn't think there was any other choice. Either I somehow knew what the expectation was, or I assumed that I was the only holdout in the clan. I went forward.

In a poor country church, dark and strange, with its candles burning strong around the altar in the heat of a backwoods Georgia August, I bowed my head at the wooden altar rail and clutched my small hands in prayer, "Dear God, save Mommy, save Daddy, save . . ." I prayed as hard as I could to keep the roof from caving in under a certain hail of fire.

The next morning, I picked up the phone at my grandparents' house and patiently navigated the party lines to call every kid I knew and invite them to the evening service. Privately, at the altar while we were being "saved" the night before, the preacher had commanded us each to call our friends. "Bring them tomorrow night," he had said. And so when we returned to church, I saw that I had snared a few prize catches, children, like me.

"But was there any discernment of the event?" JoAnne asked.

"Discernment?"

"I'm sorry, that's religious lingo. I mean, did anyone ask you about being saved? Why was it scary? What was it like to go up to the altar alone? What did it mean to you then? What did it mean later?"

That night, when my mother and I returned, I saw a couple of kids I had called—under the arms of their parents. When the minister asked us to raise our hands if we had brought guests, I raised mine high. He went around the sanctuary, acknowledging the adults by name and asking them to stand. But when he came to me he looked away and skipped to the next pew. I was appalled. I was saved! I was a fisherman! What was wrong with me? One night I had knelt at his feet while he dripped sweat on us and pronounced us saved, and the next night, I was invisible.

I don't remember any more.

"How did that affect you?"

Right away? Nothing else, except that sometime during that trip to my grandparents' I was joined by an imaginary friend. When I had to take naps on my grandparents' porch, I watched him go through the screen and play wildly around the yard. God was there, too, playing. I remembered that. I remembered needing God and talking to God.

"So this wasn't a place where people spoke in tongues?" JoAnne asked again.

Yes, my mother spoke in tongues. I remembered her telling me once. But I didn't understand. Not yet, anyway.

"It wasn't that kind of place," I said. "Besides, I think the whole system was breaking down by the time I was growing up."

I knew what JoAnne must have been thinking: Struggling against the wrong questions without the right equipment. And maybe she was correct. Much of the passion, repression, and peculiarities of Southerners probably has to do with hearing the Gospel in grotesque ways. Our animated landscapes, prejudices, and conservatism. Poor boy, I thought, making calls from your grandparents' house on the party line, saving souls and being ignored by the minister the next night because you were only a child. Not worth more than a dime or a quarter.

And I was thinking: Doesn't she understand? Can you imagine how much courage it took for me to leave that pew?

And JoAnne: Why didn't they just give those poor people a stamp or certificate saying they'd been saved and then leave them alone? Instead, little children are left feeling cheated and soon they're scared and praying to an angry God . . .

And me: No, praying to a God to protect me from the doomsayers, the detached and icy, the raging, the ignorant, the misled, the lunatics . . .

But JoAnne said nothing. It was me thinking in the silence. Remembering. At First Church, I knew, the task for serious beginners was to seek wise direction, not personal salvation. The act of "being saved" meant little or nothing here. Those days had passed at least a full century ago, when Reverend Horace Bushnell resisted the impulse to define Christianity exclusively on the basis of conversion. His theology of a more benign and loving God, a more benign and loving human nature, had marked an abrupt about-face from the angry, evangelical theology of Jonathan Edwards, which had been so powerful during my childhood and still thrived in some places around the American South. Perhaps, I thought, for JoAnne to hear one Southerner's experience from 1961, one hundred years after Bushnell reached prominence, must have struck her as oddly fascinating. It was certainly interesting to me, having never spoken of my conversion before.

Imagine that. I heard myself talking. Thirty years had passed, and as horrifying as it was, I had never spoken to anyone about that first conversion. Bizarre and frightening. I suppose for many years it had simply been unspeakable.

From Celtic Christianity came the saying "Anyone without a soul friend is like a body without a head." My new soul friend was JoAnne, no doubt. When I first went to talk to her about signing up for spiritual direction, she advised me that she was not available for emotional support. She insisted she was nothing like a psychologist. She would ask only a few questions and listen. Over time she would insist on accountability, meaning she would look to see that you did not take yourself too seriously, make sure you were paying attention to your own story, and "listening to your soul," as she would say. She would observe my comings and goings and, if I wished, help me straighten out misconceptions I had about the spiritual life. She would sometimes suggest possibilities for change, and maybe nudge me with advice. But most of the time, she would just listen.

Often, I had heard, people regained memories about their own ambiguous religious heritage when they talked to her. Former Catholics at First Church, of which there were quite a few, had particular trouble sorting through bad theology. Some people came simply needing an explanation for inexplicable events. Others told her they did not know why they wanted to see her. In any case, everyone was welcome.

When I went to her that first time, one bright spring morning, and saw her in the First Church library, standing by a window, wearing a green scarf and sipping tea, she looked suspiciously like the average, everyday psychotherapist—detached, observant, self-possessed.

Something about it seemed thrilling to me. I felt like a boy going to school for his first grade-school photograph. I thought our meeting might add a little more dimension to my life. I might come away with a bit more clarity about being alive in a moment of someone else's awareness. Everyone said JoAnne helped smooth ways that were already clear, but it was the pursuit of a new story that really piqued my interest.

"Have a seat," she had said, suddenly, motioning to a set of chairs by the window. "It's not just the two of us here, you know."

"Yes, the intellectual enlightenment," she said now. "You were saying the culture changed."

I never would have called Southern religious culture enlightened. By "changed" I probably meant "mutated." The electronic church emerged. Pentecostal megachurches sprang up on the outskirts of town. Jim and Tammy Faye Bakker moved their headquarters to Charlotte. Gains in wealth and political power among evangelicals brought them prestige and respectability. The old way was dying and, as popular as it was, the new way seemed even worse, more distant, colder, far more calculating.

I felt a knot in my stomach. In my childhood, expectations of the religious life were so enormous, so confused.

They used to say churches covered more square inches of Charlotte than they did of any city in the world. Religion had too much power there, in some ways. I had long ago recognized that a spiritual life made no sense unless it squared with reality, unless it came down to earth in a modest and simple way. But not in Charlotte. Not in my hometown.

At the same time, if I could set aside the theological problems, the dogma, and the corrupt proselytizing of fundamentalists, I always felt there was something valuable amid the clamor. Something in that first altar call still felt legitimate. It did not square with reality, but whatever I had acquired in the exchange remained an influential and energizing presence in my life.

"The born-again business is always a very public event. You stand up and walk to the altar alone, lower your head like a virgin sacrifice in front of an entire church, you say what you are told to say. You make a promise to be faithful. It is both the most private moment of your life and one of the most humiliating. Strange day. And once it's done, it is done. You put your dollar in the collection plate and then you go home. No questions asked."

"You chose not to be a hypocrite, I presume," JoAnne asked.

"How's that?"

"I mean, I guess you chose not to delude yourself into thinking you were right all the time. Not to go saved self-righteous."

I had never heard that term.

"A lot of people who are saved take on great energy and decide they are good and the world's bad," she explained. "But it sounds like you understand that life is conflict and people are conflicted and . . ."

I could feel the cool, green cushions on Granddaddy's lounge chair and look out on his farm through the screen. A current of heat rising off the ground rippled the barbed fence where the pigs ran. My imaginary friend dodged around the yard like a rabbit, bouncing high, tumbling, flying through the air, doing back-flips on Daddy's Chevrolet. God was mine and I was God's and the world was never so beautiful or serene, never so alive.

Strangely, despite the minister's images of blood and fire, I experienced a profound sense of clarity and peace. I went to the altar rail, and when it was over, I could communicate with God.

"You had a relationship with God after that?"

"No question."

"And understood as a relationship?"

"Absolutely."

"Did it change your idea of what God was like?"

What was God like? God sent me an imaginary playmate. God was on my granddaddy's farm. God and I daydreamed on Granddaddy's porch.

So the problem wasn't God. The problem was people. Once you went through with it, the preaching should have stopped. But once was never enough. My family was never satisfied to think you could be saved only once. The preachers didn't believe you. They always had more to say about it. Always another day came when you'd be asked to give up another piece of your soul—two, three, four times . . . forever, it didn't matter. Greedy and insatiable, the fundamentalists always wanted more.

After the first time I thought, "So what else do I have to do?" I'd been saved. God and I were friends. Why did they always want you again and again? It was they who always grasped for God. "Come here, God! Where did you go? Where are you now? Forgive me, Lord! Forgive me, Jesus!" Being saved meant suffering a continuous torment, in their eyes. It never meant you could enjoy life. You were called on constant alert. Always vigilant for signs of the coming Apocalypse.

I never separated the altar call from the swift events that followed. The Magical Mystery Tour. Student riots. Black armbands and placards to protest the Vietnam War. Reading Camus. Meeting Billy Pilgrim. Wire-rims and long hair. When the world seemed most out of control, those were the times it made the most sense to me. We were stardust, we were golden. We went back to the Garden.

When I was fifteen, my mother, I believe, destroyed my copy of *The Catcher in the Rye*. She burned my Ouija board. She left scripture verses on my dresser. I retaliated, invading her bookshelves of religious tracts—pernicious-sounding volumes by David Wilkerson, Billy Graham, Kathryn Kuhlman, and John Wesley—and hid the books in an old trunk in the attic. The fear they had engendered, the way they had overtaken my mother's life, their presence in our household, was more than I could tolerate.

But I could not talk about these things. Not yet. I was still too ashamed. The memories were too sad.

"Maybe I took something good from it," I said. "Somehow I think I used it to become who I am."

"And early on, how was that expressed?"

Social action? But what? Raising money for a Democrat running for city council. Standing on the streets of downtown Charlotte asking for money for Easter Seals. Harassing ROTC kids at the high school. Writing letters to the editor of the *Charlotte Observer*. Promoting desegregation and open schools, and opposing the war, in the school newspaper.

That was my interpretation of real religion—rebellion.

But did you join larger groups in social action? she asked. Did you know other kids with similar experiences? Or was this just an interpretation you made on your own? How did it connect with "being saved"?

Maybe I was just making it all up, imagining a story for my life, mapping like a child drawing lines through words in the church bulletin. *This page is a map, and this pencil line is my path, dodging hymns, skirting verses, from here . . . to here . . . to here.*

Maybe it was more complex than that. In my generation, a lot of people learned, in that sweep of ideas from the home church to the Beats to the Merry Pranksters, that we could create our own church. What else were you going to do if you felt alienated from your parents and your society? You felt God working in another direction, and you were ready for Him, saying, "Okay, God, let's get on with it! Let's trip. Let's go!"

"You must have felt different as a child," JoAnne said.

That sounded intrusive. Yes, I had always felt a certain lonely distance, a milder/hotter temperament that separated me from most. Occasionally, I met someone who understood spiritual matters the way I did. But that was so long ago. These days . . . I didn't know what I believed anymore.

"And that relationship? Have you had a continuing relationship with God?"

"No," I said

"Okay. So if I ask what's your faith now . . ."

"I would say whenever I pray now it's like casting a fishing line into the ocean. You might get a tug. You might catch a fish. You might sense nothing at all."

"All valid."

"Yes, but I'm saying I cast prayers into a black universe. Infinite space. I don't know where they go, or if they go. I don't know anything about God."

She said nothing for a moment. "There's a nuance to that word *cast*."

"I mean, it's like casting a line. Or 'casting off.' You know, launching . . ."

"Launch?"

"Pushing off from the shore. Setting off. Out to sea. Into a vast, un-knowable universe."

Maybe I tangled the line somewhere. She changed course.

"Tell me," she said, "what image do you have of God? Or do you have another word?"

I was stumped. Never thought of God as an image.

"I assume it has changed over time," she said, trying again. "Maybe that would tell us something."

God felt so big I had no image.

"I told you, I'm casting a line and God is . . ."

"Everywhere? Nowhere? Beyond?"

"God is too big."

"You sound like a mystic."

"At the moment I'm pretending to be a Congregationalist."

She laughed and looked out the window for a moment.

"If you had to put some words on that mystery, when does God feel closer than at other times? When did God ever feel especially present?"

I couldn't say.

"Then when has the Spirit touched your life?"

The question was not when. I wanted to say often, and in many ways God was present.

"Never?" she said. "Sometimes? Often?—or would 'often' be too bold?"

How should I know? We sat in silence for the longest time.

I was getting tired of this. She asked too many questions, I had too few answers.

"Always," I said, hoping to shut her up.

In 1986, while on a magazine assignment, I attended a workshop led by a best-selling Connecticut author named Scott Peck, whose book about spiritual development, *The Road Less Traveled,* was becoming a phe-nomenon. After a lengthy interview at his home, he graciously invited me to meet him and about sixty other people at a seminar in Knoxville,

Tennessee. I was unprepared for what would happen next. Over three days, I was asked to put away my notebooks and give myself over to Peck and this group in an effort, as he would say, to "build community."

I tried to tell JoAnne about the experience, as it had marked the next stage of my being "born yet again."

On the first day in Knoxville, Dr. Peck introduced everyone—most were therapists and clergy—and the sessions started with pleasant, polite conversation. With sixty people acting under few guidelines and operating with no directions but to form community, the group changed abruptly over a few hours. Civility crumbled. Organizers tried to organize. Therapists lectured. I, having completed a cursory background investigation of their "guru," let it be known, in very specific ways, that Dr. Peck was not a saint.

It is hard to say exactly what happened. My statements led to angry confrontations. I was accused of having come to "feed on Scotty's entrails." The details of what else was said are unimportant. But it would be true enough to point out that my own subjective, otherwise private judgments about Peck made people angry. As his defenders spoke, their own judgments came to light. Alternately defending and attacking, we quickly degenerated into chaos.

Peck wrote me later to say that, looking back, he thought it was a hilarious event. But at the time, after four or five hours of our haggling, Peck also acknowledged that he felt a sudden gush of back and neck pain. I remember seeing him stretched out on the floor in agony. Soon, all around the room, people began to confess and cry. They were the most awful, most honest stories I had ever heard. At the end of the day, the room was quiet for a long time, and we broke up without resolution. That night, I went back to my room and watched TV, an angry skeptic, having been vilified for telling what I thought were my own "truths."

The second day, Peck invited us to tell any dreams we might have had the night before. The dreams led again to confessions. Some people apologized to me. A quiet transformation of conscience occurred, and people told more stories about their personal failures. By the second afternoon, the group was quiet and exhausted.

"Had you ever had an experience of going head-to-head or sharing so intimately?" JoAnne asked.

"No. And it surprised me, frankly. Beneath all the turmoil and struggles, we all seemed very much alike. One person's story would always affect someone in the group, and it ricocheted. We heard a number of amazing revelations about adultering ministers, thieving therapists, alcoholic couples. I'd never heard people express so much pain."

"And you felt centered more than you had before? Maybe coming to terms with who you were, too?"

I hadn't said a word about what happened to me yet. That part was very difficult. At the moment, I was still not sure I understood.

By the second day, I felt more alienated, isolated, and excluded than on the first. Having read Peck's book, I harbored an undefinable ill will for "grace" and "God" and even the task at hand.

"And the community?" JoAnne said.

"I was moved by what happened. And I wanted to be a part of the group. But I was also so resentful that my 'truths' still had not been accepted that I wanted to walk out. Finally, at lunch that afternoon, I talked privately with one therapist, who I felt safe with."

And as I talked, I felt as if I had wandered into a safety zone. A place without judgment. She promised to help me.

Late that afternoon, I talked to the group, and as I spoke I felt that I had, for once, been received by people without malice. As I spoke about my truths and resentments and lifelong feelings of alienation, I was overwhelmed by the enormity of the silence. As I damned them and forgave them and damned them again, tears ran down my face. People reached out and listened.

I don't know if it was the presence of God I felt. I don't even know that I experienced it that way. But I do know that at the end of those three days, the world seemed different. Alive. Not metaphorically alive. Atomically alive. Every thread connected. Everything properly recognized under heaven, a group united, and a small community in accord.

The next night, after I flew home to Hartford, I dreamed about a man in a white linen suit. He was standing on the street in front of my house. My dog's body lay crumpled on the sidewalk.

"Scott Peck killed my dog!" I told my wife in the dream. "He denies it, but I know what's true. Scott Peck has killed my dog."

Later when the profile appeared in a magazine, I included a description of the workshop and the dreams. Still not knowing exactly what it meant, I reported that the experience had signified a dramatic personal change.

Soon people started to write me. One man who wrote said, "Don't you know, 'Dog' is 'God' spelled backwards."

Yes, exactly! The vindictive God, the personal God, the playful God—the God of that Georgia fundamentalist and all the Gods I ever imagined—were gone. And in its place was only a mystery and a community. Connection. The instinct for religion.

"When was this again?"

"Four or five years ago."

"And even though you say it changed your life, like going to an altar call, there was no . . ."

Right again. No process. None. I came back to Connecticut thinking, What in the world has happened to me? It affected my mind. I had dreams and visions. When I told close friends, most were skeptical. "You don't know what you're dealing with!" they'd say. Or "Let me give you this book!" But I could not deny the experience. As skeptical as I was, I was also ready to accept it as a matter of grace.

"But you also discovered a community. Which suddenly disappeared?"

"In only three days. And sometimes I still feel that loss."

"You know the story of the road to Emmaus?"

Yes, I had heard the story for the first time only a year ago at the little Presbyterian church. No one knew, but that story had begun my quest to find a church. "A small group of stinking fishermen and friends lose their center and, grieving, discover a new Messiah . . ." Something in that little church had reminded me of the experience in Knoxville, of my grandparents and our hot evenings at revival, of the first altar call. It had nothing to do with hellfire or the saving of souls. Something about the people in the story affected me, their need, their grief, the community of fishermen discovering—after the crucifixion—that a Messiah was with them still, walking alongside on the road to Emmaus.

The third turn on my spiritual path, the road to Emmaus was preached during Pentecost at a plain, unsophisticated Presbyterian church in eastern Connecticut. Hearing the story—in such a way that it almost vibrated in my heart—had led me to Windsor.

"Now this is strange, JoAnne," I said. "I've never talked to anyone about this before."

"What?" she said.

Shortly after leaving Knoxville, and then again more recently, I had begun to see certain road signs along highways, and like magic, they would come to life. The words would become animated and almost leap into my mind, rattling awake some inner connections. It sounded nearly insane as I told her, but they were as unmistakable as the call of a crow.

"For instance," I said, "you know Jan and I have been trying to get pregnant—but this was before we had any hint of infertility. We were driving home from Amherst one afternoon several weeks ago and we . . . we saw a series of flashing signs on the highway that said, EXPECT DELAYS . . ."

"And it gave you a sign?"

"Immediately. And not just me. It struck us both that way. We looked at each other and knew what it meant. The way it affected us is indescribable really. It's like other times in my life when I've prayed for growth or I've been at a place in my life where I was stuck professionally or faltering in my marriage, and I'd say, 'Okay, God, I'm ready,' and the next thing you know, I'm taking off in another direction. It sounds absurd, but—"

"You mean, you ask for bread and then wonder why you don't get a stone?"

I saw the first glint of her toughness.

"Look, I'm skeptical enough to wonder about it." I meant JoAnne, too. Who was she, after all? What did she know about God?

"What do you wonder?"

"I want to know how it works. Why does it happen? I mean, your brains goes *snap!* when you see a sign on the highway, and you think you've gotten a sign from God? Why? Why at that moment? Why that sign? Or you attend a workshop with a crowd of ministers and psychologists and—*whap!*—the world comes alive and you feel utterly connected to it. Can't you explain this with psychological concepts? Couldn't you frame it merely in terms of personal need?"

"You mean, how perverse of God that you should want something and you should get it?"

"That is not what I mean!"

"We can put up all kinds of interesting roadblocks."

Now, I thought, she was being hard to get along with. Playing both ends against the middle.

"No, I'm saying that at the base of all these experiences, I am still left wondering, 'Is there a God?' Because despite everything else, the God I feel is often so distant and big beyond imagining."

She looked away and thought for a second.

"You are a mystic," she said. "Which is exactly the opposite of being a fundamentalist, who is absolutely sure about God and even speaks for God, no problem. Am I right?"

I didn't know how to respond to that. Me, a mystic? I never considered myself anything.

"Well?" she said. "In fact, it's best that we know nothing about God or at least not be so sure we know about God. Am I right? I mean, really! Isn't it outrageous that we pretend to know anything about God? That we could pretend we understand it? But there are these strange little things that every so often flash or touch us in a place we don't understand. Like a sign on the highway. Can you say that the sign brought you back to a central place inside?"

How did she know?

"That's what these signposts do, you know," she said.

Maybe she could be trusted, I thought. Maybe she did understand.

All right, then. There was something else. I had not discussed it with anyone. Like everything else "spiritual" in my life, it seemed too strange, or perhaps too insignificant to mention.

"Let me tell you about another time," I said. This was my test.

"Okay."

Back in February when I was traveling around the valley looking for a church to write about, I had come to Windsor and met Van. I could see that he was just a regular guy and his church was just an ordinary place, but something else had happened that convinced me to stay.

"I'm listening," JoAnne said.

"Okay," I continued. "So the next thing that happened was this: I was driving on the highway on the way up here to meet with Van, just to check my impressions again, and all of a sudden I notice I'm stuck in traffic behind a truck covered with pictures of colored balloons. It's a Wonderbread truck!"

"Wonderbread!" Joanne repeated, smiling.

"And it was like an opening again. It was like the highway sign that Jan and I saw. It was like the workshop in Knoxville. I didn't expect it. I wasn't looking for it. But then it was there—this wonderful feeling in that central place. Wonderbread!"

JoAnne said nothing.

"I mean, this is absurd, isn't it?" I said.

"No. No." She was thinking. "In fact, it's all right there, isn't it? Wonder: joy. Bread: the sacraments."

I had never made those connections. Actually, it had struck me as very funny at the time. But wonderful? Maybe at that moment. But now, looking back, I was shocked. Had I really spent months looking for the right church, and finally chose First Church in Windsor on the advice of a bread truck?

Suddenly I felt that I shouldn't have told her.

But JoAnne did not seem especially interested in my signs. She said nothing. It was all too ordinary. Twenty years ago, she said, Sister Corita Kent, a friend of Daniel Berrigan's, had published a book full of road signs and advertising logos. One of them was Wonderbread.

"Hey, JoAnne," I said, "do you mean that some nun twenty years ago had these same experiences? I must be a lunatic. Do you mean there are other people like this?"

"Like what?"

"Crazy like this. People who have these weird spiritual issues. People who 'hear' road signs and 'feel' stories spring to life. I have never known what to make of it, really."

"Of course," she said. "And maybe that struggle is inevitable. Maybe it's a lot more common and less worrisome than you might think. In fact, there's a part of me that has been wanting to leap in this whole time and say to you, 'The church has not been doing its job! It should have been there all along, helping you—and people like you—to understand.' And I really believe that's true. But that's beside the point right now. Let's keep moving."

Did she mean there was more?

She sat back in her chair, crossed her legs, and listened—as quiet as the grass and stones—as I started again to talk, telling more stories than I had ever recalled.

CHAPTER EIGHT

If *God* was merely *dog* spelled backward, Van should have seen tangible signs of trouble. All spring, Daisy ransacked the kitchen and gnawed on Lucille's best furniture. She chewed holes in the Oriental rug, leaped on old ladies, and growled at new members. When the dog pounced, jaws snapping, she went straight for your crotch.

By June, Lucille's young black Lab overtook the manse like a frightening, full-blown metaphorical possibility. Lucille made an appointment for obedience classes. The grounds supervisor considered purchasing a muzzle. Van arose early every morning to run her round and round the cemetery. Nothing worked. Bound to a chain along the clothesline, Daisy managed to pulverize a wooden fence surrounding the Parkers' garbage cans and ravage Lucille's freshly mulched flower beds.

Peggy and I watched from afar, amused and enthralled. It is a plain fact of religious life that a person cannot attend a church for long without seeing signs and portents in any change. So as we watched, we concluded that Daisy's antisocial behavior must have coincided with the first salvos in the inclusive-language campaign. The dog brought into their community all the heat and fire of an Old Testament prophet.

Maybe it was not coincidence. Maybe D-O-G and G-O-D did speak as one. Daisy, the almighty "I AM." Daisy, the overactive verb. Or maybe she had been sent by God—God's only begotten pet—to turn the suburban church into Her more undomesticated domain. Every morning, jerking the minister around the cemetery in an all-out tilt, Daisy struggled to reclaim the churchyard for the greater glories of Whomever.

Watching Van set her loose to sprint through the cemetery—where she leapt across gray stones, dug atop graves, squeezed under the fence, and darted down to the river—I enjoyed a secret affection for Daisy's rebellion. Until Van needed to get back to work and the wild dog refused to mind, they were like kindred spirits dancing across the graves of elders.

"Daisy! Daaaaaai-sy! Bad dog! Come here. Come back here now! Baaaaaad dog!" Van eventually exerted control. Cowed, thumped on her wet nose, dragged whining to the clothesline, Daisy spent part of every day in chains.

"Good dog," Van would say, once she was tied.

Snap! Woof! Wiggle! Strain! Snarl!

The dog would upset garbage pails, and the minister would scurry back to the parish house, laughing to himself. For some reason, he seemed strangely delighted, secretly pleased by what his wild dog hath wrought.

When the season of Pentecost came, Bill and John sprang into action. Working secretly, organizing through phone calls and private meetings over lunch, Van's colleagues planned an adventurous service for the first Sunday in June. Once Van and Lucille left for a three-day weekend in Washington, the meetinghouse became open ground for experimental God-talk—a "sneak attack," just as Andy McCarthy's wife had predicted.

The two ministers headlined their ten-o'clock service as "The Coup of Hyphenated Names," suggesting that for one day, and one day only, Mssrs. Warner-Prouty and Gregory-Davis would deliver a full course of feminist theology.

Bill launched off with number 8, "Joyful, Joyful, We Adore Thee." A sly and deliberate choice, number 8 throttled up with the surging melody of Ludwig Van's "Hymn to Joy." He forced the congregation to rouse itself alert. The lyrics also presented numerous examples of linguistic sexism that could be reflected on during the sermon. As we sang, Bill looked so excited, I thought he might have been dancing behind the pulpit.

John stood next to him, tall and thin, dramatically dressed in a long white robe and a brightly colored Nicaraguan stole. The young outreach minister raised his lanky arms after the singing and called for silence. His prayer sounded like a chant: "Loving God . . . Creator of man *and woman* . . . in your image. Help us grow strong and learn . . . to embrace you . . . Holy *Mother* . . . Father . . . friend . . . *lover* . . . redeemer. Like a father . . . receiving wayward children . . . so you will welcome us. As a *woman* . . . searching for a lost coin . . . so you rejoice for even one soul . . . restored to wholeness."

He droned on, suggesting one new image after another like a poet playing pranks. Joan Rockwell leaned over from the balcony and gave thumbs up. Peggy Couples beamed from the tenth pew.

Hard coughs echoed like shotgun cracks when John started the Lord's Prayer: "Our *Mother,* who art in heaven . . ." A stunned silence clouded the children's message when he gathered a dozen kids around the chancel area. Speaking into a microphone, leaning down into their little faces, masking a hint of accusation at the adults in the pews, he asked: "Did it ever occur to you boys and girls that God might be a . . . *woman?*"

Bill's feminist sermon followed. Employing the same steady, bland, academic logic used by Dr. Clarkson during the Wednesday-night lectures, he tried to disguise his intention with subtle and arcane references. But it was too late. The gig was up.

Referring to the opening hymn, he expressed a long-standing appreciation for Henry Van Dyke's lyrics to Beethoven's exhilarating tune. Pointing to the hymnist's rich lode of images—*"giver of immortal gladness," "wellspring of the joy of living," "ocean depth of happy rest"*—he drove home his first point about the mysterious nature of God. Then Bill shook his head, confessing sadly: "But I'll never be able to sing, '*Father love is reigning o'er us, brother love binds man to man,*' with the same unrestrained joy that my father's voice brought to that wonderful combination of music and lyric. To hang on one image denies us and our children of a growing sense of the fullness of God."

I heard a hymnal drop. Feet shuffling. Someone snorted.

After the service, John and Bill stood on the front steps greeting lines of worshipers.

"What kind of plot did you guys hatch this morning!" one man said, pushing past Bill to escape.

"I want to tell you I didn't like that sermon one bit!" an older woman said.

"I'm sorry," Bill said.

"It hit me right here," said the next, rubbing her stomach, and twisting her mouth.

When Van returned, it was said that John and Bill had tried to "run away with the church." Those were the kindest words. Sunday-school teachers complained that children left the service hopelessly confused. Fifth- and sixth-graders came to class demanding to know why, if God was a woman, prayers ended "A-men." Elizabeth McCarthy, an intelligent and stalwart member for thirty years, called the service a personal affront.

"Van," she said, "don't these guys get it! Some of us actually *like* the image of God as an old man with a beard."

Two days later, Van started work earlier than usual. What would he do? He could take control again on Sunday. He thought about assigning number 341, "Dear Lord and Father of Mankind," or old number 8. Without making a single allusion to the words, Van could restore harmony. Old hymns often worked like a sweet antidote to soothe whatever pangs broke out during the week.

Van nosed through the lectionary for a sermon topic. But what about all the people who steadied the church? he wondered. He silently recalled them like prayer beads, enjoying a pause between names. Didn't John and Bill understand? Why disturb people who were otherwise so faithful?

He turned back to his typewriter. A full pitcher of iced tea rested atop an old wooden collection plate. A box of chocolate candies sat open on a shelf.

His office was a mess. Furnished during the 1950s with cast-offs from the Women's Club, and painted a dull, light green like lichen on concrete, the room had always looked humble and styleless. Years ago, the Women's Club had tried to smarten it up by adding a set of thin, light green chintz curtains to match the walls. But then Van had hauled in a green filing cabinet and a few green pieces of furniture, making the room, if not exactly color-coordinated, at least colored. It was overwhelmingly green. The subliminal green of hospital rooms, the flat green of a Necco wafer.

During these last days of spring, the office looked as if a storm had passed through. Strewn across bookshelves, cabinets, and tabletops were the effects of Van's failed efforts to bring springtime accords. Books that drifted from shelf to desk to floor lay open, marked, dog-eared, scrawled upon; some were bound with gaffer's tape to keep the spines aright. He had been reading eagerly for weeks. Old sermons, plucked and discarded, lay in heaps. Phone messages were strewn everywhere. Nothing looked unused, untested, or untried by his hand. His fingernails had left gouge marks on the faces of his desk drawers, evidence of a regular, hard, persistent grasp.

He paused once more over the lectionary selection for the day. The regulation of lectionaries supposedly aided ministers by providing already prescribed Old and New Testament verses to read each week. Encouraging the use of their knowledge of myth, history, and dogmas of the Church, lectionary readings were intended to bring ministers into relationship with the Word and send them back to the pulpit with an interpretation of biblical texts.

Such nonsense offended Van. The subjects sounded overly pious. Usually, the verses did not mesh. Sometimes they hit him like mismatched ingredients for a stew. The exercise reeked of hermeneutics and BS. This week's topic, for instance, was "The Experience of Suffering." Van looked at it briefly, laughed, and cast it aside.

The capital-funds drive had stalled at $690,000. Now there was a sermon topic! Talk about suffering! Going into summer, when church boards and committees recessed like Congress until September, the drive had fizzled. Once the annual stewardship campaign went into full gear in the fall, parishioners would not likely distinguish between the two. Money was money, whether it went to repairing church buildings or settling operating expenses. For most people, church donations still represented little more than a single line on the tax form. How could he persuade people to expand their scope?

Take last night's meeting of the Cabinet, for instance.

As in many congregations, the polity of First Church grew out of an interlocking maze of boards and committees. The Board of Deacons administered worship services. The Board of Christian Education ran the Sunday school and adult seminars. The Prudential Board managed property. Outreach did charities and missions. The stewardship committee raised money for the budget every year. And each one sent a member to the Cabinet. The Cabinet: the executive board, judiciary, the joint chiefs of staff. In some ways, the Cabinet represented the heart of the church, the soul of financial decision-making.

With final authority over the budget, the Cabinet sometimes made its meetings a simulacrum of backroom politics. The annual budget, like all major decisions, went before the total congregation every February, when each member could cast a vote. But for the previous eight months, hard haggling and horse-trading went on in Cabinet meetings, beginning in June with the first powwow on the budget.

That first meeting had occurred just the night before. Van had thought, when Janet Filer agreed to speak at this final Cabinet meeting before summer, that the Cabinet would be happy to hear her talk about the spiritual values of stewardship. When she offered her professional services, free of charge, for autumn's annual stewardship campaign, he had imagined a round of applause or, more likely, a formal commendation for her efforts.

But that was not how it happened at all.

"Ma-*nip*-ulation," Craig Fitch had said, accenting the second syllable. Van could still hear it.

Why didn't anyone object or step in? The church treasurer, Paul Price, sat with his arms folded. Members of the Prudential Board looked solemn and unfazed. Janet faced a general glaze of analytical stares. And then after those long, unsettling seconds, the head of the Cabinet, a stout, sleepy-eyed man, at last cleared his throat and said, "Anything else you'd like to add, Craig?"

The church treasurer looked up slowly from his reports.

It took a moment before Van realized Craig Fitch was going to step up and fend for the other side. After twenty years as a member, it was Craig's turn to lead the Committee of Three—the stewardship committee—to raise $300,000 for next year's budget. Of course, following on the heels of the capital campaign would not be easy. Especially since they still had to raise $60,000 to reach the capital-fund goal. No doubt the congregation would soon have two packs of fund-raisers dogging them for money. One led by Janet, the other by Craig.

Craig Fitch, one of the most dispassionate, square-shouldered, level-headed, middle-of-the-road men in the church, had the affection and sympathy of almost everyone present. Including Van. But why did he have to attack Janet when all she had done was say First Church had the financial wherewithal to raise half again its present budget. She had been trying to stir enthusiasm, not to criticize.

Craig's voice rose the first time he used the word, but that second time, after the chairman prodded him, Craig hit hard.

"Excuse me," he said, at last. Van watched Craig hunch over in his chair, as if in pain. "But I do have one more thought."

Craig sat up. His voice shook.

"All I am trying to say," he said, "is that I do feel that a large amount of fund-raising involves a substantial amount of *manipulation* of some members of the church. Some people respond to that kind of pressure. And some do not. So I do have some negative feelings about this process, Janet, and I'm just saying we need to approach the fall stewardship campaign more cautiously. I think most of us know this already. And I am not at all sure your involvement in a second very, very aggressive campaign will get us anywhere. In fact, I can't picture an untapped forty or fifty percent more to give to the annual budget, as you suggest. And in fact . . . in fact, I find that very hard to believe at all!"

Van saw pent-up anger send a jolt up Craig's neck. Janet's nose was twitching.

As Van's ally for more than eight months, Janet probably knew far more about the congregation's reluctance to give money than almost anyone else. By now, she had an unusual acquaintance with First Church finances. She knew misers. She knew saints. She could point out who was stingy and who was strapped. She knew the generous ones. The well-heeled, the discreetly wealthy, and all the rest. By address. By phone number. Pledge requests and donations told her who in that very room had resisted. She knew every lame excuse.

But when Craig said what he did, using that one word, *manipulation,* which sounded the second time like a taunt, Van exploded.

"Let some other people talk!" Van shouted. He whipped around to look at the dozen members of the Cabinet in the Morrell Room, and set his jaw.

"I can't believe this!" he said. "Look at you! Don't just sit there. Somebody else say something! Say something!"

He could still see Craig, glancing sheepishly down at the floor. Stunned members of the Cabinet turned to one another. A few exchanged knowing looks.

Well, that was quite a meeting, Van thought. Quite a way to end the church year! So the lectionary instructed him to preach on the experience of suffering? He could talk about suffering! Try raising $750,000 to repair your church and then $300,000 for your annual budget all in the same year! Try doing it during a recession! Try doing it when your staff has started its own campaign for Mother language in the church!

Van stood up to stretch his legs. Andy McCarthy was stalled out in the hallway talking with someone about an Indian arrowhead and clay pipe he'd found by the river. After delivering the mail, Andy sometimes dropped by to chat.

"Morning, Peggy," Andy called cheerfully, entering the secretary's office. "I was at my parents' house cutting grass and I thought there must be more interesting things to do. So I thought I'd come down here and call Holyoke College for an appointment to look at Florence Mills's papers."

"Florence Mills?" Peggy said. "What on earth?"

"Since she was treasurer of the church for forty years, I figure her papers might be worth a look."

Van listened from behind the wall.

"You mean you left your poor, seventy-five-year-old mother at home to cut the grass!"

"It's a power mower!" Andy explained.

"Andy," Peggy chided.

"Clean air, hard work—it's good for my mother."

"Oh, good grief!" she said. "Come on, you can use Bill's office to make your old calls."

The voices dwindled for a second, and then Van heard Peggy again. "Shame on you, Andy," she said.

A moment later, the intercom buzzer on his phone lit up.

"Van!" Peggy called from the office. "Henry Holcombe to see you."

"Henry!" Van shouted.

The big man poked his burr head around the corner. Henry had never quit working the fund drive.

"We just joined the Seven Hundred Club," Henry said, grinning. He pulled a few envelopes out of his coat pocket. "Seven oh-four to be exact."

"Praise the Lord!" Van said. He ushered Henry in and shut the door. Peggy could hear them teasing each other for being the new Jim and Tammy Faye Bakkers of Palisado Avenue.

When Van and Henry finished totaling the latest receipts, the door swung open again and Van said, "Keep on workin' " and Henry replied, "Keep on prayin'. "

"That guy's one of the steadiest people I know," Van told Peggy. And then he stepped out into the hall.

Elizabeth Krikorian was down in the library singing "The Sound of Music" in a Russian accent. The Krikorians, an old immigrant couple, had worked in the library twice a month for more than twenty years, stapling the church newsletter for mailings. Her thin soprano, warbling unrestrained, fell into a humming, and Van listened until she picked up the lyrics again—and then he went back to work.

Taking to his chair by the window, Van reached into the bookcase for a *Pilgrim Hymnal,* a faded copy, and opened to number 8, "Joyful, Joyful We Adore Thee," the same one Bill had used the week before. Not a bad tune, Van thought. The page showed his penciled notations up and down the margins marking every Sunday they'd sung the tune since 1968. He marked it again.

"The Experience of Suffering" was forgotten. Van flipped open his new Bible, the New Revised Standard Version, and felt its soft red cover and crackling white pages. He thumbed to a familiar verse. First Samuel 3:1–10: *Now Samuel did not yet know the Lord, and the word of the Lord had not yet been revealed to him.* But, as the story continued, Samuel had learned to hear, and he had learned how to answer, *"Speak, for your servant is listening."*

His mind drifted again. "The Lord bless you and keep you: The Lord make his face to shine upon, and be gracious unto you: The Lord lift up his countenance upon you, and give you peace. Amen."

Just a few weeks ago, Richard Carroway, a devoted member, had fallen down a set of stairs and broken his hip; his wife had needed meals and moral support. When Van called, Richard explained over the phone that he wanted to get his affairs in order, and then later, at the home, he told Van he was dying. Van stayed only for a short while, but before he left the bedside, the old fellow touched his hand and blessed him with the benediction. What had he done to deserve that? Van had buried Richard exactly a week ago, yet he still could not get the voice out of his mind.

Suddenly, Joan Rockwell's toddlers came clopping down the hallway and disappeared into Nelson Hall. Van heard Andy McCarthy on his way out, the cackling chatter of female voices coming through the front door, and Peggy calling him to hurry up with his sermon. Perhaps, he thought, he had been a little gruff and outspoken lately. But maybe that was all right. Maybe it was time for him to speak out.

Van looked down at the page curling out of the typewriter's carriage. He could count his blessings with each name that came to mind. He could hear their voices—fractious, frightened, lilting, feeble, blessing him, taking him to task.

"Samuel!" the Lord had called. *"Samuel!"*

Van looked up from his Bible's columned page. He could think of many sources for anecdotal wisdom. But the Lord had called Samuel to listen.

Van sat very still, grinding his thoughts against the verse until he heard the regular order and rhythm of a phrase that he could churn back into the full ground of his congregation on Sunday morning like a healthy composting. It didn't have to be pretty—not poetry or theology or hermeneutics. He listened only for a quiet voice nudging its way to the surface.

"We are ordinary servants," he typed.

Satisfied, settled in, he felt himself being carried. Somehow, no matter what anyone said, he knew they were being fed, comforted, and charmed at nearly every step along the way.

The Road to Emmaus

A serious human life, no matter what "religion" is invoked, can hardly begin until we see an element of illusion in what is really there, and something real in fantasies about what might be there instead.

—Northrop Frye,
The Great Code

CHAPTER NINE

One day my wife asked if I believed in miracles.

Standing in the kitchen, half-naked, ironing her blue smock and peasant dress, Jan was not so much posing a question as making a statement. She was so beautiful. But, reading the crease in her forehead, I could see she wanted to fight.

"I don't know," I said. "Define *miracles.*"

"Well," she said, "you're the one who spends all his time at TFC. You tell me."

TFC? That fucking church.

"If by *miracle,*" I said, "you mean, do I believe those good old boys down in Georgia are really seeing Jesus on a Pizza Hut billboard like it said in yesterday's newspaper, then no, I do not believe in miracles. But if you mean, do good things happen that sometimes can't be explained, then I would say yes, sometimes. I just don't call them miracles."

"I call them miracles," she said. "I think miracles happen every day. In fact, that's a great idea for your next book. A book of miracles!"

"That's a stupid idea," I said. "First, you'd have to do an investigation of each one—"

"That's not what I meant," she said.

"—and it would be far worse for us than it is now. I'd never be at home. I'd be traveling all over the world, and—"

"Forget it," she said.

"—spending most of my time with zealots and crackpots and—"

"I said, drop it!"

"Anyway, what do I know about miracles?" I said. "I don't even believe in miracles. If you asked Van or Bill or John Gregory-Davis, you'd get the same response. Nothing. It's a bad concept."

"It's not a 'concept,' " she said.

"No?" I said. "I know what you meant. *Hope* is to *menopause* as *miracle* is to *baby*. Good try, but the allegory doesn't work."

"I'm not talking about allegories! Why do you have to be so mean?"

"I'm not mean!" I said.

"Then why are you yelling at me?"

"I'm answering your question."

"I'm serious."

"Well, just don't tell me what to write! I've got enough on my mind right now."

"You?"

"Don't you think I feel this, too?"

"Feel what? You're never here."

"The loss," I said.

"The 'loss,' " she said, snidely.

"Our loss," I said.

Jan looked at me like a hunter who had her game in scope. Her blue eyes and curled lashes could be deceptive. She turned away.

"It's a great idea for a book," she said. "Why don't you do some research, and let me know what you find out."

"It'll be a miracle if we survive this," I muttered.

"What did you say?" she asked.

"I said, 'Yes, dear,' " I replied. Then, grabbing my bag, I kissed her, and left for church.

I would be flying to England in a few days. It was warm outside. On my way out the door I could hear Jan crying again. For the first time in my life, I really enjoyed going to church. Kept my spirits up. Off to the world of dreaming steeples, into the land of towering spires.

Shirtless workmen on three levels of pine scaffolding stripped dull white clapboards off the north side of the church on June 27, the morning of our departure. The pilgrimage to Dorchester, planned as a tour of First Church roots more than a year before, just happened to coincide with the start of the effort at historic preservation.

At noon, I stood alongside Andy McCarthy admiring a high brown stratum of planks that composed the interior wall of the meetinghouse. Andy jangled a handful of warm, hand-hewn nails he'd picked out of the grass and pointed to places where, more than two hundred years ago, carpenters had scored timber with Roman numerals to indicate a proper sequence for building the wall. He expected to find evidence of corn husks or hay as insulation, but their absence did not disappoint him. He was a *revisionist,* after all.

Andy squatted down and combed the grass, prospecting for more treasure. His face was grizzly from a week's growth of beard. Concentration cast a dramatic expression of concern across his face. He looked like a rock hound sorting across a field of fool's gold. I squatted next to him and thought we were probably the only two men on the trip who would wear faded blue jeans and T-shirts most of the time. His red hair was falling down in his eyes, too, like mine, but I was happy to note that, though we were probably both fashion exiles from the 1970s, at least I was not still wearing desert boots.

"Here's one!" he crowed, digging up another shard.

Initially, Andy had shown only a moderate interest in the trip. His attentions rarely strayed too far from the churchyard. But once he decided to join our group, he did spend some time trying to trace First Church roots from the West Country. Eventually, he passed several days in the Connecticut State Library archives tracking down congregational origins. Making the first return in 360 years, the First Church crowd needed its resident expert aboard, and, dutifully, Andy complied, gathering crumbs for the journey.

Reeling through microfilm documents of original First Church letters
and sermons from the seventeenth century, he found evidence of a parishioner's place in the drafting of the first colonial constitution. According to documents, Andy told me, a churchgoer named Henry
Wolcott had made notes of the Reverend Thomas Hooker's earliest sermons on church governance in Hartford. His jottings represented one of
the first articulations of the concept that the foundation of authority
should belong to the free consent of the people, the germinal idea of
American democracy. Andy found notes, taken in Wolcott's hand, doc-
umenting a sermon by Reverend Hooker from May 31, 1638—*"They
who have power to appoint officers and magistrates it is in their power also
to set the bounds and limits of the power and places unto which they may
call them"*—and guessed that the familiar idea of checks and balances
may have passed from Hooker to Wolcott to another First Church member, one Roger Ludlow, who was also principal author of the Connecticut constitution. That document was considered the first in America to
frame the idea of government by democracy.

Now Andy was saying he hoped one day to track the genesis of Amer-
ican democracy from such sources, beginning with principles for early
church governance in England during the sixteenth century, to Thomas
Hooker in Hartford, and, passing through the First Church sanctuary,
into the thoughts and precepts of Chief Justice Oliver Ellsworth of the
U.S. Supreme Court. Ellsworth, by all accounts the most famous First
Church member, had been an active participant in the Constitutional
Convention of 1787.

But this was not the year for serious research. Andy had never intended to travel the Cornwall coast in high-minded pursuit of old
truths. In fact, he was more interested in using his research skills tracing
the church's connections in America—to theologian Jonathan Edwards,
cousin of a First Church minister; to the early American poet Edward
Sill, a member from the eighteenth century; to Joseph Rainey, one of the
United States' first black congressmen, who had once lived on the campus and joined the church as its first black member; to the Underground
Railroad, which, it was believed, had used the parsonage to house run-
away slaves during the Civil War; to the celebrated inventor Christopher

Minor Spencer, a First Church member who had inspired Mark Twain's *Connecticut Yankee in King Arthur's Court;* or to one of a crowd of anonymous slaves, Hessians, and Native Americans whom Andy had identified as buried in the cemetery. He said the cemetery had already supplied him with enough good ideas to keep him "plenty busy" writing columns for the church newsletter without tackling such a heavy topic as primal origins. Too much had been made of ties to the motherland already, he believed. The hidden history of the church's American Indians, slaves, poets, war heroes, and insurgents needed more of his time than the Pilgrims did.

I couldn't believe it, though. Nothing seemed as important to me as tracking Henry Wolcott's intellectual heritage back to Dorchester, England. It could be the most significant challenge the church historian would ever tackle.

"Certainly," I said, "Andy, you are joking. You really are planning to work on this while we're there, aren't you?"

"Not this time, old buddy," he said. "This trip's strictly personal."

I peered into the box of nails he'd collected. As he dated each one and commented on the history of nail production in the eighteenth century, I snuck one out and stuffed it into my pocket as a traveling piece for good luck.

"This is an historic occasion," Andy said, loudly enough that I knew he was not talking to me. Newspaper reporters and photographers came dragging across the cemetery. Invited by Van, journalists from the *Hartford Courant* and the *Windsor Journal* came to record the occasion. They walked with Andy through the sunny graveyard. Pointing out significant markers, he introduced them to First Church history with his usual studied overview.

"Here you will find statesmen and slaves, old Puritans who lived in the 1500s, people who've fought in all our wars and lived under all our presidents. From a Supreme Court justice to the Lexington alarmers . . ."

Inside, Andy's wife, Elizabeth, was unlocking the deacons' closet behind the choir room. She pulled out a twelve-ounce bottle of VeryFine grape juice and rummaged for beeswax candles. Then she ran over to the parish house for a frozen loaf of low-cholesterol oat-bran bread and

quickly thawed it in the microwave. Probably because Lucille had suggested that we launch our journey with a Communion service, Elizabeth
fixated on details more than usual. For almost an hour, she scurried
around arranging bread, grape juice, and the finest silver settings for an
elegant table.

When Andy finished the briefing, he trotted back to the meetinghouse. He jammed his shirttail into his jeans, flipped up his clip-on sunglasses, and grabbed a pile of elegantly inscribed bulletins outlining the
farewell service.

"Our last daughter just graduated from college," Elizabeth was ex-
plaining to one of the photographers. Handing the photographer a bulletin, Andy leaned over and added, "Actually, we're going along just to
celebrate the last tuition payment. It's kind of a second honeymoon."

By one o'clock, more than seventy people squeezed into the first few
pews and stood to sing a plain melody written out in the choirmaster's
patient hand. Based on Psalm 90, the hymn was the same one First
Church ancestors sang as they began the journey to America on March
20, 1630. We read the same Bible verse (Psalm 107) that inaugurated the
founders' quest, and sang number 438, "O God Beneath Thy Guiding
Hand," all to Fran's accompaniment, while his wife, Ann, the local diva,
uncoiled high harmonic counterpoints far beyond the range of the normal human voice.

Bill Warner-Prouty read a selection from *The Writings of the Puritans,*
by Perry Miller, and noted how authors of the *Pilgrim Hymnal* had ex-
cised verses from Psalm 107 pertaining to sea travel. In the spirit of the
occasion, he set the hymnal aside and rendered the Psalm whole with
the poetic King James: *For he commanded and raised the stormy wind,
which lifted up the waves of the sea. They mounted up to heaven, they went
down to the depths.*

People in the pews began to shuffle impatiently as the ceremony
dragged on. But before allowing anyone to gather for Communion, Van
jumped up from behind the dais.

"Just briefly today I wanted to talk about traveling lightly," he said.
"Lucille and I are not doing that too well. We are making some progress.

Bonnie Wister told me she's only packed two dresses and I thought, 'She could teach us something.' "

People chuckled and craned their necks to find Bonnie among the rows. Van hitched up his baggy britches, cleared a flop of hair out of his eyes, and looked down at his notes:

"Sometimes religion poses the same problems as traveling. It can seem like a heavy burden to us, like an extra suitcase or two. But really what the people who founded this church learned, I think, is the truth of Jesus' words, *'Take my yoke upon you . . . for my yoke is easy and my burden is light.'* "

While he rattled on about Christ, the yoke, and the burden, I looked around to see if I could remember everyone's name. My companions, it seemed, would include most of the big shots: half the choir; Henry Holcombe and his wife; one of the church trustees; two officers from the Women's Club; a former Prudential Board chairman; two new members, an older couple, Barry and Doris Masters; longtime stalwarts Tony and Charlotte Gillette; a few old friends from West Hartford; and the entire Simpson family.

"We know the whole culture of this world and of this place is vastly different from what it was three hundred sixty years ago," Van was saying. "But the spirit of adventurousness and the willingness to let go and seek new places and trust that God will be with us is ever present. And I would go so far as to say that whatever is most vital in our own congregation is that same spirit, and it will be renewed both in us and in the larger congregation as we go through these next few days and weeks and months and years that follow this journey. So I hope we will find that religion is a lightening factor during our travels. We are meant to be people who travel light."

He started singing, "Let us break bread together on our knees," and it was clear that he had arranged the service so no one could escape until the bitter end.

Soon, he called us for Communion and the pews emptied. In the thick gathering we stood as one, dressed in bright, clinging, cotton-knit shirts and slacks bulging with belly packs and moneybelts, cameras

slung around our necks, hair moussed, eyes twinkling. Andy and Elizabeth handled the elements. We each tore off a plug of low-cholesterol
oat-bran bread from the spongy loaf and dipped it into a silver chalice
of VeryFine grape juice.

"One body, one family," Van said. "Amen."

With the final word, our circle suddenly broke into a raucous clatter.
Hymnals fell back into their slots, crumbs littered the floor, crinkled
bulletins floated into pews. First Church, England–bound tourists
rushed for daylight.

"I only wanted three things out of this trip," griped Doris Blevins, a
lively old Swede, as she scrambled through the crowd. "A basket of fish
and chips, a game of darts, and a warm beer. Nobody said anything to
me about 'services.' "

Peggy Couples caught Van and cornered him in the aisle.

"Don't start the trip singing 'A Hundred Bottles of Beer on the
Wall,' Van."

"Well, what are we supposed to sing!" Van exclaimed.

"Fran will get very upset."

"I'm sorry, we're not doing Bach arias for Fran!"

The crowd scattered in a parking lot behind the parish house, unlocking car trunks, hauling out massive collections of Samsonite luggage, hard-shell cases, garment bags, duffel bags, shoe sacks, purses,
backpacks, and Pullman carts, as a king-size Post Road Coach bus sat
idling and the driver watched piles of belongings grow larger and larger
until they covered a plot of ground as long and wide as the bus itself.

So much for the virtues of traveling light, I thought. They were
primed for Bond Street, Harrods, the West End theater district, Barbi-
can Hall, the Royal Opera House, and afternoon teas.

Andy McCarthy tapped his fingertips together and spoke poignantly
to a reporter: "Hope, optimism, and faith—that comes through with
this group and this embarkation. We are not people who look backward.
This is a church moving into the future!"

Wearily, I dropped my own bags in the expanding pile and heard
snickers from around the front of the bus. There they were, John

Gregory-Davis and a gaggle of his First Church supporters, a small but influential cadre of Christian radicals. They looked most amused.

"Good afternoon, ladies and gentlemen," said one, holding his finger up to my face, teasingly, like a hijacker. "There has been a slight change in the itinerary. Instead of traveling to London this evening as planned, we will be taking this flight to Managua!"

I was totally confused. If church membership indicated nothing more than an adolescent longing for immortality—to be preserved in memory and honored in perpetuity—then perhaps the desire to tour England expressed nothing more than a craving for Mother's milk. It depended on one's perspective, I supposed. Maybe Andy understood that before I did, which was why he only took a modest interest in the congregation's first sojourn to the West Country. To attain the best in life experience, I imagined, perhaps New England WASPs could do no better than to forgo a flight to Paris, delay a trip to the Himalayas, forestall an adventure in China, and travel back to the cobbled streets of the old paradise—Dorchester, Plymouth, Essex, Kent, Salisbury, and Bath. To reconsider the idea of historic succession and revel in the liberal inheritance of Protestant glories might be the ultimate satisfaction at a certain age. Better than Lourdes, more excellent than the Holy Land, the cathedrals, churches, and stone circles of England would heal the most discouraged Anglophile, so embattled lately by the pressures of multiculturalism and other trendy liberal guff.

Or maybe their need to travel was more straightforward than that. Even though Van often referred to the trip as a pilgrimage, I had noticed that our visit had been planned to overlap with the world tennis championships at Wimbledon.

Or maybe nobody really knew what Van and Lucille had in mind when they announced the trip the previous spring. For six or eight months, as Van publicized the journey, he had occasionally mentioned vague "ramifications" of the event. But nothing more. Even then, as I joined parishioners climbing aboard the big air-conditioned bus, Van merely stood at the doors, rubbing his hands together and bouncing on his toes, still looking excited but speaking with a hint of guile.

"Don't worry about a thing," he said, cracking a menacing grin. "Just for your general edification, I promise to keep you all entertained. You'll see. I have planned a few more *services.*"

As we drove to Kennedy Airport, people shared reading lists. Over the preceding year Andy said he had consumed, whole, the entire *Oxford Book of English History,* the Norton series on English literature, and the novels of Thomas Hardy, whose romances occurred in the town of Casterbridge (Dorchester), the same village where Windsor's congregation first gathered in the 1620s. Jane Allyn had devoured *The Dorset Pilgrims* by English historian Frank Thistlethwaite, and selections from a local opus, Henry Stiles's *History of Ancient Windsor.* Various members of our tour had gobbled up thick loaves like *Albion's Seed* by David Fischer, *The Last Lion* by William Manchester, P. D. James's mysteries, and complete bookshelves of English historical novels, most notably the modern West Country classic, *Sarum: A Novel of England* by Edward Rutherfurd.

I thought of Saint Augustine's eloquent term *fides quaerens intellectum*—faith in search of understanding—and began to feel a more genuine appreciation of their ardent study. The need to order the present through the past, I thought, had perhaps taken on enough significance to make the trip to England necessary. The new pilgrims had gone about the task with remarkable discipline. I was pleased to think that our money would not be squandered on mere sightseeing. At $2,200 a head, the trip would certainly signify something noteworthy and uplifting.

To their credit, the group members had planned the event at a critical moment in Protestant history. After a full decade when mainline culture had shaken under the strains of feminism, inclusive language, New Age mysticism, calls to global activism, and a general crisis of identity, the solid core of First Church seemed to have made earnest preparations for revisiting their roots. Maybe I had been wrong about them. Three hundred sixty years after the Great Migration, they had readied themselves for a proper return, asking, "Who are we now?"

Not so long ago, I thought, such a question would have sounded preposterous. Members of the church would have assumed they had no cultural particularity, no reason to examine traditions. Why, they were WASPs! Civic virtue, Americanism, and Protestantism were indivisible. It was understood, it was the air they breathed. It was all there was, for God's sake. For many years in Windsor, it had been the custom for prominent families—descendants of founders—to rent pews at church every year, as if they were purchasing season tickets to the Hartford Symphony, the stage, or the ballet. Town leaders had once accepted deaconate responsibilities for lifetime terms. Certain families, who celebrated their ancestor's accomplishments on national holidays, could just as easily have celebrated those historic occasions at the First Church altar or graveyard. Imagine being the descendant of an early Supreme Court justice, of a signer of the Constitution, or of any Windsor first family, on July Fourth, Thanksgiving, Arbor Day, or Christmas. The annual succession of national observances, in some ways, belonged more to them than to the rest of us.

Over the years, families had established a proper school of WASP folklore at the church on the green hill above the Farmington River. Venerable religious rituals, hymns, the hierarchy of power among committees—the Prudential Board, historically, having been the most dominating—all referred to the past with ultimate meanings and celebrated the excellence of the Puritan plan. "Oh God beneath thy guiding hand / Our exiled fathers crossed the sea . . ."—the very verses they sang raised mythic images from Sunday to Sunday and, in their own unchallengeable way, from generation to generation. The creation myth of First Church did not originate in the Garden of Eden, after all, but in England, and all that was pristine and virtuous came from an adventurous replanting and improvement in America. All had been well, until recently.

Although it was said within some circles that our passenger list looked remarkably like the assembly of a clique and the itinerary

sounded suspiciously like the path of just another clubby church pleasure trip, I managed to suppress my doubts. At the origins of the prov-
idential mission to America we would surely find holy ground, or at
least some certitude about where we were headed. Somewhere in the
rolling West Country, leaders of Windsor's historic congregation would
enter an old, old church and, if we were lucky, they would meet good
English cousins waiting to welcome them home.

We were in the air only a few hours, but it gave me time enough to review notes and flip through the books Andy recommended. I spent the
hours on a refresher course in the congregation's collective beginnings.

The original First Church pilgrims, it was said, spent two months
crossing the Atlantic Ocean, sailing an enormous vessel weighing more
than four hundred tons, a big boat with a modest name—the *Mary and
John*. Their young Oxford-educated minster, John Warham, had been
recruited solely for the mission, and after holding the congregation's
first service in a hospital near Plymouth Harbor, he joined them on deck
"preaching and expounding the Word of God every day during the voyage," according to the surviving diary. Prayers, psalms, and sermons
sanctified their mission every Sunday morning and afternoon. They
shared catechism on Tuesdays and Wednesdays and observed regular
"solemn days of fasting," which surprised and probably amused the
boat's secular crew. Under the plan of one of Dorchester's elder ministers, the Reverend John White, one hundred forty passengers, more than
half of them children, left Dorset's rich downs thick with sheep, laced
with crumbling Roman roads.

It was White who had chosen Warham and hand-picked members of
the new congregation for the mission overseas. A relative progressive
among his cohorts, White had a vision that was not entirely religious.
Aside from the stated purpose of spreading Christianity abroad, White
intended to open new agricultural markets in North America. He
planned to plant a new society by mixing elements of capitalism with
only a slightly more vivifying Christian creed.

Studying profiles from existing records, I could see the men and women of the *Mary and John* were not the sullen radicals of their day. Compared with separatists who disavowed the Church of England, the ocean-bound congregation appeared to have been made up of simple, moderate Puritans. They have been called the most homogeneous group of emigrants to make the Great Migration. Reverend White, whose allegiance always remained with the Church of England, was less a speculative theologian than an above-average administrator and entrepreneur. His mercantilist's desire to make a profit from the venture, as well as to spread the Gospel, revealed him to be a pragmatist—a hail-fellow-well-met.

By design, the first First Church crowd should have looked like a colony of Jacobean Englishmen in New England. The Reverend White had hoped an elite group would transplant his church. When he first advertised for subjects, he had sought a class slightly less than that of the aristocrat and burgess to form his ocean-bound congregation. Neither rebel, dissident, nor zealot would find a way onto Reverend White's roster.

As it turned out, White failed to attract the higher classes to his mission, and, eventually, no family who boarded the *Mary and John* was more than minor gentry—yeomen, West Country middle-class families and single adult men, younger sons of Dorchester merchants. These included a few schoolteachers, six master mariners, a dozen or so coopers, tanners, masons, and one surveyor. I would guess they left England for many reasons, both practical and romantic, with religious freedom playing only one small role among many. History, you know, is never so clear as mythmakers would have us believe.

After a month, the original First Church pilgrims arrived in cold North Atlantic coastal waters, apparently without life-threatening incident. The ship's captain lost his bearings, however, and anchored off Nantasket Point, many miles south of their destination on the Massachusetts Bay. Nonetheless, on Sunday, May 30, 1630, they were camped on American soil, a full two weeks before John Winthrop came sailing the *Arbella* proclaiming his resonate vision of a "city on a hill."

Unlike Winthrop, the First Church clan had no grand vision to proclaim. But five years later, the soft-spoken yeomen from Dorchester were still bound into a self-sufficient community, and their population had swollen to four times its original number. When John Winthrop's magisterial theocracy finally became too much to bear, the moderate Dorchester crowd scouted for resettlement. Still committed to the Reverend John White's simple plan of establishing a small satellite church, they slipped out of Winthrop's territory and headed south into the wilderness.

In 1635, the West Country community abandoned Massachusetts and traveled through the valley of the Great River. Near a confluence of rivers, now the Farmington and Connecticut, on a high bluff above the Farmington, they constructed a palisado (a settlement surrounded by fencing for protection from Indians) and began building homes. At the center of its thirty acres of beautiful, farmable land surrounded by hills and mile after mile of hardwood forests, the community built a simple church. Under a primitive thatched roof, the Reverend Warham and his congregation wrote a covenant for the first settlement of Connecticut. They called the town—inseparable from the church, the government, and their first industry (a granary owned and operated by the Reverend Warham)—Windsor, apparently in reference to the city on the Thames, residence of English sovereigns since the time of William the Conqueror.

Today, the Reverend John White's legacy is hardly acknowledged in England or in America. While other ministers are celebrated as important historical figures—John Winthrop, Thomas Hooker, Roger Williams—it could be said that the Reverend White is just another forgotten preacher. His intentions were never as high-minded as Winthrop's, and the leaders he assembled were folk far simpler, slower-paced, and more homespun than their neighbors of Massachusetts Bay. Three centuries after holding its first services on the deck of a sailing ship, a First Church community still meets and celebrates its beginnings. And yet in England, church documents reveal that while White saw his work sustained in America, at home he was chastised as yet another minister run amok. He was accused of siphoning off church funds for the effort, and generally criticized for running his own select foreign mission overseas.

Reverend John White was eventually run out of his church during the

English Civil War of 1642, his rectory ransacked, his books destroyed. Sadly, he died uncelebrated in 1648 and was buried under the porch of Saint Peter's Church in Dorchester, where today there is only a simple plaque commemorating forty-three years of service.

I cannot say how many of my fellow passengers knew the history of John White and the First Church pilgrims. But while I studied notes of those critical events as we crossed the Atlantic, I could tell, from conversations in nearby seats, there was little interest in recalling the story. Everyone was busy with exigencies of the moment.

"Scotch on the rocks."

"Grilled breast of chicken?"

"No, I'll have the fresh salmon."

"Isn't this blueberry cream gâteau yummy!"

After ten hours, we landed at Gatwick Airport. We were received by a beaming, slender, pink-cheeked English guide giving discreet directions to the water closet. Within moments she escorted us to an air-conditioned bus furnished with high, luxurious seats, a small kitchen, and enormous, tinted windows offering panoramic views of the tranquil, sun-dappled landscape.

"Now then, everybody comfortable?" our guide inquired as the Mercedes engine purred and the bus glided off. "We are headed for Winchester Cathedral and then to the historic town of Salisbury. Settle back and enjoy this lush, green, well-to-do section of jolly old England. Now, and for the next ten days, you won't have to think about the troubles of the world a second longer."

I put my books aside and took a seat in the back.

Paradise! One-hundred-percent comfort class! Plush velour seats lifted us high above the road so we could watch the pavement curve and narrow as we barreled down the coast. The immense, clean elegance of the English landscape, trimmed and pruned, rose up in our six-foot-tall tinted wall of windows like picture postcards from Jesus. The English countryside blurred by with gracefully tended gardens, stone cottages, and small farms, fresh green fields thick with tall grasses, sprinkled with the colors of hemp, flax, and bracken. Within the first twenty-four hours we entered ancient cathedrals as large as shopping malls, villages as orderly and quaint as Disney World. At night we settled into glazed linen sofas and blue leather club chairs facing the grand fireplace of a hotel's sitting room, and took lingering strolls in the late-evening sunlight past ten o'clock. The days quickly faded together.

"Isn't this lovely?" Andy McCarthy sighed one morning aboard the bus.

"Why, yes. Lovely."

"Most charming."

"Exquisite."

"Magnificent."

"Pleasantly nice."

We were humming along to Plymouth when Delores Wickersham used those words, *pleasantly nice,* and I realized that we had been lulled and rocked into a blissful state like infants. In our overland express the guide's steady downpour of English history, sentimental anecdotes about the queen and the royal family, and intricate explanations of the British coronation system, had affected the crowd like a soothing swill of warm milk. Over three days, with not the first mention of the church or its roots, we'd been fed a massive introduction to the history of English manners and military customs, and what's more, everyone on board seemed immensely interested in hearing more. One afternoon, after a long session of questions and answers during a ride through the Dartmoors, I peeked around my high-backed luxury seat and saw members of the tour, heads dropped back, mouths agape, dead asleep. The rest—mesmerized by the low, rolling green landscape flooding past our windows—murmured across the aisles.

"Look at that lovely mustard-colored house!"

"Splendid!"

"Look at that!"

"What is it?"

"Flax."

"That is beautiful."

"And—oh! purple primroses."

"What! Wasn't that beautiful?"

"Oh my, look at the sheep."

During the first few days people had fallen into the habit of speaking in superlatives, but now they were literally trilling an affected English accent. At Salisbury Cathedral, Lucille noticed priests walking in their robes through the gray cloisters and sounded the note of an aristocrat.

"Van," she teased, "look at those men *swishing* around in their robes. I'm going to buy you a green one to *swish* around in at home."

At Winchester Cathedral, Charlotte Porter crossed the grave of Jane Austen, a memorial to Joan of Arc, Izaak Walton's tomb, and spun around, gazing at the marble thrones and choir stalls. Elaborate chantries, medieval pulpita, the dazzling pointed arches, fantastic reredoses and lavish shrines sparkled in her eyes. Without looking at her husband, she threw up her hands and gushed: "Fred, I keep hearing this thundering voice in my head screaming, 'There shalt be no graven images before me.' "

"Well," he replied, nose pointed to the ceiling, "you could never get away with something like this in Connecticut, that's for sure."

At another glistening shrine, Henry Holcombe cornered one of the older, wealthier members at the nave. "Would you look at that scaffolding, Carl? What do you think it costs to restore a place like this, anyway?"

"Henry!" his wife whispered, "can't you quit bothering Carl about that darned capital-funds drive?"

In Salisbury, Fran Angelo stopped by the Purbeck marble tomb of Bishop Robert Bingham (1229–1246) to listen to organ swells and a well-disciplined boys' choir practicing beneath the towering spire. "The building," he pronounced solemnly, "makes the instrument."

I thought it odd that of our crowd, the only one who looked thoroughly detached and uninterested was Van. Since our departure from New York, he had drifted into the background, taking up with one small group, then another. Even the guide noticed it, and whispered to the driver once after the bus unloaded, "The old vicar's rather out to lunch, wouldn't you say?" During our second day in Salisbury I found Van wandering alone in a gift shop at the cathedral, lost in a display of plastic figurines of saints, perfumed sachet cards, and lace doilies.

"Hey, Gary!" he called. He was laughing aloud. "Did you ever see that movie with Chevy Chase called *European Vacation*?"

I didn't get it. What were we doing here? From what I understood, most of Van's travels had a purpose beyond sightseeing. He had told me stories of intimate meetings with spiritual communities in Scotland, Nicaragua, Northern Ireland, Switzerland, and France. Spiritual encounters recorded in his diaries provided an important source for his understanding of the nature of modern-day Christianity. The experiences had changed him, and at least in one case—or so he said—taught him to see the world with new eyes.

One day riding down the West Country coast, while Van was sleeping, I decided to ask Lucille about their previous trips. Lucille was the kind of person whom, if you saw her from afar, you might think of as unapproachable. She looked like the headmistress of a girls' academy. Her deportment and sense of fashion was out of the ordinary—most unlike her husband's—and her long, thin build gave her a statuesque beauty that set her apart from the crowd ("Our lady's figgah," as our guide noted, "is something to which the queen's progeny might aspire.")

In any case, I had never spent much time with Lucille. She surprised me, though. Quite a talker.

"My frank opinion," Lucille said, "is that Van has used these trips for a purpose. Did he tell you that he worked through a midlife crisis on at least one trip? Now you should check with him to make sure I have this right, but I'm virtually certain. I know the old bird pretty well."

In 1975, she said, Van took a two-week hiatus to live at Koinonia Farms, an intentional Christian community in rural Georgia. After almost twenty years in the ministry (seven years of them at First Church), he had felt his spiritual life weakening. The routine of church work, the lack of fervent belief and mission, had left him casting around for something else to do. He went to Koinonia, Lucille said, thinking he might leave the ministry. Would he be happier, for instance, living a more devout and pious life with like-minded people? Did he need a long retreat into an intentional community?

After that, she said, he had made weekend trips to the Church of the Savior in Washington, D.C. He took off for retreats with prominent Christian thinkers such as Parker Palmer and Henry Nouwen. Slowly, Van had worked through his ambivalence about the church, and decided at least to be patient for the time being.

"Whew," Lucille said, laughing. "Now that was a close one. Not that I wouldn't have gone with him. But I wasn't quite ready for that Georgia commune business." She laughed again, tipped her nose up in the air, and in a mock-British accent teased, "You know, Christologically speaking, it may have been just the thing for the vicar, but for his poor wife and family . . ."

The dreaded, celebrated midlife crisis of her minister husband had passed (I couldn't help but think of those sexy books by John Updike). But then in 1984 Van had decided that he should travel to Nicaragua. "Okay, Van," Lucille had said. "But next time, I get to pick the destination."

A nonprofit organization in Connecticut called Ploughshares led the trip. Comprised of a few nationally prominent businessmen, religious leaders, and even a United States congressman, the group committed itself to a serious study of foreign affairs. One purpose of Ploughshares' trips was to give American citizens an "immersion experience" in the politics and cultures of developing countries. In this case, members of the group would be asked to judge for themselves how U.S. foreign policy was affecting the country. Over ten days, they would meet with representatives of the Nicaraguan government, talk to U.S. embassy officials, tour the cities, live with Nicaraguan families, attend religious services, and worship together.

When Van returned, he phoned his children from the Miami airport, exhausted, jubilant, transformed. He called Lucille and briefly told her that the trip had been tantamount to "a rebirth." Then, for weeks, all he could talk about was the Christian base communities of Nicaragua, and one place, in particular, where he had experienced something like

Christ's presence among the people. Unable to articulate the associations he had made with simple Nicaraguan villagers, Van kept telling fractured stories about the trip. He would talk about religious communities where people spoke easily about their grief, where the practice of Christianity went on so naturally from day to day that he finally understood what the scriptures meant when they said the Word would be made flesh, that every Christian is a member of the same body in Christ. The stories found a way into Van's sermons and into his conversations. For a while, Lucille said, she thought he would pack up and move them to Central America.

"Van is always slow to recover from his enthusiasms," she said, and while the initial reaction had concerned her even more than it did parishioners, Van eventually sorted through the experience. He recorded his thoughts in a journal, and reflected again on how he could address the thinness of life at First Church.

The next trip: to Northern Ireland. This time, Lucille went, too. "We travel to all the famous international honeymoon spots, I tell you," Lucille said, with a snort.

Making friends with bishops and priests, they had been taken to places to watch tanks roll through the streets and see the results of terrorist actions and firebombings. Their friends tried to help Van understand the religious divisions that had led to the ongoing war, and also to fathom a faith that allowed people to go on with some peace in their lives.

Establishing friendships with Protestant or Catholic church groups never seemed to end for Van. Whether it was in Nicaragua, Northern Ireland, or South Africa (another story altogether), Van always returned home hoping to raise consciousness by signing up for an exchange program or developing a "sister" relationship between First Church and a foreign parish. After Northern Ireland, it was the Ulster Project, and over the years, as he talked in church about the people he met in Northern Ireland, his congregation eventually sponsored a number of Irish children and families to visit Windsor, to live and worship for a few weeks every summer.

In 1987, they had made the last trip, a seven-week sabbatical across

Europe. Several years earlier, through the local YMCA, Lucille had served as chaperone for a group of girls traveling to Switzerland. This time, she planned the tour so Van could make real work of the journey. After spending weeks in towns from Geneva to Zurich, Van and Lucille set off for four weeks in France to visit the Taizé community, and then to the Iona monastery in Scotland. It was during this trip, she said, that Van had compiled his notes from each out-of-country retreat over the twelve-year period.

"After wondering for so long about the authenticity of his work in First Church, he finally came to some conclusion, I think," Lucille said.

Life has to be lived where you are. When I look at the scriptures and the Word made flesh and Christ living in the midst of it all, I can see the needs at home. Windsor, where I am, for better or for worse, is where I belong. And if it can't work in Windsor, maybe it was just never meant to work.

Van had shown me the passage in his journal. It marked the last recorded piece of an outline of his midlife's journey. He had used the notes to write a book, and although it had never been published, the inspiration culled from it went into most of his sermons. In just the past few years, he had used the substance of it to lay a foundation for renewed ministry at First Church. The theme was how to cultivate an "organic" Christian community in a local parish.

Not surprisingly, I had expected this trip to England would fall neatly into that same steady pattern. I assumed Van would guide us through the Dartmoors, into Plymouth, through Dorchester, dropping pearls of wisdom. But when I said something about that to Lucille, she laughed.

"Oh, no, I hope not! Not this time!" She motioned to the back of the bus where her "old bird" had just roused himself. Van was back there rubbernecking with the rest of the folks. "This trip's a little different."

As Lucille returned to her seat next to him, I shook my head. Worst of all was the silly hat he wore, a white flop-cap that made him look like Zippy the cartoon character.

Why did he let us wander so?

"Van wants to try having morning meditations," Lucille warned on the morning of the fifth day, as the bus zoomed down the road to Plymouth. "I told him, 'That's fine, Van, but keep it short.' I'm afraid he thinks he's going to wring a lot out of it."

Our brief stopover at the home church in Dorchester had been wholly unsatisfying. Every significant, surviving artifact in Saint Peter's Church could be found dated, mounted, and described on memorial plaques gracing the walls. For a few pence, one could purchase a series of pamphlets commemorating lives of poets, architects, lords and ladies, members and celebrants since the fifteenth century.

The sanctuary looked like little more than an archaic museum, and the verger, a kind but vigilant docent. The verger greeted us, I suspect, as warmly as he would any tourists, but he never seemed to make the connection between his Anglican church and the First Church crowd. Jane Allyn circled the pews, as if trying to remember something she'd forgotten. "It looks like a nice church," said Jane, whose family had descended from one of John White's parishioners who sailed to America on the *Mary and John.* "Well ... I guess that's about it."

After a glance at John White's gravesite, we filed out to shop the National Trust stores, pubs, and museums down the block.

By the time we pulled into Plymouth late in the morning, it was rainy and cold. The guide led us through the streets chattering about Sir Walter Raleigh, Sir Francis Drake, and the Spanish armada. We followed her down to the docks and, as she talked, we searched for a plaque mentioning the *Mary and John*'s departure in 1630.

"There are the *Mayflower* steps," the guide declared, pointing from the road.

"But we're from the *Mary and John,*" said Elizabeth McCarthy.

The guide did not seem to hear. Miles Standish, she said. William Bradford ... John Winthrop ... Pilgrims who sailed in 1620 on the *Mayflower.* And here, this plaque celebrates the *Tory,* pioneer ship of the colonization of New Zealand. that one celebrates settlement of Newfoundland. Over there, June 11, 1583, commemorates ...

"But we're the *Mary and John!*" Elizabeth said.

"Oh, of course," the guide said. "One of thousands. Now, if you will look to your left, where the tower appears on that hill, the famous Drake's Island . . ."

Henry Holcombe and his wife came upon the name of one of their ancestors on the wall of the Island House, a tavern by the dock. But the Davenports, whose ancestors had settled New Haven, Connecticut; Delores Wickersham, who'd descended from the original First Church minister, John Warham himself; and the Allyns continued to look for evidence of their ancestors' presence. Alas, they found nothing, no connection to the wind-blown harbor and shuddering docks.

Moments later, we followed the guide up New Street to the Black Friars Distillery, where Van stood fumbling with some papers. Overlooking the harbor from a narrow vantage between taverns, he stood smiling. Doris Blevins had her Bible open for a reading of the story of the road to Emmaus. He had been laying for us.

"I was just asking one of the locals here if they knew anything about that hospital where our congregation first gathered here in Plymouth three hundred sixty years ago," Van said. "I got a blank stare. So I asked somebody else. And I got the same response. It seems like that hospital has been gone for quite some time, and I don't think anyone here remembers the *Mary and John.* So as we wander around this place, looking for our beginnings, I'm afraid we'll see that Plymouth has changed. As we look around this harbor, we may begin to feel disconnected or we may feel that we only have taken part in a small piece of a history that we do not yet completely understand. But I'd suggest that as we look, we consider Plymouth as a place of great connections. This is truly a crossroads of the world from which people with vision and insight have set out for centuries. To America. To Australia. To New Zealand and Newfoundland. Perhaps as we turn now and look again into the harbor, we will begin to see the whole world from this place and be reminded that we are all connected. Beyond the many plaques and dates of seemingly unrelated historical events, there is a common fabric and a common connection that may not always be apparent but is there nevertheless."

The tour guide, sensing a restlessness in the crowd, shouted out,

"Well said, vicar!" She spun on her heels and marched us back to the docks to arrange a boat trip down the River Tamar.

Van was not done. But he obediently folded his notes and followed the crowd of First Church tourists who were already fleeing down the street.

At the dock, he thanked Doris for her reading, helped old Barry Masters board, and found a place for a few older women below deck out of the cold winds. We had spent a half hour in Dorchester. Forty-five minutes at Plymouth. Soon, at the end of an hourlong boat ride down the Tamar, we would be in Cornwall for lunch, a tour of a medieval home, and a visit to a nearby church. Everywhere we turned we saw memorials celebrating England's imperial character, its sainted aristocrats and unforgotten soldiers.

"Nice going, Van," Lucille said. "You kept it short."

" 'Twas good sport," he said, mocking the accent. "Time to shove off."

He caught my eye and gave me a knowing smile. After Lucille climbed up to the deck, he leaned over and, out of earshot of the others, whispered, "I can see why the Puritans wanted to get the hell out of this place. Can't you?"

The little tourist boat puttered into Plymouth Sound and soon we were skimming through the Tamar Valley. On to the next shrine.

"Yes, yes, I know what you're thinking. Stephen *Coffin*. Wonderful name for a minister, isn't it? I shouldn't think you'd let me scare you away, though—come along now, I know some people who would love to meet you."

The Reverend Coffin greeted us near Cotehele Quay, where our boat docked and we toured a Tudor estate full of the same sorts of heraldic devices, swords, monuments, faded tapestries, hunting trophies, and pewter embellishments we'd seen all along the way. Fortunately, Priscilla Drake's uncle, who lived near Plymouth, had arranged for us to meet his vicar, the Reverend Coffin, saving us from another dreary walk through a fusty fifteenth-century English landmark smelling of mink oil and moth balls. We were invited to an afternoon event.

"We've having a fete," he said. "You know, a church fair."

From the open road, we followed the Reverend Coffin down a narrow lane and soon faced an opening into an enormous sloping grade of sumptuous lawns, a long, curling trace of high hedges, and clusters of tall oaks out of which rose an ancient, turreted, gray-green stone fortress on the slope of the Cornwall coast—a magnificent church. The Reverend Coffin looked too meager to be running such an estate. His thin, pale face and poorly trimmed hair suggested a certain dangerous inattention, I thought. But he was certainly gracious, and, so far, not at all given to lecturing us with historical details.

He opened the doors of a small stone parish house and we heard the musical sounds of church women at work. "Come inside," he said, and we joined the swell of activity, a Saturday-afternoon fund-raiser—harmless gambling games, cake sales, a lottery, and a clothes auction. Behind decripit folding tables spilling over with old clothes, toys, records, books, tools, transistor radios, candles, and coffeepots, chattering church volunteers rushed around selling castoffs. Doughy-faced men and women sorted through piles of junk. They looked just like us.

"Let me introduce some friends from America!" Reverend Coffin shouted. Suddenly the doorways filled with bright faces and hands that went up in the air waving. All activity around the tables stopped, and the parishioners turned toward our troop smiling.

"First Church, Congregational, Windsor, Connecticut. How old did you say?"

"Three sixty," Van said.

"Three hundred sixty years old."

The English folk applauded and ushered us in.

I bought a tarnished brass thermometer, Lucille purchased a piece of dusty crystal, and everyone else browsed or sipped coffee with the Anglicans. Van and the vicar, who could have easily posed as father and son, strolled through the noisy room.

"We're trying to raise money for the upkeep of these buildings, you see," the vicar said.

"A capital-funds drive?" Van asked, knowingly.

"It's a constant struggle," he said. "Actually, I have three parishes altogether. While they're all blessed with magnificent structures, we spend an unholy amount of energy on preservation."

Van drew closer and adjusted his hearing aid.

"This church, St. German's, dates from the twelfth century—I'd love for you to see it—but it's all become a rather high-pressured business, to be honest. To light it, heat it . . . to repair the roof, replace the old stones—"

"The insurance alone," Van said.

"It's astronomical!"

"I can imagine," Van said. "Our church is only three hundred and sixty years old—"

"And besides," Coffin interrupted, "I hate to ask people for money. It's not like in America, where most people attend church every week. We're forced to have these little fairs to raise money, which is not God's way, if you know what I mean. I'd much rather see them dig into their pockets and acknowledge the gifts of stewardship."

"Well, I don't know—"

"Did you know less than three percent of our people regularly worship in these grand old English churches? Talk about doing God's work! I've been here for four years after working as a missionary in Burundi—you know, Central Africa—"

"Burundi?"

"—and, my gosh, the church was alive!"

"The Third World."

"I've found that in the old colonies, you know, the Christian faith is far more vibrant than here at home. People understand what it means to give, to be faithful, to sacrifice, to educate themselves in the scripture. But here, in a very wealthy corner of the world, we hold these little fairs to sell cakes and cookies to raise money to support . . . well, what? The burden of history, I suppose."

The vicar laughed. "That's not what the church is about, now is it?"

Van patted the fellow on the shoulder.

A shout went up near the entryway and someone in a white bonnet waved a lottery ticket in the air.

"The American won a prize!" cried the verger, standing beside a display table of gifts. "Your pick, madam. Wine or biscuits?"

"Did you say that's a *local* wine?" she asked, skeptically, reaching for the biscuits.

Van turned back to Reverend Coffin.

"We're working the same garden," Van said. "You know, I think it would be very nice if you could share your story with our people."

At first the vicar looked surprised, but then he seemed to understand. "Yes," he said. "Why, yes! Of course."

After a while, we walked down a path to the church and waited in a light drizzle while First Church people straggled along carrying sacks of goodies from the fair. The vicar began our tour at the Norman west door, an impressive stone archway, seventy-four feet in width, that framed his slight figure with ring upon ring of patterned stonework. Crossing the dizzying threshold, Van and the First Church entourage entered an awesome silence, the same cool, pregnant quiet of an empty church on a Saturday at home. Beyond the vestibule we came into a glorious sculpted cavern of colored glass and gold and statuary, brilliantly lit by electric sconces, high, slitted windows, and portals. It was cool and damp inside. Every step set off an echo.

"Our story," the vicar said, "begins . . ."

The First Church crowd wandered around slowly as Coffin talked, passing from one corner of the church to another, peering into the thirteenth century font, reaching out for the wooden statue of Saint Anthony of Padua, staring into a sparkling texture of stonework and polished wood. It was a treasure trove. Beside engraved lists of pastors, priors, and bishops that began in 930 A.D., they came across plain corkboards plugged with handwritten church announcements, a sheet of names for the month's coffee rotation, an announcement for a beer-and-barbecue dinner, and crayon drawings from the Sunday School. JESSUS HEALS, said one boy's artwork, underneath a lively drawing of a dog chasing a rabbit. Soon, from the choir loft we heard music, "Ave Verum," which sounded as thin and as muffled as the notes of a calliope, childlike and sweet—a peculiar tone for such a gothic space.

"I think the vicar phoned his organist to come play for us," Lucille whispered to Van. "I heard him say he came running all the way from his home in Cornwall."

The young vicar waved clusters of our crowd to join him as he circled the sanctuary, describing the many oil paintings of kings and dukes that hung on the walls. Soon he was cracking jokes. He had us all sitting in chairs in the middle of the sanctuary when he finished the history lesson.

"And we lost the old organ in a fire twenty-five years ago," he said. "As you know, it is quite expensive to find adequate replacements if you're not wealthy, and it was a terrible expense. In fact, maintaining this church is quite a chore, overall. We recently replaced the lights at a cost of fifteen thousand pounds, and the insurance alone runs close to . . . well, I hate to say."

The vicar's voice dropped. He walked into the aisle and leaned across a chair to look at us at eye level.

"I don't know how you feel about Britain, frankly. But we are in a missionary situation."

He stopped smiling, and his voice steadied into a soft, low tone. We were captive.

"For instance, we have perhaps eight thousand people living right here in this parish of St. German's, but on Sundays we are lucky to draw a crowd of forty to church services."

The First Church crowd sounded no response.

"Yes, that's right!" Coffin said. "Didn't you know? This is common throughout England. Only three percent of the population attend church anymore. Within the institution, we're divided by factions, controversies about language and power and traditions. Outside the church, people still use the word Jesus, but mostly as a swear. Those who have picked up a bit of the Christian story consider themselves inoculated and think they no longer need us. And yet here we are, an important part of the British landscape, a significant slice of the tourist industry, a formerly wealthy and powerful force. And, ironically, now considered a bit from history, an absent anachronism."

He wound his way through our rows of wooden folding chairs. All heads turned. The rhythm of his patter, tenor, and inflection led me to think he might soon ask for a donation.

"As you continue your travels you'll see we've done a marvelous job preserving, restoring, and showing off our historical buildings," he continued. "Your vicar—Reverend Parker—tells me you will be traveling to Saint Sidwell's tomorrow, where your first minister, John Warham, was from. And no doubt, from there you'll go on to London to tour Saint Paul's Cathedral and others. You'll see wonderful examples of Gothic architecture. Fabulous icons from other eras. Important monuments from England's past. But, unfortunately, you may also see how we've failed to present the Gospel story. You probably will not hear so much about the Good News in England. You see, we can talk readily about our grand history, but it's a battle to get our people to talk about their faith or their spiritual journeys. We English have become so private and disconnected. Many of us have forgotten even how to pray in an extemporaneous way."

Reverend Coffin stood straight and then eased his way a step or two down the aisle until he was, literally, in our midst. He looked down and paused for a quiet moment. I was sure he would pass the collection plate any time now.

"Please," he said, holding his thin hands out like an offering. "You can see we have a wonderful heritage in the Christian faith. We are rich in history. But we need your help."

Here it comes, I thought.

"I trust First Church is a place alive in faith and in the hope of Christ," he said.

His voice dropped to a whisper.

"You'll pray for us, won't you? That's all I would ask. Pray for us. Won't you pray for Britain?"

There was an awful moment of embarrassment. People were looking at their shoes or at the ceiling. As soon as the vicar smiled and stood erect, our crowd nodded politely, thanked him, and scurried for the door.

CHAPTER TEN

After our luminous encounter with Reverend Coffin, the First Church pleasure bus hummed along for days like a time machine under the direction of an antic Yahweh. Historical detail and frantic touring created associations that turned our tour into an encounter I can only describe as an immersion into narrative.

In London we saw even more garish statuary of English historical figures in every block and churchyard. Smug attitudes about Americans were annoying enough, but the militaristic opulence of English churches made every sanctuary look like a shrine to the British navy. Replicas of armaments and memorials to bellicose legions filled their churches. Compulsive caretaking of history forced priests to run "Super Tours" of London's finest cathedrals. Manning cash registers and hawking plastic souvenirs, the Brothers looked like sidewalk harpies on Forty-second Street.

I tried to tell JoAnne, but the stories broke on my tongue like a tab of lysergic acid. After meeting Stephen Coffin I must have spent the next five days in England not touring, but tripping.

"You saw a number of churches, I take it?" JoAnne said. We were sitting in the First Church library again, but I could feel the bus still rumbling beneath my feet.

"Resplendent churches. In Bath, Plymouth, Salisbury . . ."

"And?"

"Empty husks."

By day, I conducted formal interviews. At night, I strolled through streets and drank beer with the men. I hoped to learn how they were, who they were, why they had come. Something indescribably sad about that. They did not see themselves as pilgrims or adventurers. They had no sense of their own congregation's mythic possibility.

"But, the church?" I would ask. "Why are you with the church?"

"Let me see if I understand this," JoAnne said. "You're saying that this Stephen Coffin fellow was like an oracle . . ."

"Yes, a ghost of the future. They go back to revisit their roots and meet this thin, pale little WASP holding out his hands—'Pray for us, won't you? Pray for Britain!' Spiritually bankrupt, handicapped by the weight of history . . ."

"I see. And the name was Coffin, did you say?"

"Spooky, isn't it?"

JoAnne thought for a second. I could see she was doubtful.

"I understand," she said.

"No, you don't. I'm saying that for most of them, our trip was nothing more than a pleasure tour. But for me—strange as it seems—I often felt like we were on the trail of something important. A secret relationship. A transcendent experience."

"It was—"

"It was about seeing your own future . . ."

On the last day, we toured the village of Windsor. Their namesake. We had come full circle. By then, people were doing anything to escape the tour: shopping sprees at Harrods; afternoons at Wimbledon for the tennis finals; trips to museums and concert halls. Every night, couples made a rush for theater tickets. On the last day Van and Lucille finally managed to pull us together to tour Windsor, and I thought my intuition about the trip had been verified.

Racing through the rain on the streets of the famously royal tourist town, our guide hustled us toward the castle for a final walk-through. Everyone made a great effort to take everything in. We paced through lavish libraries, chapels, dining rooms, and bedrooms. At last steeped in the things we had apparently come so far to admire, we toured the birthplace of English royalty—a vulgar display of excess and privilege. Welcome to the castle, the queen's estate.

"It's rather pretty," one would say.

"Elegant."

"Charming!"

"Ravishing!"

"I'd like to be a queen."

Yes, I thought, why not? Let's all pretend we're queens now. A king. A prince. Well-bred knights of the Garter.

"How'd you like to live in a place like this?" the guide asked. Our crowd cooed.

At the end, on the route back to our bus, I noticed mechanical wax figures greeting guests at the gates to the village. An exhibition titled "Royalty and Empire" offered a red-carpet walking tour through British history. *The Astonishing Moving Speaking Spectacle! They Speak. They Move. They Almost Live!"*

I kept trying to describe the scene to JoAnne, a mirrorlike image of our crowd, much as I had seen it at Saint German's. Like an apparition, I said, a ghostly premonition of the First Church future.

"I see," she said, though I was not sure she really did.

"I'm only saying this: I could sense us caught up in this narrative, just as our lives are caught up in a narrative—partly of our own making, partly of our common history, partly hidden in our subconscious—and that was both a strange and invigorating experience. It was like being led. It was a journey—a beginning, a middle, and an end."

"Do you think anyone else felt that way?" she asked.

"I don't think so."

"You must have felt rather lonely."

Yes. On the last afternoon, in fact, I had just sat by myself in a bar at the hotel and drunk beer.

I had expected that everyone would join the pilgrimage. And why not? The families who traveled with us were the pillars of the church, and yet I was left feeling like their solitary, cynical, Scots-Irish punk stowaway. Sitting by myself with a bottle of bitters in hotel bars watching the World Cup, I felt sad and lonely. By the last day, I was so miserable, I hardly noticed when Van came in to order a drink, too.

He put his hand on my shoulder and I must have started.

"Well, Gary, what've you been up to?"

"Drinking and watching TV."

"Drinking and watching TV," he repeated and chuckled. "Good." He pronounced the word with a long, silly accent, like "nude."

"By the way . . . ," he said.

I looked over and he jostled his drink.

"Iced tea," he said.

"Yes," I said.

He dropped a sheaf of papers on the table from Saint James's Church in Piccadilly.

"It looked like something you'd appreciate. I thought you'd like to see all the programs. Creation theology. Spiritual growth. They're doing lots of outreach. But don't let me bother you."

JoAnne nodded. "Van made a pastoral call," she said.

The gesture was tender and comforting. I had seen him do it with others, too, at different moments during the trip.

"In any case," I said, "we searched for roots and the roots were dead. What was the point? Why even belong to a church?"

"And did you ask anyone that question?"

I had. In the town of Bath one evening, I took a long walk with Fred Porter. A member of First Church since the fifties, an intelligent and articulate man, Fred gave me a detailed description of the church and its politics during Van's tenure. At one point, I stopped him and asked him about the trip.

"What is the point, Fred?" I asked. "Doesn't the church mean anything more to people than this?"

"As a matter of fact, Gary," he said, "the church is like a cocktail party. And Van's the host who hands newcomers a drink tray so they'll feel useful. You know, he would have made a great PR man, if he hadn't been a minister."

Maybe I was more naïve than I thought, or maybe Fred was more honest than I had expected. In any case, he sensed my surprise.

"Come now," he had said, "it's all a matter of nickels and noses, isn't it?"

"Raising money?" I asked. "Building membership?"

"What else is there?"

JoAnne showed no sense of surprise.

"So you've finally uncovered our big secret," she said.

"Which is?"

"The church is only an institution."

Yes, I thought. A flimsy institution overtaken by its own history, by the image of its dying English mother, remembered now mainly in a scattering of shrines and memorials to the former empire. But why hadn't anyone else from First Church noticed? When we returned from England, the same games were being played. People fussed about teams of carpenters who had not finished painting the old meetinghouse. The Prudential Board plotted ways to dispose of the lead paint in the playground without alerting environmental officials. Bill Warner-Prouty, finally fed up with the church's irrelevance and parochialism, was having a full-blown career crisis. And Van, although worn out from the trip, immediately returned to fund-raising.

"So, in fact, a church is not just an institution," she said, "but an institution that works against the spirit."

"Yes, but there's more."

The day after we came home, we all returned to the meetinghouse for Sunday worship. In the middle of the service, John said a short prayer for Randy Broward, a homeless man at the shelter. I had joined John visiting Randy a few times in the hospital. We had both prayed over him, and, when we realized he might be dying, tried unsuccessfully to find his relatives. After six months at First Church, I thought, it seemed odd that I still had more close relationships at the homeless shelter than at church. I said one last prayer that morning with the congregation, and then, after the service, while John and I were talking out on the parish house steps, someone came from the office to say that Randy had just died. We both knew it meant we would probably bury more of our friends before the shelter reopened in October.

I joined John to help carry Randy's casket the next morning. We stood over a weedy grave at the northeast end of a city cemetery—John, his wife, and a few of Randy's homeless friends. John cried. The guys told stories about this dead man they called Bear. And I, stepping back to a place where I could watch and sketch the scene, wondered again about where the people of First Church were. Here I was, at the end of a journey, standing over a pauper's grave.

"If this were a parable, JoAnne, what would you ask now? 'Who are the homeless here? Who are the dead?' "

"You're saying this church is not aware of its own story," JoAnne said.

"Totally. Unaware of the Christian story. Unaware of its story in history. Unaware of what happens in the world around them."

She said nothing.

"I didn't think churches existed to provide people with an excuse for pleasure trips. At least four men from John's shelter have died since Easter, and the church should be there. John says, whenever one of them dies now, 'Where is God here?' And I'm thinking we could just as easily ask that same question right here about First Church. Where is God in all this?"

JoAnne shook her head.

"Then you must be clear that that's what we're up against," she said. "And it takes a mighty amount of energy and clarity and prayer to work against an institution like this to make sure it doesn't consume us with its history and buildings and its sometimes overwhelming sense of self-importance."

Nothing could be drearier than to label church people hypocrites. I had to remember the reasons I had come here. An ordinary place. Ordinary people.

"But before we pursue that," she said, "first, tell me about you. Where are you in all this? Where is your growing edge? Where is there more that you can learn? What do you expect?"

"Community," I said.

"Well then," she said. "So maybe one of your questions to people could be, 'What keeps you in this 'community,' in this 'company of strangers'?"

"I always ask that. 'Why are you here?' "

"Do people have trouble answering?"

"All the time."

"Of course. But you're writing a book, so you know why you're here."

Was that a wisecrack? I couldn't tell.

After working for twenty years as a journalist, I had never met people who seemed so out of touch with who they were, especially while we were in England.

"Everyone?" she said.

Well, there was Andy McCarthy.

"All of you dear, sweet people . . ."

I could still hear him. Several days after our visit to Saint German's, Andy opened his heart to us one morning during Communion. He took Elizabeth's hand and said: "Maybe we haven't done such a good job of finding our roots. But I'd like to suggest that perhaps we did stumble across them and didn't recognize it when we walked into the fair at Saint German's. I have to think, 'If God—He-slash-She—is infinite and also has a sense of humor, then maybe God reshaped that place to let us see ourselves.' That was my wife Elizabeth standing behind the coffee table and Lucille selling tea and my counterpart on the board of deacons selling castoffs. I could see all of you dear, sweet people just trying to live out your quiet lives from day to day. Those are our roots, really."

Andy's lip quivered, and later when I asked him about his feelings, he said he only wanted to go on to Ireland. He felt something compelling him to go. The day before we came home, I helped him and Elizabeth carry their bags to the train station for a trip to his father's homeland.

"I thought you said you didn't get to know each other," JoAnne said.

"As the official scribe, I had reason to nose around. But, I don't know, I still felt very alone there."

"Be patient," she said. "The mystic part of your nature will help you work through this."

I was not at all sure what she meant or whether I bought this "mystic" tag.

"Sure," she said. "Maybe you feel some loneliness because you really do see life from a slightly different perspective?"

Slightly? As a journalist, my job was to see clearly, to report dispassionately. But ever since our trip to England I felt like I was hallucinating. What could I make of that?

"You're experiencing things subjectively, for a change."

"But why? That's what I'm saying, JoAnne. What's happening to me?"

"You tell me," she asked.

"What if my job is not just a job? What if I am here not simply to take notes for a book? What if I've been led to . . ."

"But isn't that what we ask for at night," she said, "when we are in the comfort of our bedclothes and about to go to sleep: 'Give me meaning in my life'? What's wrong with that?"

She smiled sweetly. She was remarkably nonjudgmental. Still, she did not seem to understand the full ramifications of my experience.

"Look, JoAnne," I said, "do you remember when we talked about Wonderbread and signs? I have another one for you."

One night after we returned from England, I was driving home late, after another series of damnable church meetings. I was thinking about the entire project—leaving the Presbyterian church, coming to First Church, traveling to England—all of it. I thought, Okay, maybe it's just bullshit. Pull yourself together. Maybe I have been duped. Too easily persuaded. Maybe the early "signs" were products of an overactive imagination, and so was the trip to England. The Reverend *Coffin,* the mechanistic *Windsor* and all the rest—a matter of self-delusion. Flim-flammed by my own mysterious need to belong somewhere.

I was on the highway, again. Talking to myself in a very self-critical way, and then, suddenly, I looked up, and I was flying under another sign.

"And?"

"The sign said PROVIDENCE!"

JoAnne threw her head back and howled with laughter.

"I'm serious," I said.

"I never thought of that one."

Why was this so goddamned funny to her? I was obviously on the verge of a breakthrough and she was laughing. I scowled and crossed my arms.

"Well," I said, "you're the 'guide.' Tell me what the hell is going on here. I didn't want to see any more 'signs.' "

"Okay, I see," she said. "This is an important issue for you."

She looked out the window and closed her eyes for a moment. "Are you still having these experiences?" she asked.

No, I had shut down. They were too much.

"But can you accept them as a gift and be grateful? Like the highway sign, PROVIDENCE?"

Strangely enough, I hadn't thought it was so weird at the time. My immediate reaction was that God was in touch. God was telling me everything was perfectly okay. I should be calmed. Reassured. I was on the right road.

"Absolutely," JoAnne said. "It is okay. All will be well. That's *providence*, yes?"

"But what about this guy Coffin? And Windsor Castle? And . . . Were they part of this . . . ?" I still didn't know what to call it.

"Just give thanks for having a questioning mind."

"You're telling me not to . . ."

"Unless you expect to become Lord of the Universe." She shot me an accusing look.

But what if there is a God? I thought. What if God roams highways poking people to look up at highway signs or lurks around England leading them to the good vicar Coffin? It was too profound to contemplate.

"If that's the case," JoAnne said, "maybe you need a break. Go fishing, play golf. Maybe that'll make you feel better."

Sounded reasonable.

She looked at me kindly, then said: "And maybe you'll soon get an idea about what it is you're so critical about. Maybe you'll learn what you mean by what is 'you' and what is 'they.' "

I was not at all sure what she meant. But I did want to bring our conversation to an end. Serendipity, grace, and the epiphanies of recent weeks added up to more than I could tolerate. There was still one more thing to discuss.

"Okay, what is it?" she asked.

"JoAnne, it's got nothing to do with anything we've talked about before. I just wonder if you know anything about adoption."

She said nothing.

For months, Jan and I had continued to quarrel about our problem. When I returned from England, she had finally seemed ready to talk seriously about adoption. Then I had misgivings again. The strain was increasingly hard on us.

JoAnne pursed her lips and looked down.

"That's interesting," she said. She slowly looked up, glanced out the window, and then stared at me.

"I know a little about it," she said. "In fact, I've just started writing a book. About this issue. It's about . . . well, it's about my life."

I left her, returning to England's ivy-cloaked highways. I again saw sculptured hedges, low Tudor buildings with pantiled roofs and window boxes bearing roses as large as bowling balls. Remembering the sweetness of rainfall in Cornwall and the musty cloakroom smells of old churches leavened my senses, and as I stopped time to recall them, I experienced a new desire to taste, smell, see, and feel again. Stepping out onto the parish house steps, I saw the New England landscape, tawdry by comparison—our fields poorly tended, woods unkempt, husbandry a lost art—grow green, suddenly lush in my sight.

I was finally seeing through the illusion of childlessness with the help of an ally who knew more about babies and adoption than I could have ever imagined. Orphaned as an infant, JoAnne knew the experience firsthand. At the moment, she was writing a book about losing her sister—and finding her again, as an adult. As my spiritual guide, as a mother of five children, as a once adopted child, she had promised to help me chart a way through ambivalence and doubt toward making a decision.

"But first," she had said, "you must forget about virtue. Give yourself a break. Quit thinking so much about the church. Be easy with grace. Discard all you ever mislearned about being good. Take time to stop time."

Outside, I sank to the parish house steps. At the beginning of summertime, at JoAnne's urging, I would rest. To dream, to drift, to let go. In the fantasy of God's grace, I was, and remained, expectant of a new life. I watched as a flock of birds descended into the churchyard. Here we go, I thought. The season of Pentecost begins. Into the heart of the most myterious fire, into the passionate flame of waiting.

Pentecost

Great innovations never come from above, they come from below—the upheaval of world and upheaval of consciousness are the same; everything is relative and doubtful. . . . It is just the people from the obscurer levels who follow the unconscious drive of the psyche. It is the derided silent folk of the land who are less infected with academic prejudices than the celebrities would be. From above they present a dreary or laughable spectacle. Yet they are impressively simple as those Galileans who were once called blessed. . . .

—Carl Jung
"The Spiritual Problem of Modern Man"

CHAPTER ELEVEN

Without the press of Christian celebrations, congregational events grew lax and happy by mid-July. The Board of Christian Education polled children about *The Joy Curriculum* on their last day before summer break and heard a resounding Bronx Cheer from K through eighth-graders. The board chairman said he interpreted their objection to the previous year's lesson plan as a "clear spiritual leading," and "henceforth," he said, "we will dump *Joy* from the church school."

Andy McCarthy's father, Dick, filled in for Fran by playing solo piano at Sunday morning services. Unlike the formal, liturgically correct pieces chosen by Francis Angelo, Dick McCarthy's relaxed repertoire masked a capricious jazz style. Slowing rhythms to a meditative pulse and draping cloudy flourishes around melodic lines, he played "Old Man River," "Mack the Knife," and "I Did It My Way" all summer without anyone noticing. I prayed and tossed back shots of Communion juice with even greater pleasure than before.

Famous celebrities like Bob Hope, Ozzie Osborne, and Bart Simpson signed the visitors' notebook in childlike script on Sundays, and Morgan Smythe, the groundskeeper, retaliated by telling kids he had discovered a "serpent" living in the church basement. It was only an eight-inch garter snake, but it scared the hell out of whoever bothered to satisfy his curiosity.

By July, Van declared that the dog-who-would-be-God was now a ready subject for conversion. Daisy not only had gnawed through some of the Parkers' best cane chairs, but she broke loose from her choker on Flag Day, raided the cemetery, and pilfered a dozen flag memorials from veterans' graves. Lucille sent her to obedience school for a week, but Daisy continued to leap on couples who came in for pre-marriage counseling, to paw wedding parties, and, once, to surprise Lucille by knocking her flat on the ground and leaving a bloody mess on the porch steps.

"I am reminded that conversion is an ongoing process," Van said one day, mixing a sedative in her bowl. Peggy and I watched him lift Daisy's limp body and put her in the car. Then he and Lucille packed the trunk and roared off for a five-week vacation at the family's twenty-acre farm in Vermont.

Those of us left were free to roam. Tobacco grew tall and flowery under white shade netting on the northern perimeters of town. Parishioners dumped their gardens' excess—tomatoes, sweet corn, and green squash—in the church office. Joan passed out butterscotch candy to nursery-school kids during the mornings. Peggy and I discovered jack-in-the-pulpit in the woods one Sunday afternoon; Bill and I watched demolition crews dynamite the old Farmington River bridge. The sound of uninhibited children's voices at lunch hour often left me standing in the hallway alert, smelling freshly baked bread from the nursery school, and wondering about this inexhaustible source of comfort that people felt in a familiar environment of donated goods and voluntary services. Silent stacks of green folding chairs and plain flesh-colored rooms with clearly marked fire exits and borrowed furniture reminded me of another era and another place.

"A place to come home to," is how Van described the church. Especially when it stood empty on hot, late afternoons, when you could see it all loosely formed, a patchwork, put-together kind of place. Barely changed since the 1950s, the church became an entanglement for someone like me who had been away for years and, for the first time, was rediscovering the pleasures of connection and dependence.

"The amazing thing about Van," Andy said, "is that he will bring this inclusive-language campaign along, and get the new addition built, put in the parking lot, drive up the outreach budget, and nobody will suspect he's done a thing. I mean, really, he's amazing."

Andy consumed the last quarter of a sauerkraut hot dog.

"Just watch. By next spring, all the 'hyphenated people' will be happy and so will the old guard. He'll push the Prudential Board's agenda without pissing off the Outreach people. Half the congregation will think the church is moving ahead and the other half will think it's preserving traditions. And the whole time Van'll be in the background using people like me to make it work. And I'll know he's using me and he'll know he's using me, and he'll know that I know. And still, every once in a while when he needs help to make something work out, he'll put his arm around me and, without sounding like an asshole, he'll say, 'Andy, we need your steady hand.' "

He took a drag on his cigarette. Sitting on the picnic table outside Bart's Luncheonette, we could get a tan, eat lunch, talk politics, have a smoke. I enjoyed his company. Long lunch hours at Bart's occurred more frequently these days, especially when Andy finished his mail route early and had nothing else to do.

"I've heard some people describe it as manipulative," he continued. "But if you have any love of politics at all, Van's very good. He's not kidding anybody. He's just trying to bring this thing along in a smooth way, from a theological angle, without stepping on toes. What's wrong with that?"

Ever since the England trip, Andy and I had developed a pretty good relationship. Most people probably thought he was a little odd, and I guess he was. I mean, how many aeronautical engineers do you find who give up their jobs at midcareer so they can move back home to become part-time mailmen and pursue the splendor of local history? But maybe that's too harsh. I know for a fact that was one reason I liked him so much. You'd never guess it, running into him after church on Sundays, but Andy McCarthy, a former guidance and control expert for NASA's space shuttle, was heavily into the timeless moment, walking the path of pure soul illumination.

Right before he and Elizabeth left for Ireland, on that very same day that he lost his way on the Brompton Road looking for a Chinese restaurant and ended up in a swanky lingerie shop, he and I sat down in a coin laundry outside our South Kensington hotel and he bared his soul. He told me he always had thought the true American religion was democracy, but when we arrived at Avesbury and he spent the afternoon walking up and down hills that formed the fabulous, mysterious stone circles, he had an experience of déjà vu that suddenly tuned him in to "the music of the spheres."

All I remembered was Elizabeth worrying about the sheep droppings while Andy raced ahead of us, saying, "Wait a minute, wait a minute!" and going from ditch to balds and back again until he was a hundred yards beyond the rest of us. The whole time, he told me later, he was saying to himself, "Wow! I've been here before."

I had waved good-bye to them at the train station when they left for Ireland. "I don't want to sound like Shirley MacLaine," Andy said at the time, "but some people do believe there is a kind of race memory such that some of the feelings of the past can be transmitted from generation to generation." What he had felt at Avesbury, he expected to rediscover in Ireland. He gave me a bear hug at the station and saluted from the window. I felt as if I had somehow earned his confidence that day, offering an ear for matters otherwise unspeakable. I understood him. I knew what he meant.

Now, back home, Andy and I had started meeting for lunch. We drove to the state archives in Hartford. We made a walking tour through the historic district. Sometimes we just wandered the territory. If nothing else, we would set up circles of chairs for the anonymous groups, sip coffee with Peggy Couples, and sneak into the meetinghouse to nose around from basement to belfry. One day, we crept into the ghostly church basement to puzzle over a mysterious seventeenth-century gravestone he had discovered. Stepping through the mucky runoff from a collapsed foundation wall and decayed brick supports, I felt like we were both making a return to childhood haunts.

"Let's walk," Andy would say, and we'd hit a trail, cross the Farming-ton River bridge, or sneak up into the church steeple for a view of the Connecticut River Valley. Thick with hardwoods, the landscape looked groomed, but in a wild way, shaped only by wind and spring floods. Andy would wax poetic from the open-air perch, imagining steamships and mule-drawn boats moving downstream on the Farmington to the Connecticut River and then up to neighboring Windsor Locks.

"The seventeenth century—the age of the Puritans. The eighteenth—the age of commerce!" he'd declare. Waving his arms from the top of the steeple, he stood precariously on a thin angle of crackling tin that was never meant to hold the weight of two men, no matter how light-headed they might be.

Sometimes our stroll through the meetinghouse overlapped with Fran's practice hours, and we would invite ourselves into the balcony. Sitting outstretched across two pews, we listened to dizzy French poly-rhythms from improvisations by Fran's old teacher, Marcel Dupré. When we were lucky, Fran would stop practicing and talk about his hal-cyon days in Paris, where he studied with Dupré, then he would demon-strate what he had learned. Sharp, neo-Gothic notes exploded in the cool stillness of the church. It was like walking into a dark movie theater in the middle of an Indiana Jones adventure movie, and leaving at the end, tingling with pleasure.

But the best times were when Andy passed the afternoon telling sto-ries. Spicing local history with personal details about his divorce, his sec-ond marriage to Elizabeth, and the early days of the space shuttle, Andy would spin from one digression to another. He talked about his child-hood in Windsor, about his famous rock 'n' roller cousin, Big Al Anderson of NRBQ, and about his job as a mailman. I especially liked hearing about his father's plan to salvage the old organ when it was re-placed by Fran's Casavant. Andy said he and his Dad hauled off several truckloads of old wood and metal pipes one day, took them home, and spent the next month paneling the family's living room with the best pieces.

"I'll never forget it," Andy said, "riding home in the car with the big C pipe strapped to the hood. Everybody on Main Street stood outside to watch because it was such a sight. The wind whistled through the pipe as we drove by blowing the longest, sweetest notes."

Still, I could not figure him. Why would a middle-aged man leave an affluent neighborhood in California, and a well-paying job, to come home to Connecticut and become a mailman?

"I made the decision right after the disaster," he told me one day. I thought he was talking about the *Challenger* explosion. He was talking about his divorce. "I took some time off and went to Long Island to visit some friends and just stayed."

This event led, naturally, to an interest in Albert Einstein's mailman. I say "naturally"—natural to Andy's way of thinking. Near the house where he stayed, it seemed, there was a post office known locally as the place where a Long Island postal worker had carried news of the development of the bomb between Einstein and Franklin Roosevelt. Given his circumstances at the time, Andy had a preexisting fascination with the decision to drop the bomb. Somehow, it turned into curiosity about the mailman.

Andy showed me his file of materials, photographs, and a limited correspondence with Alistair Cooke, who had once mentioned the mailman's service in an essay. Andy gleaned an amazing amount of detail from personal interviews with local postal workers. When he finally wrote the history, it turned out to be an above-average work of some interest to professional historians. In fact, just recently his paper had been accepted with gratitude by the Roosevelt museum in New York State and filed in the presidential archive. Andy also showed me a recent note from Alistair Cooke, who, it seemed, showed some jealousy of Andy's fine scholarship.

The way he pursued a story now was wonderful to watch. One of his best sources was Noah Reese, a sixty-year-old black printer and former police officer in Windsor who also happened to be the only black member of First Church since childhood. Some days Andy dropped by Noah's shop and interviewed him about locally famous crimes and criminals who still lived, undetected, on the outskirts of town. He had a boy's curiosity—"a beginner's mind," as Van would say—and I was charmed by it.

Windsor's unsolved murders occupied a piece of his spare time that summer. He invited me to join him on interviews with the final survivors of the old Archer-Gilligan boarding house, where a series of poisonings in 1916 had led to the famous Broadway production, *Arsenic and Old Lace*. I gave him tips about how to use a tape recorder without making interview subjects uneasy, and, in return, he shared with me selected bits from his conversations with the survivors.

In a few years, I guess, he had developed an unusual ability to sense the depth of time in these places he had come back to. It was interesting to me—Andy did not approach history in an academic way, like a trained historian, but perhaps more from the vantage of the old romantic German idea that *"das Volk dichtect,"* the tradition that says the poetry and ideas of a culture come from the interaction between the folk and the ones who speak with them. Andy could see the wonder of fleeting times. From the memories he poached and the lives of people he visited, he forged a new, more startling sense of place.

The rewards were unexpected—extravagant, sensory details. We listened to the dreadful sound of ice cracking in the river as children crossed it to church in 1910, of cannery workers pissing in the darkness of the covered bridge on the way to Sunday school, of preaching and gospel choirs resounding down Palisado Avenue at the turn of the century.

Do you remember that old lady who used to sit in her house with a revolver on Halloween? Andy would ask. Do you remember Gary Merrill who married Bette Davis? He belonged to this church. Or the time Doris Day came to town?

Did they remember? Open-air trolleys rattled up Main Street; half the town gathered for the three-hundredth birthday of First Church; hundreds of people dressed like pilgrims to launch a half-scale replica of the *Mary and John* into the Farmington River; here came the Reverend Roscoe Nelson wobbling down a dirt side street on his bicycle to visit shut-ins; the evangelist Dwight Moody came to town and converted scores of young girls one summer in the meetinghouse; the old pump organ groaned like a goat; there went the Five D's scurrying to the third pew—David, Dorothy, Daniel, Darrell, and Doris Kelly; brass band concerts blared on the green; Miss Fenton's confectionary shop drew crowds across the street; Annie Sill, Florence Mills's aunt, sang like a bird in the Sunday-school room for two hours every Saturday afternoon.

Friendly places. Life and church and town were inseparable in their memories.

One day we met eighty-eight-year-old Laura Bentley: "Down there at Norman's Garage is where the old parish house used to be. We'd have ham-and-bean suppers for ten cents a plate."

Ninety-nine-year-old Mary Bartlett: "My mother would look at the Ellsworth children every Sunday and say, 'There are eight people in that family! How can they afford it!' "

Eighty-year-old Florence Jeffries: "I remember when Reverend Nelson lost his son in the Farmington River. That was one of the great sadnesses of this church. That's why the children's choir is called the Theodore Nelson Choir today."

And Mildred Knowles: "Andy, you remember our strawberry festival! That was under Reverend Morrell. He had this church flourishing by the time he left. Two Sunday services, and church suppers. Florence Ellsworth made biscuits and I made meatloaf."

On the day we met 104-year-old Martha James at the nursing home, she told Andy her dying wish. "If you want to do anything for me, light a candle in the church and put it in the window. I don't care a thing about the old fire codes, Andy. When my time comes, you'll tell Van, won't you?"

I never saw him take a single note. I could only imagine he was doing like Van, who, during the afternoons, after three glasses of iced tea, a cup of soup, potato salad, and a slice of Mary Bartlett's rhubarb pie, would hop into his Toyota and drive around on pastoral calls. You could always expect an encounter with older couples in formal, well-dusted parlors chock full of porcelain figurines and family pictures. You would find the wall-to-wall carpet streaked with fresh vacuum-cleaner paths and a plate of cookies on a table.

"Would you like a cup of tea, Andy? Or a diet soda? Would you like a piece of fresh apple pie?"

Delighted, he would take a cookie and a cup and turn his full attention to the storyteller. At those times, Andy McCarthy looked like he had just discovered something he could not have found anywhere else in the world—in the realm of familiar faces, within the boundary of a small place, where wonder was familiar.

CHAPTER TWELVE

When I dropped in for lunch, Joan Rockwell was just climbing out of her flower garden. The yard smelled of milkweed. Jasmine flourished on the pergolas. Musk rose and deep purple clematis clustered around her, hip-high, like a crowd of toddlers. She shouted, stepped out, and walked fiercely down the blacktop waving. "Come in! Come on in! Good to see you!"

I thought she would have been dizzy from the sun, which was raw and intense by midday, but she was more rugged than that. She tossed her trowel in the grass, and met me at the back porch of the rambling red colonial home, which I had seen by a sign on the front dated from 1787. She had good biceps; a cyclist's calves; rough, dirty feet. A ring of sweat circled her brown neck. She wiped moisture from her temples with her sleeve and pulled off a starchy pair of gardening gloves.

"I hope you like curried chicken salad," she said, "because that's what we're having. You're not a vegetarian, are you? How about a cold glass of Red Zinger?"

I don't know what I expected, but coming to her house for the first time after seeing her only at church, I was surprised at the formality and fashion of things indoors. Besides its size and historical value, the home's interiors showed a sophisticated taste for upmarket furnishings. The transition from colonial to contemporary had been seamless. The extensive kitchen, with its Jenn-Air range and lustrous pine-green countertops and shelves, made room for a dozen guests. The living room, with its small ancestral hearth, slight sofa, wingback chairs, and mahogany side tables, suggested the setting for stilted dinner-parties.

Perhaps I had judged her wrong. Given her interest in yoga, foreign cultures, dreams, and the arts, I had expected to see spaces filled with Pier One imports. But there was nothing boutiquey anywhere that I could see, as she showed me through the downstairs, even in the spacious den, lightly lined with new books, bricked and tiled and lit by skylights and a generous wall of sliding glass doors that opened into a solarium. There was no Appalachian folk art, as I might have expected, no cane-and-wicker furniture, no sponged walls or faux-marble anything. Only taut upholstery, a few heirloom pieces, glazed doors with open transoms sculpted out of the walls to make the formerly tight New England quarters more open and bright. Someone—she, I assumed—had harmonized the house with a graceful sense of good proportion. It was moneyed property, for certain, in keeping with her husband's birthright inheritance from one of the Boston Brahmins.

I came to her wanting to know more about the spiritual life of the church. Three beagle puppies played on the kitchen floor while we ate, and after lunch Joan invited me into the den, where we talked for a while about Van, and her family's twenty-year association with First Church. Over the six months I'd been there, though, I knew Joan had become engaged in something other than the church. In recent months, I had heard, she had undergone a spiritual rebirth. I felt that I had seen the changes occur at a distance all spring, and secretly I wanted to know more about that, too.

Aside from our acquaintance on the healing committee and in JoAnne's group, I saw her most often during the week in Nelson Hall. Many times I would stop by to watch her leading a small army of children shrieking and squealing under the floating dome of a broad, white parachute. Children scattered while Joan instructed nursery-school teachers to fling the chute up in the air and call out directions for children to run under it, kiss, and scurry out before the parachute fell on top of them. She would keep one hand on the hem of the parachute and reach out with the other to adjust the volume on a cassette player vibrating with South African rhythms and melodies. Her guitar case rested open on the stage, and her exercise mats and large cloth bags of toys draped the piano.

"Red people! Touch cheeks!" she would shout, throwing the parachute high, while little boys and girls tagged with scarlet paper hustled from the periphery to buss at the center of the circle and hightail it out before the nylon skin trapped them underneath. "Yellow people! Touch cheeks!"

Every week for more than a decade, she had turned the auditorium into a setting for new games, an experimental playground for international music, free-spirited dance, and the teaching of peace. She showed children how to bow to each other and give the Indian greeting, *Namas te*—"I greet the God in you"—and, in Japanese, *Kaneechi wa*. She brought a foreign sound and experience into First Church. A clear, bouncing plastic globe, which found its way into many of their games, had become something like her trademark.

She and her husband had started attending First Church during the late sixties, she said. The extent of their spiritual life at that time had amounted to singing in the choir and arranging social events for a traditional Young Couples' Club. Eventually, as they and their friends grew older, had children, and spent more time at work and with their families, the group disbanded. A few, including her, went on to more esoteric interests—to the communal practice of meditation, studies of Eastern traditions and Buddhist rituals, and finally, to private shamanic journeys and intense Jungian analysis. All the while, Joan said, she and her husband had continued to serve on most of the standard church committees, sing in the choir, and run children's programs. Except for Van and Lucille and a few others, most of the people at First Church only knew her in the traditional roles she performed. Very few knew the high roads she had begun to travel.

Her husband, Owen, had watched the changes and made an effort to understand. A mainstream Republican, vested and made wealthy by his executive position in a regional banking firm, Owen Rockwell had challenged his wife about her new ideas regarding social change, personal spiritual development, and politics. She had fought back, challenging him to take a break from work for more personal, spiritual exploration. He had hesitated for a time, but then he took the risk.

Ten years ago, for instance, he joined her on a guided excursion into Soweto. Led by the same group that sponsored Van's trip to Nicaragua, Joan and Owen experienced an immersion into the apartheid culture of South Africa. The trip changed them. Besides leading to a resolution of some conflicts in their marriage, it also led First Church to establish ties with a black church outside Johannesburg. She and Owen came home pledging to change their habits. She went to work in local Nuclear Freeze campaigns, he volunteered at the homeless shelter. At the same time, Joan started to train in dance therapy and soon, every week, she found herself working with palsied and handicapped children in area hospitals. She felt passionate about the need for children to express themselves through movement, and became an exponent of what she called "healing touch." He decided that, as a banker, he needed to understand more about the problems of the poor and of the developing world, and thus his travels began.

For Joan, dancing renewed a relationship with the Spirit, who had been only a distant presence since childhood. The Spirit continued prodding her to more focused activities. She joined the healing group, and—unknown to me—danced silently and alone on Monday nights in the First Church sanctuary before our services to prepare the way for leading strangers toward the Spirit.

At the middle of middle age, after twenty years as a faithful member and good steward at First Church in Windsor, Joan kept coming to the brink of one important change after another until, all at once, the changes cascaded. Physically, I thought I could see the effect. Her hair had grown out of the bouncy bob that was common among fashionable women living west of the river, and she had begun wearing Indian jewelry—thin, beaded necklaces and finely shaped silver rings twisted into provocative figures. Her face, nicely sculptured with high cheekbones and handsome dark features, looked weathered, fluid, and expressive. More significantly, she seemed to carry a strain of some sort, an excitable tension that drew her along with a hunger for what seemed to me to be unthinkable mysteries.

At the middle of midlife, she found herself at the same historic church, living in the same historic home, worshiping the same bland, historic Father God who no longer responded or spoke to her. And it was not easy anymore for her to stay.

"I love this church and I know I'm loved by people here," she told me. "But I feel a growing separation. It has nothing to do with the ministers, who I adore, or the outreach programs, which we've carried out by fulfilling the call to reach out to the world. The problem is our language—how we image God, how we pray to God, how we praise God. The Word is subtly and centrally basic to our worship. But I am finding it increasingly painful to remain at First Church when that God is always the same old white guy in the long white beard.

"It is not, however, my nature to become alienated. So I will find a way to stay no matter how painful it becomes. The church is my home, and it was my parents' home, and it was their parents' home before them. And I will never leave it. But I will work to bring about a broadening of minds."

Joan was not alone. In fact, a number of people in the church had undergone experiences not so different from hers. Although no one ever proselytized or testified to their changes in a public way, a few of her closest friends were also undergoing a spiritual metamorphosis. Andy McCarthy's predecessor as head deacon, Drew Carroll, had experienced encounters with God that had become more and more intimate in the past few years. As he battled cancer and came through with a new understanding of the spiritual life, Drew quit his job and started studying for the ministry. Unlike Joan, he had recently left First Church.

The present chairman of the outreach committee, Ralph Stoot, had systematically tinkered with an entirely new cosmology based on a feminist interpretation of the story of Noah. A dogged, though highly imaginative, study of the story's attendant symbols—beards, rainbows, blood, and wine—had led him to declare that Noah was not a man at all, but a woman much like Mother Nature, and that "her" story had such metaphorical power that she, not Adam and Eve, deserved a place at the center of Old Testament narratives. Allison Denslow, who had helped start the healing group, actually imagined Jesus as a female Indian spirit from her childhood, a strong blond-haired woman who was called Wincondicah. There were others, too, who had broken from Protestant traditions and discovered a God larger than the one they'd been instructed to accept as children in Sunday-school classes.

As Joan talked, I had a feeling she might reveal too much of herself. She was in such a free-spirited mood, and there we were, and I knew from working with her in the healing group that it was her style to be a fairly determined psychic adventurer. Very soon, she paused, took off her sandals, and tucked her feet up under her. At that very moment I lost control of the interview.

"Now I am going to tell you a secret," she said.

No, please, I thought.

"I am a mystic," she said. "I don't use the word often because people don't understand what it is and it sounds presumptuous, so I usually say I have 'mystical tendencies.' But basically I feel a very deep spiritual connection with God in the form, sometimes, of a very, very bright light, and a love that is so powerful and so deeply connected to the earth that I can't even describe it to you."

This light, she went on, was nothing new or particular to her. She had seen it for the first time five years ago at a Lenten retreat in the meeting-house. Quite unexpectedly, while she and Van and Lucille and Ted Alford, the baseball coach, were meditating quietly, a brilliant light had filled her head. The light had flooded her body with an overwhelming sense of love, and she had felt blessed or consecrated by a presence that she had not been able to shake or forget, no matter how hard she tried.

"I wasn't falling-down crazed," she said. "But I had no context for this kind of experience, no framework. I remember the meditation ended and we all left the church like nothing had happened. I tried to tell Owen about it later, but the words sounded so hollow that I decided not to tell anyone about it ever again. And I didn't for a long time."

Over the years, Joan had continued to experience this light, sometimes in meditation, sometimes in dreams. Looking for an explanation and not knowing where else to turn, she went to a Jungian analyst, who helped her examine the psychological and religious connections. That, she said, was when she came to believe she had a gift, and about that time, the next transformation began.

"I know, for example, in an almost palpable way, that we are all connected through time and space and that our bodies are, in fact, of the earth, and that our past—including all genetic knowledge and chemistry—is only reformulated in our present. It's not something I know in my mind; it's something I experience in my life. A unity of being. And I feel very responsible for honoring it by moving out into the world and being present and connected through this light."

Thus began the interest in Central America, in healing and therapeutic massage. Underneath all that had happened for twenty years was the same subtle and profound connection.

"I want to show you something," she whispered.

God help me. What did she have in mind? Were there ghosts in the attic? Were we going to levitate? Would I have to put away my notepad?

"It's upstairs," she said.

"What's upstairs?" I said.

"A few years ago Owen started complaining because I brought a lot of photographs and pictures of women and children into the house, and I finally got mad at him and decided I needed a place of my own. Come on. I want you to see it. Not many people know it's here."

We went back through the kitchen and a formal dining room, passing paintings as dreamy as Degas's, fresh flowers in porcelain vases, a bowl of stones and a basket of onions, into the foyer and up a wide staircase.

"I got fed up!" she said, passing down a corridor past bedrooms and closets that smelled of fresh linens and boxes of clean rags. "I finally came up here and went into that storage closet where Owen kept his files and I kept my ironing board, and I threw it all away. Everything! Out of here!"

We stopped at a closed white door at the end of the hall. Her black eyes sparkled.

"This is a real risk," she said, taking a breath. "Promise me you'll respect this. It's a holy place."

She cracked the door to a tiny white room that looked like nothing more than a closet with a window, and as the opening widened, I saw icons—curled photographs of women, old toys from childhood, hand-written poems, candles, a single shelf of books, a strange clay figure, ribbons and bells and a thin woolen prayer rug.

"This is Jesus," she said, pointing to a photograph of a black man on a street in Soweto. She lit a small votive candle and pointed to a slender silver bar that rested between posts on the windowsill. "And that," she said, "is the universal tone."

I was standing in a primitive sanctuary.

"Come in! Here, let me get the door."

Joan tapped the bar with a mallet and the instrument hummed a long, high tremolo. As she turned to shut the door, I felt a trickle of sweat run down my arm. I had begun to hyperventilate.

"This is where you pray?" I asked.

"I'm not joking." She sounded a little defensive.

"No, I mean—"

A blue flag flipped up outside the window frame, and I caught a glimpse of planet Earth flying from a wooden mast. On the wall, I noticed a color satellite photograph of the planet. Then a spider's web. A naked woman, pregnant, cupped in a rope hammock. A box of matches. A butterfly trapped in plastic. And in the corner—my mind busily escaping into details—I turned again to the strange clay figure. A stump? No, a tree, of some sort. I looked again. It was a penis wrapped like a vine; and gonads; gnarly feetlike roots; and from the trunk, an old woman, arms sprung up like branches, with pendulous breasts drooping to the ground.

A long pause. We were both still.

"The tree of life," she whispered, picking it up off the floor. She held the lively figure out to me and turned it over slowly in her hands, revealing more sinewy parts.

"It's . . ." I didn't know what to say. "It looks ancient."

"Yes," she said. "It is very old. It's formed out of the psyche."

She set it down and reached for a smooth block of wood. Someone had carved the word GRATITUDE in tall, neat letters.

"My father made this for me," she said.

The word stumped me. Gratitude?

She told me more about her family, about her first experiences in church, and about a special place near her home where, as a child, she would go to daydream or build forts and hide treasures in a tree trunk— her first private sanctuary where she could talk to God. "From out of our childhoods," she said, "Owen and I are realizing more and more about the meaning of this word *gratitude*. We are learning."

She set the wooden block back on the shelf.

"You see, we have lived a privileged existence," she said.

I remembered talking to Owen once and he had said much the same thing. ("Hey, I'm fine," he had told me one night while we served dinner at the homeless shelter. "We're doing well. We're healthy. Even our dogs are fine. But maybe we're just so high diddle diddle that it's not so fine, and maybe we just need to take more risks and break out into the needs of the real world.")

Increasingly, Joan said, they both felt a strong desire to move beyond the secure confines of home and church and family. Their children were grown now and she was spending her spare time training for a new mission in Nicaragua. Owen, she said, was currently building homes for poor people in Zaire—he'd taken off two weeks from his job to make the trip—and over the last two years he'd spent every Monday night serving meals to homeless men in John Gregory-Davis's shelter.

"I've seen him there with the men," I said. "He's one of the best volunteers they've got."

"And I'm telling you I can't believe it, how the experience of gratitude has become so central in our lives. Especially since the trip to South Africa. Once you've had that experience—it's a deep experience of compassion—you must move out. If gifts have been given to us, we must move out in compassion."

I stood there not knowing what to say again. It was as if I'd never heard the words *gratitude* and *compassion*. Certainly, I'd never heard them used like that.

"Would you show me what you do here?" I asked suddenly.

"Well, I don't know if I should," she stammered.

"Sorry. I don't mean to be so abrupt. It's probably not fair to ask."

"Well, perhaps," she said, looking around. "Okay. As long as you understand, this is not a performance."

"Sure," I said. But I could see now I was expected to participate.

"Okay," Joan said. She knelt on the prayer rug and invited me to do likewise. She dropped her hands in her lap and inhaled a draught of air. I assumed the sitting position. She tapped the silver chime.

"It's a circular pattern," she said. "I draw a breath that begins in 'My Sister'—deep in my heart—through fields of yellow flowers just breaking ground . . ."

She closed her eyes and exhaled slowly, then drew a great breath again.

" 'Father' . . . up to the sun, the Father, arms of warmth and radiance . . ."

A slow exhale. Her voice deepened.

" 'Brother' . . . coming down in rain, water for the earth, who is . . ."

Exhale. Breathe.

" 'Mother' . . . the deep ground . . . through the shoulders, down the chest, into the belly, thighs and legs and feet and . . ."

Another breath.

"Sister . . . Father . . . Brother . . . Mother . . ."

We meditated for a while, but I could never catch my breath. As soon as I could do so without being rude, I broke out of the prayer.

"That's very nice," I said, "but maybe you could tell me about this mission you mentioned. Did you say you want to go to Nicaragua?"

Eventually that afternoon, Joan did tell me more than I wanted to know. I could understand her interest in working in Nicaragua better than I could her vivid encounters with the world of spirits. Listening to her, I suddenly felt swamped in a strange vocabulary, an oceanic place of unfamiliar images and emotions. Her stories led to depths where I did not feel safe—a woman's place, far beyond me—where she eventually explained more about the need for spiritual disciplines (hospitality, gratitude, compassion, faith, listening, waiting, and confession), which, as she said, "open the heart to what's holy and create a safe place for transformations to occur."

Safe place? I asked. You want to travel alone in Nicaragua, but you also want a safe place?

"You must have a safe place," she said, "wherever you go."

For example, she said, over the last six months she had been overtaken by periods of intense dreams, staggering episodes that were leading her through some kind of transition to missionary work. I remembered her dream of the crashing bus from the spiritual group, and of the baby who was herself.

Exactly the kind, she said.

Sometimes she wondered how she could have forged out of a simple, regular routine of prayer, meditation, and dance a discipline that fed a fire of nightmares and visions.

"But I am ready to go on to the next adventure," she said, "in gratitude and with a desire to serve."

I did not understand. Where was her husband in all of this?

Owen was changing, too, she said, but she didn't stop to explain. And then she went on to describe a horse from one of her dreams who had literally galloped into their backyard this morning.

I was out of my element. It sounded frightening. For the first time, I had a sense of an inner journey that required substantial risk and pain—not mine yet, thank God—and as soon as I could, I found a polite way to end the questioning, to exit the room, and leave.

"It is frightening," she had said at one point. Her words were meant to be comforting. "But I think we are all mystics, really. Light and love are inside all of us. It's there, Gary." She had touched her heart and looked me calmly in the eye. "It's right there."

Allison Denslow stood at the window by the stove clearing off dirty pots and dishes while we waited for the water to boil. Beyond the bushes outside I saw little boys dancing around a frail swing set. A jumble of scuffed rubber balls, tattered bikes, and bright, hard plastic toys were strewn across the yard.

Another day, another side of town. Allison's little blue Cape, off a narrow strip of patched side street, sat on a tight lot in the middle of a long row of other modest homes. Although we were a good distance from the church, in an integrated neighborhood close to the Hartford line, I knew we were in a First Church enclave. Another deacon, Tony Gillette, lived right across the street. Bill and Sue Warner-Prouty were just around the corner.

"You like yours black," she said, reaching for the coffee.

"Good guess," I said.

"No guess. I'm a deacon. And it's regular, not decaf, right?"

Within five minutes of greeting me at the door, Allison had poured two powerful cups of coffee and cleared off a couple of chairs in the living room so we could talk. Her two sons, three and nine, kept running through the small house, up the stairs and, slamming the screen door, out into the yard. She ignored the havoc and cheerfully batted back every question I could toss out.

"As I was saying," she said, offering me a box of cookies, "Joan and I are not close friends. Never have been and probably never will be. Nothing against her, but I'm just not into a lot of this women's spirituality stuff. It's not my issue, for one thing. And besides, I don't believe women have a corner on spirituality and being in touch with their feelings and all that. Women can be very catty . . ."

She paused and peered, smiling at me, over her large, luminous eyeglasses.

"I'm not kidding," she said. "Very catty. And when it gets down to being in touch with your feelings, women can also be extremely competitive, so I just don't bother."

"Spiritual competition?"

"Oh, I keep forgetting. You're still new at this."

"No, that's why I'm here."

"Well, look, I'm no expert, either. I just choose not to compete. Anyway, I know who I am, and I'm very human. Very human. Believe me, there are some days I go to church and I can't believe that, hey, I'm a deacon serving Communion. Know what I mean? But I'm learning all the time. I'm still trying to find myself as a child of God. . . . You want some more coffee?"

"Child of God"? I had not heard that phrase in years.

There was nothing prim or pious about Allison. Perhaps that was why I was drawn to her. Besides the fact that she attended the new healing service and served as a deacon, she did not seem like a regular church-goer. She was not only raising her children in a multireligious household (her husband, Karl, was Buddhist), but her connections with the old counterculture continued to be a guiding influence. Not that she wore beads and political buttons, as Joan did. On the contrary, at forty Allison had an angelic moon face, a neat Dutch cut, and wore stylish but conservative clothes that allowed her to blend in with the hordes of neoconservative career women who dominated the Hartford region. She was unpretentious and intelligent. Except for the "Child of God" re-mark, I'd never heard her utter a word of New Age or religious lingo—a certain sign of integrity, I thought.

"Child of God?" I said.

Allison explained: Having celebrated with half a million other chil-dren of God on Yasgur's farm near Woodstock, New York, in 1969, her earliest and most vital experience with spiritual matters expanded tradi-tional definition. It was not just church that nourished her spiritually. Although she had grown up "in the fishbowl," attending regular church services as the daughter of a headmaster at an exclusive New England prep school, life in the church had not left her blessed with the wisdom of the ages. Sometimes, she said, the church was the last place she'd look for wisdom, not to mention justice or compassion.

"You're first-generation Woodstock then," I said.

"What?"

"I was just thinking of the trip to England. Some people are *May-flower* Families and some are *Mary and John* Families."

"And I'm first-generation Woodstock?"

"Your religious birthplace. It makes me wonder why a person like you bothers to go to church," I said, slipping in my stock query.

She took a sip of coffee and sat back in her chair. I was hoping she didn't think I was totally goofy.

"You know," she said, "now that is a good question."

Just two nights before, I had asked for healing from her and our group. I thought of the moment now while she talked. I had sat in the chair at the center of a circle of chairs at the front of the church. Having participated in a half dozen healing services already, I had been surprised to hear myself make a stumbling petition. My faulty syntax ("My wife, Jan and me, well . . .") didn't deter a dozen of them from coming to my side, setting their soft hands on my back and legs and shoulders. The warm comfort of their bodies and hands seemed to find the right spot. Ted's firm grasp, Joan's gentle touch on my head, Allison's pat on the back—the feeling was one of being held, a kind of light suspension at the center of a circle.

Whether I simply needed to demonstrate an affinity for the group in order to be trusted, or whether my conversation with Joan the previous week had given me the nudge necessary to try this, I could not say at the time. But when Ted took my hands, held them firmly as he prayed, for a moment, I put away doubt. He prayed only that God help me and Jan realize that we had a lot of love between us and that our love could be sustaining at a time like this. That was all he said. No promises, no deals. No magic wand. Just one honest prayer, and then a tremendous change in temperature came when Joan set her hand on my head. An icy cold, an almost ambient disturbance suddenly flushed through my body and went away.

Allison looked at me and started to laugh.

"Hey, wait a minute, you're first-generation Woodstock, too!" she said. "With that beard and long hair, and all that bullshit about Robert Bly . . . You tell me why you're here."

"Hard to say," I muttered.

"It is pretty weird, isn't it?" she said.

"Weird" did not begin to describe it.

"Okay," she said. "I'll start. Actually, I'm a lot more physically in tune with it than verbally. I guess that only makes sense, though, given what we went through with Jason."

Jason was her oldest son.

"Until he got sick I couldn't have told you why I went to church. A lot of people come to church and they don't really even know why they're there. It's not like an intentional community where you've got to have a reason to go. I think deep down most people are yearning for some kind of connection, and they know they need more meaning in their lives, so they show up at church 'for their kids' or 'to make a few friends.' But they're really coming out of a lot of confusion until something happens that makes things perfectly clear."

"I don't understand," I said.

"Hey, that's my story. That was me for the last few years."

Two years ago, Allison had taken her oldest son, then five, to the doctor for a checkup. The doctor said Jason seemed fine except for a number of faint red dots on his neck and thighs. He took a closer look at the markings and advised Allison to make an appointment immediately at the University of Connecticut Health Center. The dots looked like petechiae, a classic sign of leukemia.

"He didn't say leukemia right away," she said. "He just said, this could be serious and we need to get some blood work and bone-marrow tests right away. Then he had the nurse do a platelet count and we went home. Later that day he called and said Jason's count was very low, and projecting ahead, he said he was afraid the signs were clear and we'd better move fast.

"Karl went crazy. He went to the medical library and got all these books, and everything he read said, well, if it wasn't leukemia, it could still be fatal. Jason's platelets were dangerously low. The reality was, How were we going to deal with this? We thought maybe he only had a few months to live. So I got an appointment for the next week and I began to sink. I mean, I sank really, really low."

Strangely enough, it had been Holy Week, not usually a time of much consequence for her. But when she realized she had made the doctor's appointment for Maundy Thursday, the juxtaposition of dates made her think about their difficulties as a spiritual issue.

"I don't think I even knew what I believed in," she said. "I knew there must be a God, but it wasn't something I ever felt strongly about. I certainly didn't know I could turn to God. And here we were a day away from Palm Sunday! Anyway, the phone calls went out. Karl was calling people and I was calling people. At one point I was talking with my father and we were both crying on the phone and he said, 'I really think you need to turn to God.' Well, you'd expect that from your father, right? Not my dad. He never said things like that. He never talked like that at home, and I really did not even know what he meant. I wasn't at a point to know how you access a spiritual power. And, frankly, I didn't want help just for Jason. I remember thinking that maybe God could heal him, but the real question was how was I going to get through this? Because I just didn't have the strength. I wasn't looking for magic. I was looking for a way to cope."

By Saturday afternoon, Allison and her husband were at home fighting. They took the phone off the hook and argued about who was at fault. They even questioned God's role in their predicament.

On Sunday morning Allison woke up early and decided she must ask someone for help. It was a very rational process, as she explained it. "I just got out of bed and knew I had to ask people to pray for us. You can't imagine how hard it was. Given my background—I was raised a very proper Congregationalist—I have such a strong reaction to fundamentalists and born-again types. But I had to ask for help. It's really very funny, in retrospect. I'd never in my life called a minister for help. I'll call a friend, but never my minister."

Fortunately, Bill Warner-Prouty was at church early that morning, following an overnight vigil with the Confirmation class. He took Allison's tearful call, and promised that he would ask people to pray for her family. It was as simple as that. She called her father and he said he would ask people to pray for them in his church, and then she phoned her brother and he said he would ask for prayers at his church, too. Finally, Allison went back to her bedroom, shut the door, and cried to God to help her. "Just like that. One very honest prayer: 'I need help!' And it was like as soon as I did that, things started to change."

By Sunday evening, Allison said, she felt a sense of peace and an unusual physical presence around her, as if she and her family were being carried.

She paused and looked at me skeptically.

"It was the most powerful spiritual experience of my life, but it sounds pretty stupid to talk about, doesn't it?"

The next morning, the results of Jason's blood tests and bone-marrow analysis showed no signs of leukemia. Doctors were relieved, though puzzled, and they prescribed prednisone to boost the platelets.

"We never did figure out what was wrong with him," Allison said, "and I wasn't about to say people's prayers or my prayers did anything to help. After a while, I just thought, 'Maybe I'm making too much of this.' But, believe me, I kept praying for a whole year and we kept watching the platelets climb, and when that year was over, I kept on praying like I never had before—honest, deep prayers. It was the beginning of faith for me, and before long, Jason was fine."

"So, that's what started your interest in healing," I said, skipping ahead.

"Actually, no. There's more," she said cautiously. "I was more of a skeptic than that. Are you sure you want to hear this?"

We poured ourselves more coffee and she went on.

As it turned out, a year later, her younger son, David, came down with Tourette's syndrome, a neurological disorder that caused uncontrollable blinking and facial tics. Again, doctors were stymied about how to treat the illness, and both Allison and Karl found themselves at odds over what to do. Karl finally called an ashram in New York, the American headquarters for his religious sect, and then he decided to take David to India for healing.

At first, Allison questioned the need for the trip, and she went to church one Sunday to ask for prayers at the eight-o'clock service. Interestingly, this time people did not respond to her.

"I should have known that people at First Church couldn't deal with anything too emotional," she said. "Actually, I didn't mean to cry during the service, but hey, it happened. I remember there were two deacons right there beside me at the Communion table, and when the tears started to come, they physically turned away from me. Andy McCarthy was one of them, which was a real surprise. You know, most people really can't handle stuff like this at all, but I thought Andy, of all people . . . Anyway, the church has its disappointments. Believe me, that was not the last time I've seen people act like that. It's not all positive and supportive, like you'd think."

A few weeks later, Karl and their youngest son flew to India and took a room in a monastery. People from all over the world had come for healing during the festival season of October and November, and each night large crowds waited outdoors at the monastery to dip a piece of sandalwood in oil, say a short prayer for healing, and toss it into a sacred fire. The night after David stood by the fire praying, his tics abated, and within a few weeks of coming home, the little boy appeared healed entirely.

"It's been more than a year now since they went to India," Allison said, "and the symptoms are pretty much gone."

"You're saying this time he was healed by praying and throwing a piece of wood in the fire?"

"I don't pretend to understand it," she said. "But, hey, you don't have to understand everything."

We talked through the afternoon, and eventually she, like Joan, began to tell me more than I wanted—or had a right—to know. Even though I sat there with pen in hand taking notes, at one point, I finally set it aside and listened.

Why would she tell me about her dreams and failures? About depression, addictions, and debts? I cannot imagine. But, like Joan's revelations, her stories soon left me with such fear that I knew, without being warned, that she and I had entered into a kind of compact. I never would have trusted a journalist like that.

I have promised not to tell. No one will ever know. I only wonder if this is the way it has been—undetected—for centuries. Trust me, I said. An oath as strong as a blood-written code.

One night, a few weeks after meeting with Allison and Joan, I had a dream: I boarded a bus filled with dirty orphans, ratty, untended toddlers bouncing on seats, leaning out windows. I found a place for myself by picking up a baby boy and setting him on my knee. I could feel everything in this child—jiggling bones and the pulse of blood, soft muscles and crackling plates of gristle. Everything good and bad in him awakened in my hands, in his scent, his pinch. I could see that he, too, was dirty and uncared-for. His wobbling head turned up and, amid the babbling on the bus, I heard his soft, high-pitched voice: "You can rely on strength from God."

I awoke and told Jan. The web at First Church had not only grown larger, but bonds had taken hold.

"Jan," I said, "can you imagine we're part of someone's regular morning prayers?"

She didn't seem to hear. Not until much later would I learn that she was having her own dreams, sharing her own stories with others. At the moment I was caught up in the thought of my new friends who had not only told me about how they prayed, but named the people on their prayer lists. There was no doubt in my mind now that we were beginning to enter into each other's lives.

The orderly, awful, clannish services of a thoroughly domesticated religion, and the oceanic experience of a mysterious God, which had been my only awareness of the infinite Spirit, finally fell away. Here was something new and wholly accessible. If certain modes of music, architecture, sermons, and prayers—the unhurried and predictable movements of the Protestant ritual—could not always reach people like me, the novelty of being in the prayers of friends and having them in mine was the hook that made a firm connection.

Imagine that, after so many years. Imagine me, suddenly having dreams about God and babies. Imagine me, praying again, like a child who knows that ways will always open.

CHAPTER THIRTEEN

Bill wheeled his white Ford slowly down the curved road that laced the graveyard. He usually made the most roundabout pass to Palisado Avenue, tires skirting monuments inscribed with familiar surnames. Squinting against the glare of the sun, he shifted his vision to view headstones scattered across acres of shaggy lawn.

With the riverbank as the southern boundary on his left, he drove west sixty yards down the esplanade. The narrow blacktop took him on Andy McCarthy's museum tour of American history—a teeming *Our Town* of ghostly inhabitants—until he reached a wire fence where the road hooked around at the back of the cemetery offering a look into the woods. He turned at the treeline. The car slowed and stopped at the grave of Ephraim Huit, John Warham's associate.

> *Heere Lyeth Ephraim Hvit, sometimes Teacher to ye chvrch of Windsor,*
>   *who dyed September 4th, 1644.*
> *Who When hee Lived Wee drew ovr vital Breath,*
> *Who When hee Dyed his dying was ovr death,*
> *Who was ye Stay of State, ye Chvrches Staff,*
> *Alas the times Forbid an EPITAPH*

Bill leaned out and peered down at the slab of red sandstone, the oldest original monument in the state. On the other side of the same slab, he could see the larger, more eloquent inscription for Huit's boss, the venerable John Warham.

"They couldn't wait to fill the other side with Warham's legacy," Bill said. "I always thought that was really interesting."

We passed the grave and I immediately knew what he meant. Bill recalled, cynically, as no one else would, that Ephraim Huit had been the great educator in the first Windsor congregation, but his legacy was overshadowed for all time by that of his boss.

Usually, the quiet of the old cemetery left Bill with a settled feeling, a sense of history, of order and succession, that became more apparent as he turned his steering wheel at the fence and came trundling back along the brow of the riverbank toward the rear of the church. The simple architecture, long and boxlike, rose clapboard upon clapboard like a lovely vision out of the turf, the symbol of an elegant idea or a virtue that belonged in his keeping. Some days, when a Haydn symphony or a Charles Ives string quartet played over his radio as he turned east, he imagined the great palladian window returned to the back wall above the pulpit where it had been torn out one hundred years ago and covered over with clapboards. He could see light spilling into the chancel as he preached, a fantasy that made him laugh as he recognized his own need for eminence and salvation. As a boy, he had always wanted to be a bishop standing in the light. Now, he wondered: Now what was he?

For ten years, Bill had done the duties Van preferred to avoid: men's breakfasts on Sundays, confirmation classes, youth retreats, and junior deacon forums. He planned the Christmas pageant. He answered his share of calls from townspeople who did not belong to a church but needed a minister to perform weddings or baptize babies or bury the dead. Of all the so-called "anonymous" groups that used the town's churches, those people who had no church affiliation were by far the largest and most demanding of a minister's time.

After ten years in the shadow of Van Parker, Bill entered his fifteenth year of ministry with as much biblical knowledge and experience as most senior ministers in the state. But he still lacked the forum of his own congregation in which to practice his ideas. A graduate of Yale University and Yale Divinity School, he was distinctly more logocentric and more formally trained than Van, and yet he continued to spend at least half his hours with children, wry and skeptical teenagers whom he guided from seventh grade into Confirmation classes during the ninth grade, and finally into inner-city tutoring programs or deaconate responsibilities in the twelfth.

Of course, Bill had middle management's typical complaints. He thought Van usurped his ideas; he was well compensated but received less credit than he deserved; he knew an ambitious side to his boss that no one else had to consider.

For all of Van's rhetoric about the church as an organism, living cell, or body of Christ, Bill believed Van practiced a "nickels and noses" ministry. Van's insistence on spending generous sums of money for Christian outreach, his interest in Central American politics and the South African antiapartheid movement, seemed only a kind of radical chic to Bill, an easy way for Van to avoid leadership on local issues, where a minister's persuasion could have far more effect. Van's interest in liberation theology and his conversion in Nicaragua struck Bill—in his most cynical moments—as "the late-twentieth-century equivalent of the old men who fought in the Spanish Civil War," an exercise in revolutionary romanticism, hyped morality and machismo. The overemphasis on the capital-funds drive and the advent of John Gregory-Davis as an outreach minister and JoAnne Taylor as spiritual director bothered Bill as well. In combination, they certainly heightened Van's reputation in the conference, but because they had appeared on the scene with such a lack of planning or foresight, they had thrown the church into a kind of crisis mode. Besides, the church did not need a larger staff or a bigger budget, Bill thought. It needed better management.

In any case, at the very time when Bill should have been gaining ground as a spiritual leader, he found it increasingly difficult to claim his own area of authority beyond childhood education. At age forty-five, Bill was mired in a career crisis.

"It's like there's this one big branch that keeps reaching out whenever

I try something new and I'm lost in the shadow again," Bill told me as we headed up Palisado Avenue.

"If it happened once in a while, that would be understandable. But time after time, I get sick of it. Van works a lot by intuition, which would be okay if he didn't keep intuiting himself into my areas. Sometimes I think it's because he just can't stand to give up control, and sometimes I think he just sees himself as this Good Shepherd and we're supposed to be his staff—literally, there to direct the congregation as he decides.

"Maybe it's not fair to say. He's got a big heart and he works from the heart, but I also think he would do well to think more about the organization as a whole. Things happen much too haphazardly around here, lurching this way and that, according to the 'spiritual leadings' of Van Parker."

Ministers in the area thought of Bill and Van as the one example where a senior minister and an associate formed a perfect coupling, the rare, steady confluence of the intellectual and the caregiver. Regarded as collegial, warm, and mutually nurturing, in truth, the two men could not have been more different or less communicative.

Unlike Van, Bill lived in the world of ideas. He knew a lot about Barth, Bultmann, Bonhoeffer, and the Niebuhrs. He could riff on topics like Americans' inability to assimilate history, the dialectic of Christianity across epochs, the Christian framework of the American commonwealth, and the contemporary absence of a functional cosmology. Depending on the group, he would groove using shibboleths from the academy, the church, or the streetcorner. Slinging academic lingo as fast as Dizzy Gillespie could triple-tongue be-bop, Bill not only translated Greek on the spot, but if necessary, he could "rap" (in the grand, old-fashioned Sunday-school tradition) about the feminization of poverty, Byzantine iconography, cartography, and liberalism's slow turn from a politics of civil rights to a politics of the common good. Dissecting ordinary church words for their Latinate derivatives, he could wail for a long while on the difference, say, between *utopia* and *arcadia,* or trace connections between *paradise* and the *millennium.* He was especially good during controversies. Turn him on at a meeting and he would both confuse and silence people by raising the standard of rhetoric several notches above the norm. He could diffuse tempers in a flash. Bill's bombast smothered arguments like dirt on fire.

Privately, some people said that ten years at Yale had left Bill with more to think about than was necessary for a minister. In some ways, it was true. His intellect separated him from the larger membership. As a natural educator in a time and place where religious education was no longer valued, Bill's job at First Church was to stand aside until needed, like a reference book. A portion of his mind was always ready to open to pages of one thick volume or another, highlighting opaque Old Testament stories and myths and academic texts that most people no longer really knew how to use anymore.

I always detected a hint of prejudice in people's attitudes about him. He might have looked like an incongruously rosy-cheeked rabbinical student, but add the mind of a social critic, a cutting wit, and the values of a pacifist, and you had a man who would never rise above suspicion in a mainline church. He, not Van, was the more likely source of the congregation's reputation for radical involvement. Bill's influence on Van was, I imagined, so subtle that Van never knew that over the years, he had leaned further and further in the direction of his associate— politically and theologically. At some level, however, I suspected that the congregation knew, and that some resented Bill's small but effective power over his boss.

Surrounded at work in an office filled with lexicons, handbooks, icons, maps, and concordances, Bill fed from deep shelves as he wrote sermons and worked on community projects. On those few occasions when Van relinquished the pulpit, or during the summer while Van was in Vermont, Bill deliberately avoided the saccharine narratives of Jesus' life, which was his boss's stock in trade, and instead delivered taut epistles based on the ancient stories of the Old Testament, lessons straight from the lectionary, lectures ripe with the bittersweet fruit of the ambiguous history of world religions and Judeo-Christian myths. On the weeks when he wasn't in the pulpit, Bill could be seen at town council meetings, lobbying the school board, or running forums on multiculturalism and school desegregation.

Actually, most churches did not want a senior minister like Bill. Within the state conference, when someone wondered why the Reverend W.-P. had not moved on to a senior position at a Connecticut church, it was said that Bill simply did not "cut the right figure"—a nice way of saying "Too radical . . . too heady . . . too willing not to kiss up to the right people."

Even so, the dilemma of what to do with Bill Warner-Prouty was only painful for Bill. Most people would not have understood that the ministry left him hard-pressed to exercise his mind. Even Van did not recognize how desperate the situation had become.

"Bill is a font of creative energy," Van would say. Case closed.

Bill was quiet as we pulled into the entrance of Delmere Woods apartments. He spotted Cloris Newberry leaning on an aluminum cane outside the front doors to the lobby.

"Your car is ready, madam," he teased.

The epitome of decorum at the age of eighty-seven, Cloris was busy fidgeting with her white gloves. She was dressed in a handsome, bright blue floral cotton dress and wore the brassy filigree of antique gold jewelry around her neck and wrists. In the sunshine, she looked like a Victorian doll. Since her husband's collapse during the spring, Bill said, Cloris had experienced a rapid deterioration of her hips and, in the absence of any immediate family help, he had offered to drive her back and forth to a surgeon in Hartford. As usual, Cloris was dressed as if the doctor's appointment would culminate in an afternoon tea or a spontaneous dinner-party invitation.

"Oh Bill," she said, as he grabbed her arm at the curb, "I'm so sorry to inconvenience you."

The usual apologies.

"Cloris—"

"But, as you know, the Rotary Club bus tends to dally—"

"That's okay, Cloris."

"—and my son, David, is working in New York for a while and can only meet me as his schedule dictates."

"So how's Ed?" Bill asked. As he took her by the hand he could smell the dry fragrance of bath powder.

Bill offered the cushion of his body for support and balance. He could forget about the church in Cloris's company. On the highway to Hartford, she could talk about anything—the weather, her husband's illness, the recent conflicts in the Middle East, the economic status of Eastern Europe. Her refined vocabulary and sweet Southern accent admitted him into the old camp of privilege. For a while he could relax in good conversation and exercise his mind, for a change.

As they sped down the interstate, she remarked on the "rigorous perspicacity" of his recent letters to the editor about the tax debate in town. She noted his "admirable proclivity" to be involved with childhood education outside the church. He inquired about her opinions on the tax issue, which, as it turned out, were tantalizingly sharp and insightful. By the time they arrived at Hartford Hospital, Bill was feeling better and Cloris was again apologizing, for "rattling on so loquaciously."

"Since Ed's illness, my mind has been like a squirrel in a cage," she said.

Bill took her to the hospital entrance and walked with her past the noisy crowds in the lobby to the elevators. On the third floor, he walked her down the hallway to the doctor's office, where she asked to be left alone to wait for the call.

People like Cloris were precious to Bill. Once the linchpin of church life, they faced the trials of old age with dignity. An illness was a matter of extreme privacy. At a certain age, they tended to hide their complaints from ministers with a fierceness and deference to authority that could only be interpreted as a proud desire not to be remembered in a state of decline. In a way, many of them entered the final years with an unblinking eye toward the funeral service itself, and this, to be honest, seemed perfectly honorable and fitting. Wasn't there something admirable about spending an entire morning just getting dressed for a doctor's appointment, especially given the likely prognosis?

The admiration was mutual. Something about Bill's honesty and interests attracted these old women. They shared a particular kind of wisdom that made them his spiritual comrades during their final years together.

As we walked downstairs to wait in the coffee shop, Bill remembered that Cloris had taken a chair by the receptionist, and from her purse, extracted a book by Thomas L. Friedman, *From Beirut to Jerusalem*, the latest Book-of-the-Month Club selection on the Middle East.

"She's obviously preparing to follow news of the war within the context of history," he said. "I'll have to make a note to ask her about that later."

After Cloris's appointment, Bill and I went to his house to pick up his son, Abe. Because Bill's wife, Sue, was taking a pottery class at Wesleyan, Bill and Abe did the men's club at the Kimberly Hall nursing home on Thursdays.

Their house was in shambles when we arrived. The front doorknob was missing, a few broken branches dangled from trees, screens were off the windows, bricks were missing from the front steps, a swarm of wasps buzzed us as we ducked into the living room.

"Standard condition for the associate's dwelling," Bill said, apologetically. He didn't have to say anything. By now, I knew as well as anyone that the Prudential Board had ignored Sue's calls to make repairs for months.

"Put away the artillery," Bill said, hearing a shuffling down the upstairs hallway. Suddenly leaping down the steps, a black, bearlike figure howled and giggled. Abe stuck a water pistol under my chin and aimed a silver-tipped dart at his Dad. He snickered and then stuck the weapons in his pockets.

"Who's the a-hole?" Abe smirked, motioning at me.

"Yo! Home-boy!" Bill said. "Break off. Chill. He's cool."

At twelve, Abe was the ultimate PK. He slung a mop of blond hair out of his eyes and tried to stare me down. As tall as his father and almost as husky, he looked like a budding Hell's Angel, an archetypal preacher's kid.

"Know anything about armored tanks?" Abe asked.

I did not.

"What about handguns?"

Apparently, I failed his test. On the ride to the nursing home, Abe sat in back musing over a book of military aircraft.

A band of docile men, curled in wheelchairs, trailing IV tubes, circled up around a table in the second-floor library when we arrived. A number of them were First Church members who had become permanent residents. Bill called them the "Men's Club," served as their formal convener, and came in once a week to read aloud from the *Hartford Courant*. While Abe drew sketches of jet fighters on strafing missions, Bill talked.

"Fellas, I've got an article here from today's *Courant* called 'Reinventing the Wheelchair,'" Bill said.

Not a single head turned. The old men fumbled with hot cups of coffee and fingered jelly doughnuts.

"Did they ever figure out how to put a whiskey bottle on the back?" asked an unshaven Irishman named Thomas, who sat stiffly in an electric wheelchair at the end of the table. Thomas did not have legs.

"That's a good question, Thomas," Bill said. "Let's find out." Bill thrashed the paper into a square to read.

"There's one thing common to them all," Thomas interrupted. "They're not built for comfort. Ask Leo!" Leo's head was slumped into his chest. "Go ahead! Ask any of 'em! You can't sit in these damn things. They won't even roll on the rugs."

"Okay," said Bill. "That's a good idea. Let's hear it. The story says a company in Windsor has reinvented the wheelchair. What do you men think about that? How would you describe your wheelchairs?"

Leo's chin lifted. "Sittin' on rocks!"

To Bill's right, 102-year-old Pierre Georgioli squirmed in his chair. Pierre, a retired Italian barber from Windsor Locks, usually had an opinion.

"They alwaya wanta dis," Pierre said, rubbing his fingers together. "I coo gimme anotha seata butta for wha? So they put anotha million buck inna the pocket? Psssh! Forget!"

"I tipped over in mine," Leo said, pushing up with his withered arms until he keened sharply toward the floor.

Bill shouted, "Don't!"

Abe looked up from his drawings.

Leo dropped back into his seat and frowned.

"You wouldn't believe how many people around here dump out of these things," Thomas said. "They fall out and break their hips. Then they lie in bed and get bedsores. Bladder goes bad."

"Medicare won't pay anything for us in here," Leo said. "They won't even pay for Tom's batteries. Will they, Tom?"

"I could go into a lot of stuff about this place," Thomas said. "These goddam things won't even roll on the carpets. And don't try to push it across the grass!"

"They paid some girls to take us outside once," Leo said.

"Butta everythinga beena cut," Pierre said. "No more go outside. Naah!"

"They tried to get volunteers, but it flopped," Thomas said.

"Whatta ya gonna doot?" Pierre said.

Bill started to read again when a nurse rolled in another one.

"Well, hello, Paul," Bill said.

"Morning, Reverend. Gentlemen! I have an announcement!" the man said. A line of bruises coursed his arms, and his legs convulsed as he talked. "Just one thing and I'll hold my peace!"

"Spit it out then, goddammit!" Thomas snarled.

"I've enjoyed being with you fellas the past four years, but on Sunday I'm leaving and I'm not coming back. My grandson's driving down to take me to Maine. Like going from hell to heaven. He said to me, 'Grandpa, now you can sit under the tree. You can sit in the sunshine.' " Paul's legs were strapped to his wheelchair and his feet were loaded down with weights. His skin was the color of a dead tree trunk. Apparently, everyone knew he was just imagining. They heard the same story every week. "Oh, I love that Maine lobster!" he said.

Thomas brashly struck a match and lit a cigarette. The rest of the men were silent.

"Well, they'll miss you, Paul," Bill said.

"Miss him?" Thomas sniffed.

"You know, that son of a bitch used to be a Hartford cop?" Leo said. "I think you must've given me a hundred tickets!"

The nurse handed Paul a cup of coffee. He clutched it with trembling hands.

"Didn't you drive a motorcycle back then, Paul?" Bill asked.

"What do you mean, 'back then'?" Thomas snapped. "You make it sound like it was two hundred years ago."

"Whatta he say?" Pierre whispered to Leo.

"I can't hear nothing," Leo said.

Paul talked about his days as a police officer, then Bill asked, "Do you want me to finish this article?"

Another man in a wheelchair next to Thomas—Frank Pease, a forty-year member of First Church—lifted his eyes.

"The first car I had was a 1919 Ford. Paid twenty dollars for it," Frank said.

"Oh! I tella wonnaful story," Pierre said. "I have a frienda fromma the olda country. A shoemake. He paya ten dollahs a month rent. I givea haircutta, shoeshine-ah, a shave-ah . . . one dollah! One dollah! Sure! A frienda mine he saya, 'Yes, we have no bananas!' "

"I'm interested in that," grumbled the man across the table from Pierre, as he looked up for the first time.

"Sure!" Pierre said. "Yes, we have no bananas!"

"I used to pay ten dollars a month for rent," said Frank Pease.

"I remember when we paid seven dollars a ton for coal," said another one, vigorously tapping the table.

"I remember you," another said suddenly pointing at Paul. "You were that son of a bitch who gave me a ticket in Hartford!"

Bill set the article aside. All around the table, the men stirred into a fleeting wakefulness. Bill conducted them to life, asking questions, pouring more hot coffee, and telling his own stories about local politics. A careless undercurrent of anger and foggy memories enlivened the conversation for the rest of the hour. The men exhausted every subject, plumbing opinions about Paul's law enforcement career, Frank Sinatra, and World War II, while Bill mediated and Abe squeezed jelly out of the remaining pastries. At the end of the hour, Bill called for adjournment and the men groaned.

"He thinka he own the place!" Pierre groused.

Bill and Abe helped roll them out of the library into the hallway, and then returned to catch up with Pierre. As was custom, Bill asked to hear Pierre's story about the barber's arrival as a young immigrant at Ellis Island, and then patiently passed the time taking stock of the many photographs of the old barber and his family, and the Sons of Italy icons displayed around his room.

After another half hour, Bill and Abe walked out into the hallway past rooms groaning with amnesiacs and the chronically ill. They had interrupted the grim routines, the daily rounds of eating, sleeping, and being taken to the toilet, without uttering a single prayer or verse of scripture.

The tinny reverberation of televisions rose in their wake, but then they heard a strong, lilting voice.

"Keeponyasmilin!" Pierre said, tapping his cane in the doorway as Bill and Abe stepped into the elevator.

"What did he say?" Abe whispered.

But Bill knew Pierre wasn't *saying* anything. He was shuffling his feet in a little dance. He was singing down the corridors.

Keeponyasmilin', Keeponyasmilin', anna dahole worla smile wid you . . .

A few weeks later, near the first of August, at the monthly Monday-night healing service, Bill stood in Van's place to serve Communion. Although we invited him many times to attend the services, he often ducked out, sometimes with a smart-alecky comment. "Sorry," he'd said once. "I guess, it'll just have to be open sores this week." But with Van gone, he was obligated to sit with us.

Priscilla thought she had finally found the proper lighting for the service—one candle, lights on in the nave and chancel, off in the balcony. She set a chair in the middle of our circle. Joan had danced alone before we arrived, to prepare the way. Allison brought fresh flowers from her garden. Andy handed out bulletins.

After Communion, Bill stood up and awkwardly made his way to the center of the circle. He sat down, dropped his head, and his shoulders slumped forward. He picked at his thumb for a moment.

"I ... My name is Bill," he stammered. "And I guess I'm here tonight because I need healing. For my ... Well, my ..."

No one ever knew what Bill was thinking. It was always a surprise. Even as he sat in the healing chair, as he paused and stumbled toward a request for intercession, we had no idea what he might say. Would he speak of the symbiosis of American religion with American culture, or say that he considered Protestantism a black comedy blending innocence and guile? Would he quote from his old professors and mentors from Yale? He seemed deep in thought.

I was probably the only one there who knew what had been on his mind lately. I wondered for a moment whether Bill might finally say publicly what he hesitated even to tell me. Could he find fault with the man so many people considered saintly? Would he say to them, as he had said to me, that Van, who preached and encouraged risk-taking, had always played a safe game as a minister? That Van had been living for twenty-two years in a handsome, historic, two-story colonial home in a prosperous Connecticut suburb where he could send his children to a refined New England prep school and retire with a good pension without ever having entered into the political or social life of any group beyond the perimeters of his parish? Would Bill say that Van was an elitist and that despite his rhetoric, he would never jeopardize his privileged status by risking the protected cloister of his community? Where, for instance, was Van when community leaders tackled the issue of desegregation in Windsor's public schools? At church, raising money. Where was Van when a rabid antitax group packed the annual town meeting in May and forced a vote to cut four million dollars from the public schools? He was at church, raising money. How many times did Van go to John Gregory-Davis's homeless shelter to serve meals and visit the homeless? Bill went, but where was Van?

Of course not. Bill could never voice such complaints among parishioners. Even though the questions kept rising more frequently, especially at mealtime with his wife or with me, and in his most private thoughts as he escaped the office to make pastoral rounds, he could not say a word to the healing group.

Instead, he sat silently with his hands dangling between his knees. Bill was on the verge of leaving the ministry, I was virtually certain of that. What could he say?

"I need direction in my life," he said. He set his elbows on his knees and cupped his head in his palms.

Priscilla, Joan, Allison, and I went to his side and placed our hands on his back and arms, head and feet, and prayed. When the prayers were done, he want back to his place in the circle next to the silver Communion tray. Others went to the chair for healing, and when it was done, Bill took the nod from Priscilla, and led us singing "Alleluia, Alleluia."

After the service, Bill disappeared quickly, and no one said a word about his petition. Not then, not later. Not in our meetings, not in our services, not even informally. For some reason, it must have been too mysterious and too profound to approach a Holy Man in need.

A few days later, I received an open invitation to join Bill and Sue and Abe on Monday nights for supper. Between the end of his day and the beginning of our evening round of church meetings, we finally had a chance to discuss his crisis in detail.

Over time, I would be with him when his mother died. I would be with him when he interviewed for a part-time job teaching social studies at the high school. I joined him for piano lessons and on pastoral calls. Soon we were sharing ideas about music and history as we made the rounds in the afternoons. At night I would bring over a bottle of wine or a six-pack of beer, and while we caroused over supper Abe would entertain us with an animal he had dissected, crude jokes, or an ever-expanding cache of toy armaments. Sue made pieces of pottery for me and Jan, and talked to me about Abe's adoption.

We were becoming good friends. In the grief over Bill's effort to decide how and when to leave the ministry, we drew closer in a once-a-week celebration around the dinner table. They were not really serious people, at all. They were not any different from you or me. They were only a family that had been a bit excluded and, in the fishbowl of church life, lonelier than anyone had a right to be.

CHAPTER FOURTEEN

Most years, Van went to Vermont with at least one project in mind. While many of his colleagues spent the summer at beachside resorts or mountain cottages writing sermons like master plots for the church year, he preferred the solitude of physical labor. He put in a well, installed a new septic system, rigged up an oil heater. Out of obligation, he launched a routine of prayer and Bible study and took a hopeless stab at hermeneutics. He reread Galatians and the Gospels that way, and one summer he studied the book of Proverbs. But the language and ideas of the Old Testament usually struck him as so hilarious that he could not maintain the effort. Before he knew it, he would be outside again, cutting brush or weeding. When he returned to Windsor in September, he would come back with a slew of home repair anecdotes but not a single theological insight.

"No insights?" I asked one day.

"Right on," he said.

I drove to Saint Johnsbury, Vermont, expecting more than that. At the time I still did not think I was unreasonable to have expectations of Holy Men. They do lead examined lived, I thought, don't they?

But I also had not come to be August's insufferable guest. My plan over two days was to spend as many hours as possible talking with Van on a screened porch overlooking his nephew's Christmas tree farm. Predictably, we would spend our time drinking iced tea and watching clouds settle over the White Mountains. I would only ask as many questions as I could without disturbing his solitude. All I wanted was the story of his spiritual journey and an explanation for whatever it was that always made him seem like such a curious mixture of saint and Protestant program director.

"You know, I used to discipline myself up here," he said, apologetically, when I arrived. "Back in my youth, I thought there were certain standards for a spiritual person—like getting up at five a.m. to pray. But I've found out that I'm really at my best, spiritually, when I'm doing something else. Like walking the dog. Or working in the yard. I used to feel guilty about it, but I'm learning not to."

It was soon plain that only one subject occupied his mind. No small business owner could have fretted more about the hardware store or restaurant or office supply shop back home than Van did about the church during vacation. And I'll be damned, I thought, if they don't all worry about the same thing: the persistent lack of capital and the need for new customers.

He could talk forever, and all day he did talk about the politics of church. He was worried about the congregation's reaction to a new doxology. He wondered how he would handle the opponents to the capital-funds campaign. He could not get his mind off the problems of his outreach committee, targeted by the treasurer for budget cuts.

Van jostled his glass, took a swig of tea. He dug his toes through the grass and his whole body relaxed.

"I feel like a kid!" he said. "I'm becoming a kid again!"

He laughed out loud, uncrossed his legs, and leaned out from his chair like a lion lunging at the bars of its cage.

"This is my second childhood!" he shouted.

After six hours, I gave up. Every time I asked a philosophical question or dug into his past, Van clasped a hand behind his head, swung one leg over the other, and talked about autumn's stewardship drive.

"Why don't we go for a walk and start again in the morning," I said, at the end of the first day.

He jumped up and grabbed his hat before I could get another word out of my mouth. "Great idea!" he crooned. "I love to walk!"

That night I bedded down in the family's guest room above the porch. I slept hard, and awoke before daylight startled by a dream.

I am in a store shopping for a computer advertised as "The Great New Technology for Everyman." A chunk-toothed salesman shows me the machine, which looks like a word processor except it lacks a keyboard. In fact, I see as he demonstrates, the casing is only a cover and as he slides it off like a vinyl rolltop, the "computer" inside is really a model of the First Church parsonage. Through the windows and doors, I can see, from Van's kitchen to his living room, banks of cleanly mounted integrated circuits, layers of silicon substrates, thin interconnections between electronic boards and microprocessors laced with stringy flywires. Mixed among advanced electronics, I see old-fashioned vacuum tubes and parts made from plain magnetic coils. Buttons on a dimly lit control panel at the center of the living room animate dozens of devices inside the meetinghouse, which sits on a pedestal at the other end of the showroom like a child's dollhouse. The salesman reaches inside, taps the keys. Suddenly lights and candles flash. Stops and pedals on the organ pop. Doors swing open and toy parishioners come to life inside the church. Perfectly synchronized, controlled from the minister's living room, the computer church functions with all the precision of a robotics factory.

The scene switches. The salesman disappears and I am alone in the dark showroom. I hit a switch on the illuminated panel and a large CRT screen appears. On the display I see a thin electric cord snaking through a weedy hayfield outside the farmhouse where we are sleeping and then an intense strobe of light shoots out of the ground like a laser. I watch the lighted cord uncoil from the ground like a vacuum hose and wind its way up onto the porch. Playing with the controls, I direct the light up the stairs and then I am looking down at Van from the perspective of the ceiling. There he is,

asleep in bed, just out of my reach, floating under the shadows of my dan-
gling light, quiet and content, stirring only occasionally in the comfort and
privacy of his own dreams.

I started awake. Maybe I had been wrong. Maybe you could only
press so far into the mystery of another person before finding yourself
again. And yet the dream was as much an enigma to me as the minister.
I sat up in bed feeling strangely embarrassed and puzzled.

By the middle of the second day, Van had avoided addressing almost every event of his life that I thought would have marked an important
point in his spiritual journey. I came away with only the sketchiest details. For instance, I knew that his father had been a prominent minister
in Hartford for twenty-nine years. But Van did not seem to remember
much about the old man except that he had a stubborn streak, proved
to be a little too radical for his congregation, and never spent quite
enough time with the family. Three of his older siblings had died trag-
ically, of cancer or by drowning at an early age, and his mother, whom
he was closest to, died while he was still in seminary. He was not able to
assess the effect of their deaths.

He did not remember the church itself as particularly important to
him as a child. "Church," he said, "was a place I went to because I was
expected to go. I remember sitting with my mother and, of course, I remember Christmas and Easter services, but I don't think I ever appreciated the deeper meaning of the place."

Neither could he recall an early conversion or a call to the ministry.
Instead, he remembered going to Middlebury College with hopes of becoming a journalist, and failing try-outs at the college newspaper. Giving up on journalism, he chose the ministry, a decision he made sound
as simple as buying a new suit. His previous parishes, in southern Ohio,
Michigan, and Massachusetts, sounded like little more than way stations
in his career. The fact that his older brother, Scudder, had started out as
a journalist and, in midcareer, switched to the ministry, did not seem to
carry much weight with him. Nor was he able to see his own ambitions
reflected in the life of his oldest daughter, a successful journalist who, at

twenty-eight, had just quit her job in Washington and was planning to take a spiritual pilgrimage through Central America. He said Lucille had been studying for a graduate degree in Christian education when they met more than thirty years ago in Cincinnati at a Bible-study seminar. But that seemed only circumstantial. I knew, independently, that his younger daughter, Beth, had just dropped out of Yale Divinity School and was making an effort to break the family pattern by leaving the ministry. But he sidestepped questions about Beth. I could see I made him uncomfortable by asking.

"My whole ministry has been like coming home," he said that morning after breakfast.

More pieties, I thought.

"Coming home to my parents and my family and reaffirming something in my background."

I would have given up by lunchtime, but I was beginning to feel desperate. Changing course, I asked again about his theological influences. After all, he had studied at Yale Divinity School during the latter years of Richard Niebuhr's tenure. I started with an easy question about neo-orthodoxy.

But Van was bored by theologians. At Yale, he said simply, Richard Niebuhr never struck him as a particularly happy person. "And I'm not a highly intellectual person. In fact, I'm grateful for the education I got at Yale, but as you know, seminary education is not geared toward the practicalities of parish life."

I was getting nowhere. Maybe sensing my frustration, Van offered to show me around the farm again before lunch.

"Sure, why not?" I said.

We started out through a freshly cut hayfield behind the house and then he lit out like a hunting dog on scent.

My father was a good pastor. One story had it that if a parishioner fell down the stairs, my father would be at the bottom to pick them up. He was equally devoted to his family, and wanted to make sure, as much as he could, that all his kids "swam."

Dad had strong opinions on a number of subjects and was never hesitant to express them. He thought FDR was a disaster, admired people who could work with their hands and make or fix things. On some issues he was very progressive, always with a pragmatic twist. He would sometimes, almost cavalierly, dismiss the opinions of experts and say that he believed the average Vermont farmer had more common sense than some of the professors who had written with such erudition on any particular subject. One day, around the time I was ordained, he sent me a book written by one of these "learned men" about how to run a parish. It had charts and diagrams and wheels within wheels. Looked pretty impressive to me. But my father's terse comment was: "Van, this may be of passing interest, but not of much value." So much for expert advice!

Dad was extremely generous in other ways, too. He was always reaching for his wallet, sending his grown children checks for this or that. It wasn't that he had all that much to give but he did it because giving was such a part of his nature.

For recreation, he liked to work in the woods at our family cottage in Sunapee and, with my mother, to take walks. He kept on walking and taking care of grounds projects when he retired to Peacham, Vermont. One time I was with him when he was digging weeds around the Peacham property and he said it reminded him of pastoral work. I can see that now.

Dad was also a great letter-writer and once he retired he developed the custom of sending out family letters to all us kids. I remember him writing to us after he developed pancreatic cancer. His only comment was, "The lazy bug has exploded in my gizzard." Now there was a diagnosis for you!

He used to say he wanted to "wear out" rather than "rust out." And I think he really did wear out, despite the cancer. He was a tall, husky man, six feet three, two hundred pounds, and always seemed pretty healthy even toward the end when he kept losing weight and started looking pretty gaunt. The last time I saw him, when he finally couldn't get out of bed, he still seemed peaceful to me. He had an almost detached manner by then, like he'd finished a job and was ready to let go. He was seventy-four when he died, and I was thirty-three.

Mother died relatively young, about the time I turned twenty-three. She was sixty-two.

People always said it was hard to take a good picture of my mother because she had such an expressive face. I didn't agree about her not taking a good picture, but I have to say, when she smiled, it always seemed to light up the place. Like Dad, she was not a pious person, in the narrow sense of the word. She did not quite fit the stereotype of a minister's wife, either. She was vital and strong. The word I associate with her is life. She was full of life.

I was starting my second year at Yale Divinity School when she went through her last illness. There were some great professors at Yale, but the best teaching I got came in those weekly visits home to see her. In our final conversation before she lapsed into a coma, she gave me a blessing. She said, "Van, I believe you have a healing personality," and then she wished me well. But that was just one of her blessings. Through her life, she blessed a whole lot of people.

All in all, I was brought up in a loving home. Mother. Father. Two older brothers. An older sister. I have many happy memories of them during my childhood: Christmas celebrations, interesting visitors from all over the place, family times on Lake Sunapee, Grandma Ordway, who was a true liberal in the best sense of the word. She was from the Scudder line of the family, a member of a missionary clan that logged, collectively, more than eleven hundred years of service in India. She lived more than four years of her life there.

Beyond the family, I always had one or two buddies, but not a great circle of friends. I never really felt like I was in the middle of things. Maybe that's the reason I have such a feeling for the underdog and the outsider today.

For whatever reasons, as a boy, I was overconscientious. If there wasn't anything to worry about, I'd invent something. I labored under the burden of perfectionism. I went to prep school as a day student since there was no tuition for day students in those days, and did fairly well academically. Managed to grab the bottom rung on the tennis team. Make a good grade or two, but graduated without distinction. And never made many friends.

College at Middlebury meant more than you'd think by looking at the surface of things. By then, I desperately wanted friends and somehow managed to find a few. But I was still awkward with people because of this self-

righteous quality. I still tended to distance myself from making real connections. It was partly insecurity, but I can see now that it was also a sign of a spiritual crisis: scrupulous to a fault, falsely proud, always wanting to handle things myself. For a while, I even pictured myself in the parable of the Prodigal Son. Was I the elder brother who lived in the house, but was also out of touch with the spirit of the household? Or was I the Prodigal, a quiet stubborn cuss who had gone off spiritually into another world? (For gosh sake, I couldn't have been the Prodigal! I didn't even drink beer!) Or maybe I was a combination of the two? In any case, the whole world looked gray to me then. Grayness and isolation.

By the fall of my sophomore year, I felt downright alienated. Both my brothers and my father had been successful in college, and I was not living up to expectations. Honestly, I was so self-conscious and tied up in myself, I couldn't see a way out, Paradoxically, it was the beginning of a spiritual reawakening, though I did not know that yet. Church and religion still seemed unimportant, though I had attended a couple of churches in town—one Baptist, another Congregational—and made friends with a few "Christian" types in my dorm. So many of the "Christians" I knew seemed ultra-pious and they distanced themselves from the world in a way I didn't like. Actually, in some ways I was just like them, but didn't know it—except for all that praying and talking about Jesus every other minute.

One day during the winter that year, when these inner struggles seemed almost overwhelming, I prayed. It wasn't any great shakes of a prayer. Just something like this: "God, I haven't done very well. I've gotten myself into a dead end and can't find a way out. Please turn me around so my life can take on a new direction so I can keep growing and changing." That was about it, praying alone in my dormitory room.

At first my parents didn't seem to know what to make of me. One weekend I came home and got really mad at my father. I told him to butt out of my life. I don't think he had any idea of what I was talking about, but he didn't say anything. He just looked terribly confused and hurt. The next day was Sunday and when he got up to preach he forgot almost the entire sermon. I wondered what the congregation thought: "Reverend Parker sure seemed to be in a hurry today!" But my mother, always the loving media-

tor, got us back together that afternoon, and there were tears both in his eyes and mine when we finally started to talk.

Sometime after that I made a commitment to the ministry. As painful and as hopeful as it was, my little prayer had been heard. So I can't say that I really made a decision to become a minister. I really don't know how it came about. Really. All I know is it seemed right. My father had said, "Van, don't do it unless you can't possibly stay out of it." So there was no burst of light, no radiant cloud. It was just very simple.

I have realized slowly over my life that a person is not meant to live in isolation. When I was young I always acted like I didn't need people when really I needed people the way a bird needs air and a fish needs water and a goat needs rocky, open spaces. I was never a "good" indivi-dual even when I wanted to be. The real Van Parker, I discovered, was a pretty irreverent cuss, silly sometimes, and free-spirited. The real Van Parker was someone who has always wanted to hug people and to be hugged in return.

So that was the beginning of my homecoming. Waking up and seeing stuff that was there all along. It has never been an intellectual event, al-though I guess I could reflect on it that way. It's just the "new birth" about which Jesus spoke, and, as time has gone on, I have sensed the image of God coming among us in Jesus, an image that has become more powerful for me and deepened over time. It's like being found, I think. Found by my father's deep, if sometimes overprotective love, by my mother's sensitivity and hu-mor, by all the people who have mysteriously been there along the way. Found by Lucille, who has been my wonderful companion, and by my chil-dren, Susan, Beth, and Doug, who seem to have forgiven me if I was some-times too preoccupied or too busy for them when they were children. Sometimes I feel like I've been found, too, by people in the church. It even happens with strangers and new friends like you.

T. S. Eliot compared conversion to coming home, didn't he? The Prodigal Son "came home to himself." The Gerasenes Demoniac was "restored to his rightful mind." The meaning of homecoming is profound. It means no longer distancing yourself from people. It has nothing to do with "being holy." It's being with God in Christ who was and remains with us. It's *standing with others in the face of a mystery. It's coming upon Christ and the cross.*

When we finished our walk, down by the lake where Van's brother was buried, and up to the road to where his in-laws and nephews kept an orchard, Van had told me none of these things. That would come, in written form, another year, long after I had left the church. Instead, we talked about the weather, and as we came within sight of the farmhouse, he seemed to be in a hurry again, wanting to finish our tour of the property and talking eagerly about weeding his garden and taking Daisy out for a run before lunch.

I packed my bag and drove back to Connecticut that afternoon more perplexed and annoyed with him than ever.

CHAPTER FIFTEEN

In Van's absence, the associates took turns in the pulpit. On Sunday, Bill accused the apostle Paul of anti-Semitism. Another Sunday, John Gregory-Davis pointed out Christ's sexist attack on the Canaanite woman in Matthew 15. John read the verse—one of those elliptical Christlike sentences ("It is not fair to take the children's food and throw it to dogs")—and made this feminist interpretation: "Jesus plainly referred to the woman as a dog. A female dog. To be perfectly clear, he called her a *bitch*."

It was just getting interesting when Van phoned from Vermont and said he was coming home early. I don't know if he had heard about his colleagues' goings-on, but he did ask Peggy to type up a "generic service" for the second Sunday in August.

"I'm getting old," he told her. "I'll probably be out of there in five years, so what the heck."

About the time neighboring farmers started spreading manure on their fields, Van gathered his belongings, said good-bye to Lucille, and drove back to town alone. If there was something suspicious about a minister returning from vacation a full week early, Van did not betray it, and if anyone asked, Peggy just said he had trouble staying in Vermont once conflicts in the Middle East heated up. "He can't get C-SPAN up there," she'd say, an explanation that seemed to satisfy most inquiries.

On his first day back, Van immediately faced the usual duties: two funerals, a call for a baptism, a list of wedding dates, an unnatural number of evening committee meetings. The faint odor of raw sewage rose like fog from a storm drain in the rear parking lot. Paul Price, the church treasurer, was making appearances in the office with increasing regularity, copying reports and planning a confrontation with the Outreach Board. But before Van could deal with anything else, he had to take care of Pauline Dunhurst.

"Peggy!" Van shouted from his office. "I've got Pauline Dunhurst scheduled this afternoon and I can't find her instructions."

"She wanted you to read 'No Man Is an Island,' " Peggy said.

"Do you have a book of poetry out there?"

"Give me a break!" she said. Pauline, who had avoided church services for ten years, usually sent at least one or two annual directives for the format of her funeral. Now that she was dead and was about to be buried, on what she had once imagined as perhaps one of the most glorious days of her life, Van could not find the file.

"When's the committal, Van?"

"Never mind, I'll stop by the library on the way to the cemetery," he mumbled.

Peggy shrugged her shoulders. "Van, Billie Duncan also came by this morning and her mother's mad at you."

"Good gosh! I've got to get over to that nursing home."

"She's been there for three months and you've only been by to see her once."

"Do you know how that goes? 'No man is an island . . .' "

"She's going home this week, Van."

He rummaged through his filing cabinet and came across an old false tooth in an envelope marked TOOTH. But nothing from Pauline.

"Peggy!" he called again.

"Now what?"

"I found my old tooth."

"What?"

"Did I leave Pauline's file on your desk?"

"Van Gorder, why do you have a tooth in an envelope? You do not act like a person who's been on vacation for five weeks."

"Four."

"Right."

"But, you know, I've decided I like coming home a little earlier in August."

"I had a vacation once!" she shouted.

"It's easier not rushing into these things," Van said.

Besides two funeral services that afternoon—the second was for a local teenage boy run over by a dump truck—Van also had a young couple coming by for premarriage counseling at five, and a strategy session with the capital-funds committee at seven. There wasn't time to meet and interview the family of the teenager, so he reached for the trusted boilerplate. He turned to the standard funeral service from the United Church of Christ *Book of Worship,* a spineless, well-worn volume held together now by a web of silver gaffer's tape.

"This thing's got everything from soup to nuts," he said, jotting down verses from Deuteronomy, Psalms, and Romans. He glanced at his watch. Maybe he could make it to the funeral a few minutes early and at least introduce himself to the boy's parents.

"Hey, Peggy!"

"Hey what?"

"Have you seen Ralph Stoot? I've got to talk to Ralph Stoot!"

Ralph was the outreach chairman.

"Working at home today," she said. "Don't you remember?"

But Van was already on the phone with the Carmen Brothers Funeral Home. Then he called the shut-ins, and then his meals and transportation committee chairman to schedule dinners for the shut-ins. By ten thirty, he had hired the funeral home's drip-fingered organist to substitute for Fran, who was still on vacation, and written a thank-you note to ninety-nine-year-old Mary Bartlett who, as usual, had picked and arranged a bouquet of fresh flowers from her garden for a parishioner's new baby. He dialed Janet Filer and told her he was referring her as a fund-raiser to other ministers in the area, and then he scheduled an appointment for her to meet the new director of stewardship for the state conference.

"We're up to seven hundred ten thousand dollars," Van told the stewardship director, "and almost every campaign Janet's done went over the top. The last one she did, the minister died in the middle of the campaign and they still made out very well!"

Van turned his calendar to the week ahead. He looked at the thin outline for his generic service, and ran a finger along the lip of his shelf scanning for inclusive-language hymnals and prayer books.

"Don't forget we need to plug in a baptismal service for Molly Morgan on Sunday," Peggy called. She could hear him humming to himself. A moment later, Van poked his head around the corner.

"Here," he said, tossing a plastic rose and a flimsy paper certificate on her desk. "Take these with my compliments."

"Van," she said, making a face, "do you care that I do not like these baptism certificates? They're cheap! And *plastic* roses! We should be ashamed!" She thumped the red petals and clucked her tongue.

"No, I do not care. But I can't tell you how much I appreciate your sharing that." He quickly slipped back to his desk.

"Plastic flowers are tacky!" she shouted.

"Hey, but the right price," he replied.

Down the hall, Bill listened. Van and Peggy had prattled on all morning. He waited until it was quiet. Then he went to Van's door.

"Bill!"

"Back from Vermont?" Bill said.

"And how was your trip to D.C.?" Van leaned over his desk, flipping through a stack of new members' cards. "That's a nice tan, by the way."

Bill's face looked as red and freckled as a homegrown tomato.

"We did the Air and Space Museum, the Space and Air Museum, the Museum of Air and Space, and then we did the FBI," Bill said. "And then we went back to the Air and Space Museum."

"No art galleries?"

"When you take a twelve-year-old to Washington you do airplanes and lethal weapons. It's gotten so you can't just take Abe somewhere anymore. You deploy him."

"He's a good boy," Van said.

A moment of discomfort settled between them when pleasantries ended. Van could never bring himself to ask about Bill's career plans, and Bill did not want to tell Van he had applied for a job in the Windsor schools. Unless they had a scheduling problem, the men rarely had much to say to each other.

"Look," Van said, "I wonder if you could handle a couple of weddings. A woman with some Christian church in Hartford called this morning and asked if we'd do hers. It kind of irritated me."

"Her church doesn't have a minister?"

"They've got a minister. She just said her church wasn't big enough, and they need to use our meetinghouse. Then she said she wanted her own 'Christian' minister, and I thought—"

"Let me guess: 'We're not Christian enough for her!' "

"Maybe I'll just jack up the price. That'll shake her off."

Bill glanced at his calendar. He had four weddings next week.

"So how's the fund drive?"

"Seven ten," Van said. Bill could tell he was back on top of it. "But you know David Hirano came up to me after the service yesterday and said he wanted a pledge card. And Henry Holcombe was standing right there and he said, 'David, people tell us this isn't the best time to raise money in the church.' And David said, 'There's never a good time to raise money. Give me one of those cards!' Now that's my kind of guy!"

Bill closed his calendar and folded his arms. Hirano was the new conference minister—Connecticut's equivalent of a Congregationalist bishop. Somehow in the spring, with everything else, Van had managed to hook him as the newest member of the church. Bill shut his eyes, briefly.

"I'm learning a lot about people this year," Van was saying. "We've got folks pleading poverty when they're making a hundred thousand a year! Well, what in the world are they spending their money on? How much do they spend eating out? How much do they spend on gifts? How much do they give to the church? The happiest people I know aren't grasping. We've got people who give one hundred or two hundred dollars a year to the church and they're complaining about every little thing. And I'm thinking, 'My God! Where have you been all these years?' "

"About the wedding . . . ," Bill said.

"What wedding?" Van said.

"That—'Christian' couple."

"Oh, never mind, I'll take care of them."

Bill let the calendar drop to his side. He turned, expressionless, and went back to his office. Sitting down at his desk, he reached out for his lectionary. The chatter started up again between offices.

"Hey, Peggy!

"Hey what?"

"Have you seen my shut-in list?"

In a week's time, Van would have the office running like a train station again, and Bill would have to find ways to spend more time at home planning lessons, or out on pastoral calls.

"Hey, Peggy! You haven't heard from Ann Daltry, have you?"

Before she could answer Van dialed another number.

"Hello, Ida? Van Parker. I'm just calling to see how Bernie's doing. . . . He died? . . . In New Hampshire. . . . It's being handled up there? . . . He was always the kind of guy who wanted to go quickly . . ."

Bill turned to the page with readings for the second Sunday in August, but he could not concentrate. A capital-funds drive, he thought, was probably a minister's toughest test. It was where you finally had to prove yourself in bed. With just a few years left in his ministry, Van must have expected the drive to reflect well on his years of good service. If it went well, they might name the new addition to the meetinghouse after him. If it failed, he would probably get only a small room in his honor.

Bill knew people who were already talking about the fund drive as Van's failure. Rumors and gossip ran like mysterious tidal currents around the church, and from what he had heard, Van's opponents were still lining up a bloc for the fall. It was like the Frisian Islands or the coastal waters of Cape Cod. In a few weeks, Bill imagined he'd see ship-wrecks scattered all around the churchyard.

"Ida Gallop called, Van," Peggy shouted.

"I know, I just talked to her."

"And you got another call from that woman in California who wants you to do her wedding."

"Oh gosh!" Van said.

"What's the matter now?"

"Why in God's name did I buy all these books?"

Bill shook his head, reached over to the radio on his windowsill, and turned up the volume.

"All these books are about the Middle Ages! Why in God's name, that was a miserable time!"

A church is a primitive institution, Bill thought. Especially under Van Parker's direction. It was far more primitive than he had ever wanted to believe.

"Van, what is this opening hymn?" Peggy asked, holding up his outline for Sunday's service.

"Something unique and original."

She looked at him curiously.

" 'Joy to the world'?"

"Joy to the world, the Lord has come . . . ,' " he sang.

"I know how it goes!"

"We can afford to be a little more freewheeling in the summer."

"It's a Christmas hymn, Van."

"But isn't it thrilling, though? It's inspirational!"

A few minutes later, Van found Pauline's notes tucked away in a file marked *Nicaragua*. He rifled a stack of inclusive-language hymnals looking for new words to the old chestnut "Dear Lord and Father of Mankind." He typed his notes and pushed away from his desk.

"Hey, Bill!" he shouted.

"Bill," he said again. Van walked into the main office and set his notes on Peggy's desk. He slipped through the supply office to the associate's door and peeked in. "Bill?"

He went into the hallway and looked around.

"Peggy," he said, "have you seen Bill?"

"Are you kidding?" she sighed. "He never tells me anything."

The concerto still played lightly from the windowsill, but the associate was gone. If, as it was said, the church was Van and Van was the church, after vacation, there was hardly room anymore for two.

By the second week in August, Van had reestablished a steady rhythm to his work. He was in constant motion. Reach for a book, refer to the Bible, type notes. Make a phone call, visit a parishioner, attend a meeting. Reach for a book, read, type, call, visit . . .

He practiced the strict rootwork of religion. Connection. Binding. Drawing together. Anything he had left behind in the spring, whether it was a ritual pattern or what he insisted on calling an "organic process," he quickly regained in August, binding the congregation back together with compulsive call-making and rounds to people's homes.

On the third Sunday in August, the annual bus trip to Tanglewood signaled the end of summer. After Van's ten-o'clock Communion meditation, he and Lucille joined more than eighty parishioners on two big buses racing north on Interstate 91 toward Lenox, Massachusetts. For years they had marked the annual renewal of Christian fellowship and *savoir vivre* by watching Leonard Bernstein conduct the Boston Symphony Orchestra at an outdoor concert. If there was an irony between the morning homily, when Van urged the congregation to be "countercultural," and the afternoon with Bernstein at Tanglewood, it passed unnoticed.

We give thanks, O God, because in your own free gift of love you have reached out to us. You have refreshed us at your table, touched our deepest needs, and called us to a life shared in memory and hope. Send us out with courage and joy in the name of Jesus Christ, that we too may become bread and peace for one another.

Bread and peace, indeed! Cold plates of mandarin orange jello, cinnamon rolls, sliced luncheon meats, and coleslaw jostled in luggage compartments as they crossed the state line. Macaroni with peas, macaroni with tuna, macaroni with potatoes, and honey-baked beans rattled in a dozen deep picnic baskets. As buses lined up near the Hawthorne Cottage in Lenox and wove their way through a crowded parking lot crammed with tailgaters, the passengers on the First Church bus passed brownies and chocolate chip cookies, fruit cups and steaming cups of coffee up and down the aisles. Old Helen Trump and Martha Locke reached under their seats to extract sloshing thermoses filled with zinfandel and sparkling wine for a pre-concert toast.

In Tanglewood's old concert shed, they watched from the fortieth row as ashen-faced Bernstein led the orchestra through Benjamin Britten's "Four Sea Interludes" and Beethoven's Seventh Symphony. The First Church crowd, peering through binoculars, saw the portly, silver-haired maestro repeatedly stumble back into the thin railing of his conductor's stand, cough into a silky red handkerchief, and drop his arms from exhaustion while orchestra members played on in alarm. Broken by emphysema and old age, Bernstein finally conducted by nodding his head in rhythm and shifting his weight from one limp leg to the other like a dancing doll on a string.

Marvelous! they said afterward. How nice! Charming! As if they had not just witnessed an imminent death, and every one of us would return the next year and the next, taking the same good seats and savoring the church ladies' favorite finger foods. No matter that within a week Bernstein announced his retirement, and shortly thereafter, he was dead. On that day, the First Church crowd sipped from Communion cups and bathed in immortal music. Pianissimo, vivace, crescendo, forte, sforzando, presto, allegro con brio!

Let us open our hearts to the presence of God's spirit, and pray that we may be true disciples of Jesus the Christ. Amen.

Late that afternoon, Van went back to the office to make a few calls and ended the day poring over news of Iraqi terrorism in the day's editions of *The New York Times* and *The Boston Globe*. The next morning, he would pull up to his typewriter stand and tap out ideas for a Rally Day sermon. Soon the children would be back at school, and for the thirty-second September in a row, Van Parker would find a new way to reassure his members that they could become the products of their own invention and, by God's grace, the church would be born again.

But the next morning, he could think of nothing original to say, and after making a few phone calls, he went home for lunch, leaving a single page of typing paper scrolled halfway out of the carriage with only the words *New New New New New* hammered boldly across the top.

New, New, New

And no one puts new wine into old wineskins; otherwise the new wine will burst the skins and will be spilled, and the skins will be destroyed. But new wine must be put into fresh wineskins. And no one after drinking old wine desires new wine, but says, "The old is good."

—Luke 5:37–39

CHAPTER SIXTEEN

On the third Monday of August, when the capital-funds committee met for the last time before Rally Day, Janet and Van went so quickly through the lists they left everybody speechless. Tony Gillette, the professional engineer who monitored receipts and disbursements, could barely keep up as they sped through the figures. Bill Warner-Prouty and Henry Holcombe sat like mute spectators at a chess tournament. Together, Janet and Van seemed to know more about people's private affairs than most accountants—or ministers—had a right to know. They haggled as if battling for the soul of the church.

Janet snapped rubber bands off two stacks of pledge cards and cut rapidly through the first deck. She called out names of people who had declined to pledge.

Cindy Brainard.

"Teaching in New York now, but home on weekends," Van said.

Dave Buckingham.

"Dave Buckingham!" Van said. "I called him last week and he said he'd give stock. The market broke three thousand today, so get him quick!"

Katherine Cooper.

"She lives in Florida, but her husband built the parish house. Definitely worth a call," Van said.

John Dunham.

"That guy should give!" Van said, and snapped up the card.

Chancey Dwyer.

"She's put out with Van because we didn't sing the right hymns at her husband's funeral," Bill said.

"She always says that," Van said. "I'll call her."

Marsha Elliot.

"Every time I phone she's got a bad cold," Janet said.

"Maybe we should call to ask how her cold is," Henry said.

"We could sic Joan Rockwell on her," Tony said. "They're both in the choir."

"Hold it a minute," Van said. "She's waiting to settle her father's estate. We can't keep asking, 'How's probate, Martha?' "

"Marsha," Bill corrected.

"Good point, Van," Janet said.

"Who else you got?" Van asked.

Phil Kreski.

"*Doctor* Phil Kreski." Janet rolled her eyes. " 'Deep pocket.' "

"I don't think so," Van said. "He's just started coming to the eight o'clock service. We'll scare him off if we hand him a pledge card right away . . ."

"Okay, then, who's next? Newton?"

"Don't bother with Bud. He'll cough it up when he's good and ready."

They handed out cards like parole officers giving assignments. The room grew so quiet that even the soft click of crickets and the rattle of car engines from the parking lot sounded intrusive.

"Now," Van said, "can we assume if we bring these in, we'll get the seven hundred fifty thousand?"

"Nope," Janet said.

"Then what about all these estates and insurance policies people keep telling us will come up?" Van asked.

"Hold on, we're not done," Janet said, breaking out a second deck. "Geoffrey Pennyweight."

They kept up the brisk pace, whittling away at members with the same blunt take. In Janet's company, Van made no effort to smooth things over with his standard homilies and screeds. They knew each other too well by now.

Jim and Cathy Palmer.

"They won't give until they see the new addition to the choir room," Van said.

Cathy Remington.

"She told me she was 'estranged from the church,' " Janet said.

"She's been a stranger to the church for as long as I can remember," Van said. "Keep going."

Martin Royce.

"I've been to see that guy four times and he keeps saying he's not ready yet," Henry said.

"Let me have that one," Van said.

John Roberts.

Tony snatched the card. "I have an appointment with him next week for a checkup," he said. "I'll just go in and say, 'Look here, Dr. Roberts, as long as I'm keeping you in business, why don't you give something to the capital-funds drive?' "

"Atta boy, Tony!" Van said.

"I'll hold him captive in his own office!"

Claudia Vanderford.

A hush fell over the room. Vanderford was perhaps the church's wealthiest member, a reclusive tobacco heiress.

"There's a story about that one, Janet," Henry explained. "You see, we didn't know quite how to approach her, since the tobacco business has been so bad lately and she's just gone through that divorce. So Van asked Joan Rockwell."

"You don't know how much Joan hates to ask for money," Van said. "She hates it! But she wrote Claudia a letter anyway and asked for thirty thousand. We never heard from her, so I prodded Joan to make a follow-up call, which wasn't too productive either. In fact, I think Joan said the old lady told her she had enough on her mind right now. We can't just send anybody over to drop by again."

"I can understand that," Janet said.

"So I'm thinking now, maybe it's time for me to go," Van said.

"A pastoral call!" Tony said. "You know, what with the divorce and all."

"Yes!" Van said. " 'Why, hello, Claudia, so sorry to hear about business and the messy divorce ... and in times like these, I know, a person needs the church ...' " Van's exaggerated tone made everyone laugh.

"Actually," Van said, "I really thought about doing that last weekend when I was driving by her house and saw her outside on a ladder painting her horse barn."

Henry said: "I know what—we could both drop by the next time and say, 'Claudia, for thirty thousand, I'll steady this ladder for you, and for sixty, I'll help you down.' "

Janet groaned.

"What's wrong with that?" Van said. "She's a tough gal. She can take it."

"Oh," Janet moaned. "You are bad. Real hardball players."

Soon Janet came to Rufus Wedemeyer. Their discussions always seemed to end with Rufus. Widowed, childless, the very model of Yankee frugality, eighty-five-year-old Rufus Wedemeyer lived in a modest neighborhood in a simple woodframe house his father had built on the southside of town, an unassuming residence for a man worth millions of dollars. Approximately seven million, by most estimates.

It was widely suspected that Rufus could have made up the difference in the capital campaign by simply donating a fraction of the interest on his investments. Instead, he played a fetching game, talking publicly about his vast holdings and the contents of his will—bequests to his girlfriend, the Masonic Home, a perpetual Rufus and Ruth Wedemeyer Scholarship Fund, and, as he would say seductively to Janet or Van when they called, "a small gift for the church."

But Rufus always refused to make it official. Whenever anyone from the church dropped by, he would spend the time vividly describing the government-sponsored hot lunches he enjoyed at the senior center for $1.25, and reflect on his contributions to the YMCA.

"So how about ten thousand?" Van finally asked one day.

"Reverend Parker," old Wedemeyer said, "Rufus has got to look out for himself. Rufus has got nobody."

Janet had heard the same story.

It seemed as if they had done all they could—the deacons had even named Rufus "deacon emeritus" and agreed to let him pass out bulletins any Sunday he felt up to it. Still Rufus refused to make the big pledge. Cagey old penny-pincher, he stoked a desire so pure and distinct that his name came to symbolize the essence of the chase.

"I'm hearing now he's telling people around town that he didn't give anything to the fund drive," Janet said.

"I think he just wants to take it all with him," Henry said. "Line his coffin with gold."

"I'll tell you one thing," Tony said. "He pulled me aside last Sunday to ask me why his plaque wasn't up outside the church."

Van looked up in alarm.

"You're talking about that handicapped parking sign?" Van said. "We better call the Prudential Board and get that thing up in time for Rally Day. I don't care if the church is painted or not, but we've got to get that plaque up!"

Janet and Henry laughed out loud.

"I've got an idea," Tony said. "What if we announce that the first person to give ten thousand dollars will have the new addition named after him?"

The Rufus Wedemeyer Memorial Choir Room sounded odd. But Henry took the card and stuffed it into his pocket anyway, a gesture that went unremarked, and called an end to a fruitful discussion.

It was really no wonder that Van wanted to introduce Janet around the Connecticut conference. By now they operated like old cronies. In fact, just that afternoon he had decided to wait a few days and then ask her advice about the fall stewardship campaign, and after that he would ask her to take over the outreach committee.

Van had spotted her as ripe for conversion a mile away. What a re-source for a church, he would say, privately. Her candor and call for self-sacrifice made the work much easier for him. She had a gift. If he could persuade her to stick with him, he thought, the two of them might finish the fund-raiser by the end of the year.

By the first of September, streetlamps in town flashed on again at seven thirty. Lines of gossip sparked to life. Doris Pritchett had heart surgery one Tuesday afternoon and by Wednesday morning everyone in the office knew—vanity of vanities!—that she had refused to remove her artificial fingernails for the operation. The minister at an historic church in a neighboring town quit after twenty years and announced that he would retire to a small town in the South. A few days later, he ran off to Florida with one of his female parishioners and his wife filed for divorce. A prominent architect hobbled into First Church one Sunday and explained that she'd taken a fall water-skiing over the weekend, but people who listened to their police scanners knew that her boyfriend had beaten her up again on Saturday night.

Nothing surprised them in the First Church office. Items-about-town traveled faster there than at either the public library or Geissler's supermarket. September always brought news, but never, ever any surprises.

I was probably the only one who had not heard the news that Joan and Owen Rockwell would pack up and leave for Nicaragua. Van had quietly slipped them one thousand dollars to help cover expenses, and then Joan and Owen disappeared for a few weeks. Even I didn't know that Joan's trip marked the start of a "discernment process," to see if she was being called by God to work in Central America. If I hadn't run into the good-bye party one day in Nelson Hall, she might have left without my knowing anything. I watched her that last day as a crowd of toddlers and parents surrounded her. She sang her last Earth songs and directed one final game of parachute plunge. A few days later, she and Owen were gone.

My other friends in the healing and spiritual groups had spent the summer experimenting with New Age ideas, and came back to church dosed up on the latest concepts. Personal myth was big. So were "legitimate" suffering, co-dependency, angels, Twelve Step programs, beta-carotene, vitamin E, Camille Paglia, Deepak Chopra, on-line computer services, and the plight of cancer victims. JoAnne had been as busy as a traffic cop, as the women she counseled went into overdrive. They were holding ritual gatherings in their vegetable gardens, running off to healing seminars, and going to howling-at-the-moon parties. Uninvited, unwanted, often begging for an opportunity, I never had a chance to see these strictly women-only events. Nor would my friends discuss them. "Poor thing," they'd say. "We just can't have a reporter around."

John Gregory-Davis, however, did tell me that his wife attended secret events out in the woods somewhere near the suburban town of Farmington. She would come home at night sometimes, he said, sweaty and exhausted, with flecks of charcoal smeared on her face, smelling of wood smoke and incense, and then she would spend the next week sanctifying each room in their house with some kind of unique ritual call for the Spirit. Sounded a lot like Joan Rockwell to me.

I also missed the night Allison went to the healing service and broke down crying.

"Did you hear what happened Monday?" she asked me one night. I happened to bump into her at the public library. I was doing some research on the use of Welch's grape juice as a sacrament.

"No," I said, "what are you talking about?"

"I lost it," she said.

"Lost what?"

"I mean, at the healing service."

Jan and I had been in Norwalk at an adoption counseling class that night. We were working hard.

"Well," she said. "I better tell you about it. I don't want you to hear it from someone else. I fell apart in the middle of the service. I didn't think I had anything on my mind when I got there, but as soon as I joined the circle, I felt like I had to go to the healing chair. And then it just came out of me—all this stuff about Karl and the kids and what I'm doing with my life or not doing with my life, and about my Dad, and problems at school."

For a long time, Allison had felt the strain of trying to live up to the expectations of her prominent family, an entire line of prosperous New Englanders, blue-blooded headmasters, doctors and distinguished professors. The men of the family had always succeeded in the professional, academic world, according to Allison, and the women were known, primarily, for having married well. No matter how hard she tried to reverse the natural order—teaching English at a private academy in West Hartford—she always felt she lacked the intellectual capacity to match the family's masculine achievers.

"So, I quit my job," she said.

"What?"

"I gave notice at the academy."

"Just like that?"

"I've been thinking about it for a long time, but at the healing service, when I asked for intercession, I just felt the most amazing presence during the prayers. I can't even describe it. Just this . . . heat. Real heat. It kind of rushed all over my body, and then I broke down sobbing. I just knew it was okay. I knew I could change and things would be all right. In fact, that's what I'm doing here right now. Checking out some books."

She had two columns of books stacked between her arms.

"AIDS," she whispered. "I'm thinking about AIDS."

Why, for God's sake! Joan had left for Central America, Allison was apparently considering a career counseling AIDS patients, and I was increasingly interested in topics like transubstantiation and the history of Welch's grape juice.

I also had been thinking all day of a passage I had read earlier in my studies. Northrop Frye, the great Canadian literary critic, once observed that "a serious human life, no matter what 'religion' is invoked, can hardly begin until we see an element of illusion in what is really there, and something real in fantasies about what might be there instead." If at the church in summertime, with the long season of Pentecost in effect, the simple idyll of the season allowed us time to wait, to play and to enjoy the regular pleasure of good company, the new season that began in September and ran through Easter brought this feeling of claustrophobia, of time running out, of the perhaps necessary, but not novel, sensation of needing to come back to something. Time to act. Go back to work. Maybe that explained why my friends were coming to turning points.

"Hey," Allison said, "it's not such a big deal, really. I'm just going to try something new. JoAnne's been pushing me for a long time to do something."

JoAnne again.

"By the way," she asked, "did you ever find out what went on at the women's retreat a few weeks ago?"

She could be absolutely terrifying sometimes. Her green eyes widened, and she looked at me giddily over her gold-rimmed glasses.

"You want to tell me?" I asked.

"Well, if you promise not to tell anybody I told you."

I promised.

She let out a stark and eerie howl, a warble that split through the library quiet like the midnight squawl of a tomcat.

"It's okay," she whispered, as heads jerked and turned our way. She covered her mouth and waved her hand to the librarians.

"Jesus! Allison," I whispered.

She looked at me seriously.

"Well, you've been wanting to know," she said.

"What the hell was that?"

"Last call of the summer loon," she said. "Now, does that freak you out or what?"

God love her! I thought. Clobbering people with her wild heart. Silly kook, soul sister number one.

I scratched up five hundred bucks for the capital-funds campaign, and pledged twenty dollars a week to the church beginning on Rally Day. I can't explain it exactly, but I did feel a little dishonest, as if I wanted to lull everyone into thinking I was just part of the crowd.

I rationalized it. Knowing what I knew about "the List" and knowing that most people probably knew a lot more about that List than they ever acknowledged, it only made sense to try. Although church membership officially required nothing, a regular deposit definitely made you a player in the game.

The first few times I wrote a check during the summer, I could not believe the easy, unexpected gambler's pleasure I felt creasing the check and tossing it into a silver plate. Maybe for the regulars throwing money away marked an adventure in self-sacrifice. It did remind me of the many times as a boy I'd seen my father crease and flick a twenty-dollar check into the plate—a small, surreptitious act he carried out with ritual precision each week at our family's Methodist church. But the payment also helped me feel better about taking a regular seat on Sundays (center pew, left balcony).

Who, I thought, would not pay twenty dollars to hear Trudy Crandall's Seeing Eye dog snore every Sunday ten minutes into Van's sermon, or to watch retarded kids scramble ecstatically out of the Amen pews during the otherwise tepid Passing of the Peace ceremony and fluster rows of prim worshipers by hugging them and shaking hands? I tried to think of my contribution as cash paid for pleasure, and I calculated a slightly improved return at tax time.

But most of all, I knew, come fall, I would join the church's private files. Along with the names of hundreds of others, I would appear on the confidential list of contributors and enjoy the privilege, more or less, of being an accredited actor in the troupe on Palisado Avenue. When Henry Holcombe personally sent me a thank-you note, only one day after the church received the five hundred, I felt a momentary sense of belonging and, even without having seen the lists with my own eyes, figured that I had placed myself securely in the middle to upper third of pledging units. Not a bad place for a beginner and, at the time, the best way I knew of disappearing into the scene before anyone began to question my commitment.

But those things were all I knew about stewardship. It was, at best, an absurd act of one day's reordered priorities. In a way, it seemed rather clubby, and in another way, I faced up to it as an obligation, the way you would with any superimposed tax. To be perfectly honest, I couldn't see what it had to do with God, at all. But then I was still learning that God often had very little to do with the life of a church.

How else could a person like me fit in? How else could I earn their trust and buy enough time to find out whatever it was I had come for? Over the next few months, I just wanted to blend in. There was always a price to pay for being intimate. Weekly dues and regular service—first steps, I imagined, in the religious discipline.

At seven thirty on Rally Day morning, Andy and Elizabeth stripped the shelves behind the choir room for Communion. They laid out six loaves of Allison Denslow's freshly baked bread, sterling silver Communion plates, hundreds of thimble-size glass cups, and a dozen white cotton napkins stored away in a Brooks Brothers shirt box. Glints of September sunlight sparkled across the table setting.

"You know, I always wondered . . . ," Andy said. He paused to reach into a cabinet. "I always wondered why we use grape juice. The whole time we were in England I kept thinking the Puritans couldn't have had access to that much grape juice."

He screwed the top off a device that looked like a seltzer bottle with a blue squeeze-bulb attachment, and used a red aluminum funnel to fill it with a cool quart of Welch's. Elizabeth stood in the open back door letting the sun warm her shoulders.

"Andy," she teased, "why do you always ask questions like that? You still act like an engineer!"

He tilted the bottle over a glass and squeezed the bulb once. A precise ounce of purple juice lipped the tiny cup.

"What's wrong with that?" he asked. "I'm always here earlier than anyone else and I do a lot more than anyone wants me to do."

He squeezed the bulb again over the next twinkling glass. "I believe in practical solutions."

"You mean like that time you tried to rope off the balcony?"

"You have to admit it was efficient."

"People had a fit!"

"It was practical."

"That was not the point!" Elizabeth said.

Andy filled a few dozen cups, then turned the task over to her. He pinched soft gobs of bread from a fragrant honey-flavored loaf until he'd crafted white mounds on two trays. Then, casually, he popped the last chunks into his mouth.

"What?" he said, chewing. Elizabeth was looking at him sternly. "You know I didn't have any breakfast."

Elizabeth spread cotton napkins over the trays and then gave Andy one to carry out into the quiet, brightening sanctuary. He winked at her as they walked past the pulpit, and whispered, "I've always wondered why we cover these with cloth. Is it an aesthetic thing or is it just to keep the flies off?"

"Good question," she whispered back. "Smarty."

Van came in just as the choir tuned up. The plum-purple and cantaloupe-orange shirts, and Crayola-colored dresses of summer had been replaced by more somber autumn hues. No one had to be told that styles changed in September.

"Sing unto the Lord a new song!" bellowed Morgan Smythe, the church's groundskeeper. His monstrous tenor overpowered the choir's lilting counterpoints. Then as he sailed into the third whole note in "song," his face burst bright red and his body shook until he gave out a beat short. "What's the matter, Morgan?" hollered a man in the bass section. "Have to stop to see if anybody was listening?"

A sense of fun and a distinctly Protestant willingness to be disciplined excited the choir. Even though it had rained the last fifteen weekends in a row, an army of terrorists had attacked Iranian oil fields, and the Red Sox had fallen two games behind in the American League pennant race, between the deacons and the choir, at ten o'clock, the way would be cleared for a new beginning. New wine in new wineskins. A new doxology. A New Jerusalem. A new confirmation class. A new song. A new heaven and a new earth. New siding. A new paint job. And the sermon, of course—Van's all-inclusive Rally Day crowd-pleaser titled, naturally, "New Things."

Van had spent weeks marshaling the logic of scripture with the Rally Day theme, orchestrating mowers, painters, and Prudential Board members to welcome the congregation back to a show of revival. Outside, members of the Prudential Board presented an exhibit on particle board titled "Work in Progress" displaying staged photographs of summer's work crews while Andy handed out eighteenth-century nails and old clapboards he'd collected during the reconstruction. The church itself, reflecting the luster of fresh paint, looked as white and new as fire-glazed porcelain.

At ten, Van ascended the pulpit, and the noisy crowds settled down to a modest chatter. After a month of Sundays, I thought I could read a pattern in the seating arrangements. Van called this a "crock," but I always thought I could count on seeing the ministers' most ardent supporters on the right; the endearing centrists in the middle; the more conservative critics on the left. In the back, crossing left to right, hidden among young families with babies and hobbled widows, sat those powerful, stoic figures who took the long view and, for unexpressable reasons, wished to be congregational guides to the future: Henry Holcombe and family at the far right corner; Paul Price, the treasurer, far left. In front, more sympathetic faces appeared, those who would willingly follow in good faith: the Gilleys and Clarkes, the Fitches and McCarthys, the Drakes and Gillettes. I found myself in the balcony surrounded by my friends from the healing committee, mothers with unruly adolescents, and aloof visitors. Van occasionally shot a skeptical glance our way, as if he knew more about the "observer's perch" than any one of us there.

"Things are happening!" he shouted, when the organ pipes clapped shut. (Rufus Wedemeyer's plaque was restored, for one). "The capital-fund drive is like a time-release capsule. I want to express my thanks to people who have led the drive—Henry, Tony, Janet . . ."

Children squirmed in their seats. One little boy stripped off his plaid bow tie and another wrested himself from his mother's grasp and wriggled off under the pews. Bill led the call to worship with a new nonsexist hymn printed on a purple bulletin insert, and sat us down again with a prayer he'd written at twelve thirty that morning while he and Abe watched a band called Faith No More on MTV—"Lift us out of our preoccupations with our own needs," he said, "awaken in us a longing to do the right thing . . ."

Trudy Crandall's Seeing Eye dog lunged into the aisle. Rowdy teenagers from the new confirmation class made faces at each other across the balcony. Mary Bartlet's little gray head, wrapped in an infrared hearing set, poked up above the third pew to pinpoint the source of the racket but turned, instead, toward the white colonnade on the pulpit surrounded by a thicket of roses, carnations, and palms left over from two weddings the day before. Oh! how she loved flowers!

Announcements ran long—healing services, the construction of a Habitat house, Bill's taxpayers' alliance, raffle tickets for sale. Then we sang two hymns, said the Lord's Prayer, and Ralph Stoot climbed into the pulpit to read the scripture lesson. *"You are the salt of the earth! . . . You are the light of the world!"*

Van felt such a rush of excitement as he stood to preach that he bobbled his notes and knocked the microphone out of its stand. He sprang up on his toes and thrashed his arms beneath the dark robe, calling out about "the old salt that has lost its taste" and the "light hid under a bushel basket that should return to the lampstand." He referred to verses about new beginnings from the Psalms, Jeremiah, and Isaiah, mentioned his daughter who was traveling in Central America, quoted critically from old gospel hymns that reflected a familiar theology based on individual salvation ("Jesus Walked with *Me*" . . . "Jesus is *My* Friend" . . . "Rock of Ages Cleft for *Me*"), and then he pointed to the need for newer, saltier, more robust hymns for community. He had not found a single song in the hymnal celebrating community rather than individual salvation. Why? he asked. What is wrong with this picture?

I watched Andy mark up the back of a visitor's card to show two new deacons how to move collection plates across the pews. By the time Van asked the congregation to bow their heads for prayer, a little girl in the balcony made the final fold in the purple insert and reached way back for the launch.

Van prayed with his eyes open. He had probably lost half the congregation at the mention of Central America. Andy spent much of his time gazing out the window. John Gregory-Davis was probably grading him down like a college professor for not challenging suburbanites to social ministry. But Van expected nothing more from them. He fumbled with the green prayer request cards and then made an invitation to a minute of silent meditation and confession.

He always felt tempted to distance himself, to laugh at the fat ladies and cackle at Della Fripp's piercing, hideously flat singing voice wailing down on him like a blue jay from the balcony. Sometimes he could look out into the meetinghouse and identify certain people by their tendencies toward transference, neurosis, denial, and midlife crisis. After twenty years, he knew them that well. Still, he did not laugh to himself or condescend. He could not do that when he saw himself like any one of them, increasingly feeling the need to begin again, too, with hope for a new start.

It had become his privilege now, in the accumulation of years, to gauge their growth as they sprang back from disappointments, recovered from disease, came to maturity, or grasped the first simple tools for the spiritual journey into midlife and beyond. Joan Rockwell had left for Nicaragua. Janet Filer had sent them on a new venture in stewardship. Every year the church would launch some people into action, into new ways of consciousness or political involvement. Who would it be this year?

And all the ordinary ones, the faithful ones, they would come back to him, too, to iron out details for a wedding or baptism or funeral service, and in the process tell him the apocryphal stories of their lives. September gatherings always reminded him that couples he married would be bringing their babies in for baptism. Some whom he had baptized fourteen years before would join Bill's Confirmation class. A few of those teenagers would come back as adults with partners for marriage, and then they would have babies, and Van would see, as he had often seen, the change again within families from one generation to the next. Even his daughters reminded him now, when they came home in August or September, that he and the church had become inseparable. As much as they preferred not to, they would tell him now, often with hurt in their voices, that they could not look back on their childhoods and separate their memory of home from the needs and celebrations of the families who filled the meetinghouse on Sundays. Van knew. He felt their frustration. He knew he had been absent. His children's pain was one of the greatest sorrows of his ministry. But he also felt a responsibility and, always, a secret pleasure in the need of his people as they returned from September to September. The choices were his, correct or not.

And out there before him, heads bowed in prayer—Janet Filer, Tony Gillette, Allison Denslow, and the mysterious opponents to the fund drive who had just come back from vacation. Competing interest groups and gossip mongers were spread around the meetinghouse like agents provocateurs. His own associate, Bill Warner-Prouty, who was spending more of his time now organizing a tax-support group in town than planning programs for the church, sat behind him, thinking only God knew what. But for some reason they kept coming back here, and they all prayed together with him now, Communion crumbs at their feet. By God's grace they would give each other another chance. All equal in the eyes of God. Heads bowed again for comfort and forgiveness.

"Dear God," he prayed aloud—he could see Rufus Wedemeyer diddling with the little hole for the Communion cup in the third pew— "Dear God . . . ," he started again. Their silence swelled up like a wound at times. He could feel a vague pain when he sensed their needs. So many people looked hunched over awkwardly in prayer.

Nick Wilton prayed without ceasing. Ever since his wife's death in the spring, he had prayed for forgiveness. He had prayed for his mistress, begged forgiveness for infidelities, sought the forgiveness of his children, remembered more now about his wife's strength and love than he could sometimes stand. Guilt? Yes, he felt that. But he also felt himself coming home, with Van's help. They had talked often about the sadness. And then, just recently, Nick had begun to remember working as an altar boy in his childhood. He recalled the time when he griped to his priest about having to be at church one Saturday morning to help with Communion when there were no parishioners around. "What's the point, Father?" Nick had asked. "There's no one here!" That had been nearly fifty years ago.

But that priest's reply haunted him now: "God's here, son."

God's here, son. Nick was at First Church now every Sunday, beaming up at Van like that young altar boy. He was helping out at the coffee hours, volunteering to work on different committees. During prayers, he always bowed down like a Boy Scout lugging a pack. Thank you, God, he prayed. Thank you for giving me a second chance.

Back in the right corner, Paul Price bowed his head, too. Even from the far corner, where Van could hardly see him. There was no mistaking that man. Tall, muscular, broad-shouldered, Paul sauntered into the office many days now with a golden-toned tan and a brown leather briefcase that matched his cotton twill fatigue shorts and khaki cotton shirt with epaulets. From the pulpit it looked like he shaved his head, too, but it was just the closely cropped profile of a corporate conservative.

Paul had transformed the job of church treasurer by projecting a professional image and playing the guardian's role as chief financial officer. He was a genuine hardball player, as they liked to say on the Prudential Board, and now, as September began, he was beginning to make it clear that he did not agree with the way the minister ran the church. From where Van stood, he could see Paul watching him. "Close enough to keep an eye on things, far enough away to avoid having to listen to Van's sermons," Paul told people.

The older ones bowed their heads, too—tidy old women who held their peace about the new hymns and praise for God Whomever. Despite the changes they heard this morning, they were not prepared to reject the nonsexist inserts. Maybe in the next few months they would stand up for the creeds they had come to cherish, for "Dear Lord and Father of All Mankind," and "Onward Christian Soldiers," for the masculine deity, the grandfather God and dear brother Jesus. Those who had volunteered for church duty through two world wars and two Pacific conflicts, who had steered sons and daughters through Confirmations during the sexual revolution and the drug culture, and shepherded husbands past faithless middle age, wondered now if Van would force them during their final days to accept strange new ideas and a change of rituals. Some of them had already decided they were not about to stand on Sunday mornings mouthing a politically correct, unoffensive, New Age language. It couldn't be Van pushing it, they thought. More likely it came from their grandchildren's Sunday-school superintendent, that red-bearded radical, Bill Warner-Prouty.

Claudia Gaither and Jack Mulvihill held hands while Van launched into the Lord's Prayer. The traditional month for weddings had switched from June to September, Van suspected, to accommodate a global warming trend, but Claudia and Jack told him they had always wanted to be married in September. Their wedding next Saturday would be the biggest event in the meetinghouse this month. Bill had counseled them throughout the summer, and Van agreed to come to the reception, even though he preferred to be mowing grass rather than wasting his time with ponderous, customized ceremonies that always tended to devour his Saturday afternoons. Claudia and Jack did not know how Van felt. Nor did they know how they had demoralized poor Fran. The desecration of the traditional wedding service with amateur guitarists playing noxious tunes like "The Wedding Song" and "Bridge over Troubled Water" was bad enough for the organist's morale, but attendant requests for odious contemporary pop/rock numbers by Billy Ocean and Elton John really brought him low.

Jack and Claudia suspected Van would ask them to join First Church as soon as they returned from their honeymoon. But that was okay. They were starting to like the idea of holding hands at First Church on Sunday mornings as "Mr. & Mrs."

At the sound of "Amen," Andy sent Allison, Tony, and the rest of the deacons down the aisles with collection plates. Everyone stood to sing the new doxology. Absent any reference to God as male, the strains jumbled, old and new, and the voices of tradition and the voices of change competed across a range of octaves. While one person sang praises to "Father, Son," another cried out, "Creator, Christ." The cacophony stirred alarm on faces in almost every pew.

A moment later Van stood with Bill at the back door, arms raised, for the benediction: "Lord, dismiss us with thy blessing. Refresh us traveling through this wilderness."

In the mystery of those forty-five minutes, I often wondered if anyone had been consoled or uplifted in the "wilderness" of worship. Leaving the balcony, I heard the head of the Pennies for Perennials committee ask the groundskeeper to plant thirty-five tulip bulbs around the church. ("Sure," Morgan said, reaching for a pack of cigarettes underneath his choir robe. "I'll plant whatever you've got, as long as I can plant 'em all in the same hole!") I overheard a few old women complaining that Bill had not bowed his head during the Lord's Prayer. Peggy Couples caught my eye and shook her head. "Same old same old," she said. John Gregory-Davis was talking to Janet about how to fight Paul Price's objections to Habitat funding again, and outside, Lucille helped serve punch and cookies on the lawn.

I circled around to the back of the church. The two new deacons stood inside by the Communion cabinet with straw baskets of drained cups and silver trays half-filled with crumbled bread. They were immobilized.

"You know I feel a little funny about this," one was saying.

"I know!" the other replied.

"What do we do with it?"

"You want to take the bread home and feed it to the ducks, but the grape juice . . ."

"I know!"

"We could just chuck it."

"Chuck it?"

As I listened, they went back and forth and finally just stood in the doorway in silence, looking out into the vast sprawl of the green graveyard as children and little parties of churchgoers toured the grounds in the light of a stunningly beautiful Sunday morning. For just a moment, until Bill Warner-Prouty happened by to stash his robe, take a pinch of bread, and wash it down with a slug of Welch's, the body of Christ once again appeared like bloody fruit in the face of those silvery plates.

The deacons quickly bagged the bread and, with a sigh of relief, brushed off their hands. The crumbs went to three little girls who came in begging for leftovers; the dirty juice cups, into a soapy tub of dishwater.

How could I ever describe a gathering like this? What was going on here? Was it beyond my imagination, or had something sacred really survived another Sunday in this plain and unobservant place?

CHAPTER SEVENTEEN

The change of seasons came slowly. Summer lingered to bless an endless round of wedding parties at the meetinghouse. With dead tree limbs trimmed away, the changing leaves seemed more charged with light. A greater stillness softened September afternoons.

Allison and Priscilla hit all the big workshops on spiritual healing around New England. I was invited but usually ducked out. Jan and I joined a class for adoptive parents in Norwalk, and the intensity of our exchanges in the car, to and from the agency, proved that we had not spent enough time together during the past months of my First Church immersion. Did we really want to adopt? Did I really want children? How would we pay the fees? How committed were we? Two hours to Norwalk and two hours back, we played the game of problem-solving.

On Monday nights I continued to visit Bill and Sue for dinner. With mounting tensions at home, I liked to have a place to come home to in Windsor. Besides, once Jan and I started the adoption process, the associate minister and his wife told me their own story in detail. One night they surprised me by revealing that Abe had been adopted, and later they mentioned Biblical accounts—the magnificent adoption story of the baby Moses, the story of Samuel, and the birth of Isaac that God provided Abraham and Sarah in old age—which had helped guide them past the trough of childlessness. They laughed about naming Abe on the way to the hospital the day he was born. Bill liked the name Abraham, from the Old Testament. Sue argued for the name Oblio, from the Harry Nilsson song "The Point." They stopped and haggled at every red light to the hospital until it was settled: Abraham Oblio Warner-Prouty. Jan and I certainly weren't having fun like that.

Now at night, after hours at adoption workshops reviewing laws and strategies, I would go upstairs to my office, shut the door, and read the Bible. I noticed a surprising disjunction in my understanding when I read the familiar tales for the first time as an adult. Never having heard them except as childhood lessons, I had no clue what an adventure they posed.

I no longer imagined sandal-shod, gray-bearded desert nomads standing near a picnic basket mired in the bulrushes. Instead, I saw a group of cunning women literally plotting Moses' adoption in defiance of governmental orders. Moses' sister, his mother, and the king's daughter arranged to bring the child up in the royal household without the king's knowledge. Thus, a prophet was born and reared.

If Moses' birth story celebrated a group of courageous women, the story of Abraham and Sarah presented the case of a courageous couple. The two old people were not the cardboard cutouts I remembered playing with in Sunday school. Sarah, at age ninety-one, must have surmounted one of the worst cases of menopause in history when she gave birth to Isaac. In an extraordinary display of faith, Sarah yielded to the will of God and gave birth to a son.

New images soon entered my prayers. I cradled the laughing baby who had spoken to me that summer in a dream. In prayer, I plotted, imagining Jan, Joan, and Allison scheming to save the child. I saw myself, in cahoots with them, sweeping the baby out of the weedy River Protestant. On other nights, I imagined sitting by a fire in the desert, listening for angels to come to the tent where Jan slept. Just as they had once come to Abraham and Sarah, they now visited us.

Still, no matter how I tried, once I had the child in arms, I never had the strength to hold on to the vision for long. Somehow, the flimsy

Sunday-school images intruded. I would lose what God might have in sight for Jan and me. The beautiful baby would vanish.

At the center of activities, JoAnne was listening. Privately or in our groups, she would suggest that Jan and I really were spiritual beings, in need of a community and liberation from the world's standards. Listen, she would say. Listen to your life.

Just as Bill saw her on Wednesdays to talk about his career, as Allison went in on Thursdays to discuss plans to work with AIDS patients, as Priscilla met her on Fridays to talk about her family, I went to her, too. Although we talked about the adoption, what I really wanted was what I assumed we all sought. Courage. Faith. Patience.

She always left me with just enough ammunition to think I could still haggle with God. Good old JoAnne. She prayed for us, too.

"And what about you?" I asked Joan Rockwell one Monday afternoon over lunch. I had been trying for weeks to catch up with her after her trip to Ocatol.

She looked tired after the three-week adventure. Slicing the last tomatoes from her garden, she kept stopping to sweep the hair out of her eyes and run back to the refrigerator to find something else for the salad. Lunch wasn't getting done. Her house was a mess. She hadn't even dressed that morning but for the same ragged blue sweats.

I could see Joan was not interested in talking to me.

"First, tell me where are you in all this stuff?" she asked. "Have you found a place for yourself in the church yet?"

I described the adoption effort and complained.

"You knew I once spent five years as an adoption counselor with the state, didn't you?" she said.

What?

"Sure," she said. "I'm always hearing about girls who want to place babies for adoption."

I sat down at her table and as she brought our plates in, I noticed her red hands. Her eyes were puffy and her face was pale. I let her offer drop, for a moment, hoping my silence would redirect the conversation back to her. I pointed to her raw knuckles.

"Oh! I baked bread for the church this morning," she said. "I get down on the floor and give it a good pounding. Makes the bread rise well, but my knuckles always swell up for a while."

Although she had been back from Nicaragua for two weeks, no one from the church had seen her. Joan and Owen were the fifth and sixth people from First Church to make the trip to Ocatol, a small town ravaged by Contra invasions. For the others who had visited, the Rockwells' observations sounded familiar themes: The hospital was like the black hole of Calcutta: dysentery, malaria, and cholera were rampant. Townspeople apparently had quit using the hospital because of the lack of medicine; the X-ray equipment was outmoded; there was only one microscope in the lab, and no centrifuge. The country itself had the highest birth rate in the western hemisphere; prenatal care was sadly lacking. Joan and Owen saw the town virtually unchanged since the first reports from church groups ten years earlier.

Still, Joan had been thrilled at the beauty of the countryside, so lush and green during the wet season. The Nicaraguans spoke passionately to her about the Christian basis for the revolution, and they invited her and Owen to attend the feast of the town's patron saint, the Virgin of the Ascension. They joined a mass in which the whole town seemed to participate. Fireworks, parades, rodeos, and religious services went on the entire week. Despite problems, the people were wonderful.

At Casa de Materna, a woman's center in town, Joan thought she could see herself working with a staff whose mission was to provide sex education, prenatal care, and midwifery for the surrounding population. Unfortunately, in just a few days, having exhausted her ability to converse in Spanish, she left Casa de Materna afraid she had failed to make a good enough impression with the staff to return. A job offer did not come immediately.

After ten days, she and Owen decided to use Ocatol as a base camp to see the rest of the country. Visiting coffee cooperatives in the hills. Touring schools. Assessing hospitals. Going into overcrowded day-care centers equipped with bomb shelters to protect children from Contra attack. She often felt unspeakably sad in the towns. But once they were back on the road, her spirits picked up again. She loved hiking through the woods, hitching rides on rusted pickup trucks, and worshiping daily with the campesinos in the Christian base communities. She and Owen traveled from town to village by day, slept on lumpy mattresses and fought off mosquitoes at night. Sometimes, when they prayed with the Nicaraguans, she felt embarrassed, pulling out her fifty-thousand-cordoba notes (two dollars, American) to drop into the collection plate. So little to her, so much to them.

Finally, on the last day, they returned to Managua for a farewell service at the famed Santa Maria de los Angeles, considered the heart of the revolutionary church in Nicaragua. Located in a neighborhood where heavy fighting had occurred during the revolution, it was adorned inside with beautiful murals depicting the history of Nicaragua from the vantage of liberation theology, the radical Christian philosophy of resistance and empowerment.

"By the last day, Owen and I were feeling closer to each other than we had in years," she told me. "This thing between us—this conflict we've had about all the recent changes I've been going through—wasn't an intellectual exercise anymore. It wasn't someone else's observations for us to discuss. I had been working hard for months to see if the dreams and experiences I'd had were really a calling to mission. Finally, I could see that Owen was beginning to understand that, to put it all together, about what it could mean for me, and what it might mean for the two of us."

Before the service in Managua, she and Owen met the minister of Riverside Church in New York, and, hearing Joan's story, he asked her to dance his sermon that afternoon. So that day, as he preached, she moved from mural to mural, dancing her way into scenes of the Nicaraguans' early gods, indigenous leaders, and Spanish conquistadors. She danced beneath brilliantly colored paintings of Archbishop Oscar Romero, Augusto Sandino, and Carlos Fonseca, the campesino Christ. By the time she reached the final set of paintings, depicting villagers resisting attacks by Contra soldiers, she no longer heard the words of the sermon.

She heard another voice inside her. She danced wildly with the Spirit, swirling, feinting, tumbling and leaping right and left. She merged with images, into scenes that surrounded her like visions.

When she slowed, as the sermon ended and the voices stopped, she looked into the faces in the church. Everyone was crying, including Owen. He was crying hardest, and at that moment she realized that he had never before seen her dance. Never. Not once.

"We were starting another journey," she told me. "I think, somehow, we both knew we were being called."

Called like a patriot? Like a soldier? Who called?

Joan pressed a napkin to her pale lips and closed her eyes. She sighed as she stood up and started clearing dishes off the table.

"Being called by God does not mean what anyone thinks it means," she said. "Owen and I came home changed, but in different ways. You know, we have different journeys, but I do not believe we can live with a cloistered sense of God. God is not only here. In Windsor. In our church. In our little community. You can't pretend that God is *our* possession."

She went to the kitchen window, walking barefoot across the floor. Her gardens flamed along the fence separating her from the nearest neighbor. The yard led to a hedge and then to a plot of woods.

"Come here," she said.

She took her hand and pushed it up into her chest. "We are a mixture of spiritual and animal. I don't want to squelch this. Although I don't always want to recognize it. But they meet right here . . ."—she pushed down into her stomach—"right here for me, in the center. The spiritual; the animal . . ."

What I did not know, she said, was this: Shortly after she had returned from Nicaragua, Priscilla invited her to attend a workshop in Boston with a Quaker mystic, John Youngblut. Building from Jungian concepts, the teacher had encouraged her to keep a journal of dreams. Consequently, for the past two weeks, Joan had experienced intense visions that had not yet finished with her.

"Sometimes all I can do is write and write and write," she said. "I get up in the middle of the night, and I think, geesh, this must be psychotic, these dreams are so terrifying. But then I also know that mystics are often writers—like Meister Eckhart and Hildegard of Bingen—so I keep at it, no matter how exhausted I am."

I looked around me. *We are in a colonial home with a baby blue mailbox out front and gardens around the sides. Joan has moved the furniture around the house so she and Owen can see different parts of the yard during the fall. She is afraid that if she leaves, even for a while, Owen will not understand, and their marriage might not survive. No matter what happened in Nicaragua, she still fears for them.*

A few days ago, she said, she called Bill and told him why she hadn't been to church for two weeks. Van, she thought, would never understand. But Bill said, "Joan, you are not crazy. You are okay. These things happen to me, too. Dreams and visions are not unusual. Listen to them. Find help, but listen to them."

She visited her therapist, and he told her to continue meditating at home. When the horse comes out of the woods again, talk to it.

"What horse?" I asked.

The imaginary animal she had seen stalking around the yard was a symbol of power, she said. Her therapist told her she must confront it. "If it continues to appear and it continues to frighten you, you must ask yourself, 'What could I do with that power? How could I use it to my own ends?' "

Early that morning, after Owen left for work, she had gone to her room to meditate. When the dark horse marched out of the woods again, arrogantly tossing its head, kicking and prancing in the grass, she wanted to go to it. In her mind, she left the house, stumbled across the backyard, and sank waist-deep in mud. The horse trotted over and offered its mane to pull her up. Her playful, dancing self, her dangerous, angry self—the horse—leaned over and hauled her up.

"How can we be friends?" she asked. "Why won't you accept me?"

She touched the stiff mane and felt a surge of power in the horse's neck. She saw that it was female, and as it trotted back toward the woods, she leapt on its back and rode hard through to a clearing like a huntsman. In a rough, grassy field they stopped and played. Joan asked again, "What do you have to teach me?" and stroked her hair. The horse bared its teeth, snorted, stomped a hoof, and raced away. Alone in the woods, Joan felt scared and betrayed.

Momentarily, the horse returned, this time saddled for a long ride. Joan climbed up and, peeking into the saddlebags, found oats, an apple, carrots, and a tomato. Here was the answer to her question. Food for the journey. Food for her, food for the animal.

"What am I supposed to do with this?" she asked me, her eyes filling with tears. "I feel weak. I can't eat. I wake up at night, and write and write and write. Everything around me feels enchanted. I think, can I endure the truth? When the time comes that I have to leave my family, leave my church, leave Windsor and go to Nicaragua, will I go to affirm something that only seems to me to be the call for salvation? Am I traveling the right path?"

"What about Owen?" I asked.

She looked so bad, I regretted having asked.

"He doesn't have a clue," she said. "He's come with me as far as anyone could. But maybe it's time to let go. That's all. Maybe he will have to let go."

It really is funny, I thought. Perceptions can change so quickly. Barriers dissolve. Geologic plates shift. It's like when people tell you there are no coincidences, and then something happens to make grace less a theological proposition than a gift. That's what I was learning, anyway, in September, among a disordered assembly of religious amateurs who, in our ignorance and need, came to church to find God and found nothing more extraordinary than a group of people, like ourselves, with large and small imaginations. Sometimes it seemed as if everyone I knew was trying, in one way or another, to learn how to let go and live again in wonder.

So I was able to keep praying, and a couple of times a month, Priscilla, Allison, Joan, and the rest of us met in a group to talk about what we were learning. It was really not as much of a "journey" as I'd expected—wandering down the hallway to JoAnne's "office" in the library. Dragging in, walking out, our groups were more like undisciplined classes, like a boys' backyard science club or a girls' secret garden society. We might have prayed for each other, prayed for strangers, listened to New Age music, and practiced guided visualizations, but most of the time, it seemed, we were playing. Playing with big concepts, playing with adult problems. But playing.

As foolish as it sounds, I rarely left one of them anymore without feeling more free-spirited, like a rebellious teenager—a "child of God" walking the beautiful flat neighborhoods of old Windsor. And, honestly, I think for any one of us, young or old, beginner or journeyman, there was no longer any other expectation than that.

CHAPTER EIGHTEEN

Paul Price entered the office on Monday morning to copy reports for the Cabinet meeting. He cleared a place on the countertop by Peggy's desk and went to work. A birthday party, a mob of kids, a garrison of bread bakers and flower arrangers came and went. Paul never once looked up.

In the adjoining office, Bill and Ralph Stoot circled a series of wall maps Ralph had drawn comparing the geography of Iran with that of northeastern Pennsylvania. Ralph, who had only recently retired, said he had discovered a diner that summer called the White Dove, located in Lord's Valley near the town of Ararat just off Interstate 81. Besides wanting to sample wine at the restaurant, Ralph wondered if there might be any similarities between the land north of Scranton and the mythological area described in the Bible as the Garden of Eden. The geography of biblical places and their reappearance in the American landscape held a peculiar fascination for Ralph. As usual, Bill could not tell whether Ralph's imagination had taken over, or if he had bumbled into something better left to fundamentalists. But Ralph produced such beautifully colored, intricately drawn wall maps that Bill had agreed to look.

They compared Pennsylvania's colored lace of scribbled rivers and roads with Bill's own maps of the Holy Land. Ralph described the findings of his etymological study, including the origins of the name Lackawanna ("It's not an Indian word at all," Ralph observed, "but a Latinate derivative of the verb *to wane*"), and details of his original feminist theory of Noah's Ark.

While Ralph eagerly scooted around the edge of his maps, next door Paul silently kept his head down in the balance sheets.

"I give up," Ralph said, finally. "I can tell you're not going to buy into this. You're no fun."

"Don't give up yet," Bill said. "Anyway, I've got my own theories. See? Look at this."

Bill opened the *Pilgrim Hymnal.* Number 358.

"We sang it at least twice this summer," Ralph said, thrumming the page.

"And we're going to sing it again. 'Rock of Ages,' " Bill said.

"So what?"

"But don't you see? It's a feminist hymn!" Bill teased.

"What?"

" 'Rock of ages, *cleft* for me . . .' Get it?"

Ralph looked perplexed.

" 'Let me *hide* myself in thee,' " Bill said, wiggling his nose. "Get it? Cleft? Cleavage? It's like this big bosom!"

Paul Price turned his head to listen, but he did not look up.

"It's a female image of God!" Bill exclaimed.

Peggy, who was trying to ignore their nonsense, suddenly spoke up. "Bill, you are ridiculous!" she said.

"He started it," Bill said, pointing at Ralph.

"Maybe you've really got something there," Ralph said.

"No, no, no! I didn't mean it. I'm just kidding. Really," Bill said. "It's supposed to be an image of Moses. The bosom's just my personal fantasy."

Paul finished at the copier, then went to work on payroll checks. Tall, tawny, muscular, dressed in his usual cleanly pressed cotton twill, Paul looked more like a college athletic director than a church treasurer. Without a word, he turned and set the checks on Peggy's desk. When Bill and Ralph walked through the door, he did not greet Ralph or look at his maps. Ralph offered a curt "Good morning, Paul," and stepped aside.

"Ah! Mr. Price," Bill said, happily. "Dear Paul Price, how gracious of you to remember me at a time like this. Your thoughtful preparation of a paycheck will allow my family sufficient resources to make our annual journey to the sands of Cape Cod."

Paul was expressionless.

"On behalf of my son, I thank you. On behalf of my wife, I thank you. On behalf of myself, I most humbly thank you."

Bill picked up the check and stuffed it into his shirt pocket.

"This will really help us out," he said, more earnestly. "Honestly, Paul, thanks. Thanks a lot."

"That's not your paycheck," Paul said firmly. "It's for the missionary society."

Bill looked again at the check. "Oh," he said. "I thought you said you'd get me an advance before our vacation next week."

Paul didn't say a word.

"I . . . I said I thought you were going to get us . . . ," Bill stammered.

Paul stared, a hard, puzzling, downward look into Bill's fuzzy face. He held him there, gazing, through an awkward silence.

"Well, Bill," Peggy said, trying to ease the tension, "at least you can be sure that your check's on the front of Paul's mind now. Isn't it, Paul?"

Paul snapped his briefcase shut. He looked at Bill, smirked, and turned toward the door. "No, it isn't," he said.

And with two steps and a final backward glare at the minister, Paul Price walked out.

In just the past year, Paul's sober control had gained a following. A number of people thought the congregation needed a firm advocate like Paul Price. Just look from one corner stake of the property to the other: painters and carpenters had spent months roaming the grounds making repairs to roofs, replacing rotted windowsills, shoring up foundations, stripping off rotted clapboards. Despite Van's sermonizing about "new things" and "new life," drain plugs in the parking lot still overflowed during hard rains, raw sewage backed up in the cemetery, water seeped through the ceiling above Bill's desk and dribbled into a plastic bucket. The Morrell Room felt like a sauna on late summer nights, and the one noisy window unit blew only hot air. Without a large, central parking area, people still pulled their cars up on graves along the hearse path in the cemetery. Visitors continued parking every Sunday, like guests at a tent revival, up and down Palisado Avenue.

Years of neglect meant someone had to collar the senior minister. As nice as he was, Van had more than a covenantal relationship with the Lord in Windsor. He also had a fiduciary responsibility to the congregation. Someone had to step in and lead with a more logical and consistent plan. Fortunately, Paul Price was willing. He was as logical and as consistent as anyone could desire.

Van had welcomed Paul onto the staff several years ago to keep the books. Even though Van considered the accountant an enigma, Paul had virtues certain members of the congregation held in high regard, traits unparalleled in his predecessors. Besides having been a member for almost twenty years, Paul Price also had enjoyed a distinguished career in financial management for aerospace companies.

Precision, professionalism, and productivity had highlighted his work as an assistant to full-time treasurers. Paul had created the congregation's first computerized bookkeeping system. He had produced concise monthly budgets for the Cabinet. As a CPA, Paul had also offered an expert's services at a bargain price. Seeing far more than the average scrivener for hire, Van eventually signed Paul onto the payroll for three thousand dollars, appointed him treasurer, and gave him a permanent slot on the Prudential Board and Cabinet. It was a pragmatic decision, Van would say, one appointment he did not have to think about twice.

And so it was that every month for two years Paul's financial reports, processed by computer, had come in on time, clean and uncluttered: comprehensive quarterly summaries of income and expenditures, lists of capital-funds projects, end-of-the-year projections. Modern principles of accounting were finally being applied to church life.

Before long he was dipping into past financial records. Paul summarized statistics and plotted trends. Overnight, he changed the job from that of a mere Sunday-afternoon bookkeeper to a professional position of real fiscal authority.

Unfortunately for Van, Paul also discovered financial irregularities, and he was not afraid to speak with the courage of his convictions. To his mind, something was not right in the First Church countinghouse. The obligation to bring to light otherwise private affairs had led him into areas where, frankly, he was not always wanted.

"Bookkeepers keep books," Paul explained to me one day. "Someone gives them a bunch of numbers and they put them into different accounts. But an accountant should be able to analyze and verbalize what those numbers mean, and the only way you can do that is by having a real understanding of exactly what transactions created those numbers. If you commingle too many things into a single account, you never really know what kinds of activities are reflected in your budget. And at First Church, when I first took over, all the requisitions for checks came through Van and Bill. They were the ones who determined the accounts. And a lot of those accounts were, shall we say, ambiguous."

Soon, Paul had examined years of murky expenditures. He identified a large number of previously nonbudgeted items, such as the annual bus trip to Tanglewood and grocery bills for the homeless shelter. Every bit of the data went into his computer. ("Quite a task," he told me, "as you might imagine," because for 358 years, all financial records of the church had been made in manuscript form.) Paul analyzed the preceding ten years' accounts, and when that was done, he had what amounted to the first clear snapshot of First Church receipts and disbursements.

"And after all that work," Paul said, "I thought it would be smart to reconstruct what had happened with our funds over time."

The computer-driven, line-item comparisons and statistical analyses turned up one puzzling trend. Every year, it seemed, a larger and larger proportion of the church budget was going directly to the Outreach Board. When Paul nosed around, he found out that around 1982 or 1983, someone on the Cabinet had initiated an informal policy, unknown to the larger congregation, that twenty percent of each year's bottom line would automatically belong to the Outreach Board. What made the policy so egregious, Paul thought, was not simply the lack of accountability, but the fact that it looked as if the formula allowed outreach proponents to siphon off money from restricted endowments set aside exclusively for use by the Sunday school and the property reserve fund. To his surprise, what at first looked like a simple accounting problem quickly became a matter of semantics.

"Two years ago," he explained, "I went to Van privately and said, 'Van, this is just not right. There is an inherent conflict from an accounting point of view if you have these endowments set aside with a strict say on how they're to be used and then a separate policy to spend x percent of the bottom line on outreach. In fact, if you exclude the basic administrative and property costs—just so you're looking at program costs—it's not just twenty percent of the bottom line we're giving away to outreach, it's more like thirty to thirty-three percent.' "

Van listened, but would not yield. The minister argued that the twenty percent formula for outreach had been an "informal" guideline agreed upon years ago at the Cabinet level. Although it looked as if outreach drew from the Florence Mills Scholarship Endowment and the Molyneaux Property Reserve Fund, the kids still received $7,000 or $8,000 every year for scholarships, as intended, and the property fund still took its $36,000 or so. As far as Van was concerned, the proportion set aside for outreach was a matter of basic Christian priorities. It was like a tithe.

Paul knew better. It was an accounting fiasco. Illogical. Underhanded. Maybe illegal.

"Van," he would argue, "it's like trying to spend the same money twice. It's not just a tithe, it's a *double* tithe. We're leaving ourselves wide open."

Van acted as if he did not understand.

"Look at it this way," Paul said. "Every year, the Outreach Board takes a standard twenty percent of the total budget. Not only is that nearly equivalent to our total investment income for the year, but if we go out and spend ten thousand dollars for a new office copier, that means we have to make an automatic twenty-percent donation to outreach. Now that's just not right."

Eventually, Van asked the church's lawyer to review conditions for the two endowments prescribed by the Mills and Molyneaux estates. When the lawyer judged the Outreach Board's formula legally acceptable, Van persuaded Paul to set aside his complaints.

The issue might have been put to rest. But in January, during discussions about the capital-funds drive, Van again promoted the idea of setting aside a percentage of money for an outreach program. Five percent of every pledge, he said, would be for Habitat for Humanity. Again Paul suspected that the congregation was being finagled. This time, instead of speaking privately with Van about the issue, he spoke out publicly at congregational meetings and with Cabinet members, trying to explain what he had discovered about disparities in the church's budget. Not everyone understood the logic of accounting procedures. But those who did were aroused with suspicions. By the time the capital campaign started, Paul's financial reports were being quoted—in some circles—with almost scriptural authority.

Paul Price spoke truth to power. Whenever Janet Filer went to church meetings and claimed that giving money to Habitat for Humanity would work as an incentive to increase pledges for the fund drive, Paul would be in the background saying, "She has no proof." In recent months, members of the Cabinet would ask Van point-blank at their meetings, "Why do we pay a five-thousand-dollar supplement, provide janitorial service, heat, and electricity, and give our entire first floor over to a nondenominational nursery school, when it is not a part of the church ministry?" Van would say, "It's a part of our outreach to the community." And Paul would pipe up: "So, why don't we pay for it out of the outreach budget?"

Sometimes, Van wondered whether the treasurer's authority might have swayed the fundamental core of the church. Janet Filer suspected Paul was not acting as an accountant at all, and told Van she thought Paul's attack on outreach reflected his own ideological agenda. In closed-door conversations about outreach, Paul would show a conservative bias. Targeting specific outreach items to cut from the budget, he would laugh and say cryptically, "You know, Van, I'm a hawk, not a dove."

Despite objections, Van could not mount an effective defense to Paul's reports. He had to admit that the Outreach Board benefited from a prearranged deal. If the church property needed expensive renovations now, people began to say, perhaps it was because the minister had spent years secretly stacking the Outreach Board with liberals who gave away a chunk of money every year to shrouded political activists and his own favorite social causes.

By mid-October, the treasurer's latest figures were about to make the rounds again, and while Paul worked in the office copying another report for the Cabinet, it was certain he had built another concise, well-modulated argument to shift the ideological foundations of the budget.

"No one had ever done a real financial analysis before I came on board," Paul explained to me that morning. "And from what I can tell, it's not really wanted by the minister."

Like most ministers, Paul thought, Van simply did not understand the world of finance. He could not blame Van, really, because religion was not supposed to be a logical activity. In fact, if you thought about it, the Christian religion was absurd and illogical. Religion reminded him of the behavior of lemmings: someone hops up and down on one foot and then someone else says, that's a pretty good idea, and then he hops up and down on one foot. Before you know it, they're all hopping up and down on one foot. And, before long, someone calls that religion.

But Paul had not given up. He had a more reality-based vision for First Church, and over the next few months, given the worsening economic climate in New England, maybe Van would begin to see its value. Some day soon, Paul thought, maybe the minister would come to his senses. In fact, after the Cabinet saw Paul's latest report, Van might, for once, be forced to take a hard look at the bottom line.

Late that afternoon, Van phoned Tony Gillette, the assistant head deacon, and asked if he could drop by. When Tony opened his front door, Van immediately noticed the ink-stained hands. Tony's eyes looked bloodshot and his shirtsleeves were bunched up around his elbows.

Over the weekend, Tony had stayed home and worked. When Van arrived, Tony was still mapping a set of concentric circles, like ripples in a pond, showing the dispersion of outreach funds from First Church into the world. Tony had little patience left for details. Besides, he was not an artist, he was an engineer, and, frankly, he preferred spending his spare time doing anything other than compiling papers about the nature of charitable giving.

At the far edge of his dining room table, Van saw where Tony had copied documents tracing the church's ideological influences—from the Catholic missions of Dorothy Day to the laws of Moses—and started an outline for a presentation to the Cabinet.

"It's a good strategy," Tony said, ushering Van into the dining room. "If I can just draw the materials together . . ."

Van acted as if he hadn't heard. He picked up a coffee cup and glanced around at a spread of empty Scotch tape cannisters, crayons, rulers, scissors, scraps of typing paper and poster board.

"What strategy?" Van said.

" 'What strategy,' " Tony repeated with a chuckle. "You know what I'm talking about. Look!" He reached for an easel pad and curled back the pages. ACTION ITEMS—OUTLINES—GOALS . . .

Van turned away.

"So I guess you've thought about Paul's figures," Van said.

"We're working against something that's very hard to put your finger on," Tony said. "With some people it must look like we're giving money away without accounting for it."

"Which we are," Van said.

"I suppose. But that's what I thought you always said Christian mission was about. Somehow I didn't think the Good Samaritan ever had to give an accounting."

Van laughed. Tony could see that he did remember. *Obfuscate.* The last time Van met with the Outreach Board during the summer, his parting advice had contained that one unambiguous note of guile.

"*When the Cabinet comes back in October,*" Van had said, "*make it look like you've thought about your budget all summer, and while Paul's still recovering from his vacation in Bermuda, go in and say, 'Look, we're all friends here. We go to the same church. And we've got this wonderful new mission statement. And here are a bunch of documents about all the exciting programs you're supporting.' Swamp 'em with paper. Confuse 'em! Obfuscate!"*

Tony snagged Van by the arm and led him over to the table to show off the confusion of circles.

"This better work," Tony said.

"It's going to be fine!" Van said, looking away, embarrassed.

"Well," Tony said. "You can see I'm not an artist."

Tony spun one of his maps on his buffed mahogany dining table.

"You're well prepared," Van said.

"Tell you what," Tony said. "Maybe you could make a few phone calls. Janet sent me a copy of Paul's most recent figures. He could make things very tough for us. Janet's going to be there tonight to lead this, so it's not really my business. I'm only there for moral support. But I'm sure she'd be happy if Joan Rockwell and John Gregory-Davis showed up, too."

Van set his cup aside. He couldn't invite outsiders into a Cabinet meeting.

"So you'll be there?"

"I offered to help."

"Okay, I'll call Janet first and see what she thinks. Maybe Joan could come. I think John might be away, but I'll call."

"Good."

Tony handed Van a map and followed him to the door.

"You know, Van," he said, "a person with Paul's background is very uneasy with our kind of mission. With the economic climate the way it is, I'm afraid this thing could turn into a crisis. Our church could become an ideological battleground."

Van patted Tony on the shoulder. "Don't worry, Tony. There's more than two ways to skin a cat," he said.

Van stepped out into the heat of the day. Playing church politics was one thing, but teaching Tony Gillette how to play hardball was going to be a challenge of an altogether higher order.

Van stuck the circle map inside his Bible, where he wouldn't have to look at it again, and drove back to the office to set up the coffee tray for the Cabinet.

It would have been no surprise if Van had fought that night to protect the outreach budget. Privately, he encouraged Tony and Janet to address the Cabinet, "obfuscate," then demand more money.

But a half hour before the Cabinet met, I watched as Van called Paul Price into his office and, after reviewing the latest financial records, told the treasurer not to lose his momentum. Without thinking twice, Van agreed, on the spot, behind closed doors, to give up the Outreach Board's twenty-percent cut, just like that.

I was shocked. I knew Janet had come fully prepared to fight for a twenty-four-percent cut. She held copies of Tony's reports with a firm grasp, and she chatted cheerfully with Cabinet members before the meeting began. She looked perfectly confident.

But once Paul's financials went around, it was apparent she would never have a chance to make a case. The treasurer's analysis showed that over the year more than three-quarters of the church's $74,000 outreach budget had disappeared into cryptically titled accounts: one, for instance, marked Ocotal (Nicaragua) Project; another called the South African Covenant. A thousand dollars went to support a low-income-housing protest march in Washington, D.C., and other hefty sums went to private colleges for unspecified causes. The rest of the outreach budget, the report showed, had spilled into the coffers of the United Church of Christ and mysterious "mission" fields around the world. If, as Paul believed, the church was exporting liberalism's agenda, supporting American farm workers' unions, and legal services for Salvadoran refugees, and abortion rights groups—as was certainly the case—there had never been any acknowledgment from the Outreach Board and certainly no accountability to the larger congregation. At the same time, Paul's report showed, the First Church building reserve fund had stagnated, making up a paltry two to four percent of each year's budget for ten years.

Devastating evidence. Once the discussion started, Janet did her best. She went after Paul's motives like a trial lawyer.

"Come on, people, look at these numbers!" Janet said. "Paul here is just trying to isolate the outreach budget from everything else. I mean, just what kind of question is being posed by this report? What is the question and who's asking it?"

The four pages, containing itemized summaries of the outreach budget, also included a section of analysis that looked like this:

	1989	1988	1987	1986	1985	... 1980
Outreach as % of Ministry, Music, Christian Ed & Outreach	30.6%	31.6%	30.4%	31.6%	30.4%	30.6%
Bld. Reserve as % of Ministry, Music, Christian Ed & Outreach	4.7%	4.8%	4.6%	5.5%	6.0%	3.4%
* Outreach as % of Bld. Reserve	554%	554%	573%	487%	443%	773%

* Outreach does not include property expenses, primarily custodial & insurance, directly related to nursery school

Janet thumped the pages. "I'm afraid the question I read here is about the buildings being starved and outreach going through the roof. And that's just not true."

"But why is outreach isolated in this budget?" Tony Gillette asked. "And by whose request is it isolated? No one else's budget is broken down like this."

"Paul's own thinking is that the buildings haven't gotten enough attention," Janet said, "and he wants us to give less to outreach and I want us to give more. I know there are some folks in our church who just think 'property,' but my whole philosophy is that as you give, it all comes back to you."

"So am I right to think that you suspect there is a basic philosophical issue being presented here by the treasurer?" Tony said. "It's not like there are any overt questions being asked here."

Janet wiggled her nose and turned the attack back on Paul. "That's right. And, Paul, I'm concerned that what you keep calling a 'technical matter' is really the basis for a philosophical discussion. And I think it's time we as a board took a closer look at what's really behind your philosophy."

Paul looked sternly at her from across the room.

"The problem is a technical one!" he said. "We are spending people's money that has been entrusted to us through endowments that are restricted, and I don't see how you can justify taking any of that. Now maybe you want to call that a philosophical problem or you can call it whatever you want, but I call it illegal! And you are playing games!"

Janet pressed her thumb to her lips and turned to Van for defense. Members of the Cabinet—chairpersons of every committee, sitting as heads of the church—silently reviewed Paul's documents. While every other committee scraped and bargained for Sunday-school books, Christmas sconces, and lightbulbs, it seemed as if the Outreach Board had managed to cut a deal against the bottom line.

Janet finally caught the minister's eye.

"Van?" she said.

But instead of coming to her rescue, Van looked over at Paul. "You know, Paul," he said, "I think maybe this twenty-percent formula is just an idol and a fetish. And, just to get us back on track, it might be wise right now if we just dropped it entirely."

Janet's face hardened as Van went on to suggest that the Cabinet challenge the Outreach Board to "make a clear case" for any increase in its budget. She turned red, but she did not say another word. The discussion ended immediately.

In minutes, the Cabinet voted to cut the outreach budget and then set an eight-percent cap on any other budget increases in the upcoming year.

"I didn't mean to play both ends against the middle," Van told Janet afterward, "but we had to get around the obstacle."

Paul left the meeting thinking that his message had finally reached Van. The reality of New England's recession had brought them all back to common sense.

"I'm mildly surprised," Paul told me. "But maybe I was finally heard."

On Sunday morning, a week after the Cabinet meeting, Lucille tried to reassure Van over breakfast. "Van, you've built up enough support in this church to take on Paul," she'd said. "You've got lots of supporters out there."

"Yeah, well, if it was up to him, we'd be getting paid with a bushel of potatoes," he said.

"Van!"

"Okay, maybe two bushels."

"You don't think people will start cutting their pledges, do you?" she asked. "Or quit coming to church?"

"I don't know," he said. "But I think we've got to keep our antenna up."

Lucille, whose circle of sources always ran deeper and broader than her husband's, had not been able to trace currents of gossip very well that year. Lucille, who always had her ears open at choir practice and at Women's Club luncheons, was afraid that if Van started bearing down again on the outreach issue, the congregation might counter by freezing Van's salary or cutting pledges or staying away from church on Sunday mornings. But when she went to choir practice that morning—with her antenna alert—she heard nothing unusual. Janet Filer was still upset with Van, but Lucille heard nothing else to indicate that his critics were out to get him anymore.

A week later, Van called the Outreach Board together again, this time for a meeting in his own living room, and advised Janet to go ahead and take the usual twenty-percent portion of the total budget and send the request directly to the treasurer.

"Don't worry about Paul," Van had said. "We'll print up Tony's charts in a brochure, write a mission statement, and spend the rest of our discretionary funds before the end of October. The majority of people in this church are behind us one hundred percent."

Of all the gossip that came and went through the First Church office in the fall, the political machinations of Van Parker struck me as the most remarkable. Good old Van Parker—outwardly as simple, honest, straightforward, and everyday a guy as you'd want to meet—was an operator.

"This church is an organism," Van said to me later, when I asked about his cagey maneuvers. "And the job of a parish minister is just to do what you can, and then let things evolve as they will. As long as I don't separate myself from people, things work out."

But I thought that was just a lot of BS from the boss man, and, frankly, I suspect he knew in his heart of hearts that it was a lot of BS, too.

CHAPTER NINETEEN

From the street I could see little figures rushing through Allison's house and hear the muffled rumble of three boys scampering and squealing from lighted room to lighted room. With doors and windows standing open to take advantage of the recent balmy weather, the children's activity repeated scenes visible up and down the block. From dinnertime to bath, certain homes erupted with the sound of adolescent laughter and rebellion.

The women who had become my spiritual pals all had families with clamoring spirits. I suspected that one reason we had started these field trips was to provide them with an escape. We met perhaps once a week on average now to practice spiritual disciplines. In addition to prayer, meditation, healing, and meetings with JoAnne, the field trip to an AIDS healing service came to represent our latest effort to leave the boundaries of First Church and venture into the unknown.

From the porch, I could see Priscilla and Nancy snatching up light jackets and pocketbooks. Allison was giving her husband, Karl, a patient push toward the stairs to get the boys ready for bed. I tried to poke my head in the door and speak to Karl, but the women breezed by so quickly I didn't have a chance.

"Come on, I'll drive," Allison said, waltzing off to the Subaru, and the three of us followed.

After nine months, they had finally grown comfortable with me as a companion. Conversation in the car turned to sex and the virus.

"Better hope your husbands aren't having an affair these days," Allison said, as we sped down the interstate. "Most people out here are totally clueless about how this stuff spreads."

"That's not what worries me," Nancy said. "We have to take so many precautions at the hospital now. You used to just worry about not spilling a bedpan. Now it's gloves and masks and glasses. Oh God! for the good old days."

"Karl's absolutely terrified about it," Allison said. "He spent three weeks doing intakes in the ER at Saint Francis, and every night he came home ready to change professions."

They agreed the problem was really much worse than it appeared on television.

"Elissa said they're selling condoms for ten cents in her dorm at UConn," Nancy said. "My poor baby!"

"You'd better hope they're selling condoms in the dorm," Allison said.

As a nurse, Nancy knew Allison was right, but she still hated the idea of her daughter stocking up on ten-cent rubbers and having sex with college boys.

"The only thing to be said for it," Allison continued, "is it's bringing the whole gay issue out. Unfortunately, it's like a double whammy for that community. We just had two gay men move in down the street and you'd think the Martians landed. None of the neighbors will even speak to them. And the stories you hear are awful."

Priscilla and Nancy didn't say anything.

"You know, I had an uncle once who had two holes in his penis," Nancy said, after a pause. Priscilla and Allison burst out laughing.

"Ouch!" I said.

"It's okay," Nancy said. "He was happily married with two point five kids."

Within minutes, we drove into the neighborhood where the healing service would take place. Priscilla spotted the Quaker meetinghouse, its

doors and windows open. Long lines of cars parked along the curb indicated a sizable crowd. Allison stopped a block away on the grassy edge
of someone's yard, and as we got out I saw a throng of people bunched
outside the entrance to the bright meetinghouse.

A large sign on the front door said, THE ONLY THING THAT STANDS BE-
TWEEN THIS CHURCH AND AIDS IS A WELCOME MAT. As we crossed the mat, I
felt a hint of pride to think of the risk we were taking. At the time, AIDS
was the disease of pariahs, as distant from the domestic concerns of First
Church as the streets of Calcutta. I hoped this visit would mark a change
for us.

For six months we had been holding our own healing services, but
the quest for orderliness and liturgical form still dominated the work.
Priscilla still seemed to think our service never sufficiently accounted for
the unexpected. Every evening we met she insisted on spending half our
time creating the right ambience. We wasted hours bothering over everything from how best to light the sanctuary to deciding how to shape
the circle. It never made sense to me. I never thought our guests would
recoil from the squeaky back door that groaned when latecomers drifted
in, or clam up if one of our hymns or creeds referred to God with a male
pronoun. But my friend was relentless in pursuit of perfection.

"Admitting you have real needs is terrifying enough without having
to worry about what happens first or where you will sit," Priscilla em-
phasized one night over my objections. "The least we can do is provide
safety in structure," she said, and little bombs went off inside my chest.
People at First Church, I assumed, were accustomed to a given symme-
try and sense of good proportion, above all else. I gave up trying to
resist.

Maybe there was good reason for Priscilla's obsession, I don't know.
Maybe it was God's path for her. But I still could not help wondering
why we continually restructured bits of scripture and prayers into an
impregnable force of propriety. The back door of the meetinghouse
would still swing open occasionally with latecomers who cared nothing
about liturgy but came with a need only to be heard. The cancer victims
in their tightly wound nylon wigs, slack-eyed men in the trauma of divorce, a girl who'd had an abortion and needed to grieve—they never

seemed to care whether the Communion loaf was adequately thawed. When somebody you knew visited the service and revealed that in the past week he had lost his job and his wife, and now felt like killing himself, would he care at all if we had put fresh flowers on the Communion table? Actually, to my mind, we never warranted a liturgy at all. The largest crowd we ever had was thirty, including eleven members of the committee. Sometimes the only ones there were just us, one of the ministers, and a couple of deacons, strong-armed into service.

Fortunately, I was not the only one exasperated. In September, Ted Alford, the baseball coach, expressed my feelings by making an oblique comment, aimed at Priscilla, about anal retentiveness. It was not an appropriate remark, but it did force the issue.

Shortly afterward, Allison and I suggested that we meet more often to encourage cohesion within the group. That was why, in September, we drove to the Kingswood Oxford Academy for guided meditations with Bernie Siegel and a hall full of cancer survivors. And this month, it was AIDS at the Quaker meetinghouse. On both occasions, Ted feigned an excuse about having to coach junior-varsity football, but we carried on without him.

So we were finally here, I thought. Taking a risk. On the edge. Out in the world. We trooped into the Quaker meetinghouse and took our seats in a small, warm worship area filled with concentric rings of rosy oaken benches. Only after we were settled did I notice my three friends fidgeting in their seats, looking around the room like gawkers at a cockfight.

Tony Gillette pecked at his keyboard and watched a colored chart bleed through the monitor. Following the plot across his computer screen, Tony saw the line dip suddenly at the notch that marked early April. It fell, then rippled at a low ebb. He wasn't expected to give a report, but the new information seemed important. After the capital campaign began, you could see a correlation between the ongoing fund drive and declining church attendance.

After three years as a deacon, Tony was still pondering the value of his service. The longer he worked at First Church, the more he found himself fiddling with charts, typing data, writing letters, and helping committees. It seemed as if he was always on the phone now talking to someone from the church—Andy McCarthy or Allison Denslow or, lately, Janet Filer and Craig Fitch about the budget. Sometimes his wife thought it was funny, considering their history.

Fifteen years ago, when they were first married, Tony had not even bothered to join his wife, Charlotte, for church on Sunday mornings. He would tease her at the breakfast table. He'd say: "I'll bet they're the kind of people who greet you at the door with a gang of sober deacons who look like the offensive line for an Irish football team. Bunch of sour, broad-backed men in dark suits with names like O'Malley and Doyle."

Charlotte would ignore it, put the kids in the car, and go off without him. After a while Tony got the message. Not that she had ever felt a great, gut-level spiritual yearning herself; but as a Windsor native, Charlotte did have bottom-line expectations about certain things. Attending First Church, she felt, should have been considered one of Tony's weekly responsibilities with the family.

"At least it's not some kind of priest-ridden bog," he would mutter later, paraphrasing James Joyce, on the drive to church.

The strangest thing, Tony thought, was that over the years at First Church he was never expected to approach the place with pious or high-minded airs. You could tackle any task with a strictly nuts-and-bolts attitude. Take the deacons: You had your seven-tray Sundays for Communion, your dripless candles for Easter, your bread bakers to call once a month, the standard setup of inflammable candles with six-inch Cape Cod colonial sconces (style no. AP-06) for Christmas. Weekly responsibilities for ceiling fans and general climate control. Check the circuit-breaker panels and fill the baptismal bowl. Occasionally you'd coordinate an eight- or ten-o'clock service. He helped Allison Denslow update lists of scripture readers and coffee-hour hosts. He called on First Church greeters, flower ladies, name-tag sources, and youth deacons. After a few years, anyone could do the job blindfolded.

So why had he agreed to put in more and more time over the last three years? For some reason, every meeting required hours of careful preparation. First, there were letters. Then he added statistical charts.

Then phone calls, and now, with the latest outreach conflicts, he was being drawn into church politics. Lately, he would leave for church at least an hour early for any event, and Charlotte would say, "Why are you going now?" And he would say, I've gotta do this or get that in place or set up chairs or talk to Van or see Andy about something. But as soon as he arrived at church, he would take out his keys and stroll over to the meetinghouse, sit down in the sanctuary, and enjoy a moment with God alone.

Tony did not think of himself as a spiritual guy. No way; he was an engineer. Water systems, hydraulics. Irrigation.

"Is that Pratt and Whitney software?" the guys on the Cabinet would ask. They teased him when he used x-y plots to document the effect of foul weather on church attendance—"Rainy-Day Christians," he'd called it—and passed out diagrams for Easter and Tenebrae drawn on professional graph paper. They laughed at his hog-headed inability to leave the chauvinist corporate lingo at work. One night after an especially sensitive discussion of intercessory prayer, he had said: "Okay, fair enough, why don't we take it up as an action item and revisit it next month. All we need now is an interface with healing on twelve October and we've got a done deal." Another time, at an early inclusive-language meeting, which he chaired because Andy was absent, he'd said, solemnly placing his foot in his mouth, "I believe inclusive language is a gentleman's prerogative." And just a week ago, after working closely with Allison Denslow on the board of deacons for three years, he tried to compliment her quick preparations for a funeral service. Quite thoughtlessly, he said, in front of the entire board: "Allison, I would gather from our conversations that you don't know too much about sports. But there's a sports metaphor I think is appropriate for this occasion. 'It ain't the size of the dog in the fight, but the size of the fight in the dog.' You can fill that in however you want."

No wonder people thought he was a redneck. How did a guy like him become part of the spiritual life of a church? But then, he had given up the old idea of God as a graybeard, and had recently started calling God "He Slash She," like some kind of New Age clown. The whole experience turned out to be more fun than he had ever imagined.

Tony tapped at the keys of his computer again, and printed out three pages of charts for the stewardship meeting. He opened another window on his blue screen, and under a file slugged PREPARATION, inserted a note under "Item 7: **For particularly well attended services, consider an eighth juice tray.**"

None of his friends could understand why he got such a kick out of church work. They kidded him about the broadcasts on WJMJ radio, where he came on after midnight, during "Kukla, Fran, and Ollie," and read a quaint homily inviting people to church on Sunday. People didn't realize it was just part of his job. Something he couldn't explain. It was the same way he couldn't explain why he spent so much time typing up pages of charts every month, or why his reports always sounded less like notes for a worship service than like a plan for overhauling an underwater feed pump. Frankly, he didn't understand it, either.

By the time Tony finished printing out a calendar for the annual stewardship drive, he had a stack of twelve charts and outlines ready for the copying machine. He opened his black ring binder, where he kept his church material, and clipped the pages into the final section.

Anyway, he was just a facilitator down there, that was all.

"Supper's ready!" Charlotte called.

But Tony had already pulled on his olive-colored Range jacket and packed his sportsman's briefcase.

"Tony! Don't you want some supper?" Charlotte called. "There's at least an hour before the meeting."

But he was gone, out the door, hustling to the car.

Across the street, the neighbors saw him tromping through the leaves with a set of files wedged snugly beneath his arm, as usual, looking like a little monk rushing off to vespers.

Young men packed the room. Many of them, gaunt and frail, talked quietly among themselves with uncommon intimacy. Anyone could immediately tell that we were the strangers, tourists in the midst of what was, reportedly, a local nomadic community of otherwise closeted gays and lesbians. We gripped our bulletins and uttered not a word.

"God of compassion . . . God of peace . . . You are ever-present."

The service began with a prayer by a fragile blond-haired man identified in the bulletin only as "John." A scripture reading followed, then
a moment of silence, then a song accompanied by electric piano and
guitar. The men's voices rose in melodic swells. There was a slow, lingering pattern in the way they phrased the lyrics, a mournful sound trans-
posed into a hymn of praise. By the third verse I heard my voice pitched
to the same haunting timbre. Six verses, seven, then eight, and I could
feel a power sweep over the room. A ruddiness returned to drawn faces,
and, after the "Amen," I found my attention heightened to every sound
and breath that ended the hymn and steadied into silence.

A small group of men and women dressed in clerical collars and
white robes gave directions about how to proceed. They sectioned the
plain room off into three parts and invited anyone who wanted healing
to meet a minister and an aide in one corner or another. But before the
service of healing could begin, we were instructed to welcome each
other with the sign of peace.

Our First Church squad hardly budged when the assembly broke to
honor its own festive conventions. Gay men and lesbians milled around
the room, hugging one another, turning to kiss lightly on the lips. They
approached our bench to welcome us to the service, too.

The liturgy was otherwise strict and forward-moving, but it had not
protected us from the strange encounter with men passing peace with a
kiss. The shock of a simple buss, man to man, left me a bit unsettled at
first, and then I was ashamed by my own embarrassing incapacity to
move a single step from our bench by the wall. We stood awkwardly.
Frozen with self-conscious smiles, offering a curt handshake and saying
our pat First Church greeting, "Peace be with you," we four had stood
up like periscopes, and down we went again.

We joined the meditation in prayer. I watched young men stand and
shuffle across the room. Many walked with canes or with the help of a
friend. They inched through the pews to a corner and folded into a hud-
dle with one of the ministers. Several minutes later, they shuffled back
to their seats, some weeping softly as others stood to take their place.
They looked like survivors of concentration camps, wispish figures with

closely cropped hair and dark eyes—small-boned, sunken, skeletal creatures. Surrounded by the dying, we bowed our heads.

One after another took a turn, and then I finally closed my eyes, too. Images of fishing nets hit the surface of a rolling ocean, drifted down through a luminous green current, and drew up around dark, human shapes. I could see nets gathering bodies of gay men and women whom I had known and loved. People I had known since grade school. People I knew who had recently come out. Friends who were still in the closet. They were more than memories and faces. I tumbled into the green water myself, and soon I was praying.

The energy of prayer, I had learned, came from waiting, listening, and giving up, all at once, until my heart was both receptive and yielding and the Spirit made its move. In an entire roomful of people, it was easy to assume that everyone might be having the same kind of experience, even though the person on your left could be reciting her mantra, the one on the right confessing a sin, the one in front checking his watch, the one across the aisle being dragged down by a gloomy or an impassive mind. I was blessed by being healthy and naïve enough to believe in a higher power, and in having a few good friends who, for God's love of cornucopia, happened to be homosexuals. The idea that my church friends did not feel as moved as I by the service, as it continued in songs and verses, never would have occurred to me. For the remainder of the time, I felt we had all been united in a healing.

And when it was done, I thought we would stay for coffee and meet the organizers. But after the final hymn, I turned and saw Priscilla bolting for the door with Nancy on her heels. Allison looked at me and shrugged. We were halfway home before anyone spoke.

The real mystery of the previous evening was not only that my small group of friends, whom I had considered authentic spiritual compatriots for six months, had suddenly and utterly turned homophobic, but that another curious event occurred simultaneously in the church library.

At the same time that Nancy and Priscilla were apparently imploding on the bench next to me at the Quaker meetinghouse, Nancy's husband, Craig, announced his resignation as chairman of the fall stewardship campaign. Paul Price joined him in a private meeting with Van and Janet and supported his decision. Craig unceremoniously handed over the financial lists and canvass notebooks to Tony Gillette and Andy McCarthy. Tony and Andy, neither of whom had ever run a church canvass before, were stunned. Van suspected that Paul Price's leadership had finally taken hold in the church.

I showed up just in time to hear Craig make his speech. Noting all the problems with trying to increase pledge percentages during a sour economy, Craig's recital of First Church ills sounded remarkably like Paul's standard message. Then, right after he tendered his resignation and blamed Janet Filer again for "manipulating" the congregation, Tony Gillette underwent a conversion.

I would not have believed it if I hadn't seen it myself. After Craig's little speech, Janet started to make a conciliatory gesture to bring him back to the committee, and then, suddenly, Tony Gillette slapped his fist into his palm, jumped out of his chair, and started circling the room, his face turning deeper shades of red.

"Craig, do you really want to know what's wrong with this church?" he cried. "I'll tell you what's really wrong with this church! It's not outreach! It's not Janet Filer! It's not Van! It's money! It's that we are so damned attached to our little budget! It's that we only have three people running the stewardship campaign every year and we follow the same tired formula without practicing the values that Van preaches to us all year long. It's that our people are not grateful for all the blessings we've been given!"

He was thumping the table with his knuckles. Quiet, shy, levelheaded Tony Gillette, an engineer who had never taken a controversial role and never shown himself to be a very spiritual person at all, suddenly seemed to have experienced a seismic shift. Everybody in the room looked surprised as they watched him roam agitatedly around the table.

"It's time to start taking this thing seriously!" he said. "It's time we started to get this message out there! Stewardship is not about raising money! Janet and Van have been trying to tell us this for the last six months. Stewardship's not about money or percentages or budgets. It's about gratitude! It's about faith! Now we can all sit here and feel sorry for ourselves or we can look at Craig's resignation as an opportunity. We can turn this thing around! But only if we ask ourselves and our congregation just who we are and—what is it you always say, Van?"

"You mean, 'Who we are and to whom we belong'?" Van said, raising his eyebrows.

"That's it! 'Who we are and to whom we belong,' " Tony repeated. "Van says it at just about every Cabinet meeting: There's more money in our congregation than we'd ever know what to do with. And it's time we went out and said so. Because money's not the problem here. Our problem is it's time we started talking about faith. And I say, damn the budget! Forget drawing up a budget. Let's go out and talk to our people about faith for a change!"

Andy McCarthy told me later that he thought at first, "Well, we've got no choice. Tony's just trying to make good of a bad situation. With two weeks before the campaign starts, it looks like he and I are the ones faced with raising money for the coming year's expenses. And there's nothing else we can do but say the hell with the budget." But then he thought, No, Tony didn't have to volunteer. Tony could have said, Okay, guys, let's volunteer Andy's wife, Elizabeth, to take Craig's place; she's done this before. He could have said, We'll let the Cabinet cut the annual increase back to eight percent and then follow the same mass-mailings-and-telephone-brigade tactic they've used for the past twenty years. But when he said, "Damn the budget!" Andy thought that maybe Tony had just announced the most revolutionary plan in First Church history.

But could they raise money without a budget? Could they really do it based on gratitude and faith alone?

Trembling with excitement, Van called it a historic moment. Janet looked dumbstruck. Andy started laughing and clapping, and all of a sudden he was wound up, too, praising Tony for inaugurating "a new concept" for stewardship, and then he hopped up out of his chair and went circling around the table, too.

"Van, just imagine what would happen if we could get people like Tony up there in the pulpit to testify every Sunday for the next twelve or fourteen weeks?" Andy said, eyes alight. "Think about it. We could get people talking about the personal meaning of giving money to the church. We could get Allison Denslow."

"Joan Rockwell!" Tony said.

"I can think of a dozen people who would be great up there. The congregation will go crazy."

"I'm ready," Tony said.

"Why not?" Van said.

"Okay," Andy said. "Van, next Sunday, save me a few minutes before the sermon, because I'm going to announce that for the first time this church is going to talk openly about money and the roof won't fall in. Because we're doing it here tonight, and, by God, the walls are still standing around us."

Craig and Paul were the only ones who looked glum.

"I guess I'm just a facts-and-figures man," Craig said sheepishly, and then he offered to stick around at least to help out with the mechanics for the first mailing of pledge cards.

Paul left in a rush. He said something about having to get home to watch the World Series, and then walked out.

The rest of them, however, kept working until ten thirty, when Tony and Andy finally volunteered to run the church's first "faith-driven campaign." Those were Janet's words—"faith-driven"—which she had trotted out every chance she could for the last nine months. Now she was finally hearing the phrase from someone else's mouth.

The meeting ended and Van went around turning off the lights. Tony talked to Andy out on the steps of the parish house. Tony said he was a little perplexed and embarrassed by how he had acted.

"I can't believe I said all that," he told Andy. "I'm really not some kind of radical nut. Believe it or not, I've spent my whole career designing water systems."

Andy went home so excited he couldn't go to bed. He woke Elizabeth and told her about Tony's conversion. The new stewardship campaign would be tremendous. Even Craig had decided to stick with it.

But then, try as he might, Andy could not remember how the new concept worked. He'd start to describe it to her and she would say, "Andy, that can't be right. No budget?"

"That doesn't make sense, does it?" he'd say.

He would start and have to stop and think again.

"Actually, I'm not sure I really understand it," Andy said. "But really, I think for the first time we're on the right track."

I had never seen anything like it. That night and the next day, even while Priscilla, Nancy, Allison, and I kept coming in anxiously to talk to him about AIDS and homophobia, Van would interrupt us and say he'd never forget what had happened the previous night. "October twenty-eighth," he said. "That date should go down forever in First Church history."

I should not have been surprised. So what if our participation in an AIDS service set off a wave of hysteria? In Windsor, garden clubs, car pools, church socials, and cocktail parties formed the venues for public discourse. Although the culture of First Church had assimilated ideas about antiques, Cézanne, Bach, and Beatrix Potter, securities and life insurance policies, there was certainly no reason to think anyone was ready to accept the notion of affectionate love—or sex—like to like. Just the image of men kissing men was far more frightening and repulsive than the plague of AIDS itself.

Nevertheless, Allison spent hours on the phone the next morning taking calls from people who had heard about our venture into the wilds of West Hartford. One woman said she knew for a fact that the AIDS healing services around Hartford had supplanted gay bars as new trysting spots for homosexuals, and that the kissing we saw at the Quaker meetinghouse would, of course, lead later to *you-know-what*.

"Just take it to its natural conclusion," the woman kept repeating.

"I do not know what you mean," Allison insisted.

"They shouldn't be kissing, for one thing, but just take it to its natural conclusion."

"What are you talking about?"

"You know!" the woman cried.

"I do not know!"

"Anal sex!"

The next thing I knew, Priscilla came in to see Van and told him she did not think it "appropriate" for First Church to sponsor an AIDS healing service. Van shut the door and reassured her that she was right, now was not the time to consider such a move. "Maybe someday," he said, "but frankly, gays and lesbians are not my issue."

While they talked, I ran into Nancy in the office and she brought it up again. It's not all homosexuals we fear, she said. "Actually, lesbians are fine."

"What?" I asked.

"Bisexuals are okay, too," she said.

"Huh?"

"It's a way to make sure you get a date on Saturday nights."

"What?"

"Bisexuals."

"You've got to be joking," I said.

"But this kissing and promiscuity in public is wrong!"

Soon, my friend who had been so reticent the night before started talking to me about homosexual sex in a most explicit and unsavory way.

When I finally got Allison on the phone, she sounded as outraged as I felt.

"It's not that First Church isn't 'ready' to handle AIDS, it's that we're too homophobic to even allow gays or lesbians into our church," she said.

While we fumed about the spiritual poverty of our healing committee and both Priscilla and Nancy said they were prepared to personally stand in our way if we even thought of pursuing an AIDS ministry for First Church, Van was ecstatic.

In just one night, everything I thought I'd learned about First Church went to shit. My friends were acting like heathens and the money-grubbers had undergone contrition, absolution, and apostolic revival. A dramatic reversal. A paradox. A contradiction. The unmasking of one illusion, the mysterious advance of another.

And I was ready to call it quits altogether.

CHAPTER TWENTY

Van washed and waxed his white Toyota in the shade by the porch one warm Monday. Autumn musk rose out of the ground like an earthy incense. Leaves fell across the churchyard. As orange as mangoes, scabby red like the peel of pomegranates. The dark limbs of maples and sycamores held full clouds of light, and between what had fallen and what held tight, spots of sunlight swirled under his hand.

His body shimmied as he spread liquid wax across the hood. Sweat stained his wrinkled red cotton shirt. Daisy snoozed at the end of her chain, nose slumped into a fresh pit, and Van's thoughts drifted to people who were finding a new passage in church or were on their way back after an absence. The next line of the congregation's story was always being written, but he didn't always realize it until he stood aside in rare moments like these, moving to the swish of a damp rag. Soon he found himself calling names like a silent canticle.

Drew Carroll. Cured of cancer at fifty-three, Drew had turned to the ministry and left First Church to take a job as education director at Thomas Hooker's old Congregational church in Hartford. The offer had come late in the spring, the night after Drew came to the First Church healing service and asked for prayers about his need to find a call. It was

Drew who had made the deal with the Cabinet ten years ago to give a portion of money every year to the outreach board, Drew who had advised Van to start the eight-o'clock service, Drew who had helped Van through the controversy of bringing a cross into the sanctuary. Who could take his place?

Of course, Allison Denslow seemed happier these days and more active. Joan Rockwell was back from Nicaragua, more spirited now. Nick Wilton was a great addition to the church. How about that confession he'd made the other night at the healing service about his wife's death? It had left everyone feeling calmed: "I'm not such a good person," he'd said, and Van had thought, as he crossed into the circle to lay hands on Nick's hunched shoulders, No, Nick, and neither am I.

And the Corts and the Williamses, two black families whom Van had gotten a bead on for new memberships. Charlie and Cindy Squires, Andy and Elizabeth McCarthy, Henry and Carol Holcombe, and now Janet Filer and Tony Gillette—as steady a conversion of time, talent and treasure as he could ever hope for—and all the silly mystics, cynics, and secularists who came and went as naturally as the change of seasons. The men and women in the Wednesday-morning Bible-study class— "Bless their hearts," he thought—they floated into focus as he scrubbed the chrome clean, and when he finally emptied the bucket and snapped his rag, they fell away, too, with the rest.

Van climbed the porch to go inside for tea when the car was done, but stopped short on the landing when he smelled something peculiar on his shoe. Always these blasted reminders. He laughed when he went back into the yard to scrape his soles across the grass. Dogs and God— *ludens in orbe terrarum*—playing over all the earth. Amen and amen.

For more than fifteen years, the Wednesday-morning Bible-study class met with good intentions in the Morrell Room. Virtually the same crowd showed up with Bibles and study guides to carry on the never-ending dialogue. Mining the text was just a ruse.

Trudy Crandall came in with her seeing-eye dog, Ara, and Kate

Thomas, who always taxied them over in her car. Alice and Buddy Brookstone, who had quit attending a few years ago when Buddy contracted cancer, came back singing the praises of vitamin C and meditation. A handful of widows—pretty Olive McAlister, Rose Lester, and Maggie Hollyfield, who was just beginning to use a cane—came as a faithful contingent. Benny Blackwell, a school crossing guard, strolled over at nine forty-five and by ten fifteen promptly fell asleep sitting upright next to Rose on the green divan. My friends, Nancy Fitch and Allison Denslow, the only middle-aged pair in the crowd, acted as resident cognoscenti, bringing a smattering of ideas from Sigmund Freud, William James, Harold Bloom, Thucydides, or whoever else they happened to be studying with Bill at the time in his evening adult Christian ed class.

Whatever they lacked in intensity, they made up for in faithfulness. Unlike any other committee or board, steady members of the Bible-study crew often remarked that their fifteen years had passed in a flash.

One morning in mid-October they were reading Ecclesiastes for the first time when Rose and Kate decided they could not go on.

"This is a depressing book," Rose said, after Van read the fourth chapter from the New Revised Standard out loud.

"You said it, Rose," Kate moaned. She reached over and touched Rose's arm. "Why did we even bother to come back this week?"

"I say, why bother with anything after reading this?" Maggie said, tapping her cane against the floor.

"Van," Rose said, "I don't understand why we're reading this study guide by Rabbi Kushner, *When All You've Ever Wanted Isn't Enough*. I think we've all had everything we wanted and it was enough."

"That's not true," Kate said. "It's just too late for us to bother anymore. Our lives are almost over anyway." Kate wrinkled her nose and made a razzing sound.

Van had not been able to read Ecclesiastes, either. *Better is a handful with quiet than two handfuls with toil and a chasing after wind. . . . Fools fold their hands and consume their own flesh. . . . Dead flies make the perfumer's ointment stink. . . .* The truth was he winced the whole time he read it at home, and by the time he finished chapters on the purposeless nature of pleasure, work, wisdom, and dreams, he had set his Bible down and groaned.

"Well, God Bless the reading of His Holy Word!" Van cried. The women laughed again. Van made such a fitful bark. They could tell he didn't care much for the old wisdom-teacher, either.

"But Van, there must be some reason it's in here," Nancy said, holding up her new red-covered copy of the NRSV. "Rabbi Kushner calls it the most dangerous book in the Bible."

Kate shook her head and patted the *Good News* Bible lying open on her lap. "He says if you do something it's vanity. If you don't do something, it's vanity. If you're smart, it's vanity. If you're stupid, it's vanity. And in the end it's all the same, whether you're rich or poor, saint or sinner. You're vain. You die. And that's that."

"He's right," Rose said.

"Of course he's right. But why dwell on it?" Kate replied.

Trudy, who had been stroking her Seeing Eye dog, rose in her seat and piped up: "I know why. It was written by Solomon. They couldn't afford not to include something by Solomon."

Van turned to Allison. "Allison, what do you think?"

Allison had the keenest mind. Besides, she knew all about hard times. She had those three boys at home. For the first time in her life, she was jobless. By any account, she knew the need of keeping your faith intact. She swept the hair out of her eyes, revealing a penetrating gaze in a thin face. She was much younger than anyone else, her complexion as light as the October moon. "I think he reflects the human condition in an honest way," she said quietly. "You realize that it wasn't my generation that invented this kind of cynicism. These feelings have existed for an awfully long time."

"That's encouraging," said Nancy, who usually agreed. "One less thing for me to feel guilty about."

"Well, I don't think it belongs in the Bible," Maggie said.

"I have a version of the Bible on tapes I bought from a group in Florida and Ecclesiastes isn't in there," Trudy said.

"Oh no!" Nancy said. "Trudy, you've hooked up with one of those evangelical outfits."

"They knew what to do with the old buzzard!" Van snorted.

"They did warn at the beginning of the tape that they left out a few books," Trudy said.

"What else did they leave out?" Maggie asked.

"Song of Solomon."

"Aha!" Nancy said. "I knew it!"

"I don't care," Trudy said. "Bill made me my own tape. Anyway, I think Ecclesiastes is just talking about the different stages of life, not the whole thing. It made me think of my son-in-law who used to buy all his clothes from the Salvation Army during the sixties and now he buys them all from Ralph Lauren. I have pictures of him when he was young and silly and wanted to show the world that clothes weren't important. He got married in Bermuda shorts and a bow tie and a plaid jacket. He wouldn't be caught dead like that now."

"That's the most amazing thing," Nancy said.

"But, don't you see, these are just the stages of life," Trudy said. Then she remembered to add, "It was a formal wedding," and then, "Oh, he's a great guy, too."

Trudy smiled. She warmed the room with her smile now. In just the last few weeks, she had completed a nine-month cycle of cancer treatments and taken off the dry blond wig she'd worn for a year. Seeing her new hair, growing black and healthy, and observing the unexpected radiance in her eyes, the rest of the group deemed her the star of Wednesday-morning Bible study. Most of them had reached the age where maintaining good health was an accomplishment, but Trudy, who had lost her eyesight to diabetes and her husband to heart disease, and now battled cancer, was nothing less than heroic. Above all, she maintained a positive attitude.

"I do like the familiar phrases," Trudy said. " 'The sun also rises' . . . 'to everything there is a season' . . . 'cast your bread upon the waters' . . . That's what it's all about."

"You're right," Van said. "He does say a few good things."

" 'Tis a pity he's become so cynical, though," Maggie said. "It seems to me that in your older years, you should have reached a point where you have some peace and serenity in your life." Maggie was seeking peace every day, reading in the library, swimming at the Y, learning to be still, even though her spine was wracked by arthritis and the pain constantly reminded her that she would probably fight a battle, just like Trudy, for the rest of her life.

"I think he's having a midlife crisis," Trudy said.

"I beg your pardon?" Maggie said.

"I just don't think he's old enough yet for peace and serenity."

"You mean Ecclesiastes is younger than we think?" Maggie said. "Van, I assumed he was in his retirement years like the rest of us."

Van threw up his hands. "I don't know a whole lot about him," he said. "I've never read this before."

True enough. Although Ecclesiastes' search for God, and the assessment of his failures, pleasures, and losses in life sounded more authentic, in some ways, than any other book in the Bible, the passages had no appeal for Van. With no mysterious visions, no trumpeting angels, no moralistic canon writ in stone, the book of Ecclesiastes reflected the ultimate futility of religion. Integrity came only through knowing the fullness of life's failures as well as its successes.

Obviously, Ecclesiastes had not been Van's idea. It sounded like one of Bill's selections. In fact, the Kushner book—an explication of Ecclesiastes—had always been one of Bill's favorites.

So Bill, who sat quietly in a corner by the window, volunteered to read the next chapters out loud—*For who knows what is good for mortals while they live the few days of their vain life, which they pass like a shadow?* . . . and *For who can tell them what will be after them under the sun?*— and when he finished, Van laughed again and snapped his Bible shut.

"This guy's a real breath of fresh air!" Van cried, and the ladies tittered. "Gosh! You know, I can't even read this stuff!"

"I think we've done the best we could do for one day," Rose said.

"I think I'm going to cry," Trudy said.

"I think we all could," Olive said.

"Isn't it time to go?" Maggie said.

With at least a half dozen chapters left, they agreed to stop for the morning, but they would stay with the book at least until Thanksgiving. Next time, they would read down to the end of chapter nine: *One bungler destroys much good.*

"Oh no!" Nancy moaned. "That reminds me—my mother-in-law is coming next week."

"Don't worry, we'll meet anyway," Trudy said.

"We'll give you an excuse to get out of the house," Kate said.

"You people are so wonderful!" Nancy said, clasping her hands to her chest. "If it weren't for you, I'd have no place to be but with my Catholic mother-in-law. This is so exciting! We've never met when she was in town before."

"See? God has spoken through your mother-in-law," Van said.

"I knew it! This is a good universe," Nancy said.

But Bill, who hadn't made a single comment all morning, was still looking at the text when Van assigned a few more chapters for the next week. Everyone agreed to start again Wednesday at ten, and although most of the class stayed for coffee at the end, Bill closed his book, got up, and left without saying a word.

The hurly-burly of commuter traffic fanned off Main Street up Palisado past the church and down Pocquonock Avenue, sweeping him along like a leaf in a stream. For hours, he made calls—from the funeral home to the nursing home to the post office to the hospitals. He was running hard.

At least twice a month, Van visited the new home of Frank Lester. Harvard Law, Class of '37. Rose never did say much about her husband in the Bible-study class, but she appreciated the ministers' help, since their children now lived out of state and she could no longer be of much service to Frank. Crippled by a stroke, he would likely live many more years, but he had lost significant control over his bowels and bladder and, as with a number of men in his predicament, at times his mind lapsed into a frightening awareness that he was in steady decline. He would probably never leave the home where church elders often spent their final days. Kimberly Hall was not such a bad place to die. But it could be lonely.

"Hi Frank," Van said, making the bedside his first stop of the afternoon. Frank must have been asleep with his ear tuned to the radio perched next to his bed. He uncurled slowly out of a fetal position and looked up. One eye drooped, his hair was matted.

"Hello, Van," he said in a quiet, child's voice. On this side of the room, he had a pleasant view out of a picture window, a calendar of Eastern birds taped to his wall, Rose's picture on his dresser. His roommate, by the door, a man wrapped in a white sheet, groaned in bed, but Frank did not seem to notice.

"Been listening to the playoffs?" Van asked. The radio was playing the first afternoon game. Van's favorite, Cincinnati, was ahead by two runs. Frank reached over and turned the volume down.

"I don't have the mind for it anymore, Van," Frank said shyly, rubbing his eyes. "Ever since the stroke, I can't remember things. I feel like a ten-year-old boy. I used to have a pretty good brain, you know. I could read and study. I can't read anymore, Van. When I was ten I could read."

He was smiling. His voice sounded so soft and sweet you would not have thought there had ever been a lawyer's command in it. Or now, despite what he said, that it had ever once sounded a complaint. Van shuffled around uneasily.

"Look," Frank said, straining to lift his sheet so Van could see, "they told me I had to put this on the bed before I go to sleep." Van saw the plastic pad under Frank's thin, white legs. "I like to sleep," he said.

Van helped Frank turn over and sit up, then searched around for something else to talk about. "Look at that bird calendar, Frank," he said. He reached down to pull the covers up again over Frank's legs. "I saw Rose at Bible study this morning. She's a good woman."

"I never knew how good until I came here," Frank said.

Van kept searching. Pictures of children. The man by the door was snoring now.

"How's your son, Frank?"

"He comes by once a month." Frank's voice sounded even smaller, more boyish. "I'm proud of him. He comes by every once in a while and we go for a ride."

"You're getting out some, Frank. That's good."

No, Frank said. He was not. He could not walk anymore. He could not remember things. He felt angry. His face went blank.

Van drew closer to the bed. Frank's roommate was turning in bed and groaning again.

"The next time your son comes to visit, you should drive by the church," he said.

Frank looked up. "Church?"

"You should see the Pierson House, Frank," Van said. "It looks brand-new. The whole place looks brand-new. We've nailed on new clapboards and slapped on a nice gray stain. We've got more painters running around there than we've got kids on the playground."

Something registered. Frank untwisted his legs, pushed himself up in bed, and fluffed his pillow. He lifted his hand, bruised by catheters, and rubbed it over his stubbled cheeks, squinting as if remembering the name of an acquaintance or a forgotten date. It took him a second and then he said: "Yes, I'm so glad the church bought the Pierson House. They used to have all kinds of people renting out rooms over there. It never made sense to me that we didn't own that property, Van. When I was on the Prudential Board I used to argue with those guys all the time and say, 'We should buy that old Pierson House and fix it up for the congregation to use.'"

"That was you?" Van said, genuinely surprised. "You mean, you were the one who did that?"

"Yeah," Frank said. He reverted back to the embarrassed smile. His body seemed to shrink. His face went blank.

"Frank?" Van said.

"Yes!"

"Frank, your grandchildren come to church now. They sit on the left-hand side, about two-thirds of the way back, right where you and Rose used to sit."

"They do?" he said, again sitting up and taking notice. "I didn't know that. Nobody told me that!"

"It's a good seat, Frank."

"That's where my father and I used to sit. That's back when they rented pews. We'd sit there every Sunday. And on Easter or Thanksgiving or any of those big days, my uncle and his family would join us. We'd all be squeezed in there like sardines, and it made my father so mad, he finally rented two pews to handle everybody."

"Well, your grandchildren sit there now," Van said.

"That's the conservative side," Frank said.

"No," Van said. "There's no pattern like that."

"Yes, there always was," Frank said. "Left-hand side. All of the conservatives sit over there. I remember. It was a good seat."

The man's mind suddenly made a jump start. Frank clicked into gear and went on to recall the first time he laid eyes on Rose. He spoke of their early days in Texas, where he started law practice, his college years at Yale College and Harvard, a half dozen presidential elections, a few big cases he fought, and then he went all the way up to his last birthday, which the family celebrated recently. He pointed to the clay flowerpots and cards standing along the sill.

"Isn't it funny, Van?" he said. "I was born in 1910, and now I think like a ten-year-old."

Van looked out the picture window at the woods in back of the nursing home. "It's getting cold outside," Van said. They both watched a wind blow leaves across the lawn. "It's the first cold day."

"Well," Frank said. "I better get up."

"And I better be going," Van said.

Frank tugged the sheets up around his neck and turned over to look out the window.

No need for a prayer, Van thought. Frank looked back and waved when Van reached the door. The radio came up again and Van almost caught the score. Sounded like Cincinnati, still ahead by one.

Late in the afternoon, on the way back from the hospital, Van wheeled his Toyota down Palisado into Ruth Bissell's shaded yard.

Ruth lived directly across from First Church, but she had not attended services for many years. At ninety-four, she did not feel a need for formal sermons anymore. Instead, she would pick her own times to climb into her immaculate '67 Chevrolet and drive very slowly from her driveway to the front of the parish house—a distance of no more than fifty yards—and park by Van's mailbox so she could check up on things. When Van dropped by, though, she would always apologize for her absences. "You know my parents were married in that church in 1887," she'd say, as if to reestablish herself as a member. "And I was married there in 1916 by Reverend Roscoe Nelson." And Van would say, "Yes, Ruth, I know. And your children were baptized there, too."

The scent of heavily oiled antiques and baked apples rose in his nostrils as he entered the house. Ruth shuffled along the cool carpets with a cane and showed him into the dim living room where her son, Walter, roared with surprise.

"Van Parker! Your buildings are looking mighty good, my man!"

They were wearing the same baggy pants and open-collared cotton shirts. Walter Bissell, a retired Episcopal bishop, looked salty and lean like a lobster fisherman, and he stood a little taller and spoke a lot louder than Van. But otherwise they made a pretty good match, Episcopalian to Congregationalist, shouting at each other for lack of proper hearing aids.

"It's coming along, isn't it," Van said proudly. "We're almost finished working on the Pierson House."

"My husband rebuilt that place when it burned," Ruth said.

"That's what I understand," Van said. "Everyone says it's structurally better than the parsonage."

"Well, it should be," she sniffed.

Van rarely had a chance to see the old bishop, since Walter was traveling now. Van liked him, despite his being an Episcopalian. Walter had an earthy quality that was unmistakably the mark of a veteran. Retired ministers had a certain appeal for Van, especially now, as the idea of his own retirement came more often to mind. Walter Bissell was never at a loss now for reminiscing and calling up old war stories.

"You know, I was a bishop for fourteen years and I'm still floating around churches in Connecticut," Walter said, "but that's where I started, right over there, with Roscoe Nelson."

"You did?" Van asked, leaning over to look through the window at the old meetinghouse.

"Yes, Don Filer and I joined the same day. We met with Roscoe a few times and one day he took us both out into the cemetery ..."

Van started to chuckle at the bishop's loud, formal delivery. He could hear every syllable.

"... and he made us touch Ephraim Huit's grave."

Van barked a laugh so hard that he took a tumble out of the wicker chair. "I'm falling out of this chair!" he said. Something cracked and Van jumped up.

"Don't worry about it, Van," Walter admonished. "It happens all the time."

"I'm afraid I broke it," Van said, moving quickly to the sofa, leaving an arm of the wicker chair hanging limply toward the floor.

"Don't worry, we'll send you a bill. As I was saying, I remember standing in the graveyard and touching base with our beginnings."

"And that's why you became a Episcopalian," Van said, chuckling again.

"Well, you Congregationalists are a scary bunch," Walter said, eyeing the broken chair.

Walter had been ordained for something like forty-seven years and had spent half his career in the town of Cheshire. He and Van belonged to the same cohort that had weathered careers through the fifties, when, as Walter said, "All you had to do was ring the bell, open the doors, and get the heck out of the way," up to the eighties, when the big mainline churches lost members in record numbers. They were comrades, in a sense.

"Van, you must have thousands over there by now," Walter said.

"About eleven hundred," Van boasted. "And we're doing this capital-fund drive, which is kind of fun."

Walter didn't betray a sign of doubt.

"We'll be building a new parking lot in front next," Van said, "and then we'll put an addition on the back of the choir room."

"On the back?" Ruth said. "Aren't there graves back there?"

"We can do it without digging anybody up," Van said.

"That's good," the bishop said, unabashed.

"Yes," Ruth said, "you'd hate to move them."

The bishop sat up, cocked his head, and licked his lips. "Yup!" he bellowed. "Van, do you know what I think? I'd just move them if I were you!"

Van looked back quizzically. "You'd do what?"

"You know, when I was in Cheshire we had to move a few graves for a new building once. Some of the old-timers were upset, but the old-timer who meant the most stood up one Sunday and said, 'I thought the church was for people who are alive, not dead. And I move that we dig 'em up!' So I did. I dug 'em up myself."

Van's eyes brightened. "Well, good for you, Walter."

"Sure did!" the bishop said. "Dug graves, found bones."

"Oh no!" his mother gasped.

"That's right, Mother. We went right down to the First National and got some beer cases and buried 'em back in the ground."

"Beer cartons?" his mother said.

"We figured they deserved something good after all that."

"Wow!" Van said.

"But then, everybody who came along for the burial service kept saying, 'Alas, poor Yorick . . .' until one of the guys got tired of it and said, 'If you people don't quit saying that, I'll hit you with my shovel.' God, it was awful!"

Van was rapt. The bishop had not cracked a smile.

"The next time we had a building campaign and had to move 'em, the undertaker said, 'You know you did it against the law the first time,' and I told him, 'I'm not going to pay you a hundred dollars a grave! There's nothing down there but bones.' But he forced the issue and we had to buy a vault."

"You did?" Van said.

"Isn't that stupid?" the bishop said, disgustedly.

"It really is," Van said.

"It's ridiculous, really," the bishop's mother said. "People like cardboard much better, anyway."

For more than an hour, they had a fine time. The bishop told stories from his career while his mother recounted the names and peculiarities of First Church ministers across an entire century.

Finally, the bishop leaned over and said, "Van, I've been trying to learn how to walk on water for almost fifty years, but I haven't gotten there yet."

Van laughed again. "Well, you dug up a cemetery. I'd say that's pretty good."

"You'd think it would help, wouldn't you," the bishop said. He actually sounded serious. "Well, the ministry's been fun. But, I'll tell you, to persuade these Yankees to give up their money, that's hard work. You know, I'll bet the biggest thing you'll be glad to get rid of when you retire is those every-member canvasses."

The bishop sat back and, in the pause, he listened very carefully.

"Of course we just had a capital-fund drive and we had good leadership," Van said. "But to tell you the truth, I'm glad it's almost over."

Walter's expression softened. "Of course you are," he said.

"And you're right," Van continued, "I will be happy if I never have to raise money for another annual budget."

The bishop looked sympathetic. He uncrossed his legs and rubbed the arms of his recliner. "Anyway, like I was saying, when I was in Cheshire," he said, "we had very little in terms of an endowment—maybe five thousand dollars—and not a single large contributor. Every year it was a hard push. It was always if you just had another ten thousand, you could put the final touch on things. In twenty-two years, we never got there. But it was still a good church, and it was moving with the Spirit and it kept on going long after I left."

"Yeah," Van said. He sat still for a second and the bishop smiled at him across the room. "Yeah, well . . ."

Ruth Bissell must have missed the moment, because her mind drifted back to another era and she started remembering a trolley car that used to stop near their house. The ministers let her talk, and then Walter stood up and walked with Van out across the dusty porch and joined him on the short walk to his car.

"Van, let me tell you one more story and then I'll leave you alone," he said. "You need to hear this. You know, I was the minister of just a small church, but the sanctuary had a huge steeple on it. Someone back in time apparently wanted people across the Connecticut River to see it above the trees and think the town was an English village or something pretentious like that, and we were supposed to be the cathedral at its center. The story was that when travelers got to town, they found out that the spire loomed over a church that was really only forty by forty feet. One day during my tenure, I recall, a prominent Anglican bishop came to visit from England and as he stood on the road and looked up at the church he turned to me and said, 'So, Walter, you've built quite a steeple there. I should think some day you will build a church.' "

Walter Bissell motioned to First Church with its square, plain, flat tower—not much more than a crow's nest on a boat. "Now, Van, you know our churches don't need big steeples," he said.

They stopped in the driveway. Walter was gazing across the street. The old First Church meetinghouse could look rather unimpressive at times—fleecy white, boxed, high and long like the body of a goose—and under a fading sky during the late afternoon, it seemed even smaller and more modest than it actually was. Without a spire, it might have been mistaken for a country courthouse or a small school. But at the moment, something in it was making the bishop's eyes sparkle.

"I used to go up there and sit in that tower as a boy," he said. "Which would drive Mother crazy. The ministers would leave a key hanging on the front door, so it was easy enough to sneak in and have the run of the place. I've been in every corner from the basement to the belfry. But you know what I remember most?"

Van shook his head.

"All my life I've never gotten away from it."

"Well, what was it, Walter?" Van asked. "Did you see a ghost or something?"

"It was a good smell," he said, taking a breath like a man entering a bakery. "A really good smell." He clamped his hands together and shut his eyes for a moment, and when he opened them he said, "That's pretty fundamental what I got there, Van. Maybe that's what makes me a little different. I'm not an Episcopalian, really. You can tell by looking at the dirt on the bottom of my feet. I'm a First Church Congregationalist."

All afternoon, the old bishop had been trying to tell Van the same thing, over and over again. Something important. To leave him with that blessing all ministers need but cannot seek. Walter winked and rubbed Van on the back. "Thanks for stopping by," he said. "It's done Mother and me a world of good."

It was sunset when Van finally left the Bissells', pulled out of the driveway, and drove across the street to the parish house. He went to the office thinking he would polish his sermon for Sunday, but he did not stay for long. He went home instead, kissed Lucille, and invited her out to a movie.

At dinner he talked about retirement, almost eagerly, she thought. Something about him seemed unusually happy and carefree.

CHAPTER TWENTY-ONE

I had expected members of the Cabinet and Prudential Board to be upset about Tony Gillette's new idea for the budget, but the cynicism spread beyond the conservatives in the church. My friends on the healing committee, with whom I felt increasingly disappointed, started talking church politics, too. The big news about the conversion of Tony Gillette, they would say, sounded like Van's usual BS.

"You're kidding!" Allison said, when Nancy told her one day about Craig's decision, again, to quit the stewardship committee.

"No, in fact, I can't believe it, either. I told him before he went to that meeting, 'Craig, maybe you can bring them back down to earth, and it'll all be worth it.' But instead of bringing them down to the earth, he flips out like the rest of them."

Allison shook her head. I was eavesdropping in the Morrell Room, as usual, as we waited for JoAnne to find a suitable nature tape to begin our November meeting of the spirituality group.

"Amazing! So you think Van's playing politics?" Allison asked.

"Well, Craig said Van had promised him there'd be no more than an eight-percent increase in the budget this year, but then Van went straight to the Cabinet last night and asked for twice that."

"I've heard," Allison said. "Everybody's saying Van let loose last night. What's gotten into him? Someone said he actually polled a bunch of churches in the conference to get their average pledge figures, and compared us to make it look like we aren't up to par."

"That's exactly what happened. And the Cabinet completely backed off. Craig said everyone was shocked. He didn't even have a clue Van was going to do that. But Van kept saying he thought people at First Church weren't grateful and he was ready to ask everyone how much money we're spending on eating out or how much we spend on vacations. Craig said he made everyone feel so guilty they didn't know what else to do. And then that Tony Gillette pitched in his two cents' worth about a 'faith-driven' budget—whatever that is—and the next thing you knew, the Cabinet voted to increase the budget twenty-one percent. I've never seen Craig so upset."

"Twenty-one percent!" Allison said. "I wouldn't want to be responsible for raising a budget like that right now."

"I told him, 'Craig, I wonder how many people on the Cabinet met their pledges last year.' So Craig being Craig, naturally he decided to do some research and—"

"And?" Allison said.

"This was really interesting," Nancy said. "He came right down here to the church office early this morning and looked through Peggy's files and found out that half the Cabinet didn't even meet their pledges last year."

"I'm not surprised. Actually, I happen to know a number of people—I'm talking brand-name people—who increase their pledge every year and then only meet about half of it."

Nancy's eyes widened.

"It's true. I'm not naming names," Allison said. "But I've got it from a very—very—reliable source."

"No!"

"That's right. You'd be amazed at the people who don't pay up. We're talking 'Mr. and Mrs. First Church.' "

"This money business has become such a pain," Nancy said.

"I know," Allison said. "One year Karl and I had some financial problems and we really couldn't afford to pledge, so I put zero down on my pledge card. A week later, Elizabeth McCarthy sent me a letter saying she hoped we weren't having problems in the family."

Nancy gasped.

"I was really upset!"

"I can't believe she had the nerve to do that."

"I was so embarrassed. Finally I had to talk to Van about it. I was in tears. I had to tell Van we just couldn't afford it."

I tried to keep my mouth shut. Priscilla Drake came into the room and sat down, and soon she was listening, wide-eyed, too.

Allison and Nancy went on with a torrent of gossip. "I know! I know!" Nancy would say, as Allison talked on, naming names, giving details about the church's financial picture and a few members' personal spending habits.

Then Nancy said: "I think Craig really got a gouge job by that Janet Filer."

"A what?" Allison asked.

"You know how she keeps driving up the costs? And Van says, 'Don't worry, we're not going over eight percent this year.' But then she comes in and tells Van to go ahead and do whatever he wants!"

"That's our Van," Allison said. "He acts like he's listening to people, but—"

"Plus, all this means Craig's trying to cut back on our budget at home. With Elissa in school and us planning Craig, Jr.'s, college, we can't afford a big pledge right now. Craig's already told me I can't use the Mastercard again until after December! Oh my God! No more books!" Nancy laughed at herself. She was a junkie for books.

"Well, don't talk to me about Janet Filer anymore," Allison said. "The church hasn't been the same since she came on the scene."

Nancy agreed. "I can't stand her."

"I can't either. I didn't like the way she ran the capital-fund campaign. I keep trying to tell Van at the deacons' meetings that people are angry about it."

"I know people who are still very upset about that."

Nancy shook her head sadly. Then she said, "Craig thinks people are afraid of Van."

"Sure," Allison said, almost casually.

"I can't imagine that!" Priscilla said, finally entering the conversation. "Van's so sweet!"

"You'd be surprised," Allison said. "A lot of people are afraid to be honest with their ministers. They clean up their homes before a minister comes to visit. They put on their best behavior. They change their entire manner."

Allison looked at me. "You've seen that, haven't you?"

I shrugged. There was no point acting any longer like I hadn't. Of course, some people acted ridiculously around ministers.

"That's just the way it is," Allison said, looking back at Priscilla. "Besides, Van is very political."

"Van?" Priscilla said. "Political?"

"Very political," Allison said, as Nancy nodded vigorously. "Watch him sometime. He's good at getting his people on one side and pulling strings to make sure things happen just the way he wants."

"Wow," Priscilla said.

"It's not that he has bad intentions, but it does keep people from speaking up and saying what's on their minds."

"That must be what happened at the Cabinet meeting," Nancy said. "Craig said he went right up to Andy McCarthy after the meeting and asked, 'Why didn't you just say this twenty-one-percent increase was too much?' And Andy said, 'I wanted to support Van.' "

"That's just it," Allison said. "People have this weird need to please their ministers."

"Gosh," Priscilla said.

"Have you ever noticed when people start to speak their minds, Van starts talking about *the Spirit?*" Allison said. " 'The Spirit! The Spirit!' If I hear him say that one more time, I'll scream!"

"Maybe Van doesn't really understand the problems people are having," Priscilla said.

"You mean financially?" Nancy said. "You're talking about the tax revolt in town and—"

"And at work," Priscilla said. "My husband didn't even get a raise this year. He usually gets eight percent but this July he didn't get anything, and then in September he only got four percent. Now his company's saying, 'Don't expect it to be any better next year.' "

"Van's not very realistic," Allison said.

"Anyway," Nancy said, "Craig was really upset after that Cabinet meeting. He's talking about leaving the church, but I don't think I could do that."

"That's interesting," Allison said, looking away.

Now that *was* interesting.

Suddenly they all looked over at me. I don't know why, exactly, but I could see an awareness on their faces that I'd been much too quiet. In fact, it was not possible now to act as if I hadn't absorbed every word.

"I guess you just got an earful," Allison said.

"Heck," I said, "I hear it all the time."

It was true. I was hearing about money all the time now. And as JoAnne popped in the wind tape and we started our morning meditation, I finally decided that I had had enough. I waited until everyone's eyes were closed, then I got up and walked out.

Van looked just awful. Sometimes at night, he would wake up feeling claustrophobic and have to get up and walk around the house. He would go home for lunch, but instead fall asleep watching the news on CNN. One Sunday, he asked the congregation to stand, hold hands, and sing "We Shall Overcome," but it created a fuss. People met him at the back door griping about having to touch each other in church and complaining about singing secular music.

Lucille told a few close friends that maybe Van had just become "too spiritual." He wasn't laughing and gregarious at work, he wasn't irreverent at home. His face looked contorted with worry, wrinkled like a punched-up feather pillow. He was anxious and more forgetful than usual.

November had started out as such a good month. Bulldozers and backhoes groaned across the edge of the cemetery laying new connectors to the town's sewer lines. A steady blitz of workers with power saws, hammers, and buckets of gray paint finished the final phase of reconstruction on the Pierson House. Prudential Board members marched around with pads and pencils noting that, where they once had seen nothing square, plumb, or level, they now could point to adjustments marked by a purple chalkline and the clean cut of a saber saw.

Of course, no one had yet replaced the rotted steps on the Parkers' front porch. Fractured cabinets and curled linoleum still marred Lucille's kitchen. Frayed phone lines and missing doorknobs were overlooked at Bill's house. Committeemen teased Van about a few cracked "nip bottles" unearthed behind the Pierson House ("C'mon, fellows," Van would joke, "I buried those back there some time ago"). Some had the audacity to question Bill's petty expenditures for leaf-raking at home and for soft drinks with the Confirmation class. But for Van, the ministers' properties were the least of his concerns. Because, despite other examples of progress around the property, the annual stewardship drive was a shambles. The new faith-driven budget had stirred up more confusion about who was in control than ever before.

Of course, Van might have been considered old-fashioned, but his rhetoric was always peppered with references to democratic principles. The question about who was in control should have been obvious by now. For years, scriptural passages about Christian community—especially from the twelfth chapter of Romans—had been his Sunday morning sutra: *For as in one body we have many members and not all the members have the same function, so we who are many are one body in Christ, and individually we are members one of another. . . .* He encouraged First Church people to be themselves, to discover themselves, to play politics and meet with a sense of abandon. To be free and feisty and celebratory, that was his mission. An authentic community must always undergo change and controversy. Who was in control? The community, of course, under guidance of the Spirit.

On the surface, his beliefs had all the appeal of a Fourth of July celebration. But democracy had its flaws. After the November Cabinet meeting, when he spoke his own mind about the congregation's financial inhibitions, Van felt the press of interest groups more than ever. Rumors swirled left, right, and center: John Gregory-Davis, for instance, had been absent more and more on Sundays; Paul Price cut his pledge by a few hundred dollars; leaders of the Women's Club, by far the largest and oldest group in the church, gossiped behind Van's back. Some people said he had turned their church into a big business with a bureaucratic structure. They said he diffused power by putting new members in high positions and developed concentrations of his own liberal-minded supporters on the boards and committees. Some of the older women who had served enough years as secretaries on those boards to know how the game was played, considered Van an "operator."

Van thought he should have earned their trust by now. Throughout his ministry he had always been pliable and equivocal. But now, as he neared his last years of service and hoped to take advantage of the good-will of his congregation, he could feel the fear. He could almost sense Paul Price on his trail. He felt hounded to put the faculty of cold reason to work.

One day Lucille made reservations to celebrate their thirty-fifth wedding anniversary with a getaway weekend special in the Berkshires. But the afternoon when they were to leave, Van rushed down to the drugstore and bought copies of *The New York Times, The Boston Globe,* and *The Hartford Courant* to take along, and then, in a flash, ran into the house to pack up books about Abraham Lincoln.

"Oh! I can see we're going to have a wild time," she said, as he tossed his papers and notebooks into the car.

The next week, Van called the Mercy Center, a seaside retreat for Congregational clergy, and signed up to meet with a spiritual director for a few days.

"It's been a tough year," he said when I caught him in the office making the arrangements.

The next evening Van came to the healing service. He led us in the Lord's Prayer and in a hymn, then served Communion using the same dry parchments of speech he always employed, "And we gather again around the table remembering the words that Jesus spoke: 'This is my body that was broken for you . . . ,'" and when it came time for prayers, he went to the chair at the center of the circle and bowed his head.

It was a low, halting voice, choked with emotion, almost inaudible and unfamiliar.

"I have no wisdom," he said. "I don't think I know how to lead anymore."

Allison, Priscilla, Nancy, Joan, Ted, and I circled around and put our hands on him. I saw his hands tremble and, once again, felt a strange heat rise.

Over the next two weeks, the Wednesday-morning Bible class remained faithful to Ecclesiastes. Van still could not contain himself through passages that sounded like bad poetry—*The toil of fools wears them out, for they do not even know the way to town* . . . —and one day after reading an especially pungent passage rife with sloth, indolence, drunkenness, curses, fools, and snares, he shouted, in an absolute whine of exasperation: "Come on, Ecclesiastes! Lighten up!"

"Poor fellow, poor guy," Trudy said.

"You meet people like this," Olive said.

"Sounds like your typical senior citizen," said Rose, who compared Ecclesiastes to a meeting of the local AARP. "All you hear about down there is arthritis," she said. "Ever notice that, Trudy?"

"You mean: 'Have you tried this? . . . Have you tried that?' "

"Sounds just like this old Ecclesiastes."

"They tell me WD40 is good for it," said Olive, who thought the women were complaining about an ailment.

"Oh it is?" Trudy said. "I'll have to get mine out from under the sink."

"What do you do," Rose asked, "ingest it or spray it on?"

Through their month of study, Bill had held them to the text. The classes had become a theological exercise, spawning the first debates I'd ever heard between the ministers. Ecclesiastes, Bill would argue, represented a step beyond most of the Bible toward a higher order of thinking, a significant change in biblical literature that foreshadowed Greek philosophy, and an approach to life based on experience, reflection, and a final distillation of wisdom.

"Ecclesiastes represents a philosophical shift," Bill said, "an approach to life mediated by thought rather than the revelation of God's will."

Bill came upon the key passage halfway into the ninth chapter, right before the famous one about time and chance happening to everyone. One gray morning, Bill read it, again, to the group: *"Go eat your bread with enjoyment, and drink your wine with a merry heart; for God has long ago approved what you do. Let your garments always be white; do not let oil be lacking on your head. Enjoy life with the wife whom you love, all the days of your life, because that is your portion in life and in your toil at which you toil under the sun. Whatever your hand finds to do, do with your might."*

But no one else could see what seemed so obviously remarkable and satisfying to Bill. They thought he had misread the passage.

"I couldn't follow that a-tall," Rose said. "Mine says, 'Eat, drink and be merry—' "

"What interpretation do you have there, Rose?" Nancy asked.

"Rose, you're still reading the *Good News*," Allison said, looking over Rose's shoulder. "Bill's using the New Revised Standard."

"There is a different emphasis," said Bill, who knew of the discrepancies. "In mine, he commends the enjoyment of life. But in the *Good News*, makes it sound like he's disapproving of gluttony."

"Eat, drink and be merry," Trudy repeated.

"The emphasis," Bill said, "should be on enjoyment—*there is nothing better under the sun than for people to eat and drink and enjoy themselves, for this will go with them in their days of toil.*"

"Sounds like good news to me," Trudy said. " 'Go barefoot in the spring!' "

"That's the disadvantage of having so many Bibles," Maggie said. "You waste energy just trying to keep up."

"If you go back and look, you'll see that Bill's translation has more words than ours," Rose said, turning to Maggie.

"I guess that means we got our money's worth, Bill," Van said, perking up. He looked over at Rose and teased: "My Bible's got more words than yours. My Bible's better than yours."

The women squealed with laughter.

"I'd never considered that possibility before," Nancy said.

"And Ecclesiastes would say that's vanity, too," Van said.

Bill rolled his eyes and went on talking. He explained what he thought about the bifurcation of body and soul, quoted Plato, and spelled out the responsibility of mature individuals to accept pain as well as joy in what he called "the shadowlands of life."

"Ecclesiastes," he said, looking at Van, "is an antidote to traditional Christian thinking. It's a refreshing challenge to the escape from reality posed by the old 'Sweet Bye and Bye.'"

"But Ecclesiastes is false Christian theology," Van said. "Where's the clarion call? Where's the Good News?"

"But this is shadowland," Bill said. "It's more novelesque, Van. He's moving us through the good and bad of life. We're being asked to reflect on its meaning. This is more about the fullness of life than simple Good News. It's existential. Just think of it this way, Van. If there is no shadowland, there is no Good News."

Van crinkled his forehead, shook his head, and twisted in his chair nervously.

"I just don't see much resurrection coming out of this. Christian thinking is based on the cross. I need some Good News!"

Bill fired back: "Don't you get it? Remember what Tillich says? Tillich says we're always attempting to remove the crucified body from the cross because we want happy endings. We lost patience passing through the valleys because we're in such a hurry to make the *Rainbow Connection* . . ."

The turn in Bill's voice had a caustic tone.

"Maybe there is a danger in trying to make Ecclesiastes into a Christian," Van said, quickly adding, "which he's not. Maybe you could say it's refreshing since he's not one of these guys with a plastic smile, but— and maybe I get impatient with people like this—but—"

"But," Bill said, "he keeps Christianity honest!"

"But he's not a guy who's terribly happy. Maybe he's more deeply serene than I can see—"

"Serenity's got nothing to do with it. There's real value here," Bill said. Then, flipping pages, he started to quote outright. *"Better is the sight of the eyes than the wandering of desire . . ."*

"I just don't see the Good News here," Van said again.

"But, Van, a mature person," Bill said, emphasizing the word *mature*, "would not deny himself the duty and clarity that comes from acknowledging difficult passages through life." He had turned to speak directly at his boss now, as Van, looking down into his Bible, scowled. "Part of becoming an adult is learning and appreciating the fact that life is marked by passages of loss and disenchantment and—"

As Bill's inflection rose, suddenly Trudy's dog sat upright, shook its head twice, and started to hack and weave and quake.

"Ara!" Trudy shouted. "Ara, stop that!"

The dog gulped, lurched its neck forward, gulped again, and, with a wrenching grunt, vomited on the rug. Van leaped to his feet, Bill grabbed the edge of the couch and looked over in alarm. For a moment, everyone craned to see what might happen next. Rose reached out and told Trudy not to move her feet.

"You old dog!" Trudy said.

"It's a wonder you didn't do this years ago, Ara," Nancy said, running off to the bathroom for paper towels.

"I always told you not to listen to us!" Trudy said, lowering her hand to find Ara's head and give it a pat. "Poor old thing."

"Does anyone want me to keep reading?" Van asked, and then he got down on his knees to mop up the mess. "What do you think Ecclesiastes would say about this? 'Life is not just walking the dog, but picking up after the dog.' "

With the floor cleaned and everyone settled again, Van started, dutifully, to read out loud: *"It is better to go into the house of mourning than to go to the house of feasting. . . . Sorrow is better than laughter . . . the heart of fools is in the house of mirth. . . . For like the crackling of thorns under a pot, so is the laughter of fools . . ."* But halfway through the chapter he started to groan again, and stopped reading early, thinking he had finished, then realized he had another page to go.

"Van, you'd better not read any more of that," Nancy said.

"Oh gosh!" he said.

"Oh my!" Trudy said.

The dog had started to snore out loud. Benny Blackwell, who had slept through the whole lesson, woke up, and Maggie, who had three different Bibles and a concordance open on her lap, began to spill books onto the floor.

Bill shut his Bible and laughed out loud. For the first time in months, he really seemed to be enjoying himself. "I guess it's time to stop this," he said. "Next week's Advent, anyway."

"On to the Good News!" Van exclaimed, and the women cheered.

The conflicts in church took a rest, finally, after Trudy's dog threw up in the Morrell Room. I thought you could mark it almost from that very moment.

Over the weeks, with the help of the Wednesday-morning Bible class, Bill and Van seemed to resolve their philosophical differences. Van seemed more relaxed and less concerned about money. Between Trudy, Rose, Maggie, Nancy, and Olive, the women beat the ministers down with common platitudes and mediated disputes about the wisdom of the Old Testament versus the New. They substituted their own sayings for the wisdom of Ecclesiastes. "Do your own thing," the ladies would say. "Be the best you can be." "Money is the root of all evil." "Eat more ice cream." "Go barefoot in the spring." "If you've got problems with your mother-in-law, just ask her to say blessing on Thanksgiving Day." After six weeks of tortuous study, the women concluded that if Ecclesiastes had only had a few good friends to talk to, he would have been a much happier man; and every week, they found a way to let Bill and Van know that they were their friends, too.

Eventually, both ministers agreed that people needed a kind of truth that reason does not teach, and after Thanksgiving Trudy summed up their studies in a sentence: "A wise person at least knows when he walks in darkness, but a fool never sees the light."

Van was singularly impressed. He praised Trudy's thought and told everyone it contained enough wisdom to win preservation on a refrigerator magnet. On Sunday morning, he repeated it in his sermon, and the one-liner entered into his conversations with parishioners for weeks.

Advent

Advent is like the hush in a theater just before the curtain rises. It is like the hazy ring around the winter moon that means the coming of snow which will turn the night to silver. Soon. But for the time being, our time, darkness is where we are.

—Frederick Buechner,
Light and Dark

CHAPTER TWENTY-TWO

Social duty regulated the church calendar during the stretch from Thanksgiving to Christmas. The smell of cinnamon filled the homes of my friends. At one warm place or another I shared meals of corned beef and cabbage, enjoyed a Sunday beer and televised football, dipped into homemade jellies and sipped bitter English tea, carved turkey and honey-sweetened ham, nibbled raisins, savored slivered almonds and figs, helped serve dark sherry in cold crystal goblets at five, and set out white lace and sterling for more formal affairs at eight. As the season of excess arrived at last, I helped myself through a half-dozen groaning boards and began to think of our Christian family as people bred of special stock, plump and peerless, like overfed ornamental fish.

Along with sumptuous meals came an outpouring of philanthropic action, which struck like a flash flood during Thanksgiving and did not let up for weeks. The parish house looked like a way station for the Red Cross. Cardboard boxes of old clothes marked for "the homeless" sat in the hallways; toys and crafts for "needy children" filled a corner of Nelson Hall. One day so many turkeys came in for distribution among "the poor" that the ministers ran out of benevolent associations who wanted the meat and finally had to call on the church's own members to take the birds home. And when the state penitentiary for women sent word that prisoners complained they were getting fat on shipments of First Church ladies' Christmas cakes, the Women's Club redoubled its efforts to knit a small mountain of mittens, shawls, caps, and scarves to distribute among inmates.

Even the Confirmation class spent hours one afternoon wrapping parcels for Latino children with AIDS. They ventured into Hartford with Bill to serve breakfast at the homeless shelter, and crossed the town's boundaries into a black neighborhood in Hartford's tough North End to work on a Habitat house. Several cold Saturdays, they raised walls and nailed headers with a black family of four building its first home. At the end of daylong shifts, they stood astride roof beams staring out across the 'hood in a quiet, pie-eyed response to mean streets below. Every Saturday for more than two months, Craig Fitch was always there, too, with a tool belt strapped to his waist and a hammer in his hand.

Nelson Hall looked more and more like a setting for a carnival. On the Sunday afternoon before Advent, a First Church event drew noisy crowds to watch deacons and deacons' wives, choir members and Sunday-school teachers model the best in New England winterwear—the annual Holiday Fashion Show. Large windows fogged over and trailed sweat while hundreds of churchgoers, surrounded by pastry-servers and coffee-pourers, ogled their friends who strutted across stage in the latest styles. The women used the Moses Room as a changing closet and lined up behind the stage, waiting for a signal to make their appearances in fragrant one-hundred-percent wool dress jackets and double-pleated trouser pants, silk beaded blouses, tapestry belts, elegant sarongs, black onyx earrings, and crisp white balloon-sleeve blouses with colorful Chinese work pants. I was surprised to see who was there among the bourgeoisie—Allison Denslow, Joan Rockwell, Sue Warner-Prouty, and Bill.

"Very oriental!" the emcee cried as the models twirled, spread their silky arms, lifted their heads, and tossed their hair like exotic birds. "Don't they look smashing, ladies?"

Bill and Sue, Joan and Allison cheered and shouted approval along with the rest, while Van, who was notably absent, worked in his office on a letter to the editor of the *Courant* objecting to plans for America to use military force in the Persian Gulf.

A few days later, on Tuesday, church members crowded into the hall again to sing with the Windsor Mad Hatters. Following a gargantuan luncheon of chocolate cakes, pecan pies, chicken and tuna casseroles, cold cuts, hot biscuits, ornamental salads, and fluorescent fruit Jell-O, the crowd settled back for two hours of homemade entertainment. Old men and women dressed like jesters sang songs from Tin Pan Alley and exchanged bowlers for colanders, stocking caps for cowboy hats, and pie plates for Dealy-Boppers while they danced across stage shaking home-made rattles and beating drums to the chant, "Hats may come and hats may go, but our hats will steal the show!"

They were intense and crazy days, and the closer we drew to Christmas, the more intense and crazy they grew. Darkness fell by midafternoon. A cold evening drizzle left Windsor's streets and rooftops covered with an icy black glaze. Cozy neighborhoods, chock-a-block with colonials, saltboxes, and quaint Cape Cod homes, sparkled with lights of a thousand white china shades and discreet electric candles shivering hyperstatically on windowsills. Religious impulses preserved and nurtured for more than three centuries spurred a pattern of behavior as regular and instinctual as veering trails of Canada geese. My friends sat up late at night dusting off classics by Dickens, Brontë, Wharton, and Hardy, and at odd moments the inheritors of tradition indulged a historical fiction as preposterous as King Arthur and his fabulous knights. The starlit journey of three wise men. The promise of angelic choirs. A virgin birth.

At times, too, when evening meetings ended and I walked through the churchyard to my car, I thought I could hear bells chiming from the meetinghouse and imagined joining carolers with a section of french horns and bassoons standing in the blue, moonlit, snowy paths of Windsor's more decorous side streets.

Something strong worked beneath the threshold of awareness, an irresistible desire calling out for magic and miracles. I could not give it a name, but there it was, circumnavigating common sense, moving quickly among us in mid-December.

Jan's year had passed in the spiritual care of the Storrs Quaker Meeting, a warm community of about fifty men and women who lived near or worked at the University of Connecticut. Every week, it seemed, she received an encouraging note in the mail, a phone call, or an invitation to dinner. A young, childless couple counseled her at times, and a wise, older couple—a retired business professor and his wife—welcomed her into their lives.

While I worked with the First Church crowd, she drew mandalas, studied Quaker history, learned massage, and practiced meditation with the Society of Friends. On Sundays while I joined the noisy congregation in Windsor, she sat quietly with Quakers. When I came home, literally at the end of my week on Sunday afternoon, Jan would always be bursting to tell me everything that had happened at meeting.

Through the fall, borrowing from the best of both disciplines, we used the Quakers' technique of creative listening to speak from the heart to each other about adopting a child, and, mindful of the traditional Protestant seasons of faith, celebrated Advent by lighting candles at the dinner table. Salvation by virgin birth had never made so much sense.

On the Sunday before Christmas, I dreamed about a baby for the last time. I held a little girl in my arms and, for once, the infant did not speak or wriggle up in the visage of a saint. I felt myself cuddling her. When I awoke, the pleasure of holding the child was really the pleasure of wrapping both arms around Jan, who was crying softly in the early morning.

Our bedroom was cold, barely bright.

She buried her head in my neck and drew up close to me.

"I had a dream," she said.

She had dreamed of a phone ringing in our house, and immediately she knew it was a pregnant woman calling to say she had chosen us to have her baby. Jan panicked, froze, and missed the call.

"The next thing I knew I was walking outside to get some tools out of the garden shed," she told me. "I could see that there had been a terrible frost during the night and it killed everything in the yard—all the flowers and vegetables were wilted in the garden . . ."

She choked back a sob, pulled away from me and wiped her face with the sheet.

"Anyway," she said, "I opened the door of the shed and the ground was covered with snakes."

"Jesus," I said. I thought we had moved past these fears.

"That's when I felt you next to me," she said. "It was like you were there but you weren't there, trying to reassure me that you'd take care of it and I shouldn't worry. So I went back out into the garden and that's when it changed."

Flowers were blooming, she said. Daffodils, dozens of them, popped up across the yard. "It was like that song we sing at the Quaker meeting."

I had not been with her to the meeting in over a year, but I did recognize the lines as she sang softly.

> *"Love like the yellow daffodils is coming through the snow*
> *Love like the yellow daffodils is coming this I know*
> *Ring out the bells of Norwich and let the winter come and go*
> *All shall be well again, I know."*

And all shall be well. And all shall be well. And all manner of things shall be well.

I held her and recalled those days in September when I would come home from church and find her on her knees in the front yard in the twilight obsessively digging holes to plant dozens of daffodils. At the time, I had assumed Jan was burying her grief under the pine trees—she put down more than two hundred bulbs, watered them tirelessly, kept the soil fertilized, laid straw. I thought it was a strange compulsion, but now I began to see.

"My dream was about faith," she said.

I didn't understand.

"We'll have our baby in the spring," she said. "When the flowers bloom."

My face turned hot, embarrassed by the sentiment and also ashamed for not wanting to recognize the need it signified. I gave her a kiss and climbed out of bed to get ready for work. For some reason, I could not talk to her anymore about childlessness and dreams. I hurried to shower, dress, and get out the door.

I quit taking notes and spent the next few days at the Windsor library working over a wrinkled plot. Too many characters. Circular narrative.

> *Minister's dog digs up fresh grave in cemetery . . . Church secretary threatens to quit . . . New deacon mistakenly hands out Pauline Dunhurst's funeral programs at Advent service . . . Outreach minister conducts a Communion service with homeless, and as the cup of wine rounds the circle, he panics because half his guests are HIV positive . . . Oh my gosh! Bill Warner-Prouty's son hangs a teddy bear from a noose in tree outside bedroom window. Neighbors alarmed. Abraham enormously amused . . . Praise the Lord! (Does this mean Jesus is coming soon?)*

Most of the stories made no sense. Someone's highly personal, life-altering experience—at an altar call, in a hospital bed, in a healing circle, on a mountaintop—always ended in ecstatic stammering or bleached religious lingo. Was this what happened when people confused God with Santa Claus? Or was it symptomatic of the problem William James described as "the terrible fluidity of self-revelation"?

I went back to earlier notes, written on index cards: "Sigmund Freud dismissed the idea of God as a fiction based on memories of our earliest relationships with our parents . . . The word *prayer* comes from the same Latin root as *precarious,* meaning 'obtained by begging,' a bit of trivia that should be useful sometime."

I carried books back to my table and turned through yet another file where I had occasionally jotted down a few of my own ideas during the year:

Conservative evangelicals represent an effort to salvage the American Dream—masking noxious "religious" doctrines in the promise of materialism, high technology, positive thinking. Middle-class members of the American mainline, however, who have also experienced the end of Progress, confront the crisis in another way. Goddesses. Gaea. Liberation theology. World myths. Could you not point to the popularity of New Age religions, ancient mythology, holistic healing, and tribalism as evidence of the decline of the American Dream? And couldn't the decline in mainline American religion be traced to that same decline? Religion was always confused with Americanism. Is not the decline of the American Dream a religious crisis, after all? What religious myth do we have if not the American Dream?

Boring shit.

I got up and blundered over to the anthropology section. Maybe something there would illuminate my experience *(The Raw and the Cooked . . . Notes on a Balinese Cockfight)*. I came back with Lévi-Strauss, set it aside, and started a list.

At First Church, I had met many kinds of people—people who took religion seriously—like Priscilla—and those who thought of religion as an intellectual game, like Bill. There were those who did not consider religion seriously, like Paul Price, and those who thought of it seriously, but never came to a church service. That was Owen Rockwell. Then there were those who took the church seriously but not religion (many of the older members), and those who took themselves seriously but thought little of either the church or religion (that was me). At last, those who took "spirituality" seriously but not "religion," which was where I finally decided to index Joan Rockwell.

I looked at the columns—names stacked like totems—and set them aside, too.

I had no idea. What was it I was looking for? If my journey into First

Church was a personal quest, was it only the desire of midlife that brought me here—wanting to have more dimension in my life, more clarity about being alive in a moment of someone else's awareness? Yes, I wanted to be someone, to make a difference, to prove I could still change, to learn the meaning of love, to learn how to love, to revive a sense of freedom, to be in parity with my parents, to learn how not to poison everything with cynicism. Wasn't that enough to know?

Here we were, I thought, too, Jan and I, in the middle of life, with all its length and responsibility, married only a few years, no longer having the buffers that come with youth—of a first marriage, of romantic love, of first jobs. Instead, now we had lingering fears and resentments—about failed marriages, failed jobs, failed dreams, about obligations and, now, almost forty, no children.

Why am I still not happy? I thought. Why am I not able to change? Why am I so irritable? Where can you go when the movies, new restaurants, and rock 'n' roll no longer warm the innermost self? To church? You've got to be kidding.

Almost an entire year had passed, and I was fully entered into the life of First Church. The effort had required habit-making, stewardship, months of practice, honesty, and persistence in finding a way into people's private lives. Asking questions. Listening intently. Prayer. Service. The guidance of a loving spiritual director. The companionship of a few equally skeptical friends. Was it not honest work, an immersion against their resistance as well as my own?

When December began with eight inches of snow and a fight in the church Cabinet, I had tagged a bumper sticker to my car that said ANTICIPATE MIRACLES, in hopes of finding a baby, and strapped a black armband around my sleeve to protest an impending war in the Middle East. Grieving and celebrating, I went back to church every day as eager as one of the natives to work and learn and rehearse the small part that I had created for myself there.

"We missed you last night at the meeting," Allison would say.

"Sure."

"No. Really. I mean, we really *missed* you."

By now, too, they were all trying to find a baby for us. Peggy had her eyes on two unwed teenage girls in town whom she happened to know were pregnant. Joan, who I had recently discovered initially came to First Church because of a miscarriage, was working her sources for adoption possibilities. Priscilla, Bill, Allison, even Janet Filer—they kept a lookout for us, too.

Why my desire sometimes seemed out of control, it was hard to say. The attraction was . . . Why, it was almost physical. It was as much a desire to be in a place as it was to comprehend the mind of God. It was the threshold experience of First Church—to enjoy the smells, the sounds, the comfort of the crowd . . . I was grateful now to know people who celebrated who I was or who I wanted to be, without, thank goodness, my ever having to announce that I was probably there, as much as anything else, out of a need to ease the panic over my own questionable place and status otherwise in the world.

I got up again from the library table and went to get the bathroom key off the circulation desk. The best tonic for tough times: Private, quiet, secluded, warm . . .

Sitting in the Windsor library's bathroom, I thought of Saint Augustine in the fourth century, "thirsting with the mouth of the heart" (*"inhiabamus ore cordis"*), answering God's call, seeing visions, moving dramatically, inexorably, toward an episode of spiritual crisis where, at once after years of searching, tormented by disembodied voices, he flings himself beneath a fig tree weeping, then hears a child nearby chanting: *"Tolle loge, tolle loge"* ("Take up and read, take up and read").

Voilà!

A religious pilgrimage was serious business.

I thought about John Bunyan. His seventeenth-century conversion story called into doubt the flash-flood transformation popularized by Augustine, and proposed an entirely new method. For Bunyan—Protestant reformer, minister, author of *Pilgrim's Progress*—a continuous battle between good and evil waged in his heart. If Augustine sought the divine embrace of God's love, then Bunyan went for nothing less than the mind of Christ. One could not help but compare the man's fractured emotional reflexes to the spring mechanism of a mousetrap popping off with a startling snap every time he imagined Satan's hand groping for his heart. In a back-and-forth war with the Devil, guilt and temptation sent the Christian warrior on a lifelong pilgrimage. Backsliding between faith and doubt. Striking an unsteady march to salvation. Conversion was not merely an event. It was an exhilarating process. Engaged in the ultimate war. Tackling grand, conflicting theological concepts. Joining history's religious virtuosi in the Parliament of Saints.

Ahhh! The most venerated models of conversion in Christianity.

Finally, Thomas Merton. Only fifty years ago, at the age of thirty-three, Merton wrote perhaps the most influential spiritual autobiography of the twentieth century, *The Seven Storey Mountain*, describing his pilgrimage as an ongoing conversion. A knockabout course with visions and voices of the Spirit. Returning to a kind of thirteenth-century monasticism, he lived and trained until he felt called to work in the ghettos of New York City. Starving for sainthood, craving nothingness, he became a Trappist monk. He turned to Buddhism. On the singular journey to selfhood, Merton concluded his lifelong quest with a strikingly ambivalent attitude toward God and the modern spiritual life—a journey without resolution or synthesis. *"Sit finis libri,"* he wrote in a dramatic conclusion, *"non finis quaerendi"* ("Let this be the end of the book, not of the searching").

The solitary hero of your own drama. Sacramentalizing the transcendent self. Translating personal events into a mythic plot.

Can you tell me whether these men made life any clearer, more agreeable, or more obscure? I did not know.

All I could think of was what the ladies in the Wednesday-morning Bible-study class might have said: "Poor Augustine, he needed a few more friends." Or the healing group, if they could have gotten their hands on one of those immortal men: "You are stuck, John. Try imaging the Spirit as a bird or a breeze." Or JoAnne's gentle counsel: "Where do you find joy, Thomas?"

I was sitting in the bathroom of the Windsor public library lost in these thoughts. Suddenly, on impulse, I drew a ballpoint pen out of my shirt pocket, and between the hairline sketch of a shaven vagina and the word SUCK, I scratched these words on the wall:

WISDOM

LOVE – DEVOTION

Well, why not? I thought. There was no longer any need to pretend otherwise.

I etched the words darker on the stall.

Maybe some day, any one of us would take comfort in a game of whist with the old ladies in Nelson Hall. Some day we all may lie blind and incontinent in a nursing home. They were public places, were they not? Public places are meant to be shared, are they not? A public place like a church will bless you with disciplines for life.

And when I was done, I buckled my britches, washed my hands, and went back to work.

Thank God for public places, I thought.

I packed my files and drove home that night feeling that I had, at last, fleshed out the feeling that weighed most heavily on my heart and finally, courageously, left my mark on the world.

CHAPTER TWENTY-THREE

I followed the highway signs to Hartford and cruised through a Hispanic neighborhood until I saw the familiar fence topped with razorwire. I circled into the lot and parked beside the sanctuary.

For almost a year, I had thought First Church would take up the cause of justice here. Some of the homeless men who returned to the shelter in October had lapsed into drunkenness, and some had disappeared into drug rehab programs. We knew five who were dead. The leaders from the springtime campaign took up shop in John's office, working his phone and photocopier to keep their effort for housing alive. Even though John gave regular reports at First Church staff meetings and kept the Outreach Board and church Cabinet informed, not a single church member offered to help in his political struggle against the city of Hartford.

I visited the shelter at least three times a week, either on the way to church or on my way home in the evenings. Even when the shelter was closed, I had visited the abandoned trailer at the railroad yards off Windsor Avenue where some of the men lived temporarily during the summertime. I had helped some of them move into the first of forty apartments that John's staff found for them during the fall.

As Christmas neared, John often talked about the "Miracle of the Immaculate," always hopeful that he and his men would find a permanent shelter to move into by spring. But the men were less certain. They knew that, come Easter, they would again be making plans to hunt the railroad yards, bridges, and parks for places to live.

I was drawn to them. I went some nights to hand out toothpaste and soap and sometimes just to talk with Bobby Ware and others, to learn how they endured indignities by caring for each other. The men who had been short-order cooks fixed breakfast. Bobby called on his contacts from the streets to stock the shelter with office furniture. The men who came out of detox sobered up long enough to volunteer at the shelter during their off hours from work. Plans for another springtime action against the city took shape.

If you wanted reality out of religion, occasion for worship in the presence of failures, and the regular expectation of miracles, this was the place. We had hot breakfasts for a week when the staff caught punks pelting homeless men with a truckload of stolen eggs. José Ortiz showed up one evening at his own memorial service, back not from the grave but from New York, and his wake turned into a welcome-home party. Those were miracles, as fine and memorable as any.

As I walked down the dank stairs, I heard the canned sound of a television. John had borrowed an old VCR and was playing *It's a Wonderful Life*. A few of the men untangled long cords of electric Christmas lights and crepe paper, making the shelter look, for once, less like a mausoleum than a carnival. José Ortiz strung lights. Cowboy Joe hung bells, bows, and tinsel around the doorframes and iron posts. Bobby Ware laced the exposed ceiling pipes with red ribbon and carried white poinsettias into the bathroom. A couple of social workers in the office cut Christmas paper, green yarn, white ribbon, and styrofoam blocks, wrapping make-believe presents and stacking the "gifts" underneath a scrawny Christmas tree that the men had managed to steal from one of the Christmas-tree lots downtown.

"Look here, man," Bobby said to me. "Scrape the ribbon with your scissors and it'll curl. Here, like this." Bobby grabbed the red strip out of my hand and pulled it across the blade.

"Detail, brother!" Cowboy Joe said to me, snatching the twisted piece and taping it to the yellow ceiling. "Devil's in the detail!"

"You guys are such a pain in the ass," I said.

While we decorated, dozens of gifts from churches and local corporations arrived that still needed to be unwrapped. Wrapped gifts could create a riot in the shelter.

Barbasol shaving cream. Balsam protein shampoo. Gold Toe socks. Caress Body Bar soap. Just days before Christmas, John could not decide if he should simply hide the presents behind the church boiler room now and pass them out gradually, unwrapped, over the year, or go ahead and risk a riot by handing them out randomly, still in Christmas paper, after the movie that night.

"Yo!" Bobby said, calling from the office. "John, there's some lady on the phone from a Catholic church in Simsbury and they got another busload of presents they want to bring over."

"Right now?" John moaned.

"Every church in Hartford County wants to give us presents," Bobby said, holding out the receiver.

"Suburbanites!" John growled. "If we didn't have a homeless problem in this country, we'd have to create one just for the holidays."

"Don't forget we've got that crowd from First Church coming by at seven thirty," Bobby said. "And the Rosary Society wants to serve supper."

"Where are they when you need them?" John said. He took the phone and spoke politely. "Wonderful!" he said. "Yes, that sounds very exciting! If you bring the presents early we can hide them and surprise the men later ..."

He dropped the phone onto the cradle and looked at the men, who were laughing outside the door.

"What the hell we gonna do with another truckload of shaving cream?" Cowboy said.

"Hide 'em in the boiler room with everything else," John said.

"Boiler room's flooded," Bobby said.

"Not again!" John said. "We aren't going to have time to unwrap them, either. And they're not just bringing shaving cream—"

"You mean, it's a mix?" Bobby asked.

"Yep, gloves, hats, long underwear—"

"We gonna have fights busting out all night," Cowboy chuckled.

The men joined social workers in the office unpacking the stacks of gifts they already had, and stuffing crumpled holiday wrapping paper into plastic garbage bags.

At four thirty, the doors opened and homeless men shuffled in from the cold. They staggered down the back stairs and the social workers sent them through a routine patdown for drugs, booze, needles, guns, and knives. Bobby took down names and ages in a ragged logbook. They never asked the men directly about AIDS, but you could see for yourself. Discarding layers of coats and sweaters, the shadowy figures passed a checkpoint and floated under the fluorescent lights. Young ones cruised the room in an excited stupor while the older ones crossed the floor declaiming incomprehensibly, seeking a corner, curling up in hard folding chairs or climbing into children's wooden school desks where they could cover their heads and blank out for a while.

Sometimes, especially on religious holidays, I couldn't come into the shelter without entering their own mystical world. Through thick clouds of cigarette smoke, I saw three men mopping up piss and blood off the concrete stairway and heard the roar of Spanish expletives and raucous laughter. I saw the first volunteer from the Rosary Society come down the stairs, too, hauling four gallon jugs of milk through the entry and shouldering his way through a crowd of drunks gathered around the old man who had fallen.

John was still in his office trying to unpack the last gift boxes of mouthwash.

"I can't believe church people don't know any better than to send mouthwash!" he said.

"Oh shit!" Bobby said. "This is eighty-percent alcohol." He shook the bottle and admired the green sparkle under the harsh lights. "Better than Night Train!"

Outside the office, rows of metal chairs lined the yellow walls, as in a high school cafeteria where chairs and tables have been pushed back for a dance. The homeless men strolled to find seats around the television set. A nasty blend of cigarette smoke, booze, sweat, urine, and stiff chemical cleansers made the rank air a kind of vaporous formaldehyde. Someone took John's cassette out of the mouth of the VCR, popped in a replacement, and shut down the lights. A few minutes later, John heard the sound of an explosion and machine guns.

"Hey!" he said, bounding from the office into the darkened basement. "What happened to the Jimmy Stewart movie?"

"Shh!" Bobby said. "The guys want to watch *The Terminator*."

John stopped in his tracks. All the seats were filled. The men, finally seated and docile, stared up at the screen.

"Power to the people, brother John," Bobby said. "Don't forget, it's Christmas."

"Yo!" Cowboy said, coming out of the office to see, too. "Schwarzenegger!"

"What kind of place is this?" John shouted. "We wrap Styrofoam presents! We unwrap Christmas gifts! We watch violent movies—"

One of the men yelled for him to shut up and another one jumped up from his chair to raise the volume. The shelter echoed with canned screams and squealing tires. Two dozen homeless men sat dead still in folding chairs, mesmerized by the TV, while green and red Christmas lights blinked across the ceiling overhead, down the metal pipes, and across the office doorway where John and Bobby and Cowboy stood.

"Merry Christmas," Bobby said, patting John on the back and stepping out to find a seat with the others.

"Yeah, man," Cowboy said, turning momentarily to look John in the eye. "Like, *feliz Navidad*."

Tony Gillette was still musing about his idea in the car when he left his office in East Hartford at five o'clock and drove home to pick up his wife and daughter for the Christmas pageant. He would drop them off at the church while he ran over to the parish house for the December Cabinet meeting. By now he thought he knew more about First Church than almost anyone other than the ministers. Although he had been a member now for twelve years, not until this fall had he ever worked to raise a budget. It was an amazing experience. One financial document, he thought, told the story more clearly than anyone could ever express with words.

Pages upon pages of names of people whom he had known for years, prominent families in town, historic addresses, phone numbers and financial accounts, had become an intimate portrait for him. When he saw them for the first time in October—My God! he'd thought—it was so embarrassing, like seeing someone you knew naked for the first time. The numbers are nothing like you'd expect, he told Charlotte. One night he opened the books to let her see, and they both gawked. Some of the big shots pledged only one hundred or two hundred dollars, and a few people—the hoi polloi—gave thousands. Ben Lacky, one of the retarded kids, pledged four hundred dollars. Nick Wilton dropped close to four thousand. That new black family whom Van snagged had started out pledging close to fifteen hundred, a remarkable commitment for newcomers.

Now, after two months of making phone calls, he could see a pattern. The numbers took on depth and shape, reflecting faith or fear, alienation or commitment. The records showed how old loud-mouthed Anne Carrington, one of the biggest critics in the church, had regularly cut her pledge over the past three years until she was now giving little more than a pittance. Jim Tyler, whose wife had died during the summer, had been only an average six-hundred-dollar-a-year pledger until recently, when Jim pulled Andy McCarthy aside at coffee hour one Sunday, and handed him a check for three thousand dollars. "Andy," Jim said, "I've really felt blessed by the church, and I'd like to try tithing this year." That blew him away. Then Georgia Kincaid's public-relations firm went into bankruptcy with the bad real estate market and although he figured that meant she would have to abandon her pledge, she still came through with one thousand dollars a year. Martin Dobbles doubled his pledge to $1,560, explaining that his life had changed after working as a volunteer at the homeless shelter. Go figure, Tony thought.

Crossing the bridge over the Connecticut River, Tony couldn't get the numbers out of his mind. He also had an idea for tonight's Cabinet meeting that would really shock them. The words had kept coming out the past week the same way again and again. Spiritual Stewardship. It had been important enough that he even went to see JoAnne Taylor about it. Tony, she said, you are seeing something important in those numbers.

Money is more than a concept, Tony thought. It's a symbol. It reflects what's in people's hearts. He could go down the lists now looking at pledge amounts and see a measure of gratitude, a desire to bring hospitality, an expression of joy. He could trace specific hopes in the way someone wanted to do a good deed. He could interpret some figures as concrete statements of faith.

If only everyone could see the lists and hear the individual stories like he had, then they would know how certain people set the most important priorities of their lives. If there had ever been a sacred code that shielded finance from the spiritual life of First Church, there was no reason to let it stand anymore. Just as soon as the Cabinet passed this evening's budget, Tony decided, he would start a new campaign. He would ignite a crusade. Janet Filer had been right all along.

If the Cabinet endorsed his simple bylaw proposal, then Tony would expand the stewardship committee from three to six people and next week he would enlist women from the healing committee to join his cause. He could hear Joan Rockwell in the pulpit on gratitude. Allison Denslow on dispossession. Priscilla Drake on the natural gifts of the Spirit. No one in his lifetime—including his father, who had been a stewardship chairman a time or two at the Catholic church—had ever dared speak the truth about money. But with the theme of Spiritual Stewardship, Tony thought he could blow the lid off. This year's stewardship campaign would mark a most remarkable change.

When he reached the meetinghouse, Tony parked his car, grabbed a thick sheaf of papers off the seat, and rushed into the church office. Andy McCarthy was standing in line behind Paul Price waiting to use the copy machine. Down the hall, Van was setting out plates of cookies. The old coffeepot gurgled and whistled like a ghostly servant.

I hurried out of the shelter and drove to First Church to catch the last of the Christmas pageant and sit in on the Cabinet meeting. Nick Wilton had joined a crowd of children still dressed in their sheep and angel costumes walking across the churchyard to the parish house. The show had ended early, and the hospitality committee had invited everyone to a simple meal.

"Grilled cheese sandwiches!" I heard Nick exclaim as we waited in line at Nelson Hall.

Tony Gillette nodded and smiled. He was watching his nine-year-old daughter leap off the stage in her pink angel costume. Somehow she managed to retain her wings every time.

"Same old burnt offerings as last year," Tony said.

The greasy sandwiches were hard-toasted, rubbery, and cold by the time Tony and Nick reached the front of the line. But Tony gratefully put two of them on a wafer-thin paper plate and invited Nick to join him at a table near the stage. Tony knew all about Nick's wife who had died. During a stewardship call, Nick had expressed his feelings of guilt and failure about his marriage. He really seemed friendly, though, and even though he was old enough to be Tony's grandfather, he had an honesty and insight about himself that was remarkable. He was also one of the largest contributors to the stewardship campaign.

Tony mentioned that he had formed a brass brand to play at Christmas parties, and last night he and his wife had organized a group to go caroling around town.

"You might want to come with us the next time we go," Tony said, but Nick didn't seem to hear.

"You know, this reminds me . . . ," Nick started to say, looking down at his plate.

But it was too noisy in the hall to talk for long. Children ran wild in their fuzzy costumes and people kept shuffling in from the pageant looking for seats. Tony took two more bites of his sandwich and, excusing himself, jumped up to find his daughter, who had disappeared behind the velvet stage curtain with a couple of sheep and a shepherd boy.

Nick got up and moved to another table. He sat down beside Paul Price.

"I was just thinking about those F-15s," Paul said. "Amazing aircraft they're using in the Gulf."

Nick said, "Can you imagine those things sweeping over the desert at six hundred miles an hour?"

"Why in my day . . . ," Paul said.

They talked about new technologies in the aerospace business, but before long, a trio of boys in Wise Men costumes ripped around the side of their table, bumped Paul, and knocked a cup of coffee out of his hand.

Paul grabbed a couple of napkins to cover the spill. "Well, that must mean it's time for me to find my grandchildren and get out of here," he said.

Nick finished cleaning up the mess and then he went from table to table, talking to people and helping clear dishes until mealtime was over. By six thirty, when Bill Warner-Prouty started mopping the floor, Nick was still there, volunteering to help fold and stack the tables. Tony was still there, too, getting ready for the Cabinet meeting.

"Quite a supper!" Nick said.

"Grilled cheese sandwiches," Tony said.

"Doesn't look like much, but it reminded me of something good," Nick said. Then he put his hand on Tony's shoulder and drew up close to look him in the eye. Tony set his briefcase down.

"You know, when I first met my wife I was just about broke," Nick said. "We were living down in North Carolina at an army base and there just wasn't any money between us. She was from a pretty poor family and the most I could afford when we went out on a date was a grilled cheese sandwich and a milkshake. And we had to share that!"

Tony smiled, and Nick tightened his grasp.

"Can you imagine that?" Nick said. His voice filled with emotion. "Doesn't that sound like some kind of a date? A grilled cheese sandwich and a milkshake. She was a good woman, Tony. Anyway, I guess I knew it at the time . . ."

Nick let go and Tony stepped back. There was an undercurrent he did not understand. The old man stared at him with an expression that looked fragile and, at the same time, mystified.

"You know, this morning?" Nick said.

Tony just listened.

"This morning when Bill gave the children's message—"

"Oh, yeah," Tony said.

As he did every year, Bill had stood in front of the pulpit on the Sunday before Christmas and set up the crèche. He had pulled a dozen wooden figures out of a large cardboard box, and the children had helped him set up the scene while he told the Christmas story.

"I've never seen so much paper flying around," Tony said.

"But do you remember they couldn't find Joseph?" Nick said.

Tony looked puzzled and shook his head.

"I didn't see it, either, at first," Nick said. "But I could tell he wasn't like the shepherds or the Wise Men. You mean, you didn't see it, either?"

No, Tony said. See what?

"It just came to me tonight while the kids were singing," Nick said.

Tony crumbled a paper plate around a half-eaten sandwich.

"Joseph had his hand on his heart," Nick said. "Didn't you see that?"

Tony smiled feebly. There was remorse in the way Nick had laughed when he said it, and now from the way he leaned over the folded table and looked down at the floor, it seemed for a moment that he might start to cry.

"Now that was something new," the old man said, looking up again, his eyes intense and sparkling. He laughed and thumped his chest. "Joseph had his hand on his heart."

The two men stood looking at each other, eye to eye, seeing in each other a hint of recognition that, for just a moment, made the silence linger.

———

While the children's pageant went on at the church, John had charted a delicate course through the most difficult night of the year. DeFiori's Funeral Home called to say they had the body of one of John's men, who had climbed up the long arm on a one-hundred-ton crane at a downtown construction site and jumped to his death. An increasing stream of early releases from local hospitals brought an unusual number of newcomers—including one howling schizophrenic, a crew of migrant workers, and two homeless boys in bloody casts—to the red steel doors of John's basement.

But now, among the faces of the homeless men whom I did know— Bobby Ware, Cowboy Joe, José Ortiz—I also saw six little girls in green velvet dresses, children who had appeared earlier that evening in the First Church Christmas pageant. The children's choir was circling the hall like figures on a merry-go-round singing "Away in a Manger," "Silent Night," "O Come All Ye Faithful," "God Rest Ye Merry, Gentlemen," "Angels We Have Heard on High," not once stopping for a pause.

Despite the horrors at the shelter, my first reaction was that the suburbanites had again exported the most abominable idea of Christian mission into the inner city. Along with their castoff old issues of *Elle, The New Yorker,* and *Metropolitan Home* magazines, Bounce static remover, Pam no-stick cooking spray, and cartons of dirty designer clothes and athletic togs (indispensable articles for any homeless man), now came the First Church Christmas carolers.

Usually, the absurdities of misplaced sentiment were never lost on the homeless men. I often watched them take delight in modeling charity-givers' ragged fashions and laughing at sweet-smelling volunteers who would suggest that their little church groups and the homeless men get together sometime for a weenie roast. And then the volunteers would run and hide in the kitchen in fear while the men ravaged the do-gooders' large, industrial-size bowls of cold pastas and chocolate mix brownies and homemade, honey-sweetened pork and beans.

But tonight, the Christmas carolers silenced the entire shelter. Some men joined the songs in Spanish and others went straight to the walls and sank to the floor. Joan Rockwell struck the stained piano keys in a corner next to John's office, setting a brisk tempo with "O Holy Night" and "White Christmas," and then the children took over the entire center of the basement, going round and round in a tighter and faster circle, raising their high-pitched voices a decibel above normal as they looked about them to see grown men breaking down in tears, slumping over tables, disappearing like shadows in the gay flicker of lights. By the time they exhausted the repertoire of holiday classics and hit "Deck the Halls," I saw the horror in one little face. As our tongues clucked "Fa la la la la," Priscilla Drake's ten-year-old daughter flinched and clutched at her mother's hand, as if she was the first to realize that it was time to go, that Joan Rockwell should quit hammering at the piano and her mother should signal us to stop after one more verse and Allison Denslow should put her hands down and be silent so every person in that shelter could be still and let the grieving go on with respect.

But they did not slow down, and even when, as I saw, the whole First Church contingent suddenly recognized what was happening all around, they did not stop singing. And when they did finish, when they completed the job they had come to do, the red and green lights flickered in the dark and the TV set remained silent while John's staff quietly passed out presents and comforted men who were crying. I could not see the men very well. Instead, I was watching Allison and Joan and Priscilla and the boys and girls of the First Church children's choir.

I didn't think you could top that one. For cynicism, nothing could beat what I had just experienced at Christmas in the homeless shelter. Everyone was so busy that no one from First Church even had a chance to speak to me. Not Joan or Allison or Priscilla, who were comforting the men, or Bill and Sue Warner-Prouty and the children, who rushed around the hall serving coffee and desserts. For the first time, as a journalist at the church, I felt invisible, receding into the far background like a speck on the wall, holding a notebook and pen, furiously taking notes, describing the scene, jotting down names, feeling distant and for some reason still uncomprehending.

Scenes passed through my mind faster than traffic on the interstate as I made the thirty-five-mile drive to Windsor the next morning. I saw faces of people caught in moments of awareness in private places. Like Nick Wilton after the supper last night. Like the children's choir singing later at the shelter. They came clearly now. Expressions of need, of desperation, of excitement, of joy—all in a fragile, disconnected flood. Even though I had registered them during only a moment, in a small but significant way, like undeveloped photographs, I had never bothered to see them whole. Now, rushing up the interstate, they came in a barrage.

Bewhiskered Andy McCarthy ran into the office one day with a poem by Edward Roland Sill that his father had set to music, tape-recorded, and given to the congregation for Christmas as a hymn for peace. Priscilla Drake, embarrassed and remorseful, came to the healing committee one night and talked courageously about her homophobia—and Ted Alford's kind, teasing reprieve: "The only reason you got so upset, Priscilla," he said, "is because you were finally alone in a room full of good-looking men and no one kissed you." Allison Denslow meeting people on Sunday mornings, arms outstretched, passing peace with a hug—a face like an angel, a desire to bring holiness to the everyday. Joan Rockwell—singing with all her might, on tiptoe, throat wide, hands in motion from the choir loft—muscles taut in her neck, eyes black and brilliant, voice precisely tuned, as bright as a bell. Nancy Fitch, in her tartan skirt, knee socks, and cable-knit sweater like a '59 grad of Swarthmore, giggling in Bible study, with expressions of fear and amusement always doing battle on her face. Her husband, Craig: the shameful tilt of his head as he bent over in the fourth pew on Sundays as if he wanted to hide after abandoning the stewardship committee in October; and Craig again, in December, ruddy-faced, showing me how to frame a door at the Habitat house on Saturday mornings.

Then I could hear their voices, too: Frank Lester, Bill's Kimberly Hall men's club, Cloris Newberry . . . Blind Trudy Crandall, the day she told the Bible-study class she could see pictures in the scars in her eyes. They were swirling around becoming faces at that moment, she said, like the hidden faces she used to see as a girl inside children's puzzles. "Sometimes I think I'll see someone I know," Trudy said, "but I don't think I know any of them right now."

In the scars in my eyes.

Even so, the ecstatic experience I'd come to expect from Christmas at First Church had been quickly reduced to delusion by mid-December.

"So you're not doing it right again," JoAnne had said when I told her one day at our first meeting in December.

Christmas is still a children's holiday here, I said. Sugar-plum fairies and reindeer. A fashion show. A tawdry Christmas singalong. Sickening sweets and season's greetings. Superficial social events. An echo of my usual complaints.

"Then tell me, where is there joy in your life?" she asked.

As we sat by the window in the library, I had stared out at the cold cemetery and tried to think of an answer. All that came to mind was the church, and I wondered again what had attracted me to this place and what had kept drawing me in. Why did I want to describe the light outside? Why did I puzzle over a language that lacked words to name qualities of illumination—not just the reflection against colored surfaces, but the full, fine body of luminescence itself? I watched it changing in every room I entered lately, and as we sat just beyond the graveyard, I could see where the morning shadows had vanished at midday. There, still stretched out at the base of gray headstones, were silvery, frozen forms on the grass, as if the shadows had not moved and even the strength of sunlight could not thaw frosted ground. Very curious, I thought. I had never noticed that before.

"Joy?" she had said, again.

"Oh. Yes," I said, trying to remember. "Joy."

When I finally pulled my car into the First Church parking lot, my heart was racing. On the way into the parish house, I peeked into the church office and Andy McCarthy waved me in.

He was there telling Peggy and Bill how he had worked out his point of view on religion one Sunday morning as a child. Andy said he had accidentally mangled the old hymn, "Gladly the Cross I'd Bear," singing, instead, "Gladly, the Cross-Eyed Bear."

"And it was like—boom!—really funny," he said. "Absurd, and I don't know, illuminating."

Bill was impressed. He had discovered the same angle on things, he said, when he was a member of a church boys' club, which called itself

The Lantern Bearers, but was always known secretly among his friends as the Lightning Bears. Peggy chuckled. That reminded her of the kids in Sunday school who insisted on beginning the Lord's Prayer, "Our Father who art in Heaven, Hollywood be thy name!"

Same old silliness, I thought.

I peeked into Van's office. He was sneezing from a wicked cold as he typed out his Christmas meditation.

I went to the foyer to check my mailbox. A small group of women were still wrapping presents in Nelson Hall, and a troop of three- and four-year-olds went stampeding around the room gleefully singing "Frosty the Snowman."

I smelled fresh popcorn in the kitchen.

When I turned and headed down the hallway to the Morrell Room, there was JoAnne waving at me from the door, holding up a paper cup of hot cider.

I knew then where I belonged, without even knowing who else had come or even bothering to think twice about what I was doing there. Ever since I had awakened that morning, I could still hear the children's choir and see my friends—the First Church do-gooders—at the shelter. When you find yourself following a light that you cannot see, and see faces that you cannot touch, and hear voices that you only recognize by remembering, I thought, then it is time to go to the place where you have been called. It is time to sit down and listen.

JoAnne struck a match and touched it to a thick, white candle. Allison was there, arms wide to give me a hug. Nancy was talking for the first time about her son's alcoholism. Joan was crying—her father had died last night. Priscilla was telling people how much she enjoyed the Christmas pageant. Lottie announced that she was engaged to be married. She said Nick Wilton had proposed to her over the weekend.

As we talked, I could feel a word rising up like a bubble out of our circle. It pressed up in my mind and swept down through my back until I started to tremble. *Hope.*

And when the music began, I covered my face and wept like a child. *O come, O come, Emmanuel / And ransom captive Israel / That mourns in lonely exile here / Until the son of God appear.*

At the end of the hour, JoAnne drew us together. She called us to stand around the coffee table, where we joined in a circle and folded our arms over each other's shoulders. I felt the comfort that I must have longed for, and realized, having finally laid aside grief for joy, that I had a place where I belonged and where I could be grateful.

"Look," JoAnne said. The faces: Allison, Joan, Priscilla, Lottie, Nancy. I saw them bowing down to watch the tiny flame's lively dance on the candletop. "There is light there."

I closed my eyes and felt a strain go through our group, across our shoulders, and then people began to pull away. I dropped back, quietly turning, too, wiping away tears, embarrassed at having gone just about as far as my stubborn little faith would allow.

Epiphany

Frankly, it is not my words that I mistrust, but your minds. I could be eloquent were I not afraid you fellows had starved your imagination to feed your bodies. I do not mean to be offensive; it is respectable to have no illusions—and safe—and profitable—and dull. Yet you, too, in your time must have known the intensity of life, that light of glamour created in the shock of trifles, as amazing as the glow of sparks struck from a cold stone—and as short-lived, alas!

—Joseph Conrad,
Lord Jim

CHAPTER TWENTY-FOUR

After Christmas, Joan Rockwell dropped out of sight for a couple of months to take Spanish-language lessons and prepare for a return to Ocatol. A yearlong job at Casa de Materna awaited her. Owen, her husband, asked a few of us to be her "discernment group," and we met with Joan regularly for six weeks to see if she had made the right decision. We joined them both in role-playing games, in which we acted out Bible stories related to mission, and quizzed her about her feelings. She was unflappable. Finally, Van offered to arrange a commissioning service for her in June, to offer her the congregation's full support and say good-bye before she left for Central America.

Allison Denslow approached her service to AIDS patients with just as much excitement. She and I attended AIDS healing services a few times through the winter, and sometimes she and Priscilla went alone. By March, she had written and illustrated a children's book about AIDS, and then enrolled in nursing courses at the local community college.

As for me, I continued following Bill and Van on their daily rounds, spent many twelve- and fifteen-hour days visiting with people at their homes and in church, attended most of the committee meetings, and practically enrolled in the Confirmation class. By springtime, I knew more people on a more intimate basis than I had in years, and felt as at home in the church offices as I did in my own house. I prayed at members' deathbeds, helped bury homeless men, heard private confessions, gave money to the poor, smoked cigarettes with the groundskeeper, gossiped and drank coffee with the church secretary.

But all that effort was like a spiraling movement until my one-year anniversary at First Church came around and I realized that I was still in the beginner's class, spiritually speaking, with everyone else. I remember thinking one day that this was, as Van had said all along, exactly how it should be. To put on a beginner's mind.

It had never been my purpose to experience another conversion. Enough of those anomalies—the doubts and bewildering proofs of God's existence, the suspension of disbelief in every transient reawakening. Those were not the ground of being, after all. There must come a time, I thought, to be gracious to myself and finally satisfy the desire to belong. I embraced the community that had been there for me all along, grateful for those who reached out, if not always wholly and unequivocally, then at least consistently in kindness when I had been most in need. There was a great and lustrous tradition of Christianity yet to encounter, more of the small, but no less significant, First Church tradition still to absorb.

Perhaps I was wrong, but the heroic pursuit by a solitary soul struck me by then as so contrived and, frankly, literary, that I could not any more imagine the value of a jackpot conversion narrative to the world than I could its consolation to the author. Certainly people endure paroxysms of doubt on the way to settling for a less ambivalent attitude about life. The heroic pursuit; the solitary soul; the agonizing life narrative: familiar ingredients of plot among seminal spiritual potboilers sometimes made me laugh out loud.

Fonts, altars, pulpits, pews . . .

But to say that I had been converted to a place alone would be insufficient. Terrifying, isn't it? To go from observer to subject to enthusiast—and not just enthusiast, but participant—was considered neither shrewd, scrupulous, nor prudent in my profession. I remember beginning by pledging not to tell my secrets, reveal my logic, or allow this story to become a personal conversion narrative. But I am telling you now that after Christmas, I did go native among the glabrous WASPs with their friable loaves and commercial juices. I gossiped with the quidnuncs, dealt hands of whist with the old ladies in Nelson Hall, shepherded a young confirmed through six months of Protestant indoctrination, and eventually played a private, supporting role in a political struggle between the homeless and Hartford city hall. At the height of the war in the Middle East, I passed out antiwar bumper stickers, joined AIDS healing services, and during the springtime helped Bill hammer political signs into churchgoers' yards calling for a hike in local taxes for public education. My only excuse was that at First Church, while a person did not have to honor a creed, take a stand, be attentive in church, or even attend services, if you did not somehow pitch in, you did not belong.

That's what it came down to in the end. Belonging. I kept telling myself this even after the deadline for my departure passed. Like everyone else, I thought I was only doing what my job required, but in the end, it was much, much simpler than that.

Endless opportunities! Great enthusiasms! I was smitten, a fallen man, convinced and in love with one peculiarly blessed and pathetic place. After my first year ended, I decided to stay.

When winter gave way to an early spring, the cottonwoods released their seeds, sending thousands of feathery pods floating on the wind beyond the cemetery into the woods. As at any place endowed with ultimate meanings, a change in the material of daily life at First Church sparked patterns of association and response—metaphorical possibilities—that explained the turn in things. Once the God I AM asserted itself as a verb, not a noun, a pursuit began like the release of cottonwood seeds. Out of the churchyard. Through the woods. Into the streets.

For weeks, people all over town admired the spruced-up campus, which did look pristine and venerable, like a shrine for suburban pilgrims. Scrubby purple azaleas sprouted around the portico, fledgling dogwoods and tender flowers planted the previous spring by the Pennies for Perennials committee began to bud. The parsonage sported a new roof. The rotted planks on the minister's front porch were replaced with hard pine. Plans to refurbish the interior of the Pierson House caught the interest of the First Church ladies' bridge club, ensuring a fashionable renewal. New fluorescent replacement bulbs illuminated every room and hallway, securing a savings of close to three thousand dollars and bringing a kind of campy pink-and-green luster to committee meetings in the Morrell Room at night.

As Holy Week came around, Van wrapped up a four-part Lenten lecture series on Abraham Lincoln, vying for an audience against Bill's series about *The Book of J.* Together, they planned a men's retreat, led a weekend seminar with a popular Christian folksinger, and added a midnight vigil service to the lineup before Easter. Soon the parish house was again abuzz with Van's enthusiastic declarations.

"You can't stop this place," he would say. "It's time to fish or cut bait. . . . The train's pulling out of the station."

The Women's Club overtook the parish house on Monday of Holy Week for its annual spring luncheon. A generation of older females kept coming in all morning to arrange tables in Nelson Hall. The spring luncheon marked unsurpassed achievements in hospitality and endurance. Mary Bartlett, who would turn one hundred years old in July, brought fresh flowers, as she had for thirty-five years. Delicate arrangements in paper cups, which she had made while sitting on her front porch with her son, Larry, arrived early in boxes. Red and white zinnias, blue salvia, scabiosa, roses, dahlias, astors, mugwort—"I don't like that name, *mugwort*," she said, setting a colorful centerpiece on one of the three serving tables. "I prefer . . . *Artemesia lectaflora.*"

Around the corner from the women's gathering, the church office sounded like the back shop of a small-town newspaper publisher. The staff worked frantically typing and copying hundreds of pages for Holy Week bulletins and newsletters.

"Van Gorder!" Peggy shouted over the din. "Did you have a funeral service last week?"

"What's that?" Van asked.

"I said, did you have a funeral service in the meetinghouse last week?

Someone left a stack of bulletins from a funeral in the church over the weekend."

"I had one Wednesday, but it was outside in the cemetery."

"Yeah, but you left the bulletins *inside*," she said.

"Oh my gosh!"

"One of the deacons passed them out by mistake yesterday morning."

"Oh my gosh!"

Peggy's comment reminded Van that he had offered to host a fiftieth wedding anniversary for the Woodstocks next week, but he just remembered that he'd also agreed to perform a graveside service in the cemetery at the same hour. How could he quietly slip from one to the other without causing a stir?

But before Van had time to think through the problem, Henry Holcombe phoned.

"Henry!" Van shouted, closing the door to the office. "How'd you make out? ... Oh, eight visits to the same person, that must be some kind of record. ... Yes ... right ... We're on the bottom of his pile? Right down there with the New England Air Museum! ... Not this year, eh? Did he say anything about ... So he'll take a look at his tax returns and see what's left. Well, you did your best. ... You're just like old man river, Henry, you just keep on rollin'. "

They were still ten thousand short in the capital-funds drive, but Van believed Paul would get it eventually. Ever since Tony Gillette had raised the annual budget—$297,500, slightly above goal—and convinced key members of the healing committee to join the new stewardship team, the message about money was getting out. Joan Rockwell had agreed to meet with every church board to talk about the value of gratitude. Allison Denslow had already given a great stewardship message in church one Sunday. Andy McCarthy was still spreading the story about the night when the Cabinet faced off against Paul Price and his supporters over a vote that came down to "faith versus hard numbers." That one was destined for lore.

Van also had brought in an outside consultant, a West Hartford attorney who worked part-time for a national group called the "Ministry of Money," and scheduled planning sessions with both the new stewardship group and the outreach committee. It also wouldn't hurt now to have Andy McCarthy as the new head of the Cabinet.

"Hey, Peggy!" Van shouted.

"Hey what?"

"When you do the programs for the Confirmation class, just make sure you don't print them on the back of those old Christmas bulletins."

"Who do you think I am?"

"I need them by tomorrow morning so we can have them for the families on Thursday."

"Van, did you know that eighty percent of ministers come from dysfunctional families?"

"What does that have to do with what we were talking about?"

"Well, did you know that?"

"Do you have proof?"

"They did a study . . ."

"They're always doing studies."

"But this one came out of Yale, and they know because they gave all these ministers psychological tests . . ."

Just that moment Priscilla and Allison hustled into the office and shut the door. They had spent the morning around the kitchen, chopping cabbage, peeling potatoes, boning masses of chicken for soup. As the old volunteers came and went with platters of food, the younger women learned that a drama had unfolded in the hall. Mary Bartlett, it was said, was upset with her old friend Florence Ellsworth for not making one hundred peach shortcakes for the luncheon, as had been the church women's custom for as long as anyone could remember.

"It's just become too much at my age!" Florence had said, and now Mary was brooding.

Just then, Joan Rockwell herded a crowd of toddlers directly outside and waited for someone to get them lollipops. Joan, dressed in a light-blue smock with large front pockets, looked like the very picture of a nursery-school teacher. You never would have thought that in a few weeks, this woman with Elmer's glue and crayon marks spotting her hands would be traveling to Nicaragua.

"Larry Bartlett!" Van said, spotting Mary's son out in the hallway talking to Peggy. Larry's shoulders crept up as Van slipped his hand around Larry's back. Larry did not turn but froze in position, as the minister's touch had caught him in mid-epithet.

"It's okay," Peggy said. "You're among friends."

Dressed in a little white golf cap and light windbreaker, Mary's son looked piqued.

"Why did you have to go and change the doxology, Van?" Larry demanded, as if he had been holding back for months. "We can't even sing 'He' in church anymore."

"You can sing whatever you want, Larry," Van said.

"Most people do," Peggy quipped.

"If you want to sing 'He' go right ahead. I think half the people in there are singing 'He.'"

"Some of them sing it pretty loud, too," Peggy said.

"And I hear you've got some committee making more changes," Larry said. "What is this? Don't you have anything better to do?"

Van laughed.

"And what's this in the bulletin now?" Larry said, waving a fresh one in his hand. "This thing says, 'You may sit or you may stand'! What's that supposed to mean? I'll sit if I want and I'll stand if I want. This is too much!"

Van let Larry rant. If he had stepped out into Nelson Hall, he would have heard similar complaints. Women were apparently railing about him at the beauty parlor, too. It was not just the doxology and new hymns, but all that publicity about Bill Warner-Prouty's pro-tax group, which had managed to call for a referendum on the town budget and was putting up signs in church members' yards all over town saying, VOTE YES! FOR WINDSOR'S FUTURE. They were peeved at the article in *The Hartford Courant* about Bill's call for draft counseling in the high school. It was bad enough that John Gregory-Davis was back in the newspaper with his homeless men making charges of malfeasance and fraud and threatening to build a tent city on the legislature's front lawn. But now there was renewed talk about the church putting up money to build a Habitat house in Windsor. Where was the head man in all this? Who was in charge anyway?

"You'd think they'd like the doxology now that it's got a little 'Triune' in it," Van said when Larry walked away. "Triune" was Bill's addition to the latest version of the doxology. " 'Triune' sounds militaristic, you'd think they'd like that."

"Van Gorder," Peggy cautioned.

"They can sing whatever they want, but it won't change anything. If they want to be reactionary, conservative . . ."

"Van!" Peggy said.

"Closed-minded, far-fetched . . ."

"Okay, Van!"

"I've still got another four or five years around here and I'm getting my ducks lined up. We're teetering on the edge of faith and fear around here. When the old gods die people are always afraid because the old gods are comfort and success. That's what I've been trying to say all along. We've got to stop living on the world's agenda! We've got to get off dead center! We've got to go to the beat of a different drummer! We are a different kettle of fish!"

"You're preaching again, Van," Peggy said, wearily.

"Yeah? Well, you're darn right!" Van said. He turned, went back to his office to get his cup of iced tea, and strode past her again, heading for lunch with the old ladies in Nelson Hall.

"Van, you can't take that beer stein into the luncheon!" Peggy shouted, but it was too late. "I hate it when he takes that thing out in public," she muttered.

As the noon hour grew near and Nelson Hall filled with the aroma of fresh chicken stew and the scent of one hundred sixty old women's perfumes, everyone on the staff stopped working and joined Van and the ladies at the spring luncheon. It was a remarkably happy scene, especially following the announcement that the club was celebrating the anniversary of Meals on Wheels, started by the women of First Church thirty years ago, and that the club's budget had surpassed the four-thousand-dollar mark for the first time.

During the applause and scattered whistles, which seemed to be loudest at the table where Bill Warner-Prouty and his wife sat, I saw Mary

Bartlett and Florence Ellsworth find each other behind the serving table. Mary in her blue cotton dress and Florence in a fully pleated green wool suit stood posed with the club's finest silver service. After the prayer, Mary turned to Florence, took her hand, smiled, and said in a most forgiving way, "Okay, Florence, you ladle, I'll serve."

The celebration lasted through the afternoon. No one seemed to notice the lack of shortcake. And all the world was right again.

Jan never mentioned the dozens of daffodils pushing up through the dirt in the front yard. Too risky. The process called "identified adoption" offered no guarantees. Birth mothers often backed out, and in this case, our social worker warned us that the woman who had called and selected us, while well-meaning, might not be the one. The "spiritual" connection the woman said she made while reading our letter in the files might have been a fluke. The word *spiritual*, our social worker reminded us, could very well be a tip-off that she was still in denial about her predicament. Furthermore, even if we did become the lawful parents, if the woman changed her mind and decided to keep the child—during the sixty days after the birth—Jan and I would have to give the baby back.

Yes, we knew. It had never been in our hands.

On Thursday morning of Holy Week, the woman called and invited us to meet her for lunch in New Haven. Jan's earring exploded as soon as we sat down at the restaurant—shattered spontaneously on her ear— and then this woman, who was already seven months' pregnant, gave us the news. "I have found the couple this child was meant for," she said. "This is your baby."

At thirty-seven, the woman said she had become pregnant unexpectedly. Because of familial and financial circumstances, she said, she could not afford to keep the child. But something had told her that the pregnancy was "meant to be."

"Now I know who I have been carrying her for," she said.

Tall, with intensely ice-blue eyes and blond hair, in gray leggings and a white cotton tunic, she looked stunning. She looked angelic, to me.

But she had a husky laugh, smoked, and drank a glass of wine before lunch—as if to let us know she was perfectly human, too—and then she handed us the sonograms.

"I wasn't sure I'd ever find you," she said.

That night, Jan and I drove to First Church for the Tenebrae service. It was a small crowd: Bill and Sue, Van and Lucille, Allison, Joan, Priscilla, Peggy, Andy and Elizabeth, Tony and Charlotte, Craig and Nancy, Nick and Evelyn . . .

"They broke bread and their eyes were opened and they recognized him. In the company of those disciples and in the company of all people who gather around the table to know Christ in the breaking of the bread, let us pray . . ."

The silence felt awesome after singing hymns and hearing the sermon. Our personal good news and the Good News of the Gospel sank in like undifferentiated parts of a whole. Surrounded by friends and strangers, secret sharers, the strong chords of Fran's performance, and the faces of familiar deacons quietly passing silver plates of bread and juice, I could feel what it meant to have been carried all along. Without knowing. Without being in control. Without having earned the right to be.

"Speak to us in silence and in all languages. Call us to be in community where we are able to be the body of Christ one to another. We ask you to reveal to us in this bread and wine, your spirit that we may discern your presence in our lives for this is the time we remind ourselves and are reminded of our faithfulness to God and God's faithfulness to us. Remembering in gratitude, let us again share the bread of life and take this cup that symbolizes our unity in Christ . . ."

The click of Communion cups, the shuffle of deacons, the vibrato of the Casavant . . . The footstep. A cough. I could not close my eyes and pray. My prayer was visible.

I looked at Jan and she squeezed my hand. She had come to believe there was a reason I came to First Church to write about the life of a congregation. God, she said, had revealed Himself to us in an overarching plan.

"We're going to have a baby," she told Van when he greeted her at the back of the church after the service.

"What did you say?" Lucille asked, having overheard.

Soon a crowd surrounded us. In their light cloth jackets, purple scarves, and warm spring hats, still clutching their bulletins, people let out quiet expressions of surprise, whispered tender endearments, hugged and kissed us.

It was this last scene of anticipation, and the foreshadowing of a biblical story's ending, that swelled in my imagination as we left the church to go home.

The church often looked like that at night—like a paper lantern from the street, as fragile as a dormant faith, until you looked back again. And when I looked back, it was far more than I had ever remembered it: larger, more luminous, more concrete, more representative and institutional, exceedingly hollow, more alive in the associations it made in my mind and memory than ever it could have been in objective reality. That was holy and precious, I thought, and we—those of us who gathered there—had been fortunate enough to act in its mystery.

On the way home I told Jan that I finally felt confident that we had been entrusted with tools of knowledge. We had a chance now to make a daily response to God's revelations and soon, we would have a regular occasion to apply whatever we had learned.

I'm sure I sounded pious and overwrought. And if I sounded a lot like Van Parker—which, in retrospect, I know I did—it should have been no surprise. Because the ability to give word to the heart was learned there. It was the miracle of a minister's love for his community, the people's love for their own congregation, and the compassionate regard for the little cosmos of an ordinary church, that brought those words into being day after day for as long as either one of us could imagine.

In May we would become parents and, at last, my journey at First Church would come to an end.

CHAPTER TWENTY-FIVE

When winter gives way to spring this year, the cottonwoods will release their seeds and the wind will blow thousands of pods beyond the First Church cemetery into streets and yards. As usual, any change in the fabric of daily life will spark patterns of association. Someone will begin the pursuit of an ongoing education and experience the propulsion of Spirit into the world.

Everyone agrees that the new addition to the meetinghouse is a splendid site for retreats and receptions. Plush and spacious, the new room, with its vaulted ceilings and tall, plentiful windows, forms a small sanctuary for the different spiritual groups. Well worth the money, it's said, and a fitting memorial to Van and Lucille's ministry. Van's work at First Church is almost done, but the congregation has already acknowledged his ministry as a true partnership, guided, in part, by his wife's counsel. The new building is named for them both.

But as Holy Week comes around again, I know of First Church only by what I read in its newsletter, which Peggy still sends. Bill Warner-Prouty, who left the ministry two years ago, teaches history at the middle school and is said to be feeling like a new person. JoAnne and John Gregory-Davis are still working at the church and the shelter. The healing committee has disbanded, but I see they have a series of retreats planned to re-reassess their service. Unfortunately, I've lost track of Janet, Joan, Allison, and Andy, but I assume they will be busy this spring planning parties and services for Van's retirement in June.

Jan and I and our daughter Ella became Congregationalists, but joined a different congregation closer to home. We are involved there, but do not feel yet like we belong. I am also working on another book—about engineering and technology—so there is little time to keep up, even with old friends, as I did for a year or so after leaving Windsor.

Ella will be four soon. When she was born, the daffodils Jan planted bloomed like magic. I found patches bursting out under trees, by the garden shed, next to the doghouse, around the garage, even in the woods—wherever Jan had stopped to pray and dig. When we brought Ella home from the hospital, three months after meeting her birth mother, our yard looked like a lawn and garden center. Soon they will bloom again, and I will be reminded of Jan's faith and the angels who came to Sarah and Abraham's tent.

I know what it sounds like. But I still do not talk about miracles. I do not talk about being born again. Or about God's Chosen People or the blessings of the Protestant church. Every spring I am reminded of what I used to think, and I am pleased to have known the people I found inside a religious community. I feel fortunate to have known my need for them and also to have felt the continued resistance in comprehending the Holy Who.

I have a lot to say about this, really. But who would believe that what looks like white bread is wonder bread; what says grape juice is wine; what is ordinary becomes mystical; what often seems to be a static, staid, dying religion is also energetic, breathing, and remarkably alive. I know the Church—the larger Church—is blessed with many people like Van Parker, Bill Warner-Prouty, JoAnne Taylor, John Gregory-Davis, Peggy Couples, and Fran Angelo, nearly all of whom have very different understandings of what it is to be a church and how to conduct worship. But they compel little places like First Church into being every day with the help of members who are like ministers, too, whether they know it or not.

No one wants to hear that. Besides, it's been said so many times before.

Most people think what is done at a mainline church is largely private. That's correct, it is. Most churches do not advertise. They do not sell a product. They are not charismatic. They do not evangelize. They do not testify. Most mainliners do not even know they have a story to tell. No wonder all the world outside assumes that what churchgoers really do well is consume lots of coffee, gossip, talk a lot of talk, hold meetings, fuss and work out compromises, sing with verve, and mix punch that looks like antifreeze. Believe me, that's true, too. I've been there, going in the same circles.

So this is what I tell people now: if you ever decide to go back to church, even despite yourself, you will eventually find yourself in a place where you can learn about mystery and timelessness. You will become part of a tradition of stories and verses and gossip greater than you can imagine. Circling and turning with a carnival of small-time saints, whose tales and homespun customs marshal wisdom out of a religious calendar, you will become a character, too, and a player in a cast.

But you do have to shop around. You do have to find the right place for yourself. A church is an institution, and each one is as different as any club, restaurant, guild, or family. I know. I was lucky.

Behind a curtain of trees that rises with the slope of a riverbank in central Connecticut, there is a place I traveled in for sixteen months. Trees obscure it during green seasons with a fabric of leaves and branches. Perched over that lacy edge, a steeple appears—simple, box-like, crossless, spire-free, plain, and ungrasping. There is a building back there, fleecy white, boxed, high and long like the body of a goose. It might be just another symbol of the plain, unchanging nature of American Protestantism. It is not.

There is a church like an enormous wooden calliope that sits at the peak of a hill beside the river in Windsor, and the light that slips across the surfaces of things every day inspires people to come. They spend their time in daydreams. They have visions, suffer silences, sing songs, dance, laugh, practice, and forget to hope. They curse and tell stories. They go round and round.

Their life is made of that raw material of daily tasks—a steady attention to the quality of life they create as well as seek. Knowing the needs of others—insisting not on a rigid schedule of disciplines, but offering a balance of activities—encouraging constancy, patience, scripture-reading, wise direction, bread-baking, communion, money-raising, service. That church is a tenacious institution. One generation's vision is the next one's tradition, the next one's problem to be resolved.

It was there I found my harbor place, where people pledged to live by remembering, and over and over and over again, experienced the miracles of wonder.

Abba abba abba! Save me from an avalanche of abstractions!

I am a poor corncrib Southerner in precious New England. I maintain an appreciation for your dovetail joints and cobbled scraps of theology. I confess a tenderness for your frozen bolts of paradox and metaphor. I have made a full immersion and taken the slow passage down the weedy River Protestant. Out to sea and back again, into the land of domestic pilgrimage.

Welcome me home! Not a pilgrim, but a churchgoer, after all. Hear my confession, oh, so strange and unoriginal.

Acknowledgments

My thanks to all at First Church in Windsor, particularly to those whose stories appear on these pages and to the staff—Van and Lucille, Bill and Sue, John and Susan, Reardon & Kusner, John Zeugner, JoAnne, Francis, and Kate—a constellation that turns and turns.

Equally important has been the help of several people who provided resources and ideas at the beginning of this process: William McKinney of the Hartford Seminary, Reverend Brian McCarthy, Dr. Steve Warner, and Dr. Stephanie H. Mullany. Flip Brophy and Pamela Dorman, I remain grateful for your fine professional guidance. Jan and I also want to express our appreciation for the friendship of the Storrs Quaker Meeting, especially during my absences from home and during the years that I have been writing.

Rick Mashburn, Mary Otto, and Sally Fleming, your counsel has been timely and uplifting.

Finally, thank God for you, Jan Winburn, and for the wild country of our marriage.

Bibliography

The following books—particularly the work of the late James Hopewell and his friends at the Hartford Seminary—have been often useful, inspiring guides in the land of domestic pilgrimage.

Ahlstrom, Sydney E. *A Religious History of American People*. New Haven: Yale Univ. Press, 1972.

Ammerman, Nancy T. *Bible Believers*. New Brunswick, N.J.: Rutgers Univ. Press, 1987.

Bellah, Robert, et al. *Habits of the Heart*. Berkeley, Calif.: Univ. of California Press, 1985.

Berger, Peter. *Rumor of Angels*. New York: Doubleday, 1969.

The Bible. New Revised Standard Version.

Brueggemann, Walter. *Finally Comes the Poet*. Minneapolis: Fortress Press, 1989.

Campbell, Joseph. *The Portable Jung*. New York: Viking Press, 1971.

Carroll, Jackson W. *As with One Authority*. Louisville, Ky.: John Knox Press, 1991.

Carroll, Jackson W., Carl S. Dudley, and William McKinney. *Handbook for Congregational Studies*. Nashville, Tenn.: Abingdon Press, 1986.

Chittister, Joan. *Wisdom Distilled from the Daily*. New York: HarperCollins, 1990.

Coles, Robert. *The Call of Stories*. Boston: Houghton Mifflin, 1989.

Crabtree, Davida Foy. *The Empowering Church*. Washington, D.C.: Alban Institute, 1989.

Dryness, William A. *How Does America Hear the Gospel?* Grand Rapids, Mich.: William B. Eerdmans, 1989.

Ducey, Michael. *Sunday Morning*. New York: Free Press, 1977.

Frye, Northrop. *The Great Code*. New York: Harcourt Brace Jovanovich, 1982.

Hall, David D. *Worlds of Wonder, Days of Judgment*. New York: Alfred A. Knopf, 1989.

387

Hauerwas, Stanley, and William H. Willimon. *Resident Aliens.* Nashville, Tenn.: Abingdon Press, 1989.

Heilman, Samuel C. *Synagogue Life.* Chicago: Univ. of Chicago Press, 1976.

Hopewell, James. *Congregation: Stories and Structures.* Philadelphia: Fortress Press, 1987.

Hordern, William E. *A Layman's Guide to Protestant Theology.* New York: Macmillan, 1968.

Joyce, James. *Dubliners.* New York: Penguin Books, 1976.

Lowry, Shirley Park. *Familiar Mysteries.* New York: Oxford Univ. Press, 1982.

MacIntyre, Alasdair. *After Virtue.* Notre Dame, Ind.: Univ. of Notre Dame Press, 1981.

Marty, Martin. *The Public Church.* New York: Crossroad, 1981.

McGuire, Meredith. *Ritual Healing in Suburban America.* New Brunswick, N.J.: Rutgers University Press, 1988.

Palmer, Parker. *The Company of Strangers.* New York: Crossroad, 1981.

Parrington, Vernon L. *The Colonial Mind.* New York: Harcourt, Brace, and World, 1927.

Peck, M. Scott. *The Different Drum.* New York: Simon and Schuster, 1987.

Roof, Wade Clark, and William McKinney. *American Mainline Religion.* New Brunswick, N.J.: Rutgers Univ. Press, 1987.

Roozen, David A., William McKinney, and Jackson W. Carroll. *Varieties of Religious Presence.* New York: Pilgrim Press, 1984.

Stiles, Henry R. *The History of Ancient Windsor.* Somersworth, N.H.: New Hampshire Publishing Co., 1976.

Stout, Harry S. *The New England Soul.* New York: Oxford Univ. Press, 1986.

Taylor, JoAnne. *Innocent Wisdom.* New York: Pilgrim Press, 1989.

Thistlethwaite, Frank. *Dorset Pilgrims.* London: Barrie & Jenkins, 1989.

Warner, Steve. *New Wine in Old Wine Skins.* Berkeley, Calif.: University of California Press, 1988.

Williams, Melvin D. *Community in a Black Pentecostal Church.* Pittsburgh: Univ. of Pittsburgh Press, 1974.

Zinsser, William, ed. *Spiritual Quests: The Art and Craft of Religious Writing.* Boston: Houghton Mifflin Co., 1988.